D0977081

ALGORITHMS

IN A NUTSHELL

QA 76.9 .A43 H45 2009
Heineman, George T.
Algorithms in a nutshell

SANTA MONICA COLLEGE
LIBRARY
1900 PICO BLVD.
SANTA MONICA, CA 90405-1628

WITHDRAWN

Other resources from O'Reilly

Related titles	Head First Object-Oriented Design and Analysis	Mastering Algorithms with C
	Head First Software Development	Programming Collective Intelligence

oreilly.com

oreilly.com is more than a complete catalog of O'Reilly books. You'll also find links to news, events, articles, weblogs, sample chapters, and code examples.

oreillynet.com is the essential portal for developers interested in open and emerging technologies, including new platforms, programming languages, and operating systems.

Conferences

O'Reilly brings diverse innovators together to nurture the ideas that spark revolutionary industries. We specialize in documenting the latest tools and systems, translating the innovator's knowledge into useful skills for those in the trenches. Visit *conferences.oreilly.com* for our upcoming events.

Safari Bookshelf (*safari.oreilly.com*) is the premier online reference library for programmers and IT professionals. Conduct searches across more than 1,000 books. Subscribers can zero in on answers to time-critical questions in a matter of seconds. Read the books on your Bookshelf from cover to cover or simply flip to the page you need. Try it today for free.

ALGORITHMS

IN A NUTSHELL

George T. Heineman, Gary Pollice, and
Stanley Selkow

O'REILLY®

Beijing • Cambridge • Farnham • Köln • Sebastopol • Taipei • Tokyo

WITHDRAWN
SANTA MONICA COLLEGE LIBRARY

Algorithms in a Nutshell

by George T. Heineman, Gary Pollice, and Stanley Selkow

Copyright © 2009 George Heineman, Gary Pollice, and Stanley Selkow. All rights reserved.
Printed in the United States of America.

Published by O'Reilly Media, Inc., 1005 Gravenstein Highway North, Sebastopol, CA 95472.

O'Reilly books may be purchased for educational, business, or sales promotional use. Online editions are also available for most titles (*safari.oreilly.com*). For more information, contact our corporate/institutional sales department: (800) 998-9938 or *corporate@oreilly.com*.

Editor: Mary Treseler
Production Editor: Rachel Monaghan
Production Services: Newgen Publishing and Data Services
Copyeditor: Genevieve d'Entremont

Proofreader: Rachel Monaghan
Indexer: John Bickelhaupt
Cover Designer: Karen Montgomery
Interior Designer: David Futato
Illustrator: Robert Romano

Printing History:

October 2008:   First Edition.

Nutshell Handbook, the Nutshell Handbook logo, and the O'Reilly logo are registered trademarks of O'Reilly Media, Inc. The *In a Nutshell* series designations, *Algorithms in a Nutshell*, the image of a hermit crab, and related trade dress are trademarks of O'Reilly Media, Inc.

Many of the designations used by manufacturers and sellers to distinguish their products are claimed as trademarks. Where those designations appear in this book, and O'Reilly Media, Inc. was aware of a trademark claim, the designations have been printed in caps or initial caps.

While every precaution has been taken in the preparation of this book, the publisher and authors assume no responsibility for errors or omissions, or for damages resulting from the use of the information contained herein.

 This book uses RepKover™, a durable and flexible lay-flat binding.

ISBN: 978-0-596-51624-6
[M]   [1/09]

Table of Contents

Preface ix

Part I.

1. Algorithms Matter **3**
Understand the Problem   4
Experiment if Necessary   5
Algorithms to the Rescue   8
Side Story   9
The Moral of the Story   10
References   11

2. The Mathematics of Algorithms **12**
Size of a Problem Instance   12
Rate of Growth of Functions   14
Analysis in the Best, Average, and Worst Cases   18
Performance Families   22
Mix of Operations   35
Benchmark Operations   36
One Final Point   38
References   38

3. Patterns and Domains **39**
  Patterns: A Communication Language   39
  Algorithm Pattern Format   41
  Pseudocode Pattern Format   42
  Design Format   43
  Empirical Evaluation Format   44
  Domains and Algorithms   46
  Floating-Point Computations   47
  Manual Memory Allocation   50
  Choosing a Programming Language   53
  References   54

Part II.

4. Sorting Algorithms **57**
  Overview   57
  Insertion Sort   63
  Median Sort   67
  Quicksort   78
  Selection Sort   85
  Heap Sort   86
  Counting Sort   91
  Bucket Sort   93
  Criteria for Choosing a Sorting Algorithm   99
  References   103

5. Searching **105**
  Overview   105
  Sequential Search   106
  Binary Search   112
  Hash-based Search   116
  Binary Tree Search   129

6. Graph Algorithms **136**
  Overview   136
  Depth-First Search   142
  Breadth-First Search   149
  Single-Source Shortest Path   153
  All Pairs Shortest Path   165
  Minimum Spanning Tree Algorithms   169
  References   171

7. Path Finding in AI **172**

Overview   172
Depth-First Search   181
Breadth-First Search   190
A*Search   194
Comparison   204
Minimax   207
NegMax   213
AlphaBeta   217
References   224

8. Network Flow Algorithms **226**

Overview   226
Maximum Flow   229
Bipartite Matching   239
Reflections on Augmenting Paths   242 •
Minimum Cost Flow   246
Transshipment   246
Transportation   247
Assignment   248
Linear Programming   249
References   250

9. Computational Geometry **251**

Overview   251
Convex Hull Scan   260
LineSweep   268
Nearest Neighbor Queries   280
Range Queries   292
References   298

Part III.

10. When All Else Fails **301**

Variations on a Theme   301
Approximation Algorithms   302
Offline Algorithms   302
Parallel Algorithms   303
Randomized Algorithms   303
Algorithms That Can Be Wrong, but with Diminishing Probability   310
References   313

11. Epilogue **314**

Overview   314

Principle: Know Your Data   314

Principle: Decompose the Problem into Smaller Problems   315

Principle: Choose the Right Data Structure   316

Principle: Add Storage to Increase Performance   317

Principle: If No Solution Is Evident, Construct a Search   318

Principle: If No Solution Is Evident, Reduce Your Problem to
Another Problem That Has a Solution   318

Principle: Writing Algorithms Is Hard—Testing Algorithms Is
Harder   319

Part IV.

Appendix: Benchmarking **323**

Index **337**

Preface

As Trinity states in the movie *The Matrix*:

> *It's the question that drives us, Neo. It's the question that brought you here.*
>
> *You know the question, just as I did.*

As authors of this book, we answer the question that has led you here:

> *Can I use algorithm X to solve my problem? If so, how do I implement it?*

You likely do not need to understand the reasons why an algorithm is correct—if you do, turn to other sources, such as the 1,180-page bible on algorithms, *Introduction to Algorithms,* Second Edition, by Thomas H. Cormen et al. (2001). There you will find lemmas, theorems, and proofs; you will find exercises and step-by-step examples showing the algorithms as they perform. Perhaps surprisingly, however, you will not find any real code, only fragments of "pseudocode," the device used by countless educational textbooks to present a high-level description of algorithms. These educational textbooks are important within the classroom, yet they fail the software practitioner because they assume it will be straightforward to develop real code from pseudocode fragments.

We intend this book to be used frequently by experienced programmers looking for appropriate solutions to their problems. Here you will find solutions to the problems you must overcome as a programmer every day. You will learn what decisions lead to an improved performance of key algorithms that are essential for the success of your software applications. You will find real code that can be adapted to your needs and solution methods that you can learn.

All algorithms are fully implemented with test suites that validate the correct implementation of the algorithms. The code is fully documented and available as a code repository addendum to this book. We rigorously followed a set of principles as we designed, implemented, and wrote this book. If these principles are meaningful to you, then you will find this book useful.

Principle: Use Real Code, Not Pseudocode

What is a practitioner to do with Figure P-1's description of the FORD-FULKERSON algorithm for computing maximum network flow?

Ford-Fulkerson Algorithm:

Input   Graph G with flow capacity c, a source node s, and a sink node t

Output A flow f from s to t which is a maximum

1. $f(u,v) \leftarrow 0$ for all edges (u,v)
2. **while** (there is a path p from s to t in G_f such that $c_f(u,v) > 0$ for all edges $(u,v) \in p$) **do**
3.   Find $c_f(p) = \min \{ c_f(u,v) \mid (u,v) \in p \}$
4.   **foreach** edge $c_f(u,v) \in p$ **do**
5. $f(u,v) \leftarrow f(u,v) + c_f(p)$ // Send flow along the path
6. $f(v,u) \leftarrow f(v,u) - c_f(p)$ // The flow might be "returned" later

end

Figure P-1. Example of pseudocode commonly found in textbooks

The algorithm description in this figure comes from Wikipedia (*http://en.wikipedia. org/wiki/Ford_Fulkerson*), and it is nearly identical to the pseudocode found in (Cormen et al., 2001). It is simply unreasonable to expect a software practitioner to produce working code from the description of FORD-FULKERSON shown here! Turn to Chapter 8 to see our code listing by comparison. We use only documented, well-designed code to describe the algorithms. Use the code we provide as-is, or include its logic in your own programming language and software system.

Some algorithm textbooks do have full real-code solutions in C or Java. Often the purpose of these textbooks is to either teach the language to a beginner or to explain how to implement abstract data types. Additionally, to include code listings within the narrow confines of a textbook page, authors routinely omit documentation and error handling, or use shortcuts never used in practice. We believe programmers can learn much from documented, well-designed code, which is why we dedicated so much effort to develop actual solutions for our algorithms.

Principle: Separate the Algorithm from the Problem Being Solved

It is hard to show the implementation for an algorithm "in the general sense" without also involving details of the specific solution. We are critical of books that show a full implementation of an algorithm yet allow the details of the specific problem to become so intertwined with the code for the generic problem that it is hard to identify the structure of the original algorithm. Even worse, many available implementations rely on sets of arrays for storing information in a way that is "simpler" to code but harder to understand. Too often, the reader will understand the concept from the supplementary text but be unable to implement it!

In our approach, we design each implementation to separate the generic algorithm from the specific problem. In Chapter 7, for example, when we describe the A*SEARCH algorithm, we use an example such as the 8-puzzle (a sliding tile puzzle with tiles numbered 1–8 in a three-by-three grid). The implementation of A*SEARCH depends only on a set of well-defined interfaces. The details of the specific 8-puzzle problem are encapsulated cleanly within classes that implement these interfaces.

We use numerous programming languages in this book and follow a strict design methodology to ensure that the code is readable and the solutions are efficient. Because of our software engineering background, it was second nature to design clear interfaces between the general algorithms and the domain-specific solutions. Coding in this way produces software that is easy to test, maintain, and expand to solve the problems at hand. One added benefit is that the modern audience can more easily read and understand the resulting descriptions of the algorithms. For select algorithms, we show how to convert the readable and efficient code that we produced into highly optimized (though less readable) code with improved performance. After all, the only time that optimization should be done is when the problem has been solved and the client demands faster code. Even then it is worth listening to C. A. R. Hoare, who stated, "Premature optimization is the root of all evil."

Principle: Introduce Just Enough Mathematics

Many treatments of algorithms focus nearly exclusively on proving the correctness of the algorithm and explaining only at a high level its details. Our focus is always on showing how the algorithm is to be implemented in practice. To this end, we only introduce the mathematics needed to understand the data structures and the control flow of the solutions.

For example, one needs to understand the properties of sets and binary trees for many algorithms. At the same time, however, there is no need to include a proof by induction on the height of a binary tree to explain how a red-black binary tree is balanced; read Chapter 13 in (Cormen et al., 2001) if you want those details. We explain the results as needed, and refer the reader to other sources to understand how to prove these results mathematically.

In this book you will learn the key terms and analytic techniques to differentiate algorithm behavior based on the data structures used and the desired functionality.

Principle: Support Mathematical Analysis Empirically

We mathematically analyze the performance of each algorithm in this book to help programmers understand the conditions under which each algorithm performs at its best. We provide live code examples, and in the accompanying code repository there are numerous JUnit (*http://sourceforge.net/projects/junit*) test cases to document the proper implementation of each algorithm. We generate benchmark performance data to provide empirical evidence regarding the performance of each algorithm.

We classify each algorithm into a specific performance family and provide benchmark data showing the execution performance to support the analysis. We avoid algorithms that are interesting only to the mathematical algorithmic designer trying to prove that an approach performs better at the expense of being impossible to implement. We execute our algorithms on a variety of programming platforms to demonstrate that the design of the algorithm—not the underlying platform—is the driving factor in efficiency.

The appendix contains the full details of our approach toward benchmarking, and can be used to independently validate the performance results we describe in this book. The advice we give you is common in the open source community: "Your mileage may vary." Although you won't be able to duplicate our results exactly, you will be able to verify the trends that we document, and we encourage you to use the same empirical approach when deciding upon algorithms for your own use.

Audience

If you were trapped on a desert island and could have only one algorithms book, we recommend the complete box set of *The Art of Computer Programming*, Volumes 1–3, by Donald Knuth (1998). Knuth describes numerous data structures and algorithms and provides exquisite treatment and analysis. Complete with historical footnotes and exercises, these books could keep a programmer active and content for decades. It would certainly be challenging, however, to put directly into practice the ideas from Knuth's book.

But you are not trapped on a desert island, are you? No, you have sluggish code that must be improved by Friday and you need to understand how to do it!

We intend our book to be your primary reference when you are faced with an algorithmic question and need to either (a) solve a particular problem, or (b) improve on the performance of an existing solution. We cover a range of existing algorithms for solving a large number of problems and adhere to the following principles:

- When describing each algorithm, we use a stylized pattern to properly frame each discussion and explain the essential points of the algorithm. By using patterns, we create a readable book whose consistent presentation shows the impact that similar design decisions have on different algorithms.

- We use a variety of languages to describe the algorithms in the book (including C, C++, Java, and Ruby). In doing so, we make concrete the discussion on algorithms and speak using languages that you are already familiar with.

- We describe the expected performance of each algorithm and empirically provide evidence that supports these claims. Whether you trust in mathematics or in demonstrable execution times, you will be persuaded.

We intend this book to be most useful to software practitioners, programmers, and designers. To meet your objectives, you need access to a quality resource that explains real solutions to real algorithms that you need to solve real problems.

You already know how to program in a variety of programming languages. You know about the essential computer science data structures, such as arrays, linked lists, stacks, queues, hash tables, binary trees, and undirected and directed graphs. You don't need to implement these data structures, since they are typically provided by code libraries.

We expect that you will use this book to learn about tried and tested solutions to solve problems efficiently. You will learn some advanced data structures and some novel ways to apply standard data structures to improve the efficiency of algorithms. Your problem-solving abilities will improve when you see the key decisions for each algorithm that make for efficient solutions.

Contents of This Book

This book is divided into three parts. Part I (Chapters 1–3) provides the mathematical introduction to algorithms necessary to properly understand the descriptions used in this book. We also describe the pattern-based style used throughout in the presentation of each algorithm. This style is carefully designed to ensure consistency, as well as to highlight the essential aspects of each algorithm. Part II contains a series of chapters (4–9), each consisting of a set of related algorithms. The individual sections of these chapters are self-contained descriptions of the algorithms.

Part III (Chapters 10 and 11) provides resources that interested readers can use to pursue these topics further. A chapter on approaches to take when "all else fails" provides helpful hints on solving problems when there is (as yet) no immediate efficient solution. We close with a discussion of important areas of study that we omitted from Part II simply because they were too advanced, too niche-oriented, or too new to have proven themselves. In Part IV, we include a benchmarking appendix that describes the approach used throughout this book to generate empirical data that supports the mathematical analysis used in each chapter. Such benchmarking is standard in the industry yet has been noticeably lacking in textbooks describing algorithms.

Conventions Used in This Book

The following typographical conventions are used in this book:

Code

> All code examples appear in this typecase.
> This code is replicated directly from the code repository and reflects real code.

Italic

> Indicates key terms used to describe algorithms and data structures. Also used when referring to variables within a pseudocode description of an example.

Constant width

   Indicates the name of actual software elements within an implementation, such as a Java class, the name of an array within a C implementation, and constants such as true or false.

SMALL CAPS

   Indicates the name of an algorithm.

We cite numerous books, articles, and websites throughout the book. These citations appear in text using parentheses, such as (Cormen et al., 2001), and each chapter closes with a listing of references used within that chapter. When the reference citation immediately follows the name of the author in the text, we do not duplicate the name in the reference. Thus, we refer to the *Art of Computer Programming* books by Donald Knuth (1998) by just including the year in parentheses.

All URLs used in the book were verified as of August 2008 and we tried to use only URLs that should be around for some time. We include small URLs, such as *http://www.oreilly.com*, directly within the text; otherwise, they appear in footnotes and within the references at the end of a chapter.

Using Code Examples

This book is here to help you get your job done. In general, you may use the code in this book in your programs and documentation. You do not need to contact us for permission unless you're reproducing a significant portion of the code. For example, writing a program that uses several chunks of code from this book does not require permission. Selling or distributing a CD-ROM of examples from O'Reilly books does require permission. Answering a question by citing this book and quoting example code does not require permission. Incorporating a significant amount of example code from this book into your product's documentation does require permission.

We appreciate, but do not require, attribution. An attribution usually includes the title, author, publisher, and ISBN. For example: "*Algorithms in a Nutshell* by George T. Heineman, Gary Pollice, and Stanley Selkow. Copyright 2009 George Heineman, Gary Pollice, and Stanley Selkow, 978-0-596-51624-6."

If you feel your use of code examples falls outside fair use or the permission given here, feel free to contact us at *permissions@oreilly.com*.

Comments and Questions

Please address comments and questions concerning this book to the publisher:

   O'Reilly Media, Inc.
   1005 Gravenstein Highway North
   Sebastopol, CA 95472
   800-998-9938 (in the United States or Canada)
   707-829-0515 (international or local)
   707-829-0104 (fax)

We have a web page for this book, where we list errata, examples, and any additional information. You can access this page at:

http://www.oreilly.com/catalog/9780596516246

To comment or ask technical questions about this book, send email to:

bookquestions@oreilly.com

For more information about our books, conferences, Resource Centers, and the O'Reilly Network, see our website at:

http://www.oreilly.com

Safari® Books Online

When you see a Safari® Books Online icon on the cover of your favorite technology book, that means the book is available online through the O'Reilly Network Safari Bookshelf.

Safari offers a solution that's better than e-books. It's a virtual library that lets you easily search thousands of top tech books, cut and paste code samples, download chapters, and find quick answers when you need the most accurate, current information. Try it for free at *http://safari.oreilly.com*.

Acknowledgments

We would like to thank the book reviewers for their attention to detail and suggestions, which improved the presentation and removed defects from earlier drafts: Alan Davidson, Scot Drysdale, Krzysztof Duleba, Gene Hughes, Murali Mani, Jeffrey Yasskin, and Daniel Yoo.

George Heineman would like to thank those who helped instill in him a passion for algorithms, including Professors Scot Drysdale (Dartmouth College) and Zvi Galil (Columbia University). As always, George thanks his wife, Jennifer, and his children, Nicholas (who always wanted to know what "notes" Daddy was working on) and Alexander (who was born as we prepared the final draft of the book).

Gary Pollice would like to thank his wife Vikki for 40 great years. He also wants to thank the WPI computer science department for a great environment and a great job.

Stanley Selkow would like to thank his wife, Deb. This book was another step on their long path together.

References

Cormen, Thomas H., Charles E. Leiserson, Ronald L. Rivest, and Clifford Stein, *Introduction to Algorithms*, Second Edition. McGraw-Hill, 2001.

Knuth, Donald E., *The Art of Computer Programming*, Volumes 1–3, Boxed Set Second Edition. Addison-Wesley Professional, 1998.

Chapter 1, *Algorithms Matter*
Chapter 2, *The Mathematics of Algorithms*
Chapter 3, *Patterns and Domains*

1

Algorithms Matter

Algorithms matter! Knowing which algorithm to apply under which set of circumstances can make a big difference in the software you produce. If you don't believe us, just read the following story about how Gary turned failure into success with a little analysis and choosing the right algorithm for the job.*

Once upon a time, Gary worked at a company with a lot of brilliant software developers. Like most organizations with a lot of bright people, there were many great ideas and people to implement them in the software products. One such person was Graham, who had been with the company from its inception. Graham came up with an idea on how to find out whether a program had any memory leaks—a common problem with C and C++ programs at the time. If a program ran long enough and had memory leaks, it would crash because it would run out of memory. Anyone who has programmed in a language that doesn't support automatic memory management and garbage collection knows this problem well.

Graham decided to build a small library that *wrapped* the operating system's memory allocation and deallocation routines, malloc( ) and free( ), with his own functions. Graham's functions recorded each memory allocation and deallocation in a data structure that could be queried when the program finished. The wrapper functions recorded the information and called the real operating system functions to perform the actual memory management. It took just a few hours for Graham to implement the solution and, *voilà*, it worked! There was just one problem: the program ran so slowly when it was instrumented with Graham's libraries that no one was willing to use it. We're talking *really* slow here. You could start up a program, go have a cup of coffee—or maybe a pot of coffee—come back, and the program would still be crawling along. This was clearly unacceptable.

---

* The names of participants and organizations, except the authors, have been changed to protect the innocent and avoid any embarrassment—or lawsuits. :-)

Now Graham was really smart when it came to understanding operating systems and how their internals work. He was an excellent programmer who could write more working code in an hour than most programmers could write in a day. He had studied algorithms, data structures, and all of the standard topics in college, so why did the code execute so much slower with the wrappers inserted? In this case, it was a problem of knowing enough to make the program work, but not thinking through the details to make it work *quickly*. Like many creative people, Graham was already thinking about his next program and didn't want to go back to his memory leak program to find out what was wrong. So, he asked Gary to take a look at it and see whether he could fix it. Gary was more of a compiler and software engineering type of guy and seemed to be pretty good at honing code to make it release-worthy.

Gary thought he'd talk to Graham about the program before he started digging into the code. That way, he might better understand how Graham structured his solution and why he chose particular implementation options.

 Before proceeding, think about what you might ask Graham. See whether you would have obtained the information that Gary did in the following section.

Understand the Problem

A good way to solve problems is to start with the big picture: understand the problem, identify potential causes, and then dig into the details. If you decide to try to solve the problem because you *think* you know the cause, you may solve the wrong problem, or you might not explore other—possibly better—answers. The first thing Gary did was ask Graham to describe the problem and his solution.

Graham said that he wanted to determine whether a program had any memory leaks. He thought the best way to find out would be to keep a record of all memory that was allocated by the program, whether it was freed before the program ended, and a record of where the allocation was requested in the user's program. His solution required him to build a small library with three functions:

malloc( )
> A wrapper around the operating system's memory allocation function

free( )
> A wrapper around the operating system's memory deallocation function

exit( )
> A wrapper around the operating system's function called when a program exits

This custom library would be linked with the program under test in such a way that the customized functions would be called instead of the operating system's functions. The custom malloc( ) and free( ) functions would keep track of each allocation and deallocation. When the program under test finished, there would be no memory leak if every allocation was subsequently deallocated. If there were any leaks, the information kept by Graham's routines would allow the programmer to find the code that caused them. When the exit( ) function was

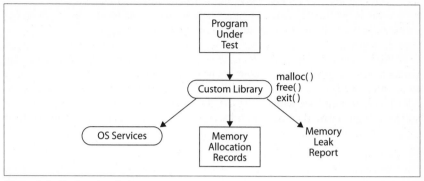

called, the custom library routine would display its results before actually exiting. Graham sketched out what his solution looked like, as shown in Figure 1-1.

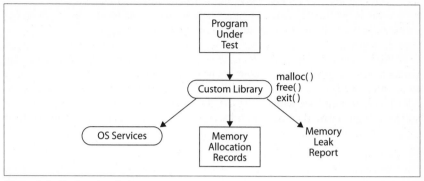

Figure 1-1. Graham's solution

The description seemed clear enough. Unless Graham was doing something terribly wrong in his code to wrap the operating system functions, it was hard to imagine that there was a performance problem in the wrapper code. If there were, then all programs would be proportionately slow. Gary asked whether there was a difference in the performance of the programs Graham had tested. Graham explained that the running profile seemed to be that small programs—those that did relatively little—all ran in acceptable time, regardless of whether they had memory leaks. However, programs that did a lot of processing and had memory leaks ran disproportionately slow.

Experiment if Necessary

Before going any further, Gary wanted to get a better understanding of the running profile of programs. He and Graham sat down and wrote some short programs to see how they ran with Graham's custom library linked in. Perhaps they could get a better understanding of the conditions that caused the problem to arise.

 What type of experiments would you run? What would your program(s) look like?

The first test program Gary and Graham wrote (ProgramA) is shown in Example 1-1.

Example 1-1. ProgramA code

```
int main(int argc, char **argv) {
  int i = 0;
  for (i = 0; i < 1000000; i++) {
    malloc(32);
  }
  exit (0);
}
```

They ran the program and waited for the results. It took several minutes to finish. Although computers were slower back then, this was clearly unacceptable. When this program finished, there were 32 MB of memory leaks. How would the program run if all of the memory allocations were deallocated? They made a simple modification to create ProgramB, shown in Example 1-2.

Example 1-2. ProgramB code

```
int main(int argc, char **argv) {
  int i = 0;
  for (i = 0; i < 1000000; i++) {
    void *x = malloc(32);
    free(x);
  }
  exit (0);
}
```

When they compiled and ran ProgramB, it completed in a few seconds. Graham was convinced that the problem was related to the number of memory allocations open when the program ended, but couldn't figure out where the problem occurred. He had searched through his code for several hours and was unable to find any problems. Gary wasn't as convinced as Graham that the problem was the number of memory leaks. He suggested one more experiment and made another modification to the program, shown as ProgramC in Example 1-3, in which the deallocations were grouped together at the end of the program.

Example 1-3. ProgramC code

```
int main(int argc, char **argv) {
  int i = 0;
  void *addrs[1000000];
  for (i = 0; i < 1000000; i++) {
    addrs[i] = malloc(32);
  }
  for (i = 0; i < 1000000; i++) {
    free(addrs[i]);
  }
  exit (0);
}
```

This program crawled along even slower than the first program! This example invalidated the theory that the number of memory leaks affected the performance of Graham's program. However, the example gave Gary an insight that led to the real problem.

It wasn't the number of memory allocations open at the end of the program that affected performance; it was the maximum number of them that were open at any single time. If memory leaks were not the only factor affecting performance, then there had to be something about the way Graham maintained the information used to determine whether there were leaks. In ProgramB, there was never more than one 32-byte chunk of memory allocated at any point during the program's execution. The first and third programs had one million open allocations.

Allocating and deallocating memory was not the issue, so the problem must be in the bookkeeping code Graham wrote to keep track of the memory.

Gary asked Graham how he kept track of the allocated memory. Graham replied that he was using a binary tree where each node was a structure that consisted of pointers to the children nodes (if any), the address of the allocated memory, the size allocated, and the place in the program where the allocation request was made. He added that he was using the memory address as the key for the nodes since there could be no duplicates, and this decision would make it easy to insert and delete records of allocated memory.

Using a binary tree is often more efficient than simply using an ordered linked list of items. If an ordered list of n items exists—and each item is equally likely to be sought—then a successful search uses, on average, about $n/2$ comparisons to find an item. Inserting into and deleting from an ordered list requires one to examine or move about $n/2$ items on average as well. Computer science textbooks would describe the performance of these operations (search, insert, and delete) as being $O(n)$, which roughly means that as the size of the list doubles, the time to perform these operations also is expected to double.[*]

Using a binary tree can deliver $O(\log n)$ performance for these same operations, although the code may be a bit more complicated to write and maintain. That is, as the size of the list doubles, the performance of these operations grows only by a constant amount. When processing 1,000,000 items, we expect to examine an average of 20 items, compared to about 500,000 if the items were contained in a list. Using a binary tree is a great choice—if the keys are distributed evenly in the tree. When the keys are not distributed evenly, the tree becomes distorted and loses those properties that make it a good choice for searching.

Knowing a bit about trees and how they behave, Gary asked Graham the $64,000 (it is logarithmic, after all) question: "Are you balancing the binary tree?" Graham's response was surprising, since he was a very good software developer. "No, why should I do that? It makes the code a lot more complex." But the fact that Graham wasn't balancing the tree was exactly the problem causing the horrible performance of his code. Can you figure out why? The malloc() routine in C allocates memory (from the heap) in order of increasing memory addresses. Not only are these addresses not evenly distributed, the order is exactly the one that leads to right-oriented trees, which behave more like linear lists than binary trees. To see why, consider the two binary trees in Figure 1-2. The (a) tree was created by inserting the numbers 1–15 in order. Its root node contains the value 1 and there is a path of 14 nodes to reach the node containing the value 15. The (b) tree was created by inserting these same numbers in the order <8, 4, 12, 2, 6, 10, 14, 1, 3, 5, 7, 9, 11, 13, 15>. In this case, the root node contains the value 8 but the paths to all other nodes in the tree are three nodes or less. As we will see in Chapter 5, the search time is directly affected by the length of the maximum path.

[*] Chapter 2 contains information about this "big O" notation.

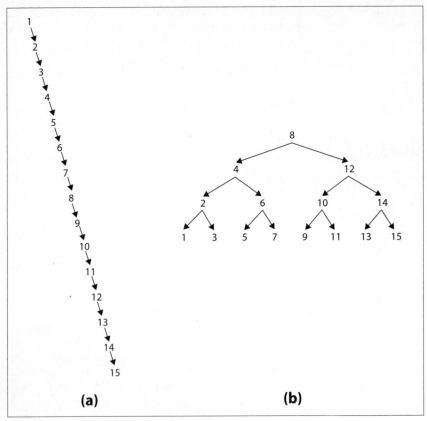

(a)   **(b)**

Figure 1-2. Constructing two sample binary trees

Algorithms to the Rescue

A balanced binary tree is a binary search tree for which the length of all paths from the root of the tree to any leaf node is as close to the same number as possible. Let's define $depth(L_i)$ to be the length of the path from the root of the tree to a leaf node L_i. In a perfectly balanced binary tree with n nodes, for any two leaf nodes, L_1 and L_2, the absolute value of the difference, $|depth(L_2)-depth(L_1)|\leq1$; also $depth(L_i)\leq\log(n)$ for any leaf node L_i.[*] Gary went to one of his algorithms books and decided to modify Graham's code so that the tree of allocation records would be balanced by making it a red-black binary tree. Red-black trees (Cormen et al., 2001) are an efficient implementation of a balanced binary tree in which given any two leaf nodes L_1 and L_2, $depth(L_2)/depth(L_1)\leq2$; also $depth(L_i)\leq2*\log_2(n+1)$ for any leaf node L_i. In other words, a red-black tree is roughly balanced, to ensure that no path is more than twice as long as any other path.

The changes took a few hours to write and test. When he was done, Gary showed Graham the result. They ran each of the three programs shown previously.

---

[*] Throughout this book, all logarithms are computed in base 2.

ProgramA and ProgramC took just a few milliseconds longer than ProgramB. The performance improvement reflected approximately a 5,000-fold speedup. This is what might be expected when you consider that the average number of nodes to visit drops from 500,000 to 20. Actually, this is an order of magnitude off: you might expect a 25,000-fold speedup, but that is offset by the computation overhead of balancing the tree. Still, the results are dramatic, and Graham's memory leak detector could be released (with Gary's modifications) in the next version of the product.

Side Story

Given the efficiency of using red-black binary trees, is it possible that the malloc() implementation itself is coded to use them? After all, the memory allocation functionality must somehow maintain the set of allocated regions so they can be safely deallocated. Also, note that each of the programs listed previously make allocation requests for 32 bytes. Does the size of the request affect the performance of malloc() and free() requests? To investigate the behavior of malloc(), we ran a set of experiments. First, we timed how long it took to allocate 4,096 chunks of n bytes, with n ranging from 1 to 2,048. Then, we timed how long it took to deallocate the same memory using three strategies:

freeUp
> In the order in which it was allocated; this is identical to ProgramC

freeDown
> In the reverse order in which it was allocated

freeScattered
> In a scattered order that ultimately frees all memory

For each value of n we ran the experiment 100 times and discarded the best and worst performing runs. Figure 1-3 contains the average results of the remaining 98 trials. As one might expect, the performance of the allocation follows a linear trend—as the size of n increases, so does the performance, proportional to n. Surprisingly, the way in which the memory is deallocated changes the performance. freeUp has the best performance, for example, while freeDown executes about four times as slowly.

The empirical evidence does not answer whether malloc() and free() use binary trees (balanced or not!) to store information; without inspecting the source for free(), there is no easy explanation for the different performance based upon the order in which the memory is deallocated.

Showing this example serves two purposes. First, the algorithm(s) behind memory allocation and deallocation are surprisingly complex, often highly tuned based upon the specific capabilities of the operating system (in this case a high-end computer). As we will learn throughout this book, various algorithms have "sweet spots" in which their performance has no equal and designers can take advantage of specific information about a problem to improve performance. Second, we also describe throughout the book different algorithms and explain why one algorithm outperforms another. We return again and again to empirically support these mathematical claims.

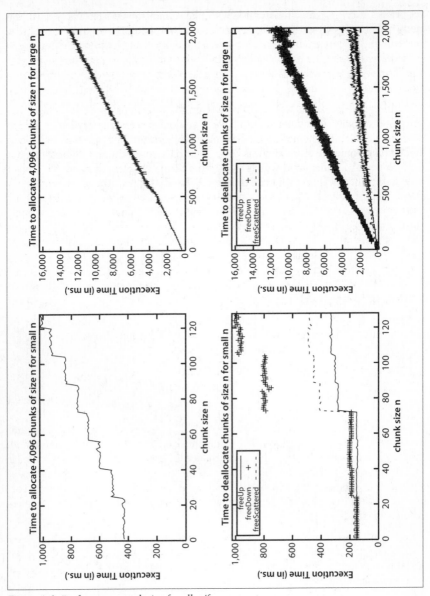

Figure 1-3. *Performance analysis of malloc/free requests*

The Moral of the Story

The previous story really happened. Algorithms do matter. You might ask whether the tree-balancing algorithm was the optimal solution for the problem. That's a great question, and one that we'll answer by asking another question: does it really matter? Finding the right algorithm is like finding the right solution to any problem. Instead of finding the perfect solution, the algorithm just has to work well enough. You must balance the cost of the solution against the value it adds. It's quite possible that Gary's implementation could be improved, either by optimizing his implementation or by using a different algorithm. However, the performance of the memory leak detection software was more than acceptable for the intended use, and any additional improvements would have been unproductive overhead.

The ability to choose an acceptable algorithm for your needs is a critical skill that any good software developer should have. You don't necessarily have to be able to perform detailed mathematical analysis on the algorithm, but you must be able to understand someone else's analysis. You don't have to invent new algorithms, but you do need to understand which algorithms fit the problem at hand. This book will help you develop these capabilities. When you have them, you've added another tool to your software development toolkit.

References

Cormen, Thomas H., Charles E. Leiserson, Ronald L. Rivest, and Clifford Stein, *Introduction to Algorithms*, Second Edition. McGraw-Hill, 2001.

2

The Mathematics of Algorithms

In choosing an algorithm to solve a problem, you are trying to predict which algorithm will be fastest for a particular data set on a particular platform (or family of platforms). Characterizing the expected computation time of an algorithm is inherently a mathematical process. In this chapter we present the mathematical tools behind this prediction of time. Readers will be able to understand the various mathematical terms throughout this book after reading this chapter.

A common theme throughout this chapter (and indeed throughout the entire book) is that all assumptions and approximations may be off by a constant, and ultimately our abstraction will ignore these constants. For all algorithms covered in this book, the constants are small for virtually all platforms.

Size of a Problem Instance

An instance of a problem is a particular input data set to which a program is applied. In most problems, the execution time of a program increases with the size of the encoding of the instance being solved. At the same time, overly compact representations (possibly using compression techniques) may unnecessarily slow down the execution of a program. It is surprisingly difficult to define the optimal way to encode an instance because problems occur in the real world and must be translated into an appropriate machine representation to be solved on a computer. Consider the two encodings shown in the upcoming sidebar, "Instances Are Encoded," for a number x.

As much as possible, we want to evaluate algorithms by assuming that the encoding of the problem instance is not the determining factor in whether the algorithm can be implemented efficiently. Although the encodings are nearly identical in size, they offer different performance on the key operation, which determines whether x has an even or odd number of 1-bits in its binary representation.

Instances Are Encoded

Suppose you are given a large number x and want to compute the parity of the number of 1s in its binary representation (that is, whether there is an even or odd number of 1s). For example, if $x=15,137,300,128$, its base 2 representation is:

x_2=1110000110010000001101111010100000

and its parity is even. We consider two possible encoding strategies:

Encoding 1 of x: 1110000110010000001101111010100000

Here, the 34-bit representation of x in base 2 is the representation of the problem and so the size of the input is $n=34$. Note that $log_2(x)$ is y≅33.82, so this encoding is optimal. However, to compute the parity of the number of 1s, every bit must be probed. The optimal time to compute the parity grows linearly with n (logarithmically with x).

x can also be encoded as an n-bit number plus an extra checksum bit that shows the parity of the number of 1s in the encoding of x.

Encoding 2 of x: 1110000110010000001101111010100000[0]

The last bit of x in Encoding 2 is a 0 reflecting the fact that x has an even number of 1s (even parity=0). For this representation, $n=35$. In either case, the size of the encoded instance, n, grows logarithmically with x. However, the time for an optimal algorithm to compute the parity of x with Encoding 1 grows logarithmically with the size of the encoding of x, and with Encoding 2 the time for an optimal algorithm is constant and doesn't depend on the size of the encoding of x.

Selecting the representation of a problem instance depends on the type and variety of operations that need to be performed. Designing efficient algorithms often starts by selecting the proper data structures in which to represent the problem to be solved, as shown in Figure 2-1.

Consider the following classic 17th century haiku by Matsuo Bashō:

古池や蛙飛込む水の音

This poem can represented by:

Encoding 1: 30-byte Unicode sequence:

E547A91CCB1A071A0908E89B4CBA5469BE85F2F1C68280732C168E381573A53EB3

Encoding 2: 40-byte Kanji string:

"furu ike ya kawazu tobikomu mizu no oto"

Encoding 3: a 3 x 18 array of characters, in translated English:

```
o  l  d     P  o  n  d
a     f  r  o  g     j  u  m  p  s     i  n  t  o
t  h  e     S  o  u  n  d     o  f     w  a  t  e  r
```

Figure 2-1. More complex encodings of a problem instance

Because we cannot formally define the size of an instance, we assume that an instance is encoded in some generally accepted, concise manner. For example, when sorting n numbers, we adopt the general convention that each of the n numbers fits into a word in the platform, and the size of an instance to be sorted is n. In case some of the numbers require more than one word—but only a constant, fixed number of words—our measure of the size of an instance is off by a constant. So an algorithm that performs a computation using integers stored in 64 bits may take twice as long as a similar algorithm coded using integers stored in 32 bits.

To store collections of information, most programming languages support arrays, contiguous regions of memory indexed by an integer i to enable rapid access to the ith element. An array is one-dimensional when each element fits into a word in the platform (for example, an array of integers, Boolean values, or characters). Some arrays extend into multiple dimensions, enabling more interesting data representations, as shown in Figure 2-1. And, as shown in the upcoming sidebar, "The Effect of Encoding on Performance," the encoding could affect an algorithm's performance.

Because of the vast differences in programming languages and computer platforms on which programs execute, algorithmic researchers accept that they are unable to compute with pinpoint accuracy the costs involved in using a particular encoding in an implementation. Therefore, they assert that performance costs that differ by a multiplicative constant are asymptotically equivalent. Although such a definition would be impractical for real-world situations (who would be satisfied to learn they must pay a bill that is 1,000 times greater than expected?), it serves as the universal means by which algorithms are compared. When implementing an algorithm as production code, attention to the details reflected in the constants is clearly warranted.

Rate of Growth of Functions

The widely accepted method for describing the behavior of an algorithm is to represent the rate of growth of its execution time as a function of the size of the input problem instance. Characterizing an algorithm's performance in this way is an abstraction that ignores details. To use this measure properly requires an awareness of the details hidden by the abstraction.

Every program is run on a *platform*, which is a general term meant to encompass:

- The computer on which the program is run, its CPU, data cache, floating-point unit (FPU), and other on-chip features
- The programming language in which the program is written, along with the compiler/interpreter and optimization settings for generated code
- The operating system
- Other processes being run in the background

One underlying assumption is that changing any of the parameters comprising a platform will change the execution time of the program by a constant factor. To place this discussion in context, we briefly discuss the SEQUENTIAL SEARCH algorithm, presented later in Chapter 5. SEQUENTIAL SEARCH examines a list of $n \geq 1$

The Effect of Encoding on Performance

Assume a program stored information about the periodic table of elements. Three questions that frequently occur are a)"What is the atomic weight of element number N?", b)"What is the atomic number of the element named X?", and c)"What is the name of element number N?". One interesting challenge for this problem is that as of January 2008, element 117 had not yet been discovered, although element 118, Ununoctium, had been.

Encoding 1 of periodic table: store two arrays, elementName[], whose ith value stores the name of the element with atomic number i, and elementWeight[], whose ith value stores the weight of the element.

Encoding 2 of periodic table: store a string of 2,626 characters representing the entire table. The first 62 characters are:

    1 H Hydrogen 1.00794
    2 He Helium 4.002602
    3 Li Lithium 6.941

The following table shows the results of 32 trials of 100,000 random query invocations (including invalid ones). We discard the best and worst results, leaving 30 trials whose average execution time (and standard deviation) are shown in milliseconds:

	Weight	Number	Name
Enc1	2.1±5.45	131.73±8.83	2.63±5.99
Enc2	635.07±41.19	1050.43±75.60	664.13±45.90

As expected, Encoding 2 offers worse performance because each query involves using string manipulaton operations. Encoding 1 can efficiently process *weight* and *name* queries but *number* queries require an unordered search through the table.

This example shows how different encodings result in vast differences in execution times. It also shows that designers must choose the operations they would like to optimize.

distinct elements, one at a time, until a desired value, v, is found. For now, assume that:

- There are n distinct elements in the list
- The element being sought, v, is in the list
- Each element in the list is equally likely to be the value v

To understand the performance of SEQUENTIAL SEARCH, we must know how many elements it examines "on average." Since v is known to be in the list and each element is equally likely to be v, the average number of examined elements, $E(n)$, is the sum of the number of elements examined for each of the n values divided by n. Mathematically:

$$E(n) = \frac{1}{n}\sum_{i=1}^{n} i = \frac{n(n+1)}{2n} = \frac{1}{2}n + \frac{1}{2}$$

Thus, SEQUENTIAL SEARCH examines about half of the elements in a list of n distinct elements subject to these assumptions. If the number of elements in the list doubles, then SEQUENTIAL SEARCH should examine about twice as many elements; the expected number of probes is a linear function of n. That is, the expected number of probes is *linear* or "about" $c*n$ for some constant c. Here, $c=1/2$. A fundamental insight of performance analysis is that the constant c is unimportant in the long run, since the most important cost factor is the size of the problem instance, n. As n gets larger and larger, the error in claiming that:

$$\frac{1}{2}n \approx \frac{1}{2}n + \frac{1}{2}$$

becomes less significant. In fact, the ratio between the two sides of this approximation approaches 1. That is:

$$\lim_{n \to \infty} \frac{\left(\frac{1}{2}n\right)}{\left(\frac{1}{2}n + \frac{1}{2}\right)} = 1$$

although the error in the estimation is significant for small values of n. In this context we say that the rate of growth of the expected number of elements that SEQUENTIAL SEARCH examines is linear. That is, we ignore the constant multiplier and are concerned only when the size of an instance is large.

When using the abstraction of the rate of growth to choose between algorithms, we must be aware of the following assumptions:

Constants matter
That's why we use supercomputers and upgrade our computers on a regular basis.

The size of n is not always large
We will see in Chapter 4 that the rate of growth of the execution time of QUICKSORT is less than the rate of growth of the execution time of INSERTION SORT. Yet INSERTION SORT outperforms QUICKSORT for small arrays on the same platform.

An algorithm's rate of growth determines how it will perform on increasingly larger problem instances. Let's apply this underlying principle to a more complex example.

Consider evaluating four sorting algorithms for a specific sorting task. The following performance data was generated by sorting a block of n random strings. For string blocks of size $n=1$–512, 50 trials were run. The best and worst performances were discarded, and the chart in Figure 2-2 shows the average running time (in microseconds) of the remaining 48 results. The variance between the runs is surprising.

One way to interpret these results is to try to design a function that will predict the performance of each algorithm on a problem instance of size n. Since it is unlikely that we will be able to guess such a function, we use commercially available software to compute a trend line with a statistical process known as

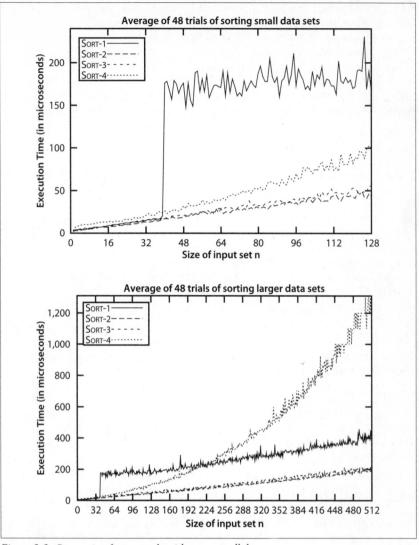

The Math of
Algorithms

Figure 2-2. Comparing four sort algorithms on small data sets

regression analysis. The "fitness" of a trend line to the actual data is based on a value between 0 and 1, known as the R^2 value. Values near 1 indicate a high fitness. For example, if $R^2 = 0.9948$, there is only a 0.52% chance that the fitness of the trend line is due to random variations in the data.

SORT-4 is clearly the worst performing of these sort algorithms. Given the 512 data points as plotted in a spreadsheet, the trend line to which the data conforms is:

$$y = 0.0053*n^2 - 0.3601*n + 39.212$$

$$R^2 = 0.9948$$

Having an R^2 confidence value so close to 1 declares this is an accurate estimate. SORT-2 offers the fastest implementation over the given range of points. Its behavior is characterized by the following trend line equation:

$$y = 0.05765^*n^*\log(n)+7.9653$$

SORT-2 marginally outperforms SORT-3 initially, and its ultimate behavior is perhaps 10% faster than SORT-3. SORT-1 shows two distinct behavioral patterns. For blocks of 39 or fewer strings, the behavior is characterized by:

$$y = 0.0016^*n^2+0.2939^*n+3.1838$$

$$R^2 = 0.9761$$

However, with 40 or more strings, the behavior is characterized by:

$$y = 0.0798^*n^*\log(n)+142.7818$$

The numeric coefficients in these equations are entirely dependent upon the *platform* on which these implementations execute. As described earlier, such incidental differences are not important. The long-term trend as n increases dominates the computation of these behaviors. Indeed, Figure 2-2 graphs the behavior using two different ranges to show that the real behavior for an algorithm may not be apparent until n gets large enough.

Algorithm designers seek to understand the behavioral differences that exist between algorithms. The source code for these algorithms is available from open source repositories, and it is instructive to see the impact of these designers' choices on the overall execution. SORT-1 reflects the performance of qsort on Linux 2.6.9. When reviewing the source code (which can be found through any of the available Linux code repositories[*]), one discovers the following comment: "Qsort routine from Bentley & McIlroy's Engineering a Sort Function." Bentley and McIlroy (1993) describe how to optimize QUICKSORT by varying the strategy for problem sizes less than 7, between 8 and 39, and for 40 and higher. It is satisfying to see that the empirical results presented here confirm the underlying implementation.

Analysis in the Best, Average, and Worst Cases

One question to ask is whether the results of the previous section will be true for all input problem instances. Perhaps SORT-2 is only successful in sorting a small number of strings. There are many ways the input could change:

- There could be 1,000,000 strings. How does an algorithm scale to large input?
- The data could be partially sorted, meaning that almost all elements are not that far from where they should be in the final sorted list.
- The input could contain duplicate values.
- Regardless of the size n of the input set, the elements could be drawn from a much smaller set and contain a significant number of duplicate values.

[*] *http://lxr.linux.no/linux+v2.6.11/fs/xfs/support/qsort.c*

Although SORT-4 from Figure 2-2 was the slowest of the four algorithms for sorting *n* random strings, it turns out to be the fastest when the data is already sorted. This advantage rapidly fades away, however, with just 16 random items out of position, as shown in Figure 2-3.

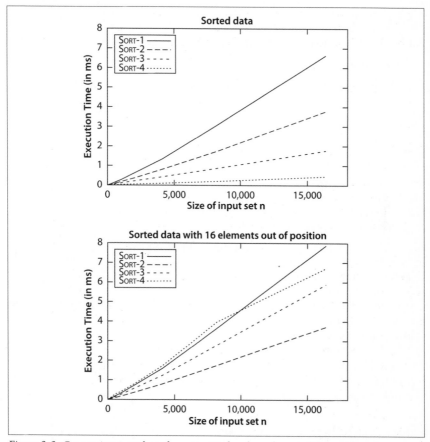

Figure 2-3. *Comparing sort algorithms on sorted and nearly sorted data*

However, suppose an input array with *n* strings is "nearly sorted"—that is, *n*/4 of the strings (25% of them) are swapped with another position just four locations away. It may come as a surprise to see in Figure 2-4 that SORT-4 outperforms the others.

The conclusion to draw is that for many problems, no single optimal algorithm exists. Choosing an algorithm depends on understanding the problem being solved and the underlying probability distribution of the instances likely to be treated, as well as the behavior of the algorithms being considered.

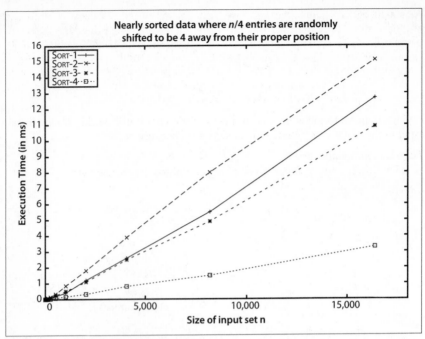

Figure 2-4. Sort-4 wins on nearly sorted data

To provide some guidance, algorithms are typically presented with three common cases in mind:

Worst-case

Defines a class of input instances for which an algorithm exhibits its worst runtime behavior. Instead of trying to identify the specific input, algorithm designers typically describe *properties* of the input that prevent an algorithm from running efficiently.

Average-case

Defines the expected behavior when executing the algorithm on random input instances. Informally, while some input problems will require greater time to complete because of some special cases, the vast majority of input problems will not. This measure describes the expectation an average user of the algorithm should have.

Best-case

Defines a class of input instances for which an algorithm exhibits its best runtime behavior. For these input instances, the algorithm does the least work. In reality, the best case rarely occurs.

By knowing the performance of an algorithm under each of these cases, you can judge whether an algorithm is appropriate for use in your specific situation.

Worst-Case

As n grows, most problems have a greater number of potential instances of size n. For any particular value of n, the work done by an algorithm or program may vary dramatically over all the instances of size n. For a given program and a given value n, the worst-case execution time is the maximum execution time, where the maximum is taken over all instances of size n.

Paying attention to the worst case is a pessimistic view of the world. We are interested in the worst-case behavior of an algorithm because of:

The desire for an answer
> This often is the easiest analysis of the complexity of an algorithm.

Real-time constraints
> If you are designing a system to aid a surgeon performing open-heart surgery, it is unacceptable for the program to execute for an unusually long time (even if such slow behavior doesn't happen "often").

More formally, if S_n is the set of instances s_i of size n, and t measures the work done by an algorithm on each instance, then work done by an algorithm on S_n in the worst case is the maximum of $t(s_i)$ over all $s_i \in S_n$. Denoting this worst-case work on S_n by $T_{wc}(n)$, the rate of growth of $T_{wc}(n)$ defines the worst-case complexity of the algorithm.

In general, there are not enough resources to compute each individual instance s_i on which to run the algorithm to determine empirically the input problem that leads to worst-case performance. Instead, an adversary tries to craft a worst-case input problem given the description of an algorithm.

Average-Case

A telephone system designed to support a large number n of telephones must, in the worst case, be able to complete all calls where $n/2$ people pick up their phones and call the other $n/2$ people. Although this system will never crash because of overload, it will be prohibitively expensive to construct. Besides, the probability that each of $n/2$ people calls a unique member of the other $n/2$ people is exceedingly small. One could design a system that is cheaper and will very rarely (possibly never) crash due to overload. But we must resort to mathematical tools to consider probabilities.

For the set of instances of size n, we associate a probability distribution Pr, which assigns a probability between 0 and 1 to each instance such that the sum, over all instances of size n, of the probability of that instance is 1. More formally, if S_n is the set of instances of size n, then:

$$\sum_{s_i \in S_n} \Pr\{s_i\} = 1$$

If t measures the work done by an algorithm on each instance, then the average-case work done by an algorithm on S_n is:

$$T_{ac}(n) = \frac{1}{|S_n|} \sum_{s_i \in S_n} t(s_i)\Pr\{s_i\}$$

That is, the actual work done on instance s_i, $t(s_i)$, is weighted with the probability that s_i will actually be presented as input. If $\Pr\{s_i\}=0$, then the actual value of $t(s_i)$ does not impact the expected work done by the program. Denoting this average-case work on S_n by $T_{ac}(n)$, then the rate of growth of $T_{ac}(n)$ defines the average-case complexity of the algorithm.

Recall that when describing the rate of growth of work or time, we consistently ignore constants. So when we say that SEQUENTIAL SEARCH of n elements takes, on average:

$$\frac{1}{2}n + \frac{1}{2}$$

probes (subject to our earlier assumptions), then by convention we simply say that subject to these assumptions, we expect SEQUENTIAL SEARCH will examine a *linear* number of elements, or *order n*.

Best-Case

Knowing the best case for an algorithm is useful even though the situation rarely occurs in practice. In many cases, it provides insight into the optimal circumstance for an algorithm. For example, the best case for SEQUENTIAL SEARCH is when it searches for a desired value, v, which ends up being the first element in the list. A slightly different approach, which we'll call COUNTING SEARCH, searches for a desired value, v, and counts the number of times that v appears in the list. If the computed count is zero, then the item was not found, so it returns false; otherwise, it returns true. Note that COUNTING SEARCH always searches through the entire list; therefore, even though its worst-case behavior is O(n)—the same as SEQUENTIAL SEARCH—its best-case behavior remains O(n), so it is unable to take advantage of either the best-case or average-case situations in which it could have performed better.

Performance Families

We compare algorithms by evaluating their performance on input data of size n. This methodology is the standard means developed over the past half-century for comparing algorithms. By doing so, we can determine which algorithms scale to solve problems of a nontrivial size by evaluating the running time needed by the algorithm in relation to the size of the provided input. A secondary form of performance evaluation is to consider how much memory or storage an algorithm needs; we address these concerns within the individual algorithm chapters, as appropriate.

We use the following classifications exclusively in this book, and they are ordered by decreasing efficiency:

- Constant
- Logarithmic
- Sublinear
- Linear
- $n \log (n)$
- Quadratic
- Exponential

We'll now present several discussions to illustrate some of these performance identifications.

Discussion 0: Constant Behavior

When analyzing the performance of the algorithms in this book, we frequently claim that some primitive operations provide constant performance. Clearly this claim is not an absolute determinant for the actual performance of the operation since we do not refer to specific hardware. For example, comparing whether two 32-bit numbers x and y are the same value should have the same performance regardless of the actual values of x and y. A constant operation is defined to have O(1) performance.

What about the performance of comparing two 256-bit numbers? Or two 1,024-bit numbers? It turns out that for a predetermined fixed size k, you can compare two k-bit numbers in constant time. The key is that the problem size (i.e., the values of the numbers x and y that are being compared) cannot grow beyond the fixed size k. We abstract the extra effort, which is multiplicative in terms of k, with the notation O(1).

Discussion 1: Log n Behavior

A bartender offers the following $10,000 bet to any patron. "I will choose a number from 1 to 1,000,000 and you can guess 20 numbers, one at a time; after each guess, I will either tell you TOO LOW, TOO HIGH, or YOU WIN. If you win in 20 questions, I give you $10,000; otherwise, you give me $10,000." Would you take this bet? You should because you can always win. Table 2-1 shows a sample scenario for the range 1–10 that asks a series of questions, reducing the problem size by about half each time.

Table 2-1. Sample behavior for guessing number from 1–10

Number	First guess	Second guess	Third guess
1	Is it 5?	Is it 2?	Is it 1?
	TOO HIGH	TOO HIGH	YOU WIN
2	Is it 5?	Is it 2?	
	TOO HIGH	YOU WIN	

Table 2-1. Sample behavior for guessing number from 1–10 (continued)

Number	First guess	Second guess	Third guess
3	Is it 5? TOO HIGH	Is it 2? TOO LOW	Is it 3? YOU WIN
4	Is it 5? TOO HIGH	Is it 2? TOO LOW	Is it 3? TOO LOW, so it must be 4
5	Is it 5? YOU WIN		
6	Is it 5? TOO LOW	Is it 8? TOO HIGH	Is it 6? YOU WIN
7	Is it 5? TOO LOW	Is it 8? TOO HIGH	Is it 6? TOO LOW, so it must be 7
8	Is it 5? TOO LOW	Is it 8? YOU WIN	
9	Is it 5? TOO LOW	Is it 8? TOO LOW	Is it 9? YOU WIN
10	Is it 5? TOO LOW	Is it 8? TOO LOW	Is it 9? TOO LOW, so it must be 10

In each turn, depending upon the specific answers from the bartender, the size of the potential range containing the hidden number is cut in about half each time. Eventually, the range of the hidden number will be limited to just one possible number; this happens after $\lceil \log (n) \rceil$ turns. The ceiling function $\lceil x \rceil$ rounds the number x up to the smallest integer greater than or equal to x. For example, if the bartender chooses a number between 1 and 10, you could guess it in $\lceil \log (10) \rceil = \lceil 3.32 \rceil$, or four guesses, as shown in the table.

This same approach works equally well for 1,000,000 numbers. In fact, the GUESSING algorithm shown in Example 2-1 works for any range [*low,high*] and determines the value of *n* in $\lceil \log (high-low+1) \rceil$ turns. If there are 1,000,000 numbers, this algorithm will locate the number in at most $\lceil \log (1,000,000) \rceil = \lceil 19.93 \rceil$, or 20 guesses (the worst case).

Example 2-1. Java code to guess number in range [low,high]

```java
// Compute number of turns when n is guaranteed to be in range [low,high].
public static int turns(int n, int low, int high) {
  int turns = 0;

  // While more than two potential numbers remain to be checked, continue.
  while (high - low ≤ 2) {
    // Prepare midpoint of [low,high] as the guess.
    turns++;
    int mid = (low + high)/2;
    if (mid == n) {
      return turns;
    } else if (mid < n) {
      low = mid + 1;
    } else {
      high = mid - 1;
```

Example 2-1. Java code to guess number in range [low,high] (continued)

```
    }
  }
  // At this point, only two numbers remain. We guess one, and if it is
  // wrong then the other one is the target. Thus only one more turn remains.
  return 1 + turns;
}
```

Logarithmic algorithms are extremely efficient because they rapidly converge on a solution. In general, these algorithms succeed because they reduce the size of the problem by about half each time. The GUESSING algorithm reaches a solution after at most $k = \lceil \log(n) \rceil$ iterations, and at the ith iteration ($i>0$), the algorithm computes a guess that is known to be within $\pm\varepsilon = 2^{k-i}$ from the actual hidden number. The quantity ε is considered the error, or uncertainty. After each iteration of the loop, ε is cut in half.

Another example showing efficient behavior is Newton's method for computing the roots of equations in one variable (in other words, for what values of x does $f(x) = 0$?). To find when $x^*\sin(x)-5^*x=\cos(x)$, set $f(x)=x^*\sin(x)-5^*x-\cos(x)$ and its derivative $f'(x)=x^*\cos(x)+\sin(x)-5-\sin(x)=x^*\cos(x)-5$. The Newton iteration computes $x_{n+1}=x_n-f(x_n)/f'(x_n)$. Starting with a "guess" that x is zero, this algorithm quickly determines an appropriate solution of $x=-0.189302759$, as shown in Table 2-2. The binary and decimal digits enclosed in brackets, [], are the accurate digits.

Table 2-2. Newton's method

n	x_n in decimal	x_n in bits (binary digits)
0	0.0	
1	−0.2	[1011111111001]00110011001100110011001100110...
2	−[0.18]8516717588...	[101111111001000001]0000101010000110110...
3	−[0.1893]59749489...	[1011111111001000000111]10011110000101101...
4	−[0.189]298621848...	[10111111110010000011101]0111011111111011...
5	−[0.18930]3058226...	[10111111110010000011011001]0101001001...
6	−[0.1893027]36274...	[10111111110010000011011000100]10011100...
7	−[0.189302759]639...	[101111111100100000111011000100101]01001...

Discussion 2: Sublinear O(n^d) Behavior for d<1

In some cases, the behavior of an algorithm is better than *linear*, yet not as efficient as *logarithmic*. As discussed in Chapter 9, the kd-tree in multiple dimensions can partition a set of *n* d-dimensional points efficiently. If the tree is balanced, the search time for range queries that conform to the axes of the points is $O(n^{1-1/d})$.

Discussion 3: Linear Performance

Some problems clearly seem to require more effort to solve than others. Any eight-year-old can evaluate 7+5 to get 12. How much harder is the problem 37+45?

In general, how hard is it to add two n-digit numbers $a_n \ldots a_1 + b_n \ldots b_1$ to result in a $c_{n+1} \ldots c_1$ digit value? The primitive operations used in this ADDITION algorithm are as follows:

$$c_i \leftarrow (a_i + b_i + carry_i) \bmod 10$$

$$carry_{i+1} \leftarrow \begin{cases} 1 \text{ if } a_i + b_i + carry_i \geq 10 \\ 0 \text{ otherwise} \end{cases}$$

A sample Java implementation of ADDITION is shown in Example 2-2, where an n-digit number is represented as an array of int values; for the examples in this section, it is assumed that each of these values is a decimal digit d such that $0 \leq d \leq 9$.

Example 2-2. Java implementation of add

```
public static void add (int[] n1, int[] n2, int[] sum) {
    int position = n1.length-1;
    int carry = 0;
    while (position >= 0) {
        int total = n1[position] + n2[position] + carry;
        sum[position+1] = total % 10;
        if (total > 9) { carry = 1; } else { carry = 0; }
        position--;
    }
    sum[0] = carry;
}
```

As long as the input problem can be stored in memory, add computes the addition of the two numbers as represented by the input integer arrays *n1* and *n2*. Would this implementation be as efficient as the following last alternative, listed in Example 2-3?

Example 2-3. Java implementation of last

```
public static void last(int[] n1, int[] n2, int[] sum) {
    int position = n1.length;
    int carry = 0;
    while (--position >= 0) {
        int total = n1[position] + n2[position] + carry;
        if (total > 9) {
            sum[position+1] = total-10;
            carry = 1;
        } else {
            sum[position+1] = total;
            carry = 0;
        }
    }
    sum[0] = carry;
}
```

Do these seemingly small implementation details affect the performance of an algorithm? Let's consider two other potential factors that can impact the algorithm's performance:

- Programming language is one factor. add and last can trivially be converted into C programs. How does the choice of language affect the algorithm's performance?
- The programs can be executed on different computers. How does the choice of computer hardware affect the algorithm's performance?

The implementations were executed 10,000 times on numbers ranging from 256 digits to 32,768 digits. For each digit size a random number of that size was generated; thereafter, for each of the 10,000 trials, these two numbers were circular shifted (one left and one right) to create two different numbers to be added. Two machines were used: a desktop PC and a high-end computer, as discussed in Chapter 10. Two different programming languages were used (C and Java). We start with the hypothesis that as the problem size doubles, the execution time for the algorithm doubles as well. We would like to also be reassured that this overall behavior occurs regardless of the machine, programming language, or implementation variation used.

Figure 2-5 contains a graph plotting problem size (shown on the X axis) against the execution time (in milliseconds) to compute 10,000 executions (shown on the Y axis). Each variation was executed on a set of configurations:

g
C version was compiled with debugging information included.

none
C version was compiled without any specific optimization.

O1, O2, O3
C version was compiled under these different optimization levels. In general, increasing numbers imply better optimization and thus better expected performance.

Java
Java version of algorithms.

PC-Java
This is the only configuration executed on a PC; the previous ones were all executed on the high-end computer.

Note how each of the computed lines for the graphs on the left side of Figure 2-5 (labeled "Desktop PC") can be approximated by a fixed linear slope, thus supporting the view that there is a linear relationship between the X and Y values. The computations using optimized code on the high-end computer cannot so simply be classified as linear, suggesting that the advanced processor has a significant impact.

Table 2-3 contains a subset of the charted data in numeric form. The code provided with this book generates this information as needed. The seventh and final column in Table 2-3 directly compares the performance times of the

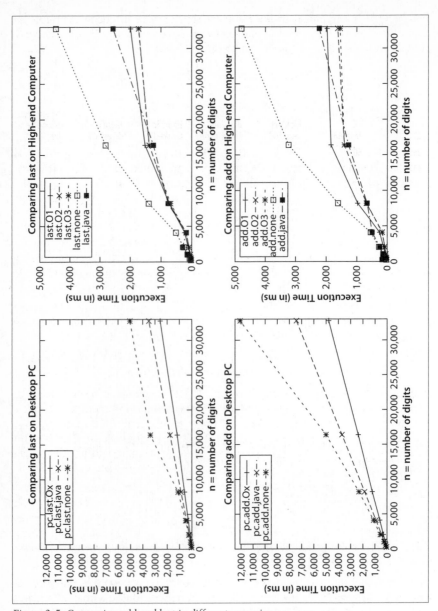

Figure 2-5. Comparing add and last in different scenarios

HighEnd-C-Last-O3 implementation,[*] as listed in the sixth column. The ratio of the performance times is nearly two, as expected. Define $t(n)$ to be the actual running time of the ADDITION algorithm on an input of size n. This growth

---

[*] That is, the C implementation of `last` when compiled using −O3 optimization level and executed on the high-end computer, as described in the appendix, which covers benchmarking.

pattern provides empirical evidence that the time in milliseconds to compute last for two n-digit numbers on the high-end computer using the C implementation with optimization level –O3 will be between $n/11$ and $n/29$.

Table 2-3. Time (in milliseconds) to execute 10,000 add/last invocations on random digits of size n

n	PC-Java-Add	HighEnd-Java-Add	HighEnd-C-Add-none	HighEnd-C-Add-O3	HighEnd-C-Last-O3	Ratio of last column by size
256	60	174	34	11	9	
512	110	36	70	22	22	2.44
1,024	220	124	139	43	43	1.95
2,048	450	250	275	87	88	2.05
4,096	921	500	550	174	180	2.05
8,192	1,861	667	1,611	696	688	3.82
16,384	3,704	1,268	3,230	1,411	1,390	2.02
32,768	7,430	2,227	4,790	1,555	1,722	1.24
65,536	17,453	2,902	9,798	3,101	3,508	2.04
131,072	35,860	12,870	20,302	7,173	7,899	2.25
262,144	68,531	22,768	41,800	14,787	16,479	2.09
524,288	175,015	31,148	82,454	29,012	32,876	2
1,048,576	505,531	64,192	162,955	55,173	63,569	1.93

Computer scientists would classify the ADDITION algorithm as being *linear* with respect to its input size n. That is, there is some constant $c>0$ such that $t(n)\leq c^*n$ for all $n>n_0$. We don't actually need to know the full details of the c or n_0 value, just that they exist. An argument can be made to establish a linear-time lower bound on the complexity of addition by showing that every digit must be examined (consider the consequences of not probing one of the digits).

For the last implementation of ADDITION, we can set c to 1/11 and choose n_0 to be 256. Other implementations of ADDITION would have different constants, yet their overall behavior would still be *linear*. This result may seem surprising given that most programmers assume that integer arithmetic is a constant time operation; however, constant time addition is achievable only when the integer representation (such as 16-bit or 64-bit) uses a fixed integer size n.

When considering differences in algorithms, the constant c is not as important as knowing the order of the algorithm. Seemingly inconsequential differences resulted in different performance. The last implementation of ADDITION is markedly more efficient after eliminating the modulo operator (%), which is notoriously slow when used with values that are not powers of 2. In this case, "% 10" is just not efficient since a division by 10 must occur, which is a costly operation on binary computers. This is not to say that we ignore the value of c. Certainly if we execute ADDITION a large number of times, even small changes to the actual value of c can have a large impact on the performance of a program.

Discussion 4: n log n Performance

A common behavior in efficient algorithms is best described by this performance family. To explain how this behavior occurs in practice, let's define $t(n)$ to represent the time that an algorithm takes to solve an input problem instance of size n. An efficient way to solve a problem is the "divide and conquer" method, in which a problem of size n is divided into (roughly equal) subproblems of size $n/2$, which are solved recursively, and their solutions merged together in some form to result in the solution to the original problem of size n. Mathematically, this can be stated as:

$t(n)=2*t(n/2)+O(n)$

That is, $t(n)$ includes the cost of the two subproblems together with no more than a linear time cost to merge the results. Now, on the right side of the equation, $t(n/2)$ is the time to solve a problem of size $n/2$; using the same logic, this can be represented as:

$t(n/2)=2*t(n/4)+O(n/2)$

and so the original equation is now:

$t(n)=2*[2*t(n/4)+O(n/2)]+O(n)$

If we expand this out once more, we see that:

$t(n)=2*[2*[2*t(n/8)+O(n/4)]+O(n/2)]+O(n)$

This last equation reduces to $t(n)=8*t(n/8)+O(3*n)$. In general, then, we can say that $t(n)=2^k*t(n/2^k)+O(k*n)$. This expansion ends when $2^k=n$, that is, when $k=\log(n)$. In the final base case when the problem size is 1, the performance $t(1)$ is a constant c. Thus we can see that the closed-form formula for $t(n)=n*c+O(n*\log(n))$. Since $n*\log(n)$ is asymptotically greater than $c*n$ for any fixed constant c, $t(n)$ can be simply written as $O(n \log n)$.

Discussion 5a: Quadratic Performance

Now consider a similar problem where two integers of size n are multiplied together. Example 2-4 shows an implementation of MULTIPLICATION, an elementary school algorithm.

Example 2-4. mult implementation of Multiplication in Java

```
public static void mult(int[] n1, int[] n2, int[] result) {
    int pos = result.length-1;

    // clear all values....
    for (int i = 0; i < result.length; i++) { result[i] = 0; }
    for (int m = n1.length-1; m>=0; m--) {
      int off = n1.length-1 - m;
      for (int n = n2.length-1; n>=0; n--,off++) {
        int prod = n1[m]*n2[n];
```

Example 2-4. mult implementation of Multiplication in Java (continued)

```
    // compute partial total by carrying previous digit's position
    result[pos-off] += prod % 10;
    result[pos-off-1] += result[pos-off]/10 + prod/10;
    result[pos-off] %= 10;
  }
 }
}
```

Once again, an alternative program is written, alt, which eliminates the need for the costly modulo operator, and skips the innermost computations when n1[m] is zero (note that alt is not shown here, but can be found in the provided code repository). The alt variation contains 203 lines of generated Java code to remove the two modulo operators. Does this variation show cost savings that validate the extra maintenance and development cost in managing this generated code?

Table 2-4 shows the behavior of these implementations of MULTIPLICATION using the same random input set used when demonstrating ADDITION. Figure 2-6 graphically depicts the performance, showing the parabolic growth curve that is the trademark of *quadratic* behavior.

Table 2-4. Time (in milliseconds) to execute 10,000 multiplications

n	Mult$_n$ (ms)	alt$_n$(ms)	mult$_{2n}$/mult$_n$
2	15	0	
4	15	15	1
8	62	15	4.13
16	297	218	4.80
32	1,187	734	4.00
64	4,516	3,953	3.80
128	19,530	11,765	4.32
256	69,828	42,844	3.58
512	273,874	176,203	3.92

Even though the alt variation is roughly 40% faster, both alt and mult exhibit the same asymptotic performance. The ratio of mult$_{2n}$/mult$_n$ is roughly 4, which demonstrates that the performance of MULTIPLICATION is *quadratic*. Let's define $t(n)$ to be the actual running time of the MULTIPLICATION algorithm on an input of size n. By this definition, there must be some constant $c>0$ such that $t(n) \leq c^*n^2$ for all $n>n_0$. We don't actually need to know the full details of the c and n_0 values, just that they exist. For the mult implementation of MULTIPLICATION on our platform, we can set c to 1.2 and choose n_0 to be 64.

Once again, individual variations in implementation are unable to "break" the inherent quadratic performance behavior of an algorithm. However, other algorithms exist (Zuras, 1994) to multiply a pair of *n*-digit numbers that are significantly faster than quadratic. These algorithms are important for applications such as data encryption, in which one frequently multiplies large integers.

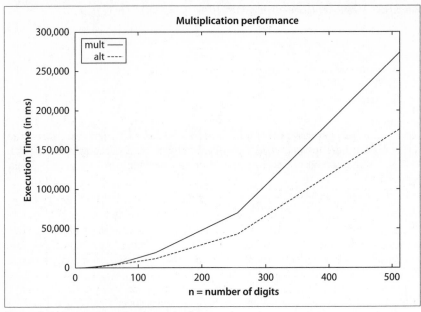

Figure 2-6. Comparison of mult versus alt

Discussion 5b: Less Obvious Performance Computations

In most cases, reading the description of an algorithm (as shown in ADDITION and MULTIPLICATION) is sufficient to classify an algorithm as being *linear* or *quadratic*. The primary indicator for *quadratic*, for example, is a nested loop structure. Some algorithms defy such straightforward analysis, however. Consider the GCD algorithm in Example 2-5, designed by Euclid to compute the greatest common divisor between two integers stored using arrays of digits.

Example 2-5. Euclid's GCD algorithm

```
public static void gcd (int a[], int b[], int gcd[]) {
    if (isZero(a)) { assign (gcd, a); return; }
    if (isZero(b)) { assign (gcd, b); return; }

    // ensure a and b are not modified
    a = copy (a);
    b = copy (b);

    while (!isZero(b)) {
        // last argument to subtract represents sign of result which
        // we can ignore since we only subtract smaller from larger.
        if (compareTo(a, b) > 0) {
            subtract (a, b, gcd, new int[1]);
            assign (a, gcd);
        } else {
            subtract (b, a, gcd, new int[1]);
            assign (b, gcd);
```

Example 2-5. Euclid's GCD algorithm (continued)

```
      }
   }

   // value held in a is the computed gcd of original (a,b)
   assign (gcd, a);
}
```

This algorithm repeatedly compares two numbers (*a* and *b*) and subtracts the smaller number from the larger until zero is reached. The implementations of the helper methods (isZero, assign, compareTo, subtract) are not shown here, but can be found in the accompanying code repository.

This algorithm produces the greatest common divisor of two numbers, but there is no clear answer as to how many iterations will be required based on the size of the input. During each pass through the loop, either *a* or *b* is reduced and never becomes negative, so we can guarantee that the algorithm will terminate, but some GCD requests take longer than others; for example, using this algorithm, gcd(1000,1) takes 999 steps! Clearly the performance of this algorithm is more sensitive to its inputs than ADDITION or MULTIPLICATION, in that there are different input instances of the same size that require very different computation times. This GCD algorithm exhibits its worst-case performance when asked to compute the GCD of $(10^n-1, 1)$; it needs to process the while loop 10^n-1 times! Since we have already shown that addition and subtraction are $O(n)$ in terms of the input size *n*, GCD requires $n*(10^n-1)$ operations of its loop. Converting this equation to base 2, we have $n*(2^{3.3219*n})-n$, which exhibits exponential performance. We classify this algorithm as $O(n*2^n)$.

The gcd implementation in Example 2-5 will be outperformed handily by the MODGCD algorithm described in Example 2-6, which relies on the modulo operator to compute the integer remainder of *a* divided by *b*.

Example 2-6. ModGCD algorithm for GCD computation

```
public static void modgcd (int a[], int b[], int gcd[]) {
   if (isZero(a)) { assign (gcd, a); return; }
   if (isZero(b)) { assign (gcd, b); return; }

   // align a and b to have same number of digits and work on copies
   a = copy(normalize(a, b.length));
   b = copy(normalize(b, a.length));

   // ensure that a is greater than b. Also return trivial gcd
   int rc = compareTo(a,b);
   if (rc == 0) { assign (gcd, a); return; }
   if (rc < 0) {
     int [] t = b;
     b = a;
     a = t;
   }

   int [] quot = new int[a.length];
   int [] remainder = new int[a.length];
```

Example 2-6. ModGCD algorithm for GCD computation (continued)

```
while (!isZero(b)) {
  int [] t = copy (b);
  divide (a, b, quot, remainder);
  assign (b, remainder);
  assign (a, t);
}

// value held in a is the computed gcd of (a,b).
assign (gcd, a);
}
```

MODGCD will arrive at a solution more rapidly because it won't waste time subtracting really small numbers from large numbers within the while loop. This difference is not simply an implementation detail; it reflects a fundamental shift in how the algorithm approaches the problem.

The computations shown in Figure 2-7 (and enumerated in Table 2-5) show the result of generating 142 random *n*-digit numbers and computing the greatest common divisor of all 10,011 pairs of these numbers.

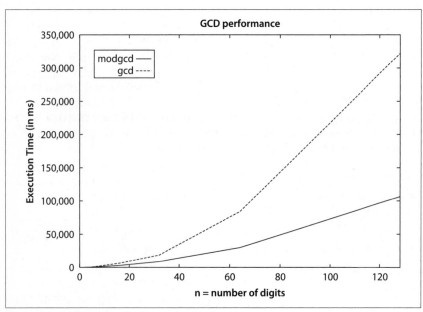

Figure 2-7. Comparison of gcd versus modgcd

Table 2-5. Time (in milliseconds) to execute 10,011 gcd computations

n	modgcd	gcd	n²/modgcd	n²/gcd	modgcd$_{2n}$/modgcd$_n$	gcd$_{2n}$/gcd$_n$
2	234	62	0.017	0.065		
4	391	250	0.041	0.064	1.67	4.03
8	1,046	1,984	0.061	0.032	2.68	7.94

n	modgcd	gcd	n^2/modgcd	n^2/gcd	modgcd$_{2n}$/ modgcd$_n$	gcd$_{2n}$/gcd$_n$
16	2,953	6,406	0.087	0.040	2.82	3.23
32	8,812	18,609	0.116	0.055	2.98	2.90
64	29,891	83,921	0.137	0.049	3.39	4.51
128	106,516	321,891	0.154	0.051	3.56	3.84

Even though the MODGCD implementation outperforms the corresponding GCD implementation by nearly 60%, the performance of MODGCD is *quadratic*, or $O(n^2)$, whereas GCD is exponential. That is, the worst-case performance of GCD (not exhibited in this small input set) is orders of magnitude slower than the worst-case performance of MODGCD.

More sophisticated algorithms for computing GCD have been designed—though most are impractical except for extremely large integers—and analysis suggests that the problem allows for more efficient algorithms.

Mix of Operations

As described earlier in the sidebar "The Effect of Encoding on Performance," a designer will have to consider multiple operations simultaneously. Not every operation can be optimized; in fact, optimizing one operation may degrade the execution of another operation. As an example, consider a data structure that contains operations *op1* and *op2*. Assume that there are two different ways by which the data structure can be implemented, A and B. For the purposes of this discussion, it is not important to know anything about the data structure or the individual methods. We construct two scenarios:

Small data sets
> On a base size of n=1,000 elements, mix together 2,000 *op1* operations with 3,000 *op2* operations.

Large data sets
> On a base size of n=100,000 elements, mix together 200,000 *op1* operations with 300,000 *op2* operations.

Table 2-6 contains the expected result of executing implementations A and B on these two data sets. The first row of the table shows that the average cost of performing *op1* on implementation A with n=1,000 sized data is assumed to be 0.008 milliseconds; the other values in the second and third columns should be interpreted similarly. The final column reflects the total expected time of execution; thus, for option A on n=1,000 sized data, we expect the time to be 2,000*0.008+3,000*0.001=16+3=19 milliseconds. Although implementation B initially outperforms the A implementation for small values of n, the situation changes dramatically when the scale of the problem increases by two orders of magnitude. Note how alternative A scales well, whereas option B performs horribly.

Table 2-6. Comparing operations from different implementations

Input Size	op1 (ms)	op2 (ms)	# op1	# op2	Total (ms)
A on 1,000	0.008	0.001	2,000	3,000	19
A on 100,000	0.0016	0.003	200,000	300,000	1,220
B on 1,000	0.001	0.001	2,000	3,000	5
B on 100,000	0.1653	0.5619	200,000	300,000	201,630

Benchmark Operations

The Scheme program in Example 2-7 computes 2^n; a sample computation of 2^{851} is shown.

Example 2-7. Expensive computations

```
;; TwoToTheN: number -> number
(define (TwoToTheN n)
  (let loop ([i n]
             [result 1])
    (if (= i 0)
        result
        (loop (sub1 i) (* 2 result)))))

;; the result of a sample computation
(TwoToTheN 851)
15015033657609400459942315391018513722623519187099007073355798781525263125238463
41589482039716066276169710803836941092523836538133260448652352292181327981032007
94538451818051546732566997782908246399595358358052523086606780893692342385292277
74479195332149248
```

In Scheme, computations are relatively independent of the underlying platform. That is, computing 2^{851} in Java or C on most platforms would cause a numeric overflow. But a fast computation in Scheme yields the result shown in the example. Is it an advantage or a disadvantage that the underlying architecture is hidden from us, abstracted away? Consider the following two hypotheses:

Hypothesis H1
Computing 2^n has consistent behavior, regardless of the value of n.

Hypothesis H2
Large numbers (such as shown previously in expanded form) can be treated in the same way as any other number, such as 123,827 or 997.

To refute hypothesis H1, we conduct 50 trials that performed 10,000 evaluations of 2^n. We discarded the best and worst performers, leaving 48 trials. The average time of these 48 trials is shown in Figure 2-8.

There is clearly a linear relationship initially, as an increasing number of multiply-by-2 operations are performed. However, once x reaches about 30, a different linear relationship takes place. For some reason, the computational performance alters once powers of 2 greater than about 30 are used.

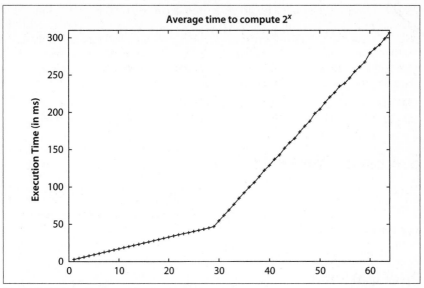

Figure 2-8. Execution times for computing 2^x

To refute hypothesis H2, we conduct an experiment that pre-computes the value of 2^n and then evaluates the time to compute $3.14159 \cdot 2^n$. We executed 50 trials that performed 10,000 evaluations of the equation $3.14159 \cdot 2^n$. We discarded the best and worst performers, leaving 48 trials. The average time of these 48 trials is shown in Figure 2-9 (these results are essentially the same, even if we multiply by 1.0000001 instead of 3.14159).

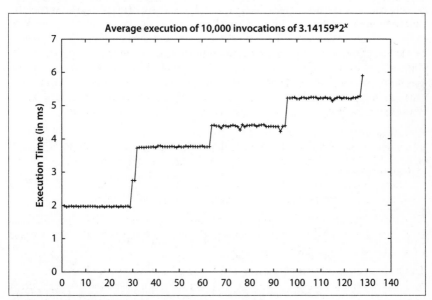

Figure 2-9. Execution times for computing large multiplication

Why do the points in Figure 2-9 not appear on a straight line? For what value of x does the line break? The multiplication operation (*) appears to be overloaded. It does different things depending upon whether the numbers being multiplied are floating-point numbers, or integers that each fit into a single word of the machine, or integers that are so large that they must each be stored in several words of the machine, or some combination of these.

The first break in the plot occurs for $x=\{30,31\}$, which cannot easily be explained. The remaining plateaus offer more conventional explanations, since they occur at the values (32, 64, 96, 128), which represent the size of the word on the computer on which the trials were executed (namely, one, two, three, or four 32-bit words). As the numbers require more and more words of space to be stored, the time needed to perform multiplication also increases.

A benchmark operation is essential to an algorithm, such that counting executions of the benchmark operation offers a good prediction of the execution time of a program. The benchmark operation of TwoToTheN is *, the multiplication operation.

One Final Point

We have simplified the presentation of the "Big O" notation in this book. For example, when discussing the behavior of the ADDITION algorithm that is *linear* with respect to its input size n, we argued that there exists some constant $c>0$ such that $t(n) \leq c*n$ for all $n>n_0$; recall that $t(n)$ represents the actual running time of ADDITION. By this reasoning, we claim the performance of ADDITION is $O(n)$. The careful reader will note that we could just as easily have used a function $f(n)=c*2^n$ that grows more rapidly than $c*n$. Indeed, although it is technically accurate to claim that ADDITION is $O(2^n)$, such a statement provides very little information (it would be like saying that you need no more than one week to perform a five-minute task). To explain why, consider the notation $\Omega(g(n))$, which declares that $g(n) \leq t(n)$ is a lower bound for the actual running time. One can often compute both the upper (O) and lower (Ω) bound for the execution time of an algorithm, in which case the appropriate notation to use is $\Theta(f(n))$, which asserts that $f(n)$ is asymptotically both an upper bound (as is the case for $O(f(n))$) and a lower bound for $t(n)$.

We chose the more informal (and widely accepted use) of $O(f(n))$ to simplify the presentations and analyses. We ensure that when discussing algorithmic behavior, there is no better $f'(n)$ that can be used to classify the algorithms we have identified as $O(f(n))$.

References

Bentley, Jon Louis and M. Douglas McIlroy, "Engineering a Sort Function," *Software—Practice and Experience*, 23(11): 1249–1265, 1993, *http://citeseer.ist.psu.edu/bentley93engineering.html*.

Zuras, D. "More on Squaring and Multiplying Large Integers," *IEEE Transactions on Computers*, 43(8): 899–908, 1994, *http://doi.ieeecomputersociety.org/10.1109/12.295852*.

3

Patterns and Domains

We build software to solve problems. During the decades since the first programmed computer printed answers to previously unapproachable problems—such as computing the 400,052,412,247th digit of π—programmers have written countless programs to solve numerous problems. Programmers spent hours happily writing code to solve the problem at hand, while at the same time others also were coding solutions to identical, or very similar, problems. There are several reasons programmers create unique solutions rather than seeking an existing solution. One reason, of course, is the tendency to believe that we can always build a better mousetrap. Programming for many of us has the same appeal that the game of chess has for chess aficionados. Some reasons are more important than others when considering why programmers continue to write the same solutions for problems from scratch:

- The programmer doesn't realize that the problem has already been solved. We'll look into this further when we discuss problem domains.

- Even if the programmer knows the problem has been solved in similar cases, it's not clear that the existing code will actually fit the specific problem facing the programmer.

- It's not easy to find code that really solves the problem at hand or code that can be easily modified to solve that problem.

Patterns: A Communication Language

In the late 1980s, a few visionary software developers began looking for new ways to communicate their designs with one another. Some of them happened upon a work by Christopher Alexander, a professor of architecture at the University of California, Berkeley, called *A Pattern Language: Towns, Buildings, Construction* (1977). In this seminal work, Alexander developed a theory for describing architectural design. In 1987, Kent Beck and Ward Cunningham, two well-known leaders of the object-oriented paradigm, introduced the idea of applying design patterns to programming at that year's Conference on Object-Oriented Programming Systems, Languages, and Applications (OOPSLA). The idea caught on and people began to think about software design patterns. In 1995, the seminal Gang of Four (GoF) book, *Design Patterns: Elements of Reusable Object-Oriented Software* (Gamma et al., 1995) was published, and a frenzy of research activity and application of patterns began.

As with any good idea, the software industry embraced patterns and their use became ubiquitous, to the point where everything could be described by a pattern. Using coding standards was a pattern. Sitting together with a partner to debug a program was a pattern. Well, you get the idea. Patterns are a great way to communicate precisely and concisely well-formed concepts. We will—at the risk of applying patterns to yet another area of computer science—use patterns as a way to communicate the algorithms in this book.

Before describing how we structure the pattern language for the algorithms herein, let's look at what a pattern is and why it's so good. We prefer the following definition for design patterns:

> A design pattern is a proven solution to a commonly occurring problem.

This definition is short and conveys the absolute essence of design patterns. First and foremost, a design pattern is a solution to a real problem. In fact, it's a solution to a general set of problems. But, a pattern is not a template where you simply fill in the blanks. It is an approach, or a plan, for solving a particular class of problems. Armed with a set of design patterns in your toolbox, you are on your way to becoming a master craftsman of software design.

We can think of algorithms in different ways. Many practitioners are happy to look up an algorithm in a book or on some website, copy some code, run it, maybe even test it, and then move on to the next task. In our opinion, this process does not improve one's understanding of algorithms. In fact, this approach can lead you down the wrong path where you select a specific implementation of an algorithm. Remember how in Chapter 1 Graham blindly selected a binary tree and didn't bother to balance it? That's what can happen when you just take the first idea that seems to solve your problem.

So, the question is, how do you locate the right algorithm for the job quickly and understand it well enough to ensure that you've made a good choice? Patterns can help. Algorithms are, in fact, proven solutions to known problems, so they fit our definition of a pattern.

The Form of an Algorithm Pattern

Design patterns are typically presented in a stylized manner that makes it easy to understand and communicate to others. Not all pattern writers or books on patterns agree on the specific form, but they have many elements in common. We have adopted a style for presenting algorithms as patterns that we believe will be effective for the reader. Feel free to recast them to your favorite form if that helps you get a better understanding of the material.

Each algorithm is presented using a fixed set of sections that conform to our pattern language. Sometimes a section may be omitted if it adds no value to the algorithm description. Sometimes we may add another section to the description to illuminate a particular point.

Algorithm Pattern Format

Each algorithm is presented using the following pattern sections:

Name
> A descriptive name for the algorithm. We use this name to communicate concisely the algorithm to others. For example, if we talk about using a SEQUENTIAL SEARCH, it conveys exactly what type of search algorithm we are talking about. The name of each algorithm is always shown in SMALL CAPS; all words typeset this way in this book refer to an algorithm.

Synopsis
> A high-level description of the algorithm and what it is designed to do.

Context
> A description of a problem that illustrates the "sweet spot" for the algorithm.

Forces
> A description of the properties of the problem/solution that must be addressed and maintained for a successful implementation. They are the things that would cause you to choose this algorithm specifically.

Solution
> The algorithm description using real working code with documentation. Where appropriate, UML class diagrams are also included.

Consequences
> Identifies and discusses the advantages/disadvantages and anti-patterns for this algorithm.

Analysis
> A synopsis of the analysis of the algorithm, including performance data as well as other data that helps the reader understand the behavior of the algorithm. Although the analysis section is not meant to "prove" the described performance of an algorithm, readers should be able to understand why the algorithm behaves as it does. We will provide references to actual texts that present the appropriate lemmas and proofs to explain why the algorithms behave as described.

Related algorithms
> Presents either slight variations of the algorithm or different alternatives.

The real power of using such a template for the algorithms is that you can quickly compare and contrast different algorithms. At the same time, you can identify commonalities in seemingly different algorithms.

Pseudocode Pattern Format

Each algorithm in this book is presented with code examples that show an implementation in a major programming language, such as C, C++, Java, Scheme, and Ruby. For readers who are not familiar with all of these languages, we first introduce each algorithm in pseudocode with a small example showing its execution.

Consider the sample fact sheet shown in Figure 3-1. Each algorithm is named, and its performance is clearly marked for all three behavior cases (best, average, and worst). The upper-right corner of the fact sheet lists a set of concepts used by the algorithm. This is a place that can be used to rapidly see commonalities among different algorithms (e.g., "these two algorithms use a priority queue").

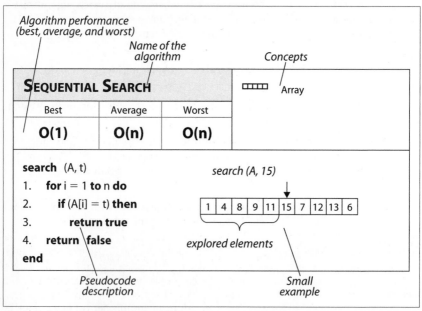

Figure 3-1. Sequential Search fact sheet

The "glyphs" that appear in this region of the fact sheet are depicted in Figure 3-2. Some of these concepts relate to the data structure(s) used by the algorithm (e.g., "Queue"), while others refer to an overall approach to solving the problem (e.g., "Divide and Conquer").

The pseudocode description is intentionally kept brief and should fill up no more than 3/4 of a page. Keywords and function names are described in boldface text. All variables are in lowercase characters, whereas arrays are capitalized and their elements are referred to using $A[i]$ notation. The indentation in the pseudocode describes the scope of conditional if statements and looping while and for statements. All statements within a function are numbered for reference (if necessary) in descriptions in the individual chapters.

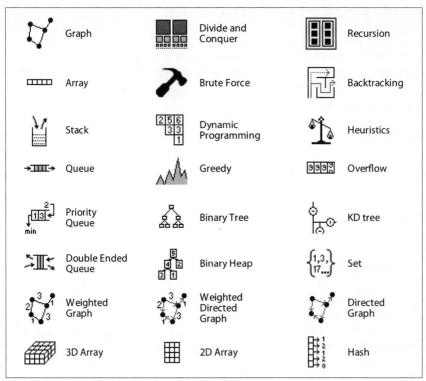

Figure 3-2. Glyphs for identifying algorithmic concepts

You should refer first to the fact sheet and use it as a reference when reading the provided source code implementations. Within the fact sheet, a small example is used to better explain the execution of the algorithm. In general, to show the dynamic behavior of the algorithms, the individual steps of the example are shown vertically in sequence, representing time moving "downward" on the fact sheet.

Design Format

We provide a set of UML class diagrams for solutions that are coded in Java or C++. These diagrams are a helpful aid to understanding code that takes advantage of class inheritance and polymorphism. Figure 3-3 contains a sample class diagram showing the relationship between a superclass SegmentTreeNode and two subclasses, DefaultSegmentTreeNode and StoredIntervalsNode, that extend SegmentTreeNode using inheritance (as identified by the arrows terminating in triangles). Each class box has two parts: the upper part lists instance variables, and the lower part lists instance methods. The leading symbols for each declared attribute or method are significant:

 # (protected)
Declares that the attribute or method is visible to the class or any of its subclasses; if the underlying implementation is Java, then the attribute or method is also visible to classes within the same package. Note that in our C++ implementations, we do not use multiple inheritance or friend classes, so the semantics are nearly identical.

~ (package-private)
Declares that the attribute or method is visible only to classes within the same package; used only by Java designs.

− (private)
Declares that the attribute is visible only to the class itself in which the attribute is defined. We intentionally do not list in the class diagram any private methods that may exist.

+ (public)
Declares that the attribute or method is visible and accessible to anyone. Public attributes are, in general, assumed to be "final" as well, implying that they are constant even within the same class.

Class methods declare their return type (which may be void) and parameter list (which may be empty). Constructor methods have the same name as the class within which they are defined. Destructor methods (only in C++) can be identified by the "~" symbol in their name. Naturally the reader may be confused between a C++ destructor and a Java package-private method, since they use the same symbol. Look to the accompanying text in the algorithm chapters, which will help differentiate these two situations.

In Java, there is an additional type of relationship between a class and an interface that the class implements. For example, SegmentTreeNode implements IInterval, which means that SegmentTreeNode must complete the implementation of methods specified only in IInterval. This relationship is depicted in Figure 3-3 by means of a dashed line terminating in an open triangle.

Empirical Evaluation Format

The implementations of the algorithms are all executed with a series of benchmark problems, appropriate for each individual algorithm. The appendix provides more detail on the mechanisms used for timing purposes. In general, we execute all algorithms on two different platforms: a common desktop environment and a high-end Linux cluster. Together these provide a range within which most systems should exist. To properly evaluate the performance, a test suite is composed of a set of k individual trials (typically $k \geq 10$). The best and worst performers are discarded as outliers, the remaining $k-2$ trials are aggregated, and the average and standard deviations are computed. Tables are shown with problem size instances ranging from $n=2$ to 2^{20}.

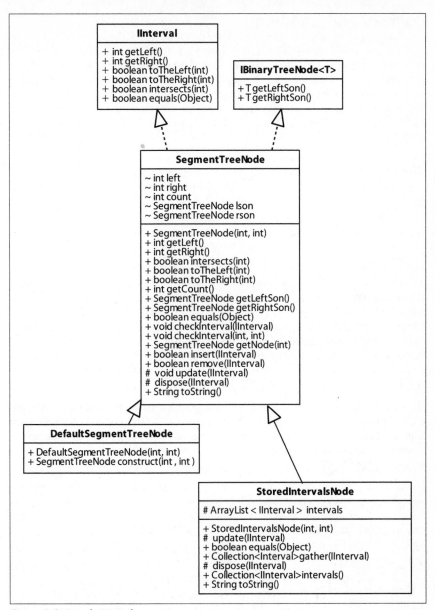

Figure 3-3. Sample UML diagram

Domains and Algorithms

Domains became popular in the late 1980s when researchers began to explore how object-oriented principles could be used to promote software reuse. In the context of reuse, domains are application areas that share common traits. Each domain has its own vocabulary that provides a language to describe the domain. The language helps design systems and reusable components that are appropriate for the particular domain. Domain-specific languages (DSLs) are used to model domains to generate domain-specific software, rather than construct it manually.

Algorithms, like applications, have domains. These domains are orthogonal to specific application domains. Algorithm domains provide us with knowledge about the application domains that are most amenable to certain types of algorithms. For example, if one is developing an application to access web services from a mobile phone, it would be appropriate to use algorithms optimized for space usage and external storage rather than simply the best overall time performance.

Algorithm domains are not as well defined as application domains; they are more general and span several application domains. Algorithm domains map more closely to standard computer science areas. We see, for example, search and graph traversal algorithms used frequently in artificial intelligence applications, whereas numerical algorithms seldom appear in such applications. Database management systems have their own set of algorithms that appear frequently, as do most other application domains.

In our algorithm patterns we do not indicate any specific domain set for each algorithm, since no standard algorithm domain categorization exists. The context for each algorithm does, however, offer the reader a particular domain where the algorithm fits well. As one becomes familiar with algorithms and thinking of algorithms in terms of patterns, a natural taxonomy that maps application domains to algorithm domains emerges.

Developing the mapping between algorithm domains and application domains is an interesting and important research area. Obtaining an appropriate taxonomy will aid us to develop and generate better software components and applications. Researchers are applying advanced mathematical analysis to develop the categorizations (Algorithm Formalization, 2007).

From a practitioner's viewpoint, algorithm categorization comes from experiential tales, or war stories (Skiena, 1998). These informal anecdotes give the practitioner a more intuitive insight and confidence about when to use a particular type of algorithm. The literature, both academic and industrial, is full of such war stories about algorithms, and we encourage you to develop your own. Such an exercise can help you internalize the algorithms and make you a better software developer. The beauty of algorithms is that the connection between algorithm domains and applicability is continually expanding. New algorithms are being developed, but possibly more importantly, new applications for existing algorithms are being discovered. Thinking of algorithm domains helps you manage this ever-complex relationship.

Floating-Point Computations

Computers are finite machines that have been designed to perform basic computations on values stored in registers by a Central Processing Unit (CPU). The size of these registers has evolved as computer architectures have grown from the popular 8-bit Intel processors from the 1970s to today's widespread acceptance of 64-bit architectures (such as Intel's Itanium and Sun Microsystems Sparc processor). The CPU often supports basic operations—such as ADD, MULT, DIVIDE, and SUB—over integer values stored within these registers. Floating Point Units (FPUs) can efficiently process floating-point computations according to the IEEE Standard for Binary Floating-Point Arithmetic (IEEE 754).

Computations over integer-based values (such as Booleans, 8-bit shorts, and 16- and 32-bit integers) have traditionally been the most efficient computations performed by the processor. Efficient programs that execute on computer architectures often take advantage of the performance differential between integer-based and floating point–based arithmetic. There are important issues that developers must be aware of when programming using floating-point arithmetic (Goldberg, 1991). Next we focus on the important issues that we consider in the algorithms and supporting code for this book.

Rounding Error

Any computation using floating-point values may introduce rounding errors because of the nature of the floating-point representation. In general, a floating-point number is a finite representation that is designed to approximate a real number whose representation may be infinite. Table 3-1 shows information about floating-point representations and the specific representation for the value 3.88f.

Table 3-1. Floating-point representation

Primitive type	Sign	Exponent	Mantissa
Float	1 bit	8 bits	23 bits
Double	1 bit	11 bits	52 bits

Sample Representation of 3.88 as (0x407851ec)

```
01000000  01111000  01010001  11101100  (total of 32 bits)
s         mmmmmmm   mmmmmmmm  mmmmmmmm
 eeeeeee  e
```

The next three consecutive floating-point representations (and values) are:

0x407851ec	3.88
0x407851ed	3.8800004
0x407851ee	3.8800006
0x407851ef	3.8800008

Here are the floating-point values for three randomly chosen 32-bit values:

0x1aec9fae	9.786529E-23
0x622be970	7.9280355E20
0x18a4775b	4.2513525E-24

One bit is used for the sign, 8 bits form the exponent, and 23 bits form the mantissa (also known as the *significand*). In the Java float representation, "the power of two can be determined by interpreting the exponent bits as a positive number, and then subtracting a bias from the positive number. For a float, the bias is 126" (Venners, 1996). The exponent stored is 128, so the actual exponent value is 128–126, or 2.

To achieve the greatest precision, the mantissa is always normalized so that the leftmost digit is always 1, so it is implied. In the previous example, the mantissa is .[1]11110000101000111101100 = [1/2] + 1/4 + 1/8 + 1/16 + 1/32 + 1/1,024 + 1/4,096 + 1/65,536 + 1/131,072 + 1/262,144 + 1/524,288 + 1/2,097,152 + 1/4,194,304, which evaluates exactly to 0.9700000286102294921875 if the full sum of fractions is carried out.

Thus, when storing 3.88f using this representation, the approximate value is $+1*0.9700000286102294921875*2^2$, which is exactly 3.88000011444091796875. The error inherent in the value is ~0.0000001. The most common way of describing floating-point error is to use the term *relative error*, which computes the ratio of the absolute error with the desired value. Here, the relative error is 0.0000001144091796875/3.88, or 2.9E–8. It is quite common for these relative errors to be less than 1 part per million.

Comparing Values

Because floating-point values are only approximate, even the most simple operations in floating point become suspect. Consider the following statement:

```
if (x == y) {
}
```

Is it truly the case that these two floating-point numbers must be exactly equal? Or it is sufficient for them to be simply approximately equal (for which we use the symbol ≅)? Could it ever occur that two values are different though close enough that they should be considered to be the same? Given three points $p_0=(a,b)$, $p_1=(c,d)$ and $p_2=(e,f)$ in the Cartesian plane, they define an ordered pair of two line segments (p_0,p_1) and (p_1,p_2). We can use the computation $(c-a)(f-b)-(d-b)(e-a)$ to determine whether these two line segments are collinear (i.e., on the same line). If the value of this expression is zero, then the two segments are collinear. To show how floating-point errors can occur in computations in Java, consider the three points in Table 3-2.

Table 3-2. Floating-point arithmetic errors

	float	double
a=1/3	0.33333334	0.3333333333333333
b=5/3	1.6666666	1.6666666666666667
c=33	33.0	33.0
d=165	165.0	165.0
e=19	19.0	19.0
f=95	95.0	95.0
(c–a)*(f–b) – (d–b)*(e–a)	4.8828125 E–4	–4.547473508864641 E–13

Dutcher - setchy
reduction of IO.
EoF
h = 65
setchy gets everything

As you can readily determine, these three points are collinear on the line $y=5*x$. When computing floating-point calculations, however, the errors inherent in floating-point arithmetic affect the computation. Using floats as the values, the calculation results in 0.00048828125; using doubles, the computed value is actually a very small negative number! Now we could introduce a small value δ to determine $\cong$ between two floating-point values. Under this scheme, if $|a-b|<\delta$, then we consider a and b to be equal. However, it may be the case that $x\cong y$ and $y\cong z$, but it might not be the case that $x\cong z$. This breaks the principle of Transitivity and makes it really challenging to write correct code.

Special Quantities

While all possible 64-bit values could represent valid floating-point numbers, the IEEE standard defines several values that are interpreted as special numbers (and are often not able to participate in the standard mathematical computations, such as ADD or MULT), shown in Table 3-3. These values have been designed to make it easier to recover from common errors, such as divide by zero, square root of a negative number, overflow of computations, and underflow of computations. Note that the values of positive zero and negative zero are also included in this table, even though they can be used in computations.

Table 3-3. Special IEEE 754 quantities

Special quantity	64-bit IEEE 754 representation
Positive infinity	0x7ff0000000000000L
Negative infinity	0xfff0000000000000L
Not a number (NaN)	0x7ff0000000000001L through 0x7fffffffffffffffL and 0xfff0000000000001L through 0xffffffffffffffffL
Negative zero	0x8000000000000000
Positive zero	0x0000000000000000

These special quantities are the result of computations that go outside the acceptable bounds. For example, the quantity positive infinity could result from the Java computation double x=1/0.0. As an interesting aside, the Java virtual machine would throw java.lang.ArithmeticException if the statement had instead read double x=1/0, since this expression computes the integer division of two numbers.

Performance

It is commonly accepted that computations over integer values will be more efficient than their floating-point counterparts. Table 3-4 lists the computation times of 10,000,000 operations on our high-end performance platform. A 1996 Sparc Ultra-2 machine generated the values in the third column. As you can see, the performance of individual operations can vary significantly from one platform to another.

Table 3-4. Performance computations of 10,000,000 operations

Operation	Linux i686 (time in seconds)	Sparc Ultra-2 (time in seconds)	High-end computer (time in seconds)
32-bit integer CMP	0.0337	0.811	0.0553
32-bit integer MUL	0.0421	2.372	0.0723
32-bit float MUL	0.1032	1.236	0.0666
64-bit double MUL	0.1028	1.406	0.0864
32-bit float DIV	0.1814	1.657	0.0768
64-bit double DIV	0.1813	2.172	0.1005
128-bit double MUL	0.2765	36.891	0.2447
32-bit integer DIV	0.2468	3.104	0.3061
32-bit double SQRT	0.2749	3.184	0.2414

Manual Memory Allocation

Most modern programming languages allow the programmer to allocate dynamic memory from the Heap (as opposed to the Stack) during the execution of a program. Consider the C program in Example 3-1.

Example 3-1. Sample program that allocates memory

```
#include <stdlib.h>
#include <string.h>

void f(char *inner) {
  char temp[11];
  strcpy (temp, "algorithms");
  int i;

  for (i=0; i<11; i++) {
    inner[i] = temp[i];
  }
}

int main (int argc, char **argv) {
  char *ar1 = malloc(132);
  char *ar2 = malloc(132);
  int i = 17, j;

  f (ar2);
  return 0;
}
```

When the program executes, variables that are local to a function (such as argc, and argv for main) are assigned to locations on the Execution Stack, which stores the progress of the program execution. Dynamically allocated memory (such as ar1 in main) is instead stored on the Heap, a separate region of memory available for allocation. The address of the variable determines where the memory can be found. In the example, one possible assignment of variables (on a Linux i686) is shown in Table 3-5.

Table 3-5. Addresses for symbols and variables

f variables	Addresses	main variables	Addresses	Global symbols	Addresses
f.inner	3221222728	main.argc	3221222796	&f	4195576
f.temp	3221222704	main.argv	3221222784	&main	4195648
f.i	3221222700	main.ar1	3221222776		
		main.ar2	3221222768		
		main.i	3221222764		
		main.j	3221222760		
		*main.ar1	5246992		
		*main.ar2	5247136		

Note how the address values are all near one another, signifying that they are co-located. The address of *main.ar1 is drawn from the Heap. In the traditional computational paradigm, the Stack grows "downward" in memory, while the Heap grows "upward" as shown in Figure 3-4.

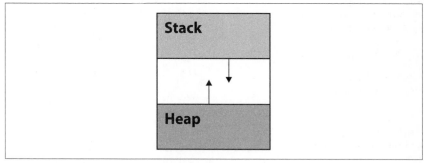

Figure 3-4. Stack and Heap dynamic behavior

The addresses reveal this behavior since the computation proceeds from main( ) to f( ) and the addresses of the variables steadily decrease. If the Stack grows too large, a program crashes because the memory for the individual stack frames will overwrite memory that should be safely protected in the heap. When this cross-over occurs depends upon the hardware platform and the initial memory allocated for the operating system process.

In Example 3-2, the infinite recursion caused a "Segmentation Fault" at the 393,060th recursive call, after the execution Stack had grown to over 12,577,888 bytes in size.

Example 3-2. Code exhibiting infinite recursion

```
#include <stdio.h>

int f(int n) {
  printf (" n %d[%u] \n", n, &n);
  return f(n+1);
}
```

Example 3-2. Code exhibiting infinite recursion (continued)

```
int main (int argc, char **argv) {
  return f(0);
}
```

As a program executes, by calling and returning from functions, the execution Stack grows and shrinks. All memory stored on the Stack is thus reclaimed automatically. However, memory stored in the Heap is under control of the programmer and will only be released explicitly. In most cases, when a program fails to release the memory, it may yet continue to function properly (when the program terminates, the memory that it used is reclaimed by the operating system).

A program can run out of Heap space (although typically this is a sign of a serious defect) if the Heap grows so large that it risks interfering with the execution Stack. Consider the program in Example 3-3, which repeatedly generates new allocated strings in memory.

Example 3-3. Code with memory leak

```
#include <stdio.h>
#include <string.h>
#include <stdlib.h>

/** Return string "abcdef" as "fabcde". */
char *cycle (char *s) {
  int n = strlen(s);
  char *u = malloc (n+1);
  strncpy (u, s+1, n-1);
  u[n-1] = s[0];
  u[n] = '\0';
  return u;
}

int main (int argc, char **argv) {
  char *s = strdup ("ThisStringHas25Characters");
  int num=0;

  for (;;) {
    printf ("%d\n", ++num);
    s = cycle(s);
  }
}
```

The `malloc` invocation requests a fixed set of memory (in bytes) from the memory allocation system. If there is sufficient Heap space, the address of the allocated memory is returned to the programmer (otherwise the null address 0x0 is returned). In the example, no attempt is made to release memory, and after 356,331,411 iterations, the program was manually terminated.* Since each

---

* Be careful when executing this code on a shared machine, because it will temporarily consume all CPU and operating system resources until the program eventually terminates.

---

pass allocates 26 bytes of memory, this program terminated after nearly 15.9 gigabytes of allocated memory on a machine with 16 gigabytes of available memory. To properly release memory once it is no longer needed (as determined by the programmer), the program must free the memory, which returns the allocated memory to the Heap for future use.

Choosing a Programming Language

Throughout this book we use a variety of programming languages to illustrate the algorithms. No single language is the right one to use in all circumstances. Too often, a specific programming language is used simply because it was used on a similar project. Since you are interested in algorithms, it is likely that you also want to ensure that your implementations run as fast as possible. This level of fine-tuning or optimization is beyond the scope of this book, though we describe several instances where carefully designed code optimizations result in impressive performance benefits. Choosing a language often depends on a number of factors:

Garbage collection versus manual memory allocation
> In the previous section we described low-level details about the way information is stored as a C program executes. Using the standard memory allocation packages available, most C programmers are used to allocating memory as needed, and freeing it when done. An alternative approach is to use a language such as Java or Scheme that provides built-in garbage collection to manage allocated memory. Garbage collection technology is increasingly efficient, and there are existing packages available to enable even C programs to integrate garbage collection with the default memory allocation schemes.

Bytecode interpretation versus compiled code
> The common perception is that compiled code will outperform interpreted code every time. In Java, for example, the Java compiler produces byte code that is interpreted and executed by the JVM. You should seriously consider whether using a language such as Java will improve the understanding of the code as it is written, even though there may be a runtime penalty in using that code.

Dynamic versus static typing
> Statically typed languages enforce the rules of types to detect errors during compilation, which should improve productivity because errors are caught immediately rather than at runtime. For strongly typed functional languages, such as ML, there is a common perception in the functional language community that most defects can be prevented by the proper application of the type system. Dynamic typed languages are often interpreted and variable values are known only at runtime, and therefore cannot be checked statically. Many scripting languages offer dynamic typing.

References

Alexander, Christopher, *A Pattern Language: Towns, Buildings, Construction*. Oxford University Press, USA, 1977.

"Algorithm Formalization," Software Engineering Institute, last modified January 11, 2007, *http://www.sei.cmu.edu/str/descriptions/algorithm.html*, accessed June 9, 2008.

Gamma, Erich, Richard Helm, Ralph Johnson, and John M. Vlissides, *Design Patterns: Elements of Reusable Object-Oriented Software*. Addison-Wesley Professional, 1995.

Goldberg, David, "What Every Computer Scientist Should Know About Floating-Point Arithmetic." *ACM Computing Surveys*, March 1991, *http://docs.sun.com/source/806-3568/ncg_goldberg.html*.

Skiena, Steve S., *The Algorithm Design Manual*. Springer, 1998.

Venners, Bill, "Floating Point Arithmetic: Floating-Point Support in the Java Virtual Machine." *JavaWorld*, 1996, *http://www.artima.com/underthehood/floating.html*.

Chapter 4, *Sorting Algorithms*

Chapter 5, *Searching*

Chapter 6, *Graph Algorithms*

Chapter 7, *Path Finding in AI*

Chapter 8, *Network Flow Algorithms*

Chapter 9, *Computational Geometry*

4

Sorting Algorithms

Overview

Given the list of states in Figure 4-1, how fast can you determine whether the state "Wyoming" is in the list? Perhaps you can answer this question in less than a second. How long would this task take in a list of 1,000 words? A good guess would be 100 seconds, since the problem size has increased 100-fold. Now, given the same list of states, can you determine the number of states whose names end in the letter s? This task is surprisingly easy because you can quickly see that the states are sorted in increasing order by their last character. If the list contained 1,000 words ordered similarly, the task would likely require only a few additional seconds because you can take advantage of the order of words in the list.

Alabama
Florida
Alaska
Rhode Island
Delaware
Maine
Wyoming
Texas
Kansas
Vermont

Figure 4-1. List of 10 states

Numerous computations and tasks become simple by properly sorting information in advance. The search for efficient sorting algorithms dominated the early days of computing. Indeed, much of the early research in algorithms focused on sorting collections of data that were too large for the computers of the day to store in memory. Because computers are incredibly more powerful and faster than the computers of 50 years ago, the size of the data sets being processed is now on the order of terabytes of information. Although you may not be called upon to sort such huge data sets, you will likely need to sort perhaps tens or hundreds of thousands of items. In this chapter, we cover the most important sorting algorithms and present results from our benchmarks to give specific guidance on which algorithm is best suited for your particular problem.

Terminology

A collection of comparable elements A is presented to be sorted; we use the notations $A[i]$ and a_i to refer to the ith element of the collection. By convention, the first element in the collection is considered to be $A[0]$. For notational convenience, we define $A[low, low+n)$ to be the subcollection $A[low]$ ... $A[low+n-1]$ of n elements, whereas $A[low, low+n]$ describes the subcollection $A[low]$ ... $A[low+n]$ of $n+1$ elements.

To sort a collection, the intent is to order the elements A such that if $A[i]<A[j]$, then $i<j$. If there are duplicate elements, then in the resulting ordered collection these elements must be contiguous; that is, if $A[i]=A[j]$ in a sorted collection, then there can be no k such that $i<k<j$ and $A[i]\neq A[k]$.

The sorted collection A must be a permutation of the elements that originally formed A. In the algorithms presented here, the sorting is done "in place" for efficiency, although one might simply wish to generate a new sorted collection from an unordered collection.

Representation

The collection may already be stored in the computer's random access memory (RAM), but it might simply exist in a file on the filesystem, known as secondary storage. The collection may be archived in part on tertiary storage, which may require extra processing time just to locate the information; in addition, the information may need to be copied to secondary storage before it can be processed. Examples of tertiary storage include tape libraries and optical jukeboxes.

Information stored in RAM typically takes one of two forms: pointer-based or value-based. Assume one wants to sort the strings "eagle," "cat," "ant," "dog," and "ball." Using pointer-based storage, shown in Figure 4-2, an array of information (the contiguous boxes) contains pointers to the actual information (i.e., the strings in ovals) rather than storing the information itself. Such an approach enables arbitrarily complex records to be stored and sorted.

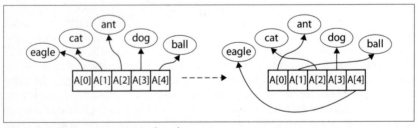

Figure 4-2. Sorting using pointer-based storage

By contrast, value-based storage packs a collection of n elements into record blocks of a fixed size, s (suitable for tertiary or secondary storage). Figure 4-3 shows how to store the same information shown in Figure 4-2 using a contiguous block of storage containing a set of rows of exactly $s=5$ bytes each. In this example the information is shown as strings, but it could be any collection of structured, record-based information. The "¬" character represents the termination of the string; in this encoding, strings of length s do not have a terminating character. The information is contiguous and can be viewed as a one-dimensional array $B[0,n{*}s)$. Note that $B[r{*}s+c]$ is the cth letter of the rth word (where $c{\geq}0$ and $r{\geq}0$); also, the ith element of the collection (for $i{\geq}0$) is the subarray $B[i{*}s,(i+1){*}s)$.

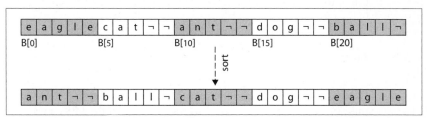

Figure 4-3. Sorting using value-based storage

Information is written to secondary storage usually as a value-based contiguous collection of bytes. It is possible to store "pointers" of a sort on secondary storage by using integer values to refer to offset position locations within files on disk. The algorithms in this chapter can also be written to work with disk-based information simply by implementing swap functions that transpose bytes within the files on disk; however, the resulting performance will differ because of the increased input/output costs in accessing secondary storage.

Whether pointer-based or value-based, a sorting algorithm updates the information (in both cases, the boxes) so that the entries $A[0]$ ... $A[n–1]$ are ordered. For convenience, in the rest of this chapter we use the $A[i]$ notation to represent the ith element, even when value-based storage is being used.

Comparable Elements

The elements in the collection being compared must admit a total ordering. That is, for any two elements p and q in a collection, exactly one of the following three predicates is true: $p=q$, $p<q$, or $p>q$. Commonly sorted primitive types include integers, floating-point values, and characters. When composite elements are sorted (such as strings of characters) then a lexicographical ordering is imposed on each individual element of the composite, thus reducing a complex sort into individual sorts on primitive types. For example, the word "alphabet" is considered to be less than "alternate" but greater than "alligator" by comparing each individual letter, from left to right, until a word runs out of characters or an individual character in one word is less than or greater than its partner in the other word (thus "ant" is less than "anthem"). This question of ordering is far from simple when considering capitalization (is "A" greater than "a"?), diacritical marks (is "è" less than "ê"?) and diphthongs (is "æ" less than "a"?). Note that the powerful Unicode standard (see *http://www.unicode.org/versions/latest*) uses encodings, such as UTF-16, to represent each individual character using up to four bytes. The Unicode Consortium (*www.unicode.org*) has developed a sorting standard (known as "the collation algorithm") that handles the wide variety of ordering rules found in different languages and cultures (Davis and Whistler, 2008).

For the algorithms presented in this chapter we assume the existence of a comparator function, called cmp, which compares elements p to q and returns 0 if $p=q$, a negative number if $p<q$, and a positive number if $p>q$. If the elements are complex records, the cmp function might only compare a "key" value of the elements. For example, an airport terminal has video displays showing outbound flights in ascending order of the destination city or departure time while flight numbers appear to be unordered.

Stable Sorting

When the comparator function cmp determines that two elements a_i and a_j in the original unordered collection are equal, it may be important to maintain their relative ordering in the sorted set; that is, if $i<j$, then the final location for a_i must be to the left of the final location for a_j. Sorting algorithms that guarantee this property are considered to be *stable*. For example, the top of Figure 4-4 shows an original collection A of flight information already sorted by time of flight during the day (regardless of airline or destination city). If this collection A is sorted using a comparator function, cmpDestination, that orders flights by destination city, one possible result is shown on the bottom of Figure 4-4.

Destination	Airline	Flight	Sched
Buffalo	Air Tran	549	10:42 AM
Atlanta	Delta	1097	11:00 AM
Baltimore	Southwest	836	11:05 AM
Atlanta	Air Tran	872	11:15 AM
Atlanta	Delta	28	12:00 PM
Boston	Delta	1056	12:05 PM
Baltimore	Southwest	216	12:20 PM
Austin	Southwest	1045	1:05 PM
Albany	Southwest	482	1:20 PM
Boston	Air Tran	515	1:21 PM
Baltimore	Southwest	272	1:40 PM
Atlanta	Alltalia	3429	1:50 PM

Destination	Airline	Flight	Sched
Albany	Southwest	482	1:20 PM
Atlanta	Delta	1097	11:00 AM
Atlanta	Air Tran	872	11:15 AM
Atlanta	Delta	28	12:00 PM
Atlanta	Alltalia	3429	1:50 PM
Austin	Southwest	1045	1:05 PM
Baltimore	Southwest	836	11:05 AM
Baltimore	Southwest	216	12:20 PM
Baltimore	Southwest	272	1:40 PM
Boston	Delta	1056	12:05 PM
Boston	Air Tran	515	1:21 PM
Buffalo	Air Tran	549	10:42 AM

Figure 4-4. Stable sort of airport terminal information

You will note that all flights that have the same destination city are sorted also by their scheduled departure time; thus, the sort algorithm exhibited stability on this collection. An unstable algorithm pays no attention to the relationships between element locations in the original collection (it might maintain relative ordering, but it also might not).

Analysis Techniques

When discussing sorting, invariably one must explain for an algorithm its best-case, worst-case, and average-case performance (as discussed in Chapter 2). The latter is typically hardest to accurately quantify and relies on advanced mathematical techniques and estimation. Also, it assumes a reasonable understanding of the likelihood that the input may be partially sorted. Even when an algorithm has been shown to have a desirable average-case cost, its implementation may simply be impractical. Each sorting algorithm in this chapter is analyzed both by its theoretic behavior and by its actual behavior in practice.

A fundamental result in computer science is that no algorithm that sorts by comparing elements can do better than $O(n \log n)$ performance in the average or worst case. We now sketch a proof. Given n items, there are $n!$ permutations of these elements. Every algorithm that sorts by pairwise comparisons corresponds to an underlying binary decision tree. The leaves of the tree correspond to an underlying permutation, and every permutation must have at least one leaf in the tree. The vertices on a path from the root to a leaf correspond to a sequence of comparisons. The *height* of such a tree is the number of comparison nodes in the longest path from the root to a leaf node; for example, the height of the tree in Figure 4-5 is 5 since only five comparisons are needed in all cases (although in four cases only four comparisons are needed).

Construct a binary decision tree where each internal node of the tree represents a comparison $a_i \leq a_j$ and the leaves of the tree represent one of the $n!$ permutations. To sort a set of n elements, start at the root and evaluate the statements shown in each node. Traverse to the left child when the statement is true; otherwise, traverse to the right child. Figure 4-5 shows a sample decision tree for four elements.

There are numerous binary decision trees that one could construct. Nonetheless, we assert that given any such binary decision tree for comparing n elements, we can compute its minimum height h; that is, there must be some leaf node that requires h comparison nodes in the tree from the root to that leaf. Consider a complete binary tree of height h in which all non-leaf nodes have both a left and right child. This tree contains a total of $n=2^h-1$ nodes and height $h=\log(n+1)$; if the tree is not complete, it could be unbalanced in strange ways, but we know that $h \geq \lceil \log(n+1) \rceil$.[*] Any binary decision tree with $n!$ leaf nodes already demonstrates it has at least $n!$ nodes in total. We need only compute $h=\lceil \log(n!) \rceil$ to determine the height of any such binary decision tree. We take advantage of the following properties of logarithms: $\log(a*b)=\log(a)+\log(b)$ and $\log(x^y)=y*\log(x)$.

---

[*] Recall that if x is not already an integer, the ceiling function $\lceil x \rceil$ returns the smallest integer not less than x (e.g., it rounds the value of x to the next higher integer).

$h = \log(n!) = \log(n^*(n-1)^*(n-2)^* ... ^*2^*1)$

$h > \log(n^*(n-1)^*(n-2)^* ... ^*n/2)$

$h > \log((n/2)^{n/2})$

$h > (n/2)^* \log(n/2)$

$h > (n/2)^* (\log(n) - 1)$

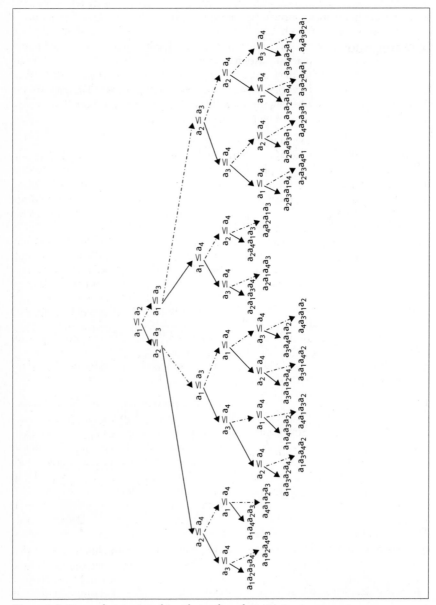

Figure 4-5. Binary decision tree for ordering four elements

Thus $h>(n/2)^*(\log(n)-1)$. What does this mean? Well, given n elements to be sorted, there will be at least one path from the root to a leaf of size h, which means that an algorithm that sorts by comparison requires at least this many comparisons to sort the n elements. Note that h is computed by a function $f(n)$; here in particular, $f(n)=(1/2)^*n^*\log(n)-n/2$, which means that any sorting algorithm using comparisons will require on the order of $O(n \log n)$ comparisons to sort. In the later section "Bucket Sort," we present an alternative sorting algorithm that does not rely solely on comparing elements, and can therefore achieve better performance under specific conditions.

Common Input

For each sorting algorithm, we assume the input resides in memory, either as a value-based contiguous block of memory or an array of pointers that point to the elements to be sorted. For maximum generality, we assume the existence of a comparison function cmp(p,q), as described earlier.

Insertion Sort

In the card game Bridge, each player is dealt 13 cards, all face down. One way to arrange a hand is to pick up the cards one at a time and insert each card into the hand. The invariant to maintain is that the cards in the hand are always sorted by suit and then by rank within the same suit. Start by picking up a single card to form a hand that is (trivially) already sorted. For each card picked up, find the correct place to insert the card into the hand, thus maintaining the invariant that the cards in the hand are sorted. When all the cards are placed, the invariant establishes that the algorithm works. When you hold cards in your hand, it is easy to insert a card into its proper position because the other cards are just pushed aside a bit to accept the new card. When the collection is stored in memory, however, a sorting algorithm must do more work to manually move information, in order to open up space for an element to be inserted.

The pseudocode in Figure 4-6 describes how INSERTION SORT repeatedly invokes the insert helper function to ensure that $A[0,i]$ is properly sorted; eventually, i reaches the rightmost element, sorting A entirely. Figure 4-7 shows how INSERTION SORT operates on a small, unordered collection A of size $n=16$. The 15 rows that follow depict the state of A after each pass. A is sorted "in place" by incrementing $pos=1$ up to $n-1$ and inserting the element $A[pos]$ into its rightful position in the growing sorted region $A[0,pos]$, demarcated on the right by a bold vertical line. The elements shaded in gray were shifted to the right to make way for the inserted element; in total, INSERTION SORT executed 60 transpositions (a movement of just one place by an element).

Context

Use INSERTION SORT when you have a small number of elements to sort or the elements in the initial collection are already "nearly sorted." Determining when the array is "small enough" varies from one machine to another and by programming language. Indeed, even the type of element being compared may be significant.

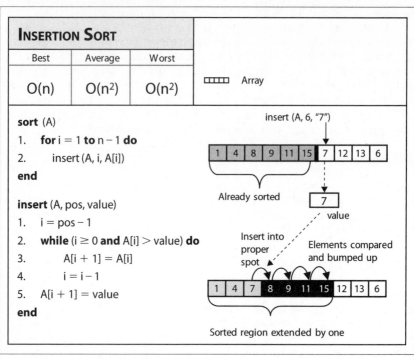

Figure 4-6. *Insertion Sort fact sheet*

15	09	08	01	04	11	07	12	13	06	05	03	16	02	10	14
09	15	08	01	04	11	07	12	13	06	05	03	16	02	10	14
08	09	15	01	04	11	07	12	13	06	05	03	16	02	10	14
01	08	09	15	04	11	07	12	13	06	05	03	16	02	10	14
01	04	08	09	15	11	07	12	13	06	05	03	16	02	10	14
01	04	08	09	11	15	07	12	13	06	05	03	16	02	10	14
01	04	07	08	09	11	15	12	13	06	05	03	16	02	10	14
01	04	07	08	09	11	12	15	13	06	05	03	16	02	10	14
01	04	07	08	09	11	12	13	15	06	05	03	16	02	10	14
01	04	06	07	08	09	11	12	13	15	05	03	16	02	10	14
01	04	05	06	07	08	09	11	12	13	15	03	16	02	10	14
01	03	04	05	06	07	08	09	11	12	13	15	16	02	10	14
01	03	04	05	06	07	08	09	11	12	13	15	16	02	10	14
01	02	03	04	05	06	07	08	09	11	12	13	15	16	10	14
01	02	03	04	05	06	07	08	09	10	11	12	13	15	16	14
01	02	03	04	05	06	07	08	09	10	11	12	13	14	15	16

Figure 4-7. *The progression of Insertion Sort on a small array*

Forces

INSERTION SORT need only set aside space for a single element to function properly. For a pointer-based representation, this is trivial; for a value-based
representation, one need only allocate enough memory to store a value (requiring
a fixed s bytes, as described in the earlier section "Representation") for the duration of the sort, after which it can be freed. There are no complicated nested loops
to implement, and a generic function can be written to sort many different types
of elements simply through the use of a cmp comparator function. For value-based
representations, most language libraries offer a block memory move function to
make the algorithm more efficient.

Solution

When the information is stored using pointers, the C program in Example 4-1
sorts an array ar with items that can be compared using a provided comparison
function, cmp.

Example 4-1. Insertion Sort with pointer-based values

```
void sortPointers (void **ar, int n,
                   int(*cmp)(const void *,const void *)) {
  int j;
  for (j = 1; j < n; j++) {
    int i = j-1;
    void *value = ar[j];
    while (i >= 0 && cmp(ar[i], value)> 0) {
      ar[i+1] = ar[i];
      i--;
    }

    ar[i+1] = value;
  }
}
```

When *A* is represented using value-based storage, it is packed into *n* rows of a
fixed element size of *s* bytes. Manipulating the values requires a comparison function as well as the means to copy values from one location to another.
Example 4-2 shows a suitable C program that uses memmove to transfer the underlying bytes efficiently for a set of contiguous entries in *A*.

Example 4-2. Insertion Sort using value-based information

```
void sortValues (void *base, int n, int s,
                 int(*cmp)(const void *, const void *)) {
  int j;
  void *saved = malloc (s);
  for (j = 1; j < n; j++) {
    /* start at end, work backward until smaller element or i < 0. */
    int i = j-1;
    void *value = base + j*s;
    while (i >= 0 && cmp(base + i*s, value) > 0) { i--; }
```

Example 4-2. Insertion Sort using value-based information (continued)

```
    /* If already in place, no movement needed. Otherwise save value to be
     * inserted and move as a LARGE block intervening values.  Then insert
     * into proper position. */
    if (++i == j) continue;

    memmove (saved, value, s);
    memmove (base+(i+1)*s, base+i*s, s*(j-i));
    memmove (base+i*s, saved, s);
  }
  free (saved);
}
```

Consequences

Given the example in Figure 4-7, INSERTION SORT needed to transpose 60 elements that were already in sorted order. Since there were 15 passes made over the array, on average four elements were moved during each pass. The optimal performance occurs when the array is already sorted, and arrays sorted in reverse order naturally produce the worst performance for INSERTION SORT. If the array is already "mostly sorted," INSERTION SORT does well because there is less need to transpose the elements.

Analysis

In the best case, each of the n items is in its proper place and thus INSERTION SORT takes linear time, or $O(n)$. This may seem to be a trivial point to raise (how often are you going to sort a set of already sorted elements?), but it is important because INSERTION SORT is the only sorting algorithm based on comparisons discussed in this chapter that has this behavior.

Much real-world data is already "partially sorted," so optimism and realism might coincide to make INSERTION SORT an effective algorithm for much real-world data. But sadly, if every input permutation is equally likely, then the probability of having optimal data (every item being in its proper position) is only $1/n!$; for $n=10$, the odds are already 3.6 million to one. Note that the efficiency of INSERTION SORT increases when duplicate items are present, since there are fewer swaps to perform.

Unfortunately, INSERTION SORT suffers from being too conservative for "random data." If all n items are distinct and the array is "random" (all permutations of the data are equally likely), then each item starts on average $n/3$ positions in the array from its final resting place.[*] So in the average case and worst case, each of the n items must be transposed a linear number of positions, and INSERTION SORT will take quadratic time, or $O(n^2)$.

INSERTION SORT operates inefficiently for value-based data because of the amount of memory that must be shifted to make room for a new value.

---

[*] The program numTranspositions in the code repository empirically validates this claim for small n up to 12; also see Trivedi (2001).

Table 4-1 contains direct comparisons between a naïve implementation of value-based INSERTION SORT and the implementation from Example 4-2. Here 10 random trials of sorting n elements were conducted, and the best and worst results were discarded. This table shows the average of the remaining eight runs. Note how the implementation improves by using a block memory move rather than individual memory swapping. Still, as the array size doubles, the performance time approximately quadruples, validating the $O(n^2)$ behavior of INSERTION SORT. Even with the bulk move improvement, INSERTION SORT still remains quadratic since the performance of INSERTION SORT using bulk moves is a fixed multiplicative constant (nearly 1/7) of the naïve INSERTION SORT. The problem with INSERTION SORT is that it belongs to a conservative class of algorithms (called *local transposition sorts*) in which each element moves only one position at a time.

Table 4-1. Insertion Sort bulk move versus Insertion Sort (in seconds)

n	Insertion Sort bulk move (B_n)	Naïve Insertion Sort (S_n)	Ratio B_{2n}/B_n	Ratio S_{2n}/S_n
1,024	0.0055	0.0258		
2,048	0.0249	0.0965	4.5273	3.7403
4,096	0.0932	0.3845	3.7430	3.9845
8,192	0.3864	1.305	4.1459	3.3940
16,384	1.3582	3.4932	3.5150	2.6768
32,768	3.4676	12.062	2.5531	3.4530
65,536	15.5357	48.3826	4.4802	4.0112
131,072	106.2702	200.5416	6.8404	4.1449

When INSERTION SORT operates over pointer-based input, swapping elements is more efficient; the compiler can even generate optimized code to minimize costly memory accesses.

Median Sort

Divide and conquer, a common approach in computer science, solves a problem by dividing it into two independent subproblems, each about half the size of the original problem. Consider the MEDIAN SORT algorithm (Figure 4-8) that sorts an array A of $n \geq 1$ elements by swapping the median element $A[me]$ with the middle element of A (lines 2–4), creating a left and right half of the array. MEDIAN SORT then swaps elements in the left half that are larger than $A[mid]$ with elements in the right half that are smaller or equal to $A[mid]$ (lines 5–8). This subdivides the original array into two distinct subarrays of about half the size that each need to be sorted. Then MEDIAN SORT is recursively applied on each subarray (lines 9–10).

A full example of MEDIAN SORT in action is shown in Figure 4-9, in which each row corresponds to a recursive invocation of the algorithm. At each step, there are twice as many problems to solve, but each problem size has been cut in about half.

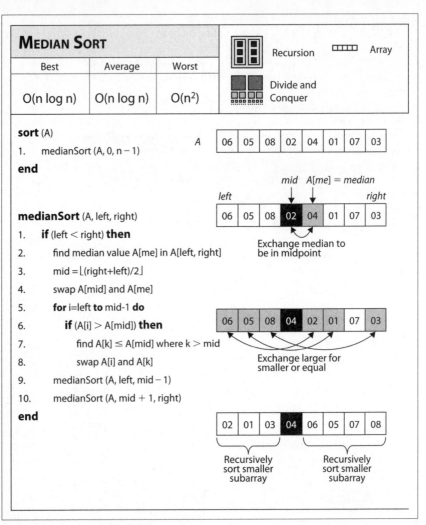

MEDIAN SORT			Recursion ▭▭▭ Array
Best	Average	Worst	Divide and Conquer
O(n log n)	O(n log n)	O(n²)	

sort (A)
1.   medianSort (A, 0, n − 1)
end

A | 06 | 05 | 08 | 02 | 04 | 01 | 07 | 03 |

                                    mid   A[me] = median
                           left   ↓   ↓   right

medianSort (A, left, right) | 06 | 05 | 08 | **02** | 04 | 01 | 07 | 03 |
1.   **if** (left < right) **then**
2.   find median value A[me] in A[left, right]   Exchange median to
3.   mid = ⌊(right+left)/2⌋   be in midpoint
4.   swap A[mid] and A[me]
5.   **for** i=left **to** mid-1 **do**
6.   **if** (A[i] > A[mid]) **then** | 06 | 05 | 08 | **04** | 02 | 01 | 07 | 03 |
7.   find A[k] ≤ A[mid] where k > mid
8.   swap A[i] and A[k]   Exchange larger for
9.   medianSort (A, left, mid − 1)   smaller or equal
10.   medianSort (A, mid + 1, right)
end

| 02 | 01 | 03 | **04** | 06 | 05 | 07 | 08 |
       ⌣   ⌣
   Recursively   Recursively
   sort smaller   sort smaller
   subarray   subarray

Figure 4-8. Median Sort fact sheet

Since the subproblems are independent of each other, the final sorted result is produced once the recursion ends.

The initial unsorted array is shown in the line labeled 1a, and the selected median element, *A[me]*, is identified by a gray square. *A[me]* is swapped (line 1b) with the midpoint element (shown in the black square), and the larger elements (shown as the gray squares in line 1b to the left of the midpoint) are swapped with the smaller or equal elements (shown as gray squares in line 1b to the right of the midpoint) to produce the divided array in line 1c. In the recursive step, each of the smaller subarrays is sorted, and the progress (on each subarray) is shown in lines 2a–2c, 3a–3c, and 4a–4c.

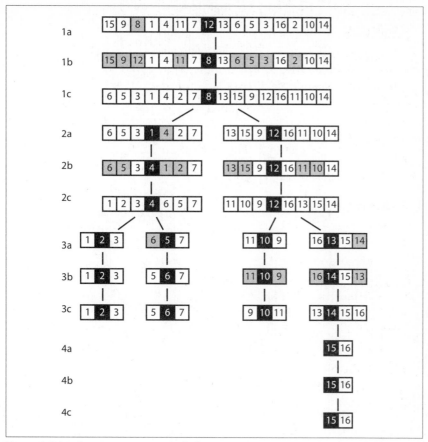

Figure 4-9. Median Sort in action on small array

Context

Implementing MEDIAN SORT depends on efficiently selecting the median element from an unsorted array. As is typical in computer science, instead of answering this question, we answer a different question, which ultimately provides us with a solution to our original question. Imagine someone provided you with a function p = partition (left, right, pivotIndex), which selects the element $A[pivotIndex]$ to be a special *pivot* value that partitions $A[left,right]$ into a first half whose elements are smaller or equal to *pivot* and a second half whose elements are larger or equal to *pivot*. Note that $left \leq pivotIndex \leq right$, and the value p returned is the location within the subarray $A[left,right]$ where *pivot* is ultimately stored. A C implementation of partition is shown in Example 4-3.

Example 4-3. C implementation to partition ar[left,right] around a given pivot element

```
/**
 * In linear time, group the subarray ar[left, right] around a pivot
 * element pivot=ar[pivotIndex] by storing pivot into its proper
 * location, store, within the subarray (whose location is returned
 * by this function) and ensuring that all ar[left,store) <= pivot and
 * all ar[store+1,right] > pivot.
 */
int partition (void **ar, int(*cmp)(const void *,const void *),
               int left, int right, int pivotIndex) {
  int idx, store;
  void *pivot = ar[pivotIndex];

  /* move pivot to the end of the array */
  void *tmp = ar[right];
  ar[right] = ar[pivotIndex];
  ar[pivotIndex] = tmp;

  /* all values <= pivot are moved to front of array and pivot inserted
   * just after them. */
  store = left;
  for (idx = left; idx < right; idx++) {
    if (cmp(ar[idx], pivot) <= 0) {
      tmp = ar[idx];
      ar[idx] = ar[store];
      ar[store] = tmp;
      store++;
    }
  }

  tmp = ar[right];
  ar[right] = ar[store];
  ar[store] = tmp;
  return store;
}
```

How can we use partition to select the median efficiently? First, let's review the results of this method, as shown on a sample unsorted array of 16 elements. The first step is to swap the *pivot* with the rightmost element. As the loop in partition executes, the key variables from the implementation are shown in Figure 4-10. store is the location identified by the circle. Each successive row in Figure 4-10 shows when the loop in partition identifies, from left to right, an element $A[idx]$ that is smaller than or equal to the *pivot* (which in this case is the element "06"). Once there are no more elements smaller than or equal to *pivot*, the element in the last computed store is swapped with the rightmost element, thus safely placing the *pivot* in place.

After partition(0,15,9) executes and returns the location $p=5$ of the *pivot* value, you can see that $A[left,p)$ are all less than or equal to *pivot*, whereas $A[p+1,right]$

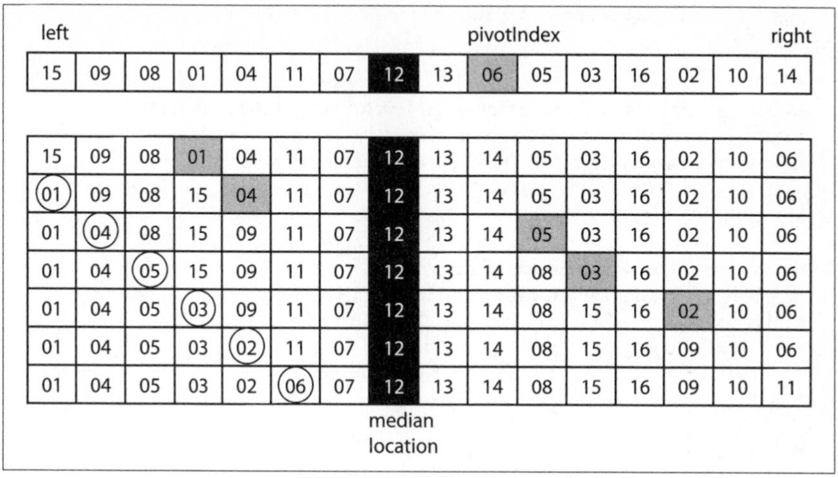

left							pivotIndex								right
15	09	08	01	04	11	07	12	13	06	05	03	16	02	10	14

15	09	08	01	04	11	07	12	13	14	05	03	16	02	10	06
(01)	09	08	15	04	11	07	12	13	14	05	03	16	02	10	06
01	(04)	08	15	09	11	07	12	13	14	05	03	16	02	10	06
01	04	(05)	15	09	11	07	12	13	14	08	03	16	02	10	06
01	04	05	(03)	09	11	07	12	13	14	08	15	16	02	10	06
01	04	05	03	(02)	11	07	12	13	14	08	15	16	09	10	06
01	04	05	03	02	(06)	07	12	13	14	08	15	16	09	10	11

median
location

Figure 4-10. partition(0, 15, 9) returns 5 and updates A accordingly

are all greater than or equal to *pivot*. How has this made any progress in selecting the median value? Note that *p* is to the left of the calculated location where the median will ultimately end up in the sorted list (identified as the blackened array element labeled "median location"). Therefore, none of the elements to the left of *p* can be the median value! We only need to recursively invoke partition (this time with a different A[*pivotIndex*] on the right half, A[*p*+1,*right*]) until it returns *p*=median location.

Note that partition effectively organizes the array into two distinct subarrays without actually sorting the individual elements. partition returns the index *p* of the pivot, and this can be used to identify the *k*th element recursively in A[*left*,*right*] for any 1≤*k*≤*right*–*left*+1, as follows:

if k=p+1
> The selected pivot element is the *k*th value (recall that array indices start counting at 0, but *k* starts counting at 1).

if k<p+1
> The *k*th element of A is the *k*th element of A[*left*,*p*].

if k>p+1
> The *k*th element of A is the (*k*–*p*)th element of A[*p*+1,*right*].

In Figure 4-10, the goal is to locate the median value of *A*, or in other words, the *k*=8th largest element. Since the invocation of partition returns *p*=5, we next recursively search for the second smallest element in A[*p*+1,*right*].

Such a definition lends itself to a recursive solution, but it can also be defined iteratively where a tail-recursive function instead can be implemented within a loop (see the code repository for the example). selectKth is an average-case linear time function that returns the location of the *k*th element in array *ar* given a suitable *pivotIndex*; its implementation is shown in Example 4-4.

Example 4-4. selectKth recursive implementation in C

```
/**
 * Average-case linear time recursive algorithm to find position of kth
 * element in ar, which is modified as this computation proceeds.
 * Note 1 <= k <= right-left+1. The comparison function, cmp, is
 * needed to properly compare elements. Worst-case is quadratic, O(n^2).
 */
int selectKth (void **ar, int(*cmp)(const void *,const void *),
               int k, int left, int right) {
  int idx = selectPivotIndex (ar, left, right);
  int pivotIndex = partition (ar, cmp, left, right, idx);
  if (left+k-1 == pivotIndex) { return pivotIndex; }

  /* continue the loop, narrowing the range as appropriate. If we are within
   * the left-hand side of the pivot then k can stay the same. */
  if (left+k-1 < pivotIndex) {
    return selectKth (ar, cmp, k, left, pivotIndex-1);
  } else {
    return selectKth (ar, cmp, k - (pivotIndex-left+1), pivotIndex+1, right);
  }
}
```

The selectKth function must select a *pivotIndex* for A[*left,right*] to use during the recursion. Many strategies exist, including:

- Select the first location (*left*) or the last location (*right*).
- Select a random location (*left≤random≤right*).

If the *pivotIndex* repeatedly is chosen poorly, then selectKth degrades in the worst case to $O(n^2)$; however, its best- and average-case performance is linear, or $O(n)$.

Forces

Because of the specific tail-recursive structure of selectKth, a nonrecursive implementation is straightforward.

Solution

Now connecting this discussion back to MEDIAN SORT, you might be surprised to note that selectKth works regardless of the *pivotIndex* value selected! In addition, when selectKth returns, there is no need to perform lines 5–8 (in Figure 4-8) of the MEDIAN SORT algorithm, because partition has already done this work. That is, the elements in the left half are all smaller or equal to the median, whereas the elements in the right half are all greater or equal to the median.

The MEDIAN SORT function is shown in Example 4-5 and is invoked on A[0,*n*–1].

Example 4-5. Median Sort implementation in C

```
/**
 * Sort array ar[left,right] using medianSort method.
 * The comparison function, cmp, is needed to properly compare elements.
 */
```

Example 4-5. Median Sort implementation in C (continued)

```c
void mediansort (void **ar, int(*cmp)(const void *,const void *),
                int left, int right) {
  /* if the subarray to be sorted has 1 (or fewer!) elements, done. */
  if (right <= left) { return; }

  /* get midpoint and median element position (1<=k<=right-left-1). */
  int mid = (right - left + 1)/2;
  int me = selectKth (ar, cmp, mid+1, left, right);

  mediansort (ar, cmp, left, left+mid-1);
  mediansort (ar, cmp, left+mid+1, right);
}
```

Consequences

MEDIAN SORT does more work than it should. Although the generated subproblems are optimal (since they are both about half the size of the original problem), the extra cost in producing these subproblems adds up. As we will see in the upcoming section on "Quicksort," it is sufficient to select *pivotIndex* randomly, which should avoid degenerate cases (which might happen if the original array is already mostly sorted).

Analysis

MEDIAN SORT guarantees that the recursive subproblems being solved are nearly identical in size. This means the average-case performance of MEDIAN SORT is $O(n \log n)$. However, in the worst case, the partition function executes in $O(n^2)$, which would force MEDIAN SORT to degrade to $O(n^2)$. Thus, even though the subproblems being recursively sorted are ideal, the overall performance suffers when considering n items already in sorted order. We ran MEDIAN SORT using a randomized selectPivotIndex function against this worst-case example where selectPivotIndex always returned the leftmost index. Ten trials were run, and the best and worst results were discarded; the averages of the remaining eight runs for these two variations are shown in the first two columns of Table 4-2. Observe that in the worst case, as the problem size doubles, the time to complete MEDIAN SORT multiplies more than fourfold, the classic indicator for $O(n^2)$ quadratic performance.

Table 4-2. Performance (in seconds) of Median Sort in the worst case

n	Randomized pivot selection	Leftmost pivot selection	Blum-Floyd-Pratt-Rivest-Tarjan pivot selection
256	0.000088	0.000444	0.00017
512	0.000213	0.0024	0.000436
1,024	0.000543	0.0105	0.0011
2,048	0.0012	0.0414	0.0029
4,096	0.0032	0.19	0.0072
8,192	0.0065	0.716	0.0156
16,384	0.0069	1.882	0.0354

Table 4-2. Performance (in seconds) of Median Sort in the worst case (continued)

n	Randomized pivot selection	Leftmost pivot selection	Blum-Floyd-Pratt-Rivest-Tarjan pivot selection
32,768	0.0187	9.0479	0.0388
65,536	0.0743	47.3768	0.1065
131,072	0.0981	236.629	0.361

It seems, therefore, that any sorting algorithm that depends upon partition must suffer from having a worst-case performance degrade to $O(n^2)$. Indeed, for this reason we assign this worst case when presenting the MEDIAN SORT fact sheet in Figure 4-8.

Fortunately there is a linear time selection for selectKth that will ensure that the worst-case performance remains $O(n \log n)$. The selection algorithm is known as the BLUM-FLOYD-PRATT-RIVEST-TARJAN (BFPRT) algorithm (Blum et al., 1973); its performance is shown in the final column in Table 4-2. On uniformly randomized data, 10 trials of increasing problem size were executed, and the best and worst performing results were discarded. Table 4-3 shows the performance of MEDIAN SORT using the different approaches for partitioning the subarrays. The computed trend line for the randomized pivot selection in the average case (shown in Table 4-3) is:

$$1.82^*10^{-7}{}^*n^*\log (n)$$

whereas BFPRT shows a trend line of:

$$2.35^*10^{-6}{}^*n^*\log (n)$$

Table 4-3. Performance (in seconds) of Median Sort in average case

n	Randomized pivot selection	Leftmost pivot selection	Blum-Floyd-Pratt-Rivest-Tarjan pivot selection
256	0.00009	0.000116	0.000245
512	0.000197	0.000299	0.000557
1,024	0.000445	0.0012	0.0019
2,048	0.0013	0.0035	0.0041
4,096	0.0031	0.0103	0.0128
8,192	0.0082	0.0294	0.0256
16,384	0.018	0.0744	0.0547
32,768	0.0439	0.2213	0.4084
65,536	0.071	0.459	0.5186
131,072	0.149	1.8131	3.9691

Because the constants for the more complicated BFPRT algorithm are higher, it runs about 10 times as slowly, and yet both execution times are $O(n \log n)$ in the average case.

The BFPRT selection algorithm is able to provide guaranteed performance by its ability to locate a value in an unordered set that is a reasonable approximation to the actual median of that set. In brief, BFPRT groups the elements of the array of n elements into $n/4$ groups of elements of four elements (and ignores up to three elements that don't fit into a group of size 4*). BFPRT then locates the median of each of these four-element groups. What does this step cost? From the binary decision tree discussed earlier in Figure 4-5, you may recall that only five comparisons are needed to order four elements, thus this step costs a maximum of $(n/4)*5=1.25*n$, which is still $O(n)$. Given these groupings of four elements, the median value of each group is its third element. If we treat the median values of all of these $n/4$ groups as a set M, then the computed median value (me) of M is a good approximation of the median value of the original set A. The trick to BFPRT is to recursively apply BFPRT to the set M. Coding the algorithm is interesting (in our implementation shown in Example 4-6 we minimize element swaps by recursively inspecting elements that are a fixed distance, gap, apart). Note that $3*n/8$ of the elements in A are demonstrably less than or equal to me, while $2*n/8$ are demonstrably greater than or equal to me. Thus we are guaranteed on the recursive invocation of partition no worse than a 37.5% versus 75% split on the left and right subarrays during its recursive execution. This guarantee ensures that the overall worst-case performance of BFPRT is $O(n)$.

Example 4-6. Blum-Floyd-Pratt-Rivest-Tarjan implementation in C

```c
#define SWAP(a,p1,p2,type) { \
    type _tmp__ = a[p1];      \
    a[p1] = a[p2];            \
    a[p2] = _tmp__;           \
  }


/* determine median of four elements in array
 *    ar[left], ar[left+gap], ar[left+gap*2], ar[left+gap*3]
 * and ensure that ar[left+gap*2] contains this median value once done.
 */
static void medianOfFour(void **ar, int left, int gap,
                         int(*cmp)(const void *,const void *)) {
  int pos1=left, pos2, pos3, pos4;
  void *a1 = ar[pos1];
  void *a2 = ar[pos2=pos1+gap];
  void *a3 = ar[pos3=pos2+gap];
  void *a4 = ar[pos4=pos3+gap];

  if (cmp(a1, a2) <= 0) {
    if (cmp(a2, a3) <= 0) {
      if (cmp(a2, a4) <= 0) {
        if (cmp(a3, a4) > 0) {
          SWAP(ar,pos3,pos4,void *);
        }
      } else {
        SWAP(ar,pos2,pos3,void *);
      }
```

---

* The BFPRT algorithm as described in the literature divides the set into groups of size 5, but in benchmark tests our code using groups of size 4 is faster.

Example 4-6. Blum-Floyd-Pratt-Rivest-Tarjan implementation in C (continued)

```c
    } else {
      if (cmp(a1, a3) <= 0) {
        if (cmp(a3, a4) <= 0) {
          if (cmp(a2, a4) <= 0) {
            SWAP(ar,pos2,pos3,void *);
          } else {
            SWAP(ar,pos3,pos4,void *);
          }
        }
      } else {
        if (cmp(a1, a4) <= 0) {
          if (cmp(a2, a4) <= 0) {
            SWAP(ar,pos2,pos3,void *);
          } else {
            SWAP(ar,pos3,pos4,void *);
          }
        } else {
          SWAP(ar,pos1,pos3,void *);
        }
      }
    }
  } else {
    if (cmp(a1, a3) <= 0) {
      if (cmp(a1, a4) <= 0) {
        if (cmp(a3, a4) > 0) {
          SWAP(ar,pos3,pos4,void *);
        }
      } else {
      }
    } else {
      if (cmp(a2, a3) <= 0) {
        if (cmp(a3, a4) <= 0) {
          if (cmp(a1, a4) <= 0) {
            SWAP(ar,pos1,pos3,void *);
          } else {
            SWAP(ar,pos3,pos4,void *);
          }
        }
      } else {
        if (cmp(a2, a4) <= 0) {
          if (cmp(a1, a4) <= 0) {
            SWAP(ar,pos1,pos3,void *);
          } else {
            SWAP(ar,pos3,pos4,void *);
          }
        } else {
          SWAP(ar,pos2,pos3,void *);
        }
      }
    }
  }
}
```

Example 4-6. Blum-Floyd-Pratt-Rivest-Tarjan implementation in C (continued)

```
/* specialized insertion sort elements with spaced gap. */
static void _insertion (void **ar, int(*cmp)(const void *,const void *),
                int low, int right, int gap) {
  int loc;
  for (loc = low+gap; loc <= right; loc += gap) {
    int i = loc-gap;
    void *value = ar[loc];
    while (i >= low && cmp(ar[i], value)> 0) {
      ar[i+gap] = ar[i];
      i -= gap;
    }
    ar[i+gap] = value;
  }
}

/**
 * Find suitable pivotIndex to use for ar[left,right] with closed bound
 * on both sides. Goal is to consider groups of size b. In this code, b=4.
 * In the original BFPRT algorithm, b=5.
 *
 * 1. Divide the elements into floor(n/b) groups of b elements and
 *    find median value of each of these groups. Consider this set of
 *    all medians to be the set M.
 *
 * 2. If |M| > b, then recursively apply until <=b groups are left
 *
 * 3. In the base case of the recursion, simply use INSERTION SORT to sort
 *    remaining <=b median values and choose the median of this sorted set.
 */
static int medianOfMedians (void **ar, int(*cmp)(const void *,const void *),
                        int left, int right, int gap) {
  int s, num;
  int span = 4*gap;

  /* not enough for a group? Insertion sort and return median.  */
  num = (right - left + 1) / span;
  if (num == 0) {
    _insertion (ar, cmp, left, right, gap);          /* BASE CASE */
    num = (right - left + 1)/gap;
    return left + gap*(num-1)/2;
  }

  /* set up all median values of groups of elements */
  for (s = left; s+span < right; s += span) {
    medianOfFour(ar, s, gap, cmp);
  }

  /* Recursively apply to subarray [left, s-1] with increased gap if
   * enough groupings remain, otherwise INSERTION SORT and return median */
  if (num < 4) {
    _insertion (ar, cmp, left+span/2, right, span);   /* BASE CASE */
    return left + num*span/2;
```

```
  } else {
    return medianOfMedians (ar, cmp, left+span/2, s-1, span);
  }
}

/**
 * Linear worst-case time algorithm to find median in ar[left,right]. The
 * comparison function, cmp, is needed to compare elements.
 */
int selectMedian (void **ar, int(*cmp)(const void *,const void *),
                  int left, int right) {
  int k = (right-left+1)/2;
  while (k > 0) {
    /* Choose index around which to partition. */
    int idx = medianOfMedians (ar, cmp, left, right, 1);

    /**
     * Partition input array around the median of medians x. If kth
     * largest is found, return absolute index; otherwise narrow to
     * find kth smallest in A[left,pivotIndex-1] or (k-p)-th
     * in A[pivotIndex+1,right].
     */
    int pivotIndex = partition (ar, cmp, left, right, idx);

    /* Note that k is in range 0 <=k <= right-left while the returned
       pivotIndex is in range left <= pivotIndex <= right. */
    int p = left+k;
    if (p == pivotIndex) {
      return pivotIndex;
    } else if (p < pivotIndex) {
      right = pivotIndex-1;
    } else {
      k = k - (pivotIndex-left+1);
      left = pivotIndex+1;
    }
  }
  /* If we get here, then left=right, so just return one as median. */
  return left;
}
```

Quicksort

If we reflect on the performance of MEDIAN SORT, we see that a random choice of pivotIndex still enables the average-case performance of selectKth to operate in linear time. Is it possible to simplify the algorithm without incurring an extra performance penalty? Would the simpler implementation perhaps be faster in some situations? The QUICKSORT algorithm, first introduced by C.A.R. Hoare, is indeed simpler than MEDIAN SORT, although it uses many of the same concepts, which is why we introduced MEDIAN SORT first.

In QUICKSORT, we no longer seek the median value, and instead select an element according to some strategy (sometimes randomly, sometimes the leftmost, sometimes the middle one) to partition an array into subarrays. Thus QUICKSORT has two steps, as shown in Figure 4-11. The array is partitioned around a *pivot* value, creating a left subarray that contains elements less than or equal to the *pivot*, and a right subarray that contains elements greater than or equal to the *pivot*. Each of these subarrays is then recursively sorted.

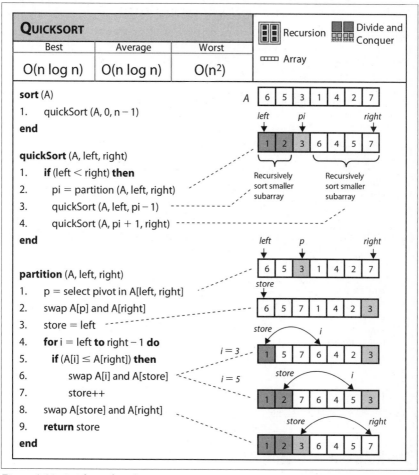

Figure 4-11. Quicksort fact sheet

The random nature of the algorithm as described makes it a challenge to prove that the average-case performance is still O(*n* log *n*). We do not cover here the advanced mathematical analytic tools needed to prove this result, but further details on this topic are available in (Cormen et al., 2001).

Figure 4-12 shows QUICKSORT in action. Each of the black squares in the figure represents a pivot selection in line 1 of partition. The first pivot selected is "2", which turns out to be a poor choice since it produces two subarrays of size 1 and size 14. During the next recursive invocation of QUICKSORT on the right subarray, "12" is selected to be the pivot, which produces two subarrays of size 9 and 4, respectively. Already you can see the benefit of using partition since the last four elements in the array are, in fact, the largest four elements. Because of the random nature of the pivot selection, different behaviors are possible. In a different execution, shown in Figure 4-13, the first selected pivot nicely subdivides the problem into two more-or-less comparable tasks.

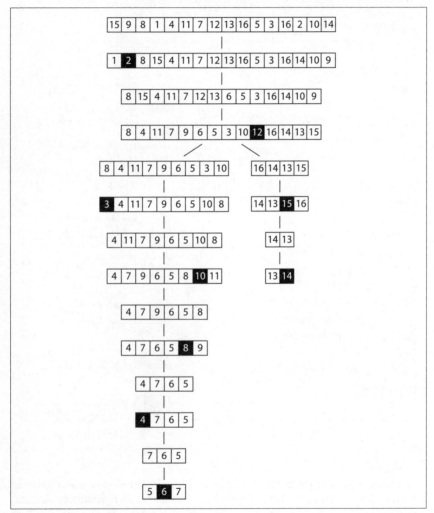

Figure 4-12. Sample Quicksort execution

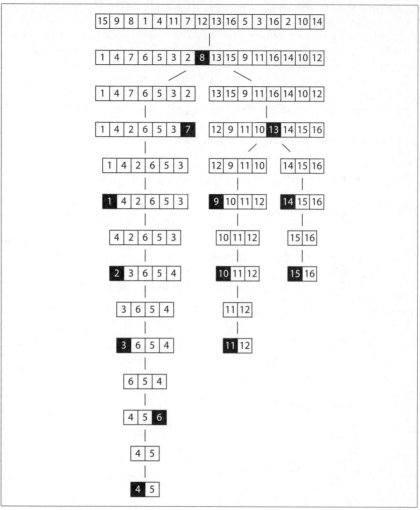

Figure 4-13. A different Quicksort behavior

Context

QUICKSORT exhibits worst-case quadratic behavior if the partitioning at each recursive step only divides a collection of n elements into an "empty" and "large" set, where one of these sets has no elements and the other has $n-1$ (note that the pivot element provides the last of the n elements, so no element is lost).

The choice of *pivot* strongly influences the relative sizes of the two subarrays after the execution of partition. Instead of just choosing *pivot* to be a random element, one can choose it to be the median (middle value) of k random elements for some odd k. Later, in the "Variations" section, we discuss different strategies for selecting the *pivot*.

Solution

The QUICKSORT implementation shown in Example 4-7 can be defined in terms of the functions already presented in "Median Sort." We use a standard optimization technique that uses INSERTION SORT when the size of the subarray to be sorted falls below a predetermined minimum size.

Example 4-7. Quicksort implementation in C

```
/**
 * Sort array ar[left,right] using Quicksort method.
 * The comparison function, cmp, is needed to properly compare elements.
 */
void do_qsort (void **ar, int(*cmp)(const void *,const void *),
               int left, int right) {
  int pivotIndex;
  if (right <= left) { return; }

  /* partition */
  pivotIndex = selectPivotIndex (ar, left, right);
  pivotIndex = partition (ar, cmp, left, right, pivotIndex);

  if (pivotIndex-1-left <= minSize) {
    insertion (ar, cmp, left, pivotIndex-1);
  } else {
    do_qsort (ar, cmp, left, pivotIndex-1);
  }
  if (right-pivotIndex-1 <= minSize) {
    insertion (ar, cmp, pivotIndex+1, right);
  } else {
    do_qsort (ar, cmp, pivotIndex+1, right);
  }
}

/**  Qsort straight */
void sortPointers (void **vals, int total_elems,
                   int(*cmp)(const void *,const void *)) {
  do_qsort (vals, cmp, 0, total_elems-1);
}
```

The choice of *pivot* is made by the external method selectPivotIndex(ar, left, right), which provides the array element for which to partition.

Consequences

Surprisingly, the random algorithm for selecting a pivot enables QUICKSORT to provide an average-case performance that usually outperforms other sorting algorithms. In addition, there are numerous enhancements and optimizations researched for QUICKSORT that have wrought the most efficiency out of any sorting algorithm. The various options are discussed in detail later, in the upcoming "Variations" section.

Analysis

In the ideal case, partition divides the original array in half; if this behavior is consistent for each recursion, then the resulting behavior produces the same results as MEDIAN SORT without incurring an additional performance penalty. Let's define $t(n)$ to be the time to perform QUICKSORT on an array of n elements. Because QUICKSORT is recursive, we can state that:

$$t(n) = 2^*t(n/2)+O(n)$$

where $O(n)$ captures the linear work needed to partition the subarrays. As shown in Chapter 2, algorithms that behave according to this $t(n)$ definition have performance of $O(n \log n)$. QUICKSORT is empirically faster than MEDIAN SORT simply because the constants abstracted by $O(n)$ are smaller. There is less overhead for QUICKSORT because it does not have to find the median element when constructing the subproblems; indeed, even a randomly selected *pivot* is shown, in practice, to suffice, and this requires only a single execution of partition for each recursive invocation of QUICKSORT (whereas MEDIAN SORT might need to recursively invoke partition multiple times when it seeks to compute the median element).

In the worst case, the largest or the smallest item is picked as the pivot. When this happens, QUICKSORT makes a pass over all elements in the array (in linear time) to sort just a single item in the array. In the worst case, this process is repeated $n-1$ times, resulting in $O(n^2)$ worst-case behavior.

Variations

QUICKSORT is the sorting method of choice on most systems. On Unix- and Linux-based systems, there is a built-in library function called qsort.[*] Often, the operating system uses optimized versions of the default QUICKSORT algorithm. Two of the commonly cited sources for optimizations are by Sedgewick (1978) and Bentley and McIlroy (1993).

Various optimizations include:

- Create a stack that stores the subtasks to be processed to eliminate recursion.
- Choose the pivot based upon median-of-three.
- Set minimum partition size to use INSERTION SORT instead (which varies by implementation and machine architecture; for example, on the Sun4 architecture the minimum value is set to 4 based on empirical evaluation).
- When processing subarrays, push larger partition onto the stack first to minimize the total size of the stack by ensuring that the smaller problem is worked on first.

It is important to recognize that none of these optimizations will eliminate the $O(n^2)$ worst-case behavior of QUICKSORT. The only way to ensure an $O(n \log n)$ worst-case performance is to use a selection algorithm such as BFPRT, described

---

[*] It is instructive that some versions of the Linux operating system implement qsort using HEAP SORT, discussed in the upcoming section "Heap Sort."

in Example 4-6, although this will result in a degraded average-case performance. If a true O(*n* log *n*) worst-case performance is required, consider using HEAP SORT, discussed in the next section.

Picking a pivot

Selecting the pivot element from a subarray A[*left*,*left+n*) must be an efficient operation; it shouldn't require checking all *n* elements of the subarray. Some alternatives are:

- Select first or last: A[*left*] or A[*left+n*–1]
- Select random element in A[*left*,*left+n*–1]
- Select median-of-*k*: the middle value of *k* random elements in A[*left*,*left+n*–1]

Often one chooses *k*=3, and, not surprisingly, this variation is known as median-of-three. Sedgewick reports that this approach returns an improvement of 5%, but note that some arrangements of data will force even this alternative into subpar performance (Musser, 1997). A median-of-five pivot selection has also been used. Performing further computation to identify the proper pivot is rarely able to provide beneficial results because of the incurred costs, which make the algorithm approach MEDIAN SORT in performance (indeed, MEDIAN SORT takes this variation to the extreme by selecting the median-of-*n*).

Processing the partition

In the partition method shown in Example 4-3, elements less than or equal to the selected pivot are inserted toward the front of the subarray. This approach might skew the size of the subarrays for the recursive step if the selected pivot has many duplicate elements in the array. One way to reduce the imbalance is to place elements equal to the pivot alternatively in the first subarray and second subarray.

Processing subarrays

QUICKSORT usually yields two recursive invocations of QUICKSORT on smaller subarrays. While processing one, the activation record of the other is pushed onto the execution stack. If the larger subarray is processed first, it is possible to have a linear number of activation records on the stack at the same time (although modern compilers may eliminate this observed overhead). To minimize the possible depth of the stack, process the smaller subarray first.

If the depth of the system stack is a foreseeable issue, then perhaps QUICKSORT is not appropriate for your application. One way to break the impasse is to use a stack data structure to store the set of subproblems to be solved, rather than relying on recursion.

Using simpler insertion technique for small subarrays

On small arrays, INSERTION SORT is faster than QUICKSORT, but even when used on large arrays, QUICKSORT ultimately decomposes the problem to require numerous small subarrays to be sorted. One commonly used technique to improve the recursive performance QUICKSORT is to invoke QUICKSORT for large subarrays only, and use INSERTION SORT for small ones, as shown in Example 4-7.

Sedgewick (1978) suggests that a combination of median-of-three and using INSERTION SORT for small subarrays offers a speedup of 20–25% over pure QUICKSORT.

IntroSort

Switching to INSERTION SORT for small subarrays is a local decision that is made based upon the size of the subarray. Musser (1997) introduced a QUICKSORT variation called INTROSORT, which monitors the recursive depth of QUICKSORT to ensure efficient processing. If the depth of the QUICKSORT recursion exceeds log (n) levels, then INTROSORT switches to HEAP SORT. The SGI implementation of the C++ Standard Template Library uses INTROSORT as its default sorting mechanism (*http://www.sgi.com/tech/stl/sort.html*).

Selection Sort

Given a pile of cards with numbers on them, a common way to sort the pile is to select and remove the largest card, and then repeat the process until all cards are gone. This approach describes SELECTION SORT, which sorts in place the elements in $A[0,n)$, as shown in Example 4-8.

Example 4-8. Selection Sort implementation in C

```c
static int selectMax (void **ar, int left, int right,
                      int (*cmp)(const void *,const void *)) {
  int  maxPos = left;
  int  i = left;
  while (++i <= right) {
    if (cmp(ar[i], ar[maxPos])> 0) {
      maxPos = i;
    }
  }

  return maxPos;
}

void sortPointers (void **ar, int n,
              int(*cmp)(const void *,const void *)) {
  int i;

  /* repeatedly select max in A[0,i] and swap with proper position */
  for (i = n-1; i >=1; i--) {
    int maxPos = selectMax (ar, 0, i, cmp);
    if (maxPos != i) {
      void *tmp = ar[i];
      ar[i] = ar[maxPos];
      ar[maxPos] = tmp;
    }
  }
}
```

SELECTION SORT is the slowest of all the sorting algorithms described in this chapter; it requires quadratic time even in the best case (i.e., when the array is already sorted). It repeatedly performs almost the same task without learning anything from one iteration to the next. Selecting the largest element, *max*, in *A* takes *n*–1 comparisons, and selecting the second largest element, *second*, takes *n*–2 comparisons—not much progress! Many of these comparisons are wasted, because if an element is smaller than *second*, it can't possibly be the largest element and therefore had no impact on the computation for *max*. Instead of presenting more details on this poorly performing algorithm, we now consider HEAP SORT, which shows how to more effectively apply the principle behind SELECTION SORT.

Heap Sort

We always need at least *n*–1 comparisons to find the largest element in an array $A[0,n)$, but we want to minimize the number of elements that are compared directly to it. In sports, tournaments are used to find the "best" team from a field of *n* teams without forcing the ultimate winner to play all other *n*–1 teams. One of the most popular basketball events in the United States is the NCAA champion-ship tournament, where essentially a set of 64 college teams compete for the championship title.[*] The ultimate champion team plays five teams before reaching the final determining game, and so that team must win six games. It is no coinci-dence that 6=log (64). HEAP SORT shows how to apply this behavior to sort a set of elements; its pseudocode description is shown in Figure 4-14.

A heap is a binary tree whose structure ensures two properties:

Shape property
    A leaf node at depth $k>0$ can exist only if all 2^{k-1} nodes at depth $k-1$ exist. Additionally, nodes at a partially filled level must be added "from left to right."

Heap property
    Each node in the tree contains a value greater than or equal to either of its two children, if it has any.

The sample heap labeled (a) in Figure 4-15 satisfies these properties. The root of the binary tree must contain the largest element in the tree; however, note that the smallest element can be any of the leaf nodes. Although the ordering information in the binary tree is limited to the fact that a node is greater than either of its chil-dren, HEAP SORT shows how to take advantage of the shape property to efficiently sort an array of elements.

Given the rigid structure imposed by the shape property, a heap can be stored in an array *A* without losing any of its structural information. Illustration (b) in Figure 4-15 shows an integer label assigned to each node in the heap. The root is labeled 0. For a node with label *i*, its left child (should it exist) is labeled $2*i+1$; its right child (should it exist) is labeled $2*i+2$. Similarly, for a non-root node labeled *i*, its parent node is labeled $\lfloor (i-1)/2 \rfloor$. Using this labeling scheme, we can store the

---

[*] Actually, there are 65 teams, with a "buy-in" game to eliminate one team at the start of the tournament.

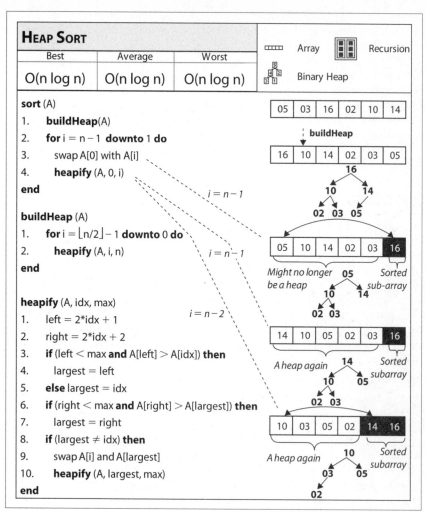

Figure 4-14. Heap Sort fact sheet

heap in an array by storing the element value for a node in the array position identified by the node's label. The array shown in illustration (c) in Figure 4-15 represents the heap shown in that figure. The order of the elements within A can be simply read from left to right as deeper levels of the tree are explored.

HEAP SORT sorts an array by first converting that array "in place" into a heap. Indeed, the heap shown in Figure 4-15 results by executing buildHeap (whose pseudocode is shown in Figure 4-14) on an already sorted array. The progress of buildHeap is shown in Figure 4-16. Each numbered row in this figure shows the result of executing heapify on the initial array from the midway point of $\lfloor n/2 \rfloor - 1$ down to the leftmost index 0. heapify (A, i, n) updates A to ensure that element $A[i]$ is swapped with the larger of its two children, $A[2*i+1]$ and $A[2*i+2]$, should either one be larger than $A[i]$. If the swap occurs, heapify recursively checks the grandchildren

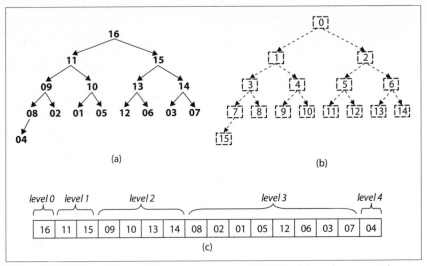

Figure 4-15. (a) Sample heap of 16 unique elements; (b) labels of these elements; (c) heap stored in an array

(and so on) to properly maintain the Heap property for A. As you can see, large numbers are eventually "lifted up" in the resulting heap (which means they are swapped in A with smaller elements to the left). The grayed squares in Figure 4-16 depict the elements swapped in line 9 of heapify.

HEAP SORT sorts an array A of size n by treating it as two distinct subarrays, $A[0,m)$ and $A[m,n)$, which represent a heap of size m and a sorted subarray of $n-m$ elements, respectively. As i iterates from $n-1$ down to 1, HEAP SORT grows the sorted subarray $A[i,n)$ downward by swapping the largest element in the heap (at position $A[0]$) with $A[i]$ (line 3 of sort in Figure 4-14); it then reconstructs $A[0,i)$ to be a valid heap by executing heapify (whose pseudocode is shown in Figure 4-14). The resulting non-empty subarray $A[i,n)$ will be sorted because the largest element in the heap represented in $A[0,i)$ is guaranteed to be smaller than any element in the sorted subarray $A[i,n)$.

Context

HEAP SORT is not a stable sort. Because it moves elements around quite frequently, it should not be used for value-based data.

Forces

HEAP SORT avoids many of the nasty (almost embarrassing!) cases that cause QUICKSORT to perform badly. Nonetheless, in the average case QUICKSORT outperforms HEAP SORT.

Solution

A sample implementation in C is shown in Example 4-9.

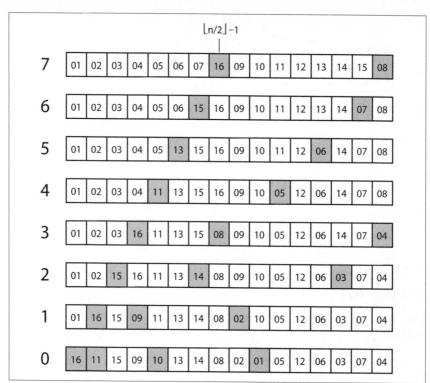

Figure 4-16. buildHeap operating on an initially sorted array

Example 4-9. Heap Sort implementation in C

```c
static void heapify (void **ar, int(*cmp)(const void *,const void *),
                     int idx, int max) {
  int left  = 2*idx + 1;
  int right = 2*idx + 2;
  int largest;

  /* Find largest element of A[idx], A[left], and A[right]. *
  if (left < max && cmp (ar[left], ar[idx]) > 0) {
    largest = left;
  } else {
    largest = idx;
  }

  if (right < max && cmp(ar[right], ar[largest]) > 0) {
    largest = right;
  }

  /* If largest is not already the parent then swap and propagate. */
  if (largest != idx) {
    void *tmp;
    tmp = ar[idx];
```

Example 4-9. Heap Sort implementation in C (continued)

```c
      ar[idx] = ar[largest];
      ar[largest] = tmp;

      heapify(ar, cmp, largest, max);
  }
}

static void buildHeap (void **ar,
                       int(*cmp)(const void *,const void *), int n) {
  int i;
  for (i = n/2-1; i>=0; i--) {
    heapify (ar, cmp, i, n);
  }
}

void sortPointers (void **ar, int n,
                   int(*cmp)(const void *,const void *)) {
  int i;
  buildHeap (ar, cmp, n);
  for (i = n-1; i >= 1; i--) {
  void *tmp;
  tmp = ar[0];
  ar[0] = ar[i];
  ar[i] = tmp;

    heapify (ar, cmp, 0, i);
  }
}
```

HEAP SORT succeeds because of the heapify function. It is used in two distinct places, although it serves the same purpose each time.

Analysis

heapify is the central operation in HEAP SORT. In buildHeap, it is called $\lfloor n/2 \rfloor - 1$ times, and during the actual sort it is called $n-1$ times, for a total of $\lfloor 3{*}n/2 \rfloor - 2$ times. As you can see, it is a recursive operation that executes a fixed number of computations until the end of the heap is reached. Because of the shape property, the depth of the heap will always be $\lfloor \log n \rfloor$, where n is the number of elements in the heap. The resulting performance, therefore, is bounded by $(\lfloor 3{*}n/2 \rfloor - 2){*}\lfloor \log n \rfloor$, which is $O(n \log n)$.

Variations

Non-recursive HEAP SORT implementations are available, and Table 4-4 presents a benchmark comparison on running 1,000 randomized trials of both implementations, discarding the best and worst performances of each. The average of the remaining runs is shown for both implementations.

Table 4-4. Performance comparison of non-recursive variation (in seconds)

n	Non-recursive Heap Sort	Recursive Heap Sort
16,384	0.0118	0.0112
32,768	0.0328	0.0323
65,536	0.0922	0.0945
131,072	0.2419	0.2508
262,144	0.5652	0.6117
524,288	1.0611	1.1413
1,048,576	2.0867	2.2669
2,097,152	4.9065	5.3249

Counting Sort

An accountant is responsible for reviewing the books for a small restaurant. Each night when the restaurant closes, the owner records the total sales for the day and prints a receipt showing the date and the total. These receipts are tossed into a large box. At the end of the year, the accountant reviews the receipts in the box to see whether any are missing. As you can imagine, the receipts in the box are in no particular order.

The accountant could sort all receipts in ascending order by date and then review the sorted collection. As an alternative, she could grab a blank calendar for the year and, one by one, pull receipts from the box and mark those calendar days with an X. Once the box is empty, the accountant need only review the calendar to see the days that were not marked. Note that at no point in this second alternative are two receipts ever compared with each other. If the restaurant were open for 60 years and the accountant had calendars for each year, this approach would not be efficient if there were only five receipts in the box; however, it would be efficient if 20,000 receipts were in the box. The density of possible elements that actually appear in the data set determines the efficiency of this approach.

At the beginning of this chapter, we proved that no sorting algorithm can sort n elements in better than O(n log n) time if comparing elements. Surprisingly, there are other ways of sorting elements if you know something about those elements in advance. For example, assume that you are asked to sort n elements, but you are told that each element is a value in the range [0,k), where k is much smaller than n. You can take advantage of the situation to produce a linear—O(n)—sorting algorithm, known as COUNTING SORT.

Context

COUNTING SORT, as illustrated in Figure 4-17, does not require a comparison function and is best used for sorting integers from a fixed range [0,k). It can also be used whenever a total ordering of k elements can be determined and a unique integer $0 \leq i < k$ can be assigned for those k elements. For example, if sorting a set of fractions of the form $1/p$ (where p is an integer) whose maximum denominator p is k, then each fraction $1/p$ can be assigned the unique value $k-p$.

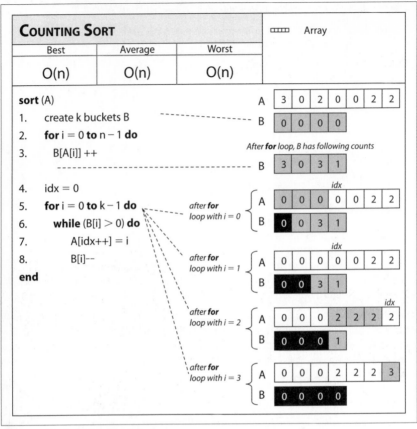

Figure 4-17. Counting Sort fact sheet

Forces

COUNTING SORT succeeds only because the k values form a total ordering for the elements.

Solution

COUNTING SORT creates k buckets that store the number of times the kth element was seen in the input array. COUNTING SORT then makes two passes over the input array. During the first pass, COUNTING SORT increments the count of the kth bucket. In the second pass, COUNTING SORT overwrites the original array by processing the count values in the total ordering provided by k buckets. The COUNTING SORT implementation in Example 4-10 relies on the calling function to determine the proper value for k.

Example 4-10. Counting Sort implementation

```
/** Sort the n elements in ar, drawn from the values [0,k). */
int countingSort (int *ar, int n, int k) {
  int i, idx = 0;
  int *B = calloc (k, sizeof (int));

  for (i = 0; i < n; i++) {
    B[ar[i]]++;
  }

  for (i = 0; i < k; i++) {
    while (B[i]-- > 0) {
      ar[idx++] = i;
    }
  }

  free(B);
}
```

Analysis

COUNTING SORT makes two passes over the entire array. The first processes each of the n elements in the input array. In the second pass, the inner while loop is executed $B[i]$ times for each of the $0 \leq i < k$ buckets; thus the statement ar[idx++] executes exactly n times. Together, the key statements in the implementation execute a total of 2^*n times, resulting in a total performance of $O(n)$.

COUNTING SORT can only be used in limited situations because of the constraints that the elements in the array being sorted are drawn from a limited set of k elements. We now discuss BUCKET SORT, which relaxes the constraint that each element to be sorted maps to a single bucket.

Bucket Sort

COUNTING SORT succeeds by constructing a much smaller set of k values in which to count the n elements in the set. Given a set of n elements, BUCKET SORT constructs a set of n buckets into which the elements of the input set are partitioned; BUCKET SORT thus reduces its processing costs at the expense of this extra space. If a hash function, hash(A_i), is provided that uniformly partitions the input set of n elements into these n buckets, then BUCKET SORT as described in Figure 4-18 can sort, in the worst case, in $O(n)$ time. You can use BUCKET SORT if the following two properties hold:

Uniform distribution
> The input data must be uniformly distributed for a given range. Based on this distribution, n buckets are created to evenly partition the input range.

Ordered hash function
> The buckets must be ordered. That is, if $i < j$, then elements inserted into bucket b_i are lexicographically smaller than elements in bucket b_j.

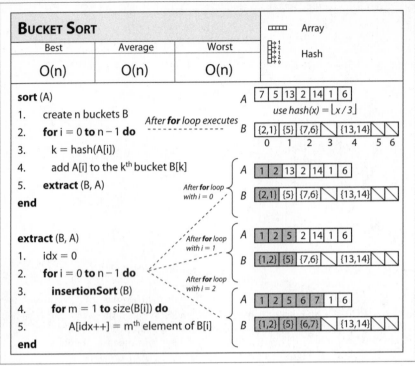

Figure 4-18. Bucket Sort fact sheet

BUCKET SORT is not appropriate for sorting arbitrary strings, for example; however, it could be used to sort a set of uniformly distributed floating-point numbers in the range [0,1).

Once all elements to be sorted are inserted into the buckets, BUCKET SORT extracts the values from left to right using INSERTION SORT on the contents of each bucket. This orders the elements in each respective bucket as the values from the buckets are extracted from left to right to repopulate the original array.

Context

BUCKET SORT is the fastest sort when the elements to be sorted can be uniformly partitioned using a fast hashing function.

Forces

If storage space is not important and the elements admit to an immediate total ordering, BUCKET SORT can take advantage of this extra knowledge for impressive cost savings.

Solution

In the C implementation for BUCKET SORT, shown in Example 4-11, each bucket stores a linked list of elements that were hashed to that bucket. The functions numBuckets and hash are provided externally, based upon the input set.

Example 4-11. Bucket Sort implementation in C

```c
extern int hash(void *elt);
extern int numBuckets(int numElements);

/* linked list of elements in bucket. */
typedef struct entry {
  void         *element;
  struct entry *next;
} ENTRY;

/* maintain count of entries in each bucket and pointer to its first entry */
typedef struct {
  int          size;
  ENTRY        *head;
} BUCKET;

/* Allocation of buckets and the number of buckets allocated */
static BUCKET *buckets = 0;
static int num = 0;

/** One by one remove and overwrite ar */
void extract (BUCKET *buckets, int(*cmp)(const void *,const void *),
              void **ar, int n) {
  int i, low;
  int idx = 0;
  for (i = 0; i < num; i++) {
    ENTRY *ptr, *tmp;
    if (buckets[i].size == 0) continue;   /* empty bucket */

    ptr = buckets[i].head;
    if (buckets[i].size == 1) {
      ar[idx++] = ptr->element;
      free (ptr);
      buckets[i].size = 0;
      continue;
    }

    /* insertion sort where elements are drawn from linked list and
     * inserted into array. Linked lists are released. */
    low = idx;
    ar[idx++] = ptr->element;
    tmp = ptr;
    ptr = ptr->next;
    free (tmp);
```

Example 4-11. Bucket Sort implementation in C (continued)

```c
    while (ptr != NULL) {
      int i = idx-1;
      while (i >= low && cmp (ar[i], ptr->element) > 0) {
        ar[i+1] = ar[i];
        i--;
      }
      ar[i+1] = ptr->element;
      tmp = ptr;
      ptr = ptr->next;
      free(tmp);
      idx++;
    }
    buckets[i].size = 0;
  }
}

void sortPointers (void **ar, int n,
                   int(*cmp)(const void *,const void *)) {
  int i;
  num = numBuckets(n);
  buckets = (BUCKET *) calloc (num, sizeof (BUCKET));
  for (i = 0; i < n; i++) {
    int k = hash(ar[i]);

    /** Insert each element and increment counts */
    ENTRY *e = (ENTRY *) calloc (1, sizeof (ENTRY));
    e->element = ar[i];
    if (buckets[k].head == NULL) {
      buckets[k].head = e;
    } else {
      e->next = buckets[k].head;
      buckets[k].head = e;
    }

    buckets[k].size++;
  }

  /* now read out and overwrite ar. */
  extract (buckets, cmp, ar, n);

  free (buckets);
}
```

For numbers drawn uniformly from [0,1), Example 4-12 contains sample implementations of the hash and numBuckets functions to use.

Example 4-12. hash and numBuckets functions for [0,1) range

```c
static int num;

/** Number of buckets to use is the same as the number of elements. */
int numBuckets(int numElements) {
```

Example 4-12. hash and numBuckets functions for [0,1) range (continued)

```
  num = numElements;
  return numElements;
}

/**
 * Hash function to identify bucket number from element. Customized
 * to properly encode elements in order within the buckets. Range of
 * numbers is from [0,1), so we subdivide into buckets of size 1/num;
 */
int hash(double *d) {
  int bucket = num*(*d);
  return bucket;
}
```

The buckets could also be stored using fixed arrays that are reallocated when the buckets become full, but the linked list implementation is about 30–40% faster.

Analysis

In the sortPointers function of Example 4-11, each element in the input is inserted into its associated bucket based upon the provided hash function; this takes linear, or O(n), time. The elements in the buckets are not sorted, but because of the careful design of the hash function, we know that all elements in bucket b_i are smaller than the elements in bucket b_j, if $i<j$.

As the values are extracted from the buckets and written back into the input array, INSERTION SORT is used when a bucket contains more than a single element. For BUCKET SORT to exhibit O(n) behavior, we must guarantee that the total time to sort each of these buckets is also O(n). Let's define n_i to be the number of elements partitioned in bucket b_i. We can treat n_i as a random variable (using statistical theory). Now consider the expected value $E[n_i]$ of n_i. Each element in the input set has probability $p=1/n$ of being inserted into a given bucket because each of these elements is uniformly drawn from the range [0,1). Therefore, $E[n_i]=n*p=n*(1/n)=1$, while the variance $Var[n_i]=n*p*(1-p)=(1-1/n)$. It is important to consider the variance since some buckets will be empty, and others may have more than one element; we need to be sure that no bucket has too many elements. Once again, we resort to statistical theory, which provides the following equation for random variables:

$$E[n_i^2] = Var[n_i] + E^2[n_i]$$

From this equation we can compute the expected value of n_i^2. This is critical because it is the factor that determines the cost of INSERTION SORT, which runs in a worst case of O(n^2). We compute $E[n_i^2]=(1-1/n)+1=(2-1/n)$, which shows that $E[n_i^2]$ is a constant. This means that when we sum up the costs of executing INSERTION SORT on all n buckets, the expected performance cost remains O(n).

Variations

In HASH SORT, each bucket reflects a unique hash code value returned by the hash function used on each element. Instead of creating n buckets, HASH SORT creates a suitably large number of buckets k into which the elements are partitioned; as k grows in size, the performance of HASH SORT improves. The key to HASH SORT is a hashing function hash(e) that returns an integer for each element e such that hash(a_i)≤hash(a_j) if a_i≤a_j.

The hash function hash(e) defined in Example 4-13 operates over elements containing just lowercase letters. It converts the first three characters of the string into a value (in base 26), and so for the string "abcdefgh," its first three characters ("abc") are extracted and converted into the value 0*676+1*26+2=28. This string is thus inserted into the bucket labeled 28.

Example 4-13. hash and numBuckets functions for Hash Sort

```
/** Number of buckets to use. */
int numBuckets(int numElements) {
  return 26*26*26;
}


/**
 * Hash function to identify bucket number from element. Customized
 * to properly encode elements in order within the buckets.
 */
int hash(void *elt) {

  return (((char*)elt)[0] - 'a')*676 +
         (((char*)elt)[1] - 'a')*26 +
         (((char*)elt)[2] - 'a');
}
```

The performance of HASH SORT for various bucket sizes and input sets is shown in Table 4-5. We show comparable sorting times for QUICKSORT using the median-of-three approach for selecting the pivotIndex.

Table 4-5. Sample performance for Hash Sort with different numbers of buckets, compared with Quicksort (in seconds)

n	26 buckets	676 buckets	17,576 buckets	Quicksort
16	0.000007	0.000026	0.000353	0.000006
32	0.00001	0.000037	0.000401	0.000007
64	0.000015	0.000031	0.000466	0.000016
128	0.000025	0.000042	0.000613	0.000031
256	0.000051	0.000062	0.00062	0.000045
512	0.000108	0.000093	0.000683	0.000098
1,024	0.000337	0.000176	0.0011	0.000282
2,048	0.0011	0.000456	0.0013	0.000637
4,096	0.0038	0.0012	0.0018	0.0017
8,192	0.0116	0.0027	0.0033	0.0037
16,384	0.048	0.0077	0.0069	0.009
32,768	0.2004	0.0224	0.0162	0.0207
65,536	0.8783	0.0682	0.0351	0.0525
131,072	2.5426	0.1136	0.0515	0.1151

Note that with 17,576 buckets, HASH SORT outperforms QUICKSORT for $n>$ 8,192 items (and this trend continues with increasing n). However, with only 676 buckets, once $n>32,768$ (for an average of 48 elements per bucket), HASH SORT begins its inevitable slowdown with the accumulated cost of executing INSERTION SORT on increasingly larger sets. Indeed, with only 26 buckets, once $n>256$, HASH SORT begins to quadruple its performance as the problem size doubles, showing how too few buckets leads to $O(n^2)$ performance.

Criteria for Choosing a Sorting Algorithm

To choose a sorting algorithm, consider the qualitative criteria in Table 4-6. These may help your initial decision, but you likely will need more quantitative measures to guide you.

Table 4-6. Criteria for choosing a sorting algorithm

Criteria	Sorting algorithm
Only a few items	INSERTION SORT
Items are mostly sorted already	INSERTION SORT
Concerned about worst-case scenarios	HEAP SORT
Interested in a good average-case result	QUICKSORT
Items are drawn from a dense universe	BUCKET SORT
Desire to write as little code as possible	INSERTION SORT

To choose the appropriate algorithm for different data, you need to know some properties about your input data. We created several benchmark data sets on which to show how the algorithms presented in this chapter compare with one another. Note that the actual values of the generated tables are less important because they reflect the specific hardware on which the benchmarks were run. Instead, you should pay attention to the relative performance of the algorithms on the corresponding data sets:

Random strings

Throughout this chapter, we have demonstrated performance of sorting algorithms when sorting 26-character strings that are permutations of the letters in the alphabet. Given there are $n!$ such strings, or roughly $4.03*10^{26}$ strings, there are few duplicate strings in our sample data sets. In addition, the cost of comparing elements is not constant, because of the occasional need to compare multiple characters.

Double precision floating-point values

Using available pseudorandom generators available on most operating systems, we generate a set of random numbers from the range [0,1). There are essentially no duplicate values in the sample data set and the cost of comparing two elements is a fixed constant.

The input data provided to the sorting algorithms can be preprocessed to ensure some of the following properties (not all are compatible):

Sorted
> The input elements can be presorted into ascending order (the ultimate goal) or in descending order.

Killer median-of-three
> Musser (1997) discovered an ordering that ensures that QUICKSORT requires $O(n^2)$ comparisons when using median-of-three to choose a pivot.

Nearly sorted
> Given a set of sorted data, we can select k pairs of elements to swap and the distance d with which to swap (or 0 if any two pairs can be swapped). Using this capability, you can construct input sets that might more closely match your input set.

The upcoming tables are ordered left to right, based upon how well the algorithms perform on the final row in the table. Each section has four tables, showing performance results under the four different situations outlined earlier in this chapter.

String Benchmark Results

Because INSERTION SORT and SELECTION SORT are the two slowest algorithms in this chapter on randomly uniform data (by several orders of magnitude) we omit these algorithms from Tables 4-7 through 4-11. However, it is worth repeating that on sorted data (Table 4-8) and nearly sorted data (Tables 4-10 and 4-11) INSERTION SORT will outperform the other algorithms, often by an order of magnitude. To produce the results shown in Tables 4-7 through 4-11, we executed each trial 100 times on the high-end computer and discarded the best and worst performers. The average of the remaining 98 trials is shown in these tables. The columns labeled QUICKSORT BFPRT[4] MINSIZE=4 refer to a QUICKSORT implementation that uses BFPRT (with groups of 4) to select the partition value and which switches to INSERTION SORT when a subarray to be sorted has four or fewer elements.

Table 4-7. Performance results (in seconds) on random 26-letter permutations of the alphabet

n	Hash Sort 17,576 buckets	Quicksort median-of-three	Heap Sort	Median Sort	Quicksort BFPRT[4] minSize=4
4,096	0.0012	0.0011	0.0013	0.0023	0.0041
8,192	0.002	0.0024	0.0031	0.005	0.0096
16,384	0.0044	0.0056	0.0073	0.0112	0.022
32,768	0.0103	0.014	0.0218	0.0281	0.0556
65,536	0.0241	0.0342	0.0649	0.0708	0.1429
131,072	0.0534	0.0814	0.1748	0.1748	0.359

Table 4-8. Performance (in seconds) on ordered random 26-letter permutations of the alphabet

n	Hash Sort 17,576 buckets	Quicksort median-of-three	Heap Sort	Median Sort	Quicksort BFPRT[4] minSize=4
4,096	0.0011	0.0007	0.0012	0.002	0.0031
8,192	0.0019	0.0015	0.0027	0.0042	0.007

Table 4-8. Performance (in seconds) on ordered random 26-letter permutations of the alphabet (continued)

n	Hash Sort 17,576 buckets	Quicksort median-of-three	Heap Sort	Median Sort	Quicksort BFPRT[4] minSize=4
16,384	0.0037	0.0036	0.0062	0.0094	0.0161
32,768	0.0074	0.0082	0.0157	0.0216	0.0381
65,536	0.0161	0.0184	0.0369	0.049	0.0873
131,072	0.0348	0.0406	0.0809	0.1105	0.2001

Table 4-9. Performance (in seconds) on killer median data

n	Hash Sort 17,576 buckets	Heap Sort	Median Sort	Quicksort BFPRT[4] minSize=4	Quicksort median-of-three[a]
4,096	0.0011	0.0012	0.0021	0.0039	0.0473
8,192	0.0019	0.0028	0.0045	0.0087	0.1993
16,384	0.0038	0.0066	0.0101	0.0194	0.8542
32,768	0.0077	0.0179	0.024	0.0472	4.083
65,536	0.0171	0.0439	0.056	0.1127	17.1604
131,072	0.038	0.1004	0.1292	0.2646	77.4519

[a] Because the performance of QUICKSORT median-of-three degrades so quickly, only 10 trials were executed; the table shows the average of eight runs once the best and worst performers were discarded.

Table 4-10. Performance (in seconds) on 16 random pairs of elements swapped eight locations away

n	Hash Sort 17,576 buckets	Quicksort median-of-three	Heap Sort	Median Sort	Quicksort BFPRT[4] minSize=4
4,096	0.0011	0.0007	0.0012	0.002	0.0031
8,192	0.0019	0.0015	0.0027	0.0042	0.007
16,384	0.0038	0.0035	0.0063	0.0094	0.0161
32,768	0.0072	0.0081	0.0155	0.0216	0.038
65,536	0.0151	0.0182	0.0364	0.0491	0.0871
131,072	0.0332	0.0402	0.08	0.1108	0.2015

Table 4-11. Performance (in seconds) on n/4 random pairs of elements swapped four locations away

n	Hash Sort 17,576 buckets	Quicksort median-of-three	Heap Sort	Median Sort	Quicksort BFPRT[4] minSize=4
4,096	0.0011	0.0008	0.0012	0.002	0.0035
8,192	0.0019	0.0019	0.0028	0.0044	0.0078
16,384	0.0039	0.0044	0.0064	0.0096	0.0175
32,768	0.0073	0.01	0.0162	0.0221	0.0417

Table 4-11. Performance (in seconds) on n/4 random pairs of elements swapped four locations away (continued)

n	Hash Sort 17,576 buckets	Quicksort median-of-three	Heap Sort	Median Sort	Quicksort BFPRT[4] minSize=4
65,536	0.0151	0.024	0.0374	0.0505	0.0979
131,072	0.0333	0.0618	0.0816	0.1126	0.2257

Double Benchmark Results

The benchmarks using double floating-point values (Tables 4-12 through 4-16) eliminate much of the overhead that was simply associated with string comparisons. Once again, we omit INSERTION SORT and SELECTION SORT from these tables.

Table 4-12. Performance (in seconds) on random floating-point values

n	Bucket Sort	Quicksort median-of-three	Median Sort	Heap Sort	Quicksort BFPRT[4] minSize=4
4,096	0.0009	0.0009	0.0017	0.0012	0.0003
8,192	0.0017	0.002	0.0039	0.0029	0.0069
16,384	0.0041	0.0043	0.0084	0.0065	0.0157
32,768	0.0101	0.0106	0.0196	0.0173	0.039
65,536	0.0247	0.0268	0.0512	0.0527	0.1019
131,072	0.0543	0.0678	0.1354	0.1477	0.26623

Table 4-13. Performance (in seconds) on ordered floating-point values

n	Bucket Sort	Heap Sort	Median Sort	Quicksort median-of-three	Quicksort BFPRT[4] minSize=4
4,096	0.0007	0.0011	0.0015	0.0012	0.0018
8,192	0.0015	0.0024	0.0032	0.0025	0.004
16,384	0.0035	0.0052	0.0067	0.0055	0.0089
32,768	0.0073	0.0127	0.015	0.0133	0.0208
65,536	0.0145	0.0299	0.0336	0.0306	0.0483
131,072	0.0291	0.065	0.0737	0.0823	0.1113

Table 4-14. Performance (in seconds) on killer median data

n	Bucket Sort	Heap Sort	Median Sort	Quicksort median-of-three	Quicksort BFPRT[4] minSize=4
4,096	0.0008	0.0011	0.0015	0.0015	0.0025
8,192	0.0016	0.0024	0.0034	0.0033	0.0056
16,384	0.0035	0.0053	0.0071	0.0076	0.0122

Table 4-14. Performance (in seconds) on killer median data (continued)

n	Bucket Sort	Heap Sort	Median Sort	Quicksort median-of-three	Quicksort BFPRT[4] minSize=4
32,768	0.0079	0.0134	0.0164	0.0192	0.0286
65,536	0.0157	0.0356	0.0376	0.0527	0.0686
131,072	0.0315	0.0816	0.0854	0.1281	0.1599

Table 4-15. Performance (in seconds) on 16 random pairs of elements swapped eight locations away

n	Bucket Sort	Heap Sort	Median Sort	Quicksort median-of-three	Quicksort BFPRT[4] minSize=4
4,096	0.0007	0.0011	0.0015	0.0012	0.0018
8,192	0.0015	0.0024	0.0032	0.0025	0.004
16,384	0.0035	0.0051	0.0067	0.0054	0.0089
32,768	0.0071	0.0127	0.0151	0.0133	0.0209
65,536	0.0142	0.0299	0.0336	0.0306	0.0482
131,072	0.0284	0.065	0.0744	0.0825	0.111

Table 4-16. Performance (in seconds) on n/4 random pairs of elements swapped four locations away

n	Bucket Sort	Heap Sort	Quicksort median-of-three	Median Sort	Quicksort BFPRT[4] minSize=4
4,096	0.0001	0.0014	0.0015	0.0019	0.005
8,192	0.0022	0.0035	0.0032	0.0052	0.012
16,384	0.0056	0.0083	0.0079	0.0099	0.0264
32,768	0.0118	0.0189	0.0189	0.0248	0.0593
65,536	0.0238	0.0476	0.045	0.0534	0.129
131,072	0.0464	0.1038	0.1065	0.1152	0.2754

References

Bentley, Jon Louis and M. Douglas McIlroy, "Engineering a Sort Function," *Software—Practice and Experience*, 23(11): 1249–1265, 1993, *http://citeseer.ist. psu.edu/bentley93engineering.html*.

Blum, Manuel, Robert Floyd, Vaughan Pratt, Ronald Rivest, and Robert Tarjan, "Time bounds for selection." *Journal of Computer and System Sciences*, 7(4): 448–461, 1973.

Cormen, Thomas H., Charles E. Leiserson, Ronald L. Rivest, and Clifford Stein, *Introduction to Algorithms*, Second Edition. McGraw-Hill, 2001.

Davis, Mark and Ken Whistler, "Unicode Collation Algorithm, Unicode Technical Standard #10," March 2008, *http://unicode.org/reports/tr10/.*

Gilreath, William, "Hash sort: A linear time complexity multiple-dimensional sort algorithm." Proceedings of First Southern Symposium on Computing, December 1998, *http://www.citebase.org/abstract?id=oai:arXiv.org:cs/0408040.*

Musser, David, "Introspective sorting and selection algorithms." *Software—Practice and Experience*, 27(8): 983–993, 1997.

Sedgewick, Robert, "Implementing Quicksort Programs." *Communications ACM*, 21: 847–857, 1978.

Trivedi, Kishor Shridharbhai, *Probability and Statistics with Reliability, Queueing, and Computer Science Applications*, Second Edition. Wiley-Interscience Publishing, 2001.

5

Searching

Overview

Given a collection C of elements, there are three fundamental queries one might ask:

Existence: Does C contain a target element t?
Given a collection C, one often simply wants to know whether the collection already contains a given value, t. The response to such a query is true if an element exists in the collection that matches the desired target t, or false if this is not the case.

Retrieval: Return the element in C that matches the target element t
When complex elements are stored in a collection, the definition of a "matching" element can be based on a key value for the element or a subset of that element's attributes. For example, when searching a collection of information for the department of motor vehicles, one might only need to provide the driver's license number to retrieve the full information for that licensed driver.

Associative lookup: Return information associated in collection C with the target key element k
It is common to store additional pieces of information for complex structures. One can associate additional information with each key element k in the collection, which can be retrieved (or manipulated) as needed.

For the algorithms discussed in this chapter we assume the existence of a set U that contains values $e \in U$ being sought. The collection C contains elements drawn from U, and the target element being sought, t, is a member of U. If t is instead a key value, then we consider U to be the set of potential key values, $k \in U$, and the collection C may contain more complex elements. Note that duplicate values may exist within C, so it cannot be treated as a set (which only supports unique membership).

As we will see, it is important to know whether one can randomly access any individual element in C or whether one can only iterate over the elements one by one. When the collection allows for indexing of arbitrary elements, we use the notation A to represent the collection and the notation $A[i]$ to represent the ith element of A. By convention, we use the value nil to represent an element not in U; such a value is useful when a search is asked to return a specific element in a collection but that element is not present. In general, we assume it is impossible to search for nil in a collection—that is, $t \neq$ nil.

The algorithms in this chapter describe specific ways to structure data to more efficiently process these kinds of queries. One approach to consider is to order the collection C using the sorting algorithms covered in Chapter 4. As we will see, the efficiency of the queries does improve, but there are other costs involved in maintaining a sorted collection, especially when there may be frequent insertions or deletions of elements in the collection. You should choose an appropriate structure that not only speeds up the performance of individual queries but also reduces the overall cost of maintaining the collection structure in the face of both dynamic access and repeated queries.

Sequential Search

SEQUENTIAL SEARCH, also called *linear search*, is the simplest of all searching algorithms. It is a brute-force approach to locating a single target value, t, in some collection, C. It finds t by starting at the first element of the collection and examining each subsequent element until either the matching element is found or each element of the collection has been examined.

Consider the case of a moderate-size restaurant with 10–20 tables that requires reservations for all customers. The restaurant is close to a large medical center, and many of its customers are medical staff of the center or family members of patients at the center. The restaurant advertises that they will locate any patron in case of emergency and deliver messages to that person promptly. When customers are seated at a designated table, the hostess records the names of the customers with that table and erases the names when the party leaves. To locate a patron in the restaurant at any given moment, the hostess simply scans through the information for the collection of tables.

Input/Output

There must be some way to obtain each element from the collection being searched; the order is not important. If a collection A supports indexing, then an index value i can be used to retrieve element $A[i]$. Often a collection C is accessible by using a read-only *iterator* that retrieves each element from C (as, for example, a database cursor in response to an SQL query). Accessing the elements by the iterator is described in the lower half of Figure 5-1.

Input

The input consists of a collection, C, of $n \geq 0$ elements and a target item, t, that is sought.

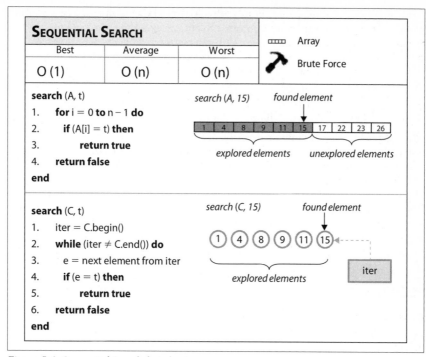

SEQUENTIAL SEARCH

Best	Average	Worst
O (1)	O (n)	O (n)

⎕⎕⎕⎕ Array

🔨 Brute Force

search (A, t)

1.   **for** i = 0 **to** n − 1 **do**
2.   **if** (A[i] = t) **then**
3.   **return true**
4.   **return false**
end

search (A, 15)   found element

| 1 | 4 | 8 | 9 | 11 | 15 | 17 | 22 | 23 | 26 |

explored elements   unexplored elements

search (C, t)

1.   iter = C.begin()
2.   **while** (iter ≠ C.end()) **do**
3.   e = next element from iter
4.   **if** (e = t) **then**
5.   **return true**
6.   **return false**
end

search (C, 15)   found element

① ④ ⑧ ⑨ ⑪ ⑮

explored elements

iter

Figure 5-1. Sequential Search fact sheet

Output

Returns true if *t* belongs to *C*, and false otherwise.

Context

Sometimes you need to locate an element in a collection. You may have to find elements in the collection frequently, and the collection may or may not be ordered. With no further knowledge about the information that might be in the collection, SEQUENTIAL SEARCH gets the job done in a brute-force manner. It is the only search algorithm you can use if the collection is accessible only through an iterator that returns the elements of the collection one at a time.

Forces

SEQUENTIAL SEARCH might be the most effective search method, depending upon *n*, the number of elements in the collection *C*, and the number of times you will perform such a search. If *n* is relatively small or you won't be performing the search over *C* often, the cost of sorting the elements or using a complex data structure might outweigh the resulting benefits.

If the collection is unordered and stored as a linked list, then inserting an element is a constant time operation (simply append to the end of the list or prepend to the beginning). Frequent insertions into an array-based collection require dynamic array management, which is either provided by the underlying programming language or requires specific attention by the programmer. In both cases, the expected time to find an element is $O(n)$; thus, removing an element takes at least $O(n)$.

SEQUENTIAL SEARCH places the fewest restrictions on the type of elements you can search. The only requirement is that there must be a match function to determine whether the target element being searched for matches an element in the collection; often this functionality is delegated to the elements themselves. No additional ordering is required.

Solution

Often the implementation of SEQUENTIAL SEARCH is trivial. If the collection is stored as an array, you need only start at the first element of the array and compare it to the target, t. If it matches, return true. If not, go to the next element and continue until you find the element you're looking for. If you reach the end of the array without success, return false.

The Ruby code in Example 5-1 searches sequentially through an array of elements.

Example 5-1. Sequential Search in Ruby

```
def sequentialSearch(collection, t)
  collection.each {
    |i| if i == t then return true; end
  }
  return false
end
```

The code is disarmingly simple. The function takes in a collection and the target item t being sought. The collection can be an array or any other collection that supports the each method in Ruby. Elements involved in the search must support the == operator; otherwise, you need to use one of the other types of equality operators supported in Ruby. This same example written in Java is shown in Example 5-2. The SequentialSearch generic class has a type parameter, T, that specifies the elements in the collection; T must provide a valid equals(Object o) method.

Example 5-2. Sequential Search in Java

```
package algs.model.search;
import java.util.Iterator;
public class SequentialSearch<T> {

    /** Apply the brute-force Sequential Search algorithm to search the
     * indexed collection (of type T) for the given target item. */
    public boolean sequentialSearch (T[] collection, T t) {
        for (T item : collection) {
            if (item.equals(t)) {
                return true;
            }
```

Example 5-2. Sequential Search in Java (continued)

```
        }
        return false;
    }

    /** Apply the brute-force Sequential Search algorithm to search the
     * iterable collection (of type T) for the given target item. */
    public boolean sequentialSearch (Iterable<T> collection, T t) {
        Iterator<T> iter = collection.iterator();
        while (iter.hasNext()) {
            if (iter.next().equals(t)) {
                return true;
            }
        }
        return false;
    }
}
```

A C implementation of SEQUENTIAL SORT is shown in Example 5-3, where the collection is stored in an array (ar) and the comparison function cmp returns 0 if two elements match.

Example 5-3. C implementation of Sequential Sort

```
int search (void *t, int(*cmp)(const void *,const void *)) {
  int i;
  for (i = 0; i < n; i++) {
    if (!cmp(ar[i], t)) {
      return 1;
    }
  }
  return 0;
}
```

Consequences

For small collections of unordered elements, SEQUENTIAL SEARCH is easy to implement and reasonably efficient. The worst case is when you search for an item not in the collection, since you must inspect every element in the collection. If the predominant result of a search is false, you may want to consider a different search algorithm, even when the collection is relatively small.

Sometimes, you may have an indexed collection that has "holes" in it. That is, there are index values in the collection where no element is stored.[*] In this case, you must add code to your implementation to check each index value, in order to ensure that there is an element in it. We would modify the code in Example 5-1 with an additional check, as shown in Example 5-4.

---

[*] To be more precise, a collection *A* may have its ith element $A[i]$ equal to the special value nil. It is quite rare for collections accessed using iterators to emit nil values.

Example 5-4. Sequential search with check for empty slot

```
def sequentialSearch(collection, t)
  collection.each {
    |i| if (i != nil) && (i == t) then return true; end
  }
  return false
end
```

If time is critical and the collection is large, this extra comparison incurred for each element will be noticeable, and so there is another solution. Instead of placing a nil value in an empty slot, place a specially identified element known as the *sentinel*. The sentinel always returns false when tested for equality to any item. For example, if the searched-for *t* is known to be a positive integer, you might use −1 as a sentinel to avoid the extra comparison.[*]

Analysis

If the item being sought belongs to the collection and is equally likely to be found at any of its indexed locations (alternatively, if it is equally likely to be emitted by an iterator at any position), then on average SEQUENTIAL SEARCH probes

$$\frac{1}{2}n + \frac{1}{2}$$

elements (as we presented in Chapter 2). That is, you will inspect about half the elements in the collection for each item you find. The best case is when the item being sought is the first element in the collection. This algorithm exhibits linear growth in the average and worst cases. If you double the size of the collection, this should approximately double the amount of time spent searching.

To show SEQUENTIAL SEARCH in action, we construct an ordered collection of the *n* integers in the range [1,*n*]. Although the collection is ordered, this information is not used by the searching code. We ran a suite of 100 trials; in each trial we execute 1,000 queries for a random target *t*, and of these 1,000 queries, 1,000*p are guaranteed to find *t* in the collection (indeed, the target *t* is negative for failed searches). We aggregate the time to execute these queries and discarded the best and worst performing trials. Table 5-1 shows the average of the remaining 98 trials at four specific *p* values. Note how the execution time approximately doubles as the size of the collection doubles. You should also observe that for each collection size *n*, the worst performance occurs in the final column where the target *t* does not exist in the collection.

Table 5-1. Sequential Search performance (in seconds)

n	p=1.0	p=0.5	p=0.25	p=0.0
4,096	0.0081	0.0106	0.0111	0.0138
8,192	0.016	0.0223	0.0236	0.0297

---

[*] In Ruby, you have the advantage that nil can be used as a comparison value for any object. So the extra comparison in Example 5-4 is really not needed.

Table 5-1. Sequential Search performance (in seconds) (continued)

n	p=1.0	p=0.5	p=0.25	p=0.0
16,384	0.0324	0.0486	0.0524	0.0629
32,768	0.0624	0.0958	0.1141	0.1263
65,536	0.1304	0.2065	0.226	0.226
131,072	0.2627	0.3625	0.3779	0.4387

In the best case, the first element in the collection is the desired target item, which performs in O(1) constant time. The worst case for SEQUENTIAL SEARCH occurs when you always search for an item not in the collection. In this case, you must examine all elements in the collection, resulting in O(n) performance. In the average case (as covered in Chapter 2 and shown in the table), the performance is O(n).

Variations

When the target element being sought is not uniformly distributed, there are variations that have been shown at times to improve upon SEQUENTIAL SEARCH without imposing an excessive burden on the programmer. Intuitively we want the elements that reside near the front of the collection to be those that are most likely to be sought. If you know something about the target items being sought (especially the order in which you are looking for them), then perhaps the following strategies can improve the performance of SEQUENTIAL SEARCH. These strategies are useful only for indexed collections that can be modified as the search progresses:

Move to front on success
> This strategy is suitable if there is an increased likelihood that an item t being searched for will be searched again. When t is found at location i, move the elements from A[0,i–1] to A[1,i], and move t into A[0]. This intuition is the basis for Most-Recently-Used (MRU) paging algorithms.

Move up on success
> This strategy is suitable if there is an increased likelihood that an item t being searched for will be searched again; additionally, there is a desire to avoid the cost of moving lots of elements. When t is found at location i, swap element A[i–1] with A[i] (except when i is already at the front of the collection). Intuitively, as items are found more frequently, they eventually "bubble" their way to the head of the collection with very little overhead (just a single array swap).

Move to end on success
> If an individual element is unlikely to be searched for multiple times, then moving it to the end when it is found will improve the performance of future searches. Move A[i+1,n] to A[i,n–1], and move the found item into A[n–1].

These variations all perform differently, based upon the probabilities of the individual search terms. Choosing one of these depends on a significant understanding of your data collections and the items being sought. Analyzing such algorithms is notoriously difficult, and requires mathematical techniques more advanced than those presented in this book.

Searching

Binary Search

BINARY SEARCH (Figure 5-2) delivers better performance than SEQUENTIAL SEARCH by sorting the elements in the collection in advance of the query. BINARY SEARCH divides the sorted collection in half until the sought-for item is found, or until it is determined that the item cannot be present in the smaller collection.

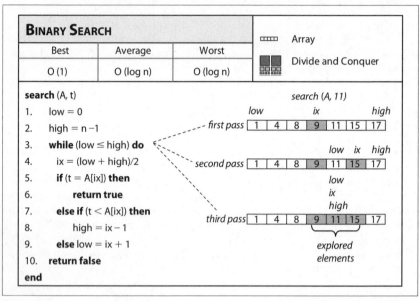

Figure 5-2. Binary Search fact sheet

Assume you have the telephone book for New York City and you need to find the phone number for "David Mamet." If you use SEQUENTIAL SEARCH as your algorithm, you might spend the better part of an afternoon trying to find the phone number; worse, you would have to read every entry in the phone book before determining whether the number is unlisted. Clearly, such an approach fails to take advantage of the ordered arrangement of names in the phone book. As an alternative, you would likely open the phone book to a page about halfway and see whether "David Mamet" is on that page. If the entry for "David Mamet" is on that page, then you are done; if not, and "Mamet" comes earlier in the alphabet than any last name on the page, you need only search through the first half of the phone book. Otherwise, you need to search through the back half of the phone book. This process is a "divide and conquer" strategy that rapidly locates the desired target. Note that if you get to a page on which "Mamet" should appear (if it were a listed phone number) but it actually does not, then you know—without looking at any other page—that Mamet's phone number is not present in the phone book.

Input/Output

The input to BINARY SEARCH is an indexed collection A of elements. Each element $A[i]$ has a *key* value k_i that can be used to identify the element. These keys are totally ordered, which means that given two keys, k_i and k_j, either $k_i<k_j$, $k_i=k_j$, or $k_i>k_j$. We construct a data structure that holds the elements (or pointers to the elements) and preserves the ordering of the keys. We must also be able to divide the data structure into subsets as we search, so that we solve the search problem in a "divide and conquer" manner. The output to BINARY SEARCH is either true or false.

Context

Whether searching through a set of numbers or a list of names ordered alphabetically, the method works. It can be shown that a logarithmic number of probes is necessary in the worst case.

Forces

The keys for the elements in the collection must admit a total ordering that lets you test whether an element is "greater than or equal" to another. Different types of data structures support binary searching. If the collection is static, the elements can be placed into an array. This makes it easy to navigate through the collection. However, if you need to add or remove elements from the collection, this approach becomes unwieldy. There are several structures one can use; one of the best known is the binary tree, discussed later in "Variations."

Solution

Given an ordered collection of elements as an array, the Java code in Example 5-5 shows a parameterized implementation of BINARY SEARCH for any base type T (using the capability of Java generics). Java provides the java.util.Comparable interface that contains a single method, compareTo. Any class that correctly implements this interface guarantees a total ordering of its instances.

Example 5-5. Binary Search implementation in Java

```
package algs.model.search;

/**
 * Binary Search given a pre-sorted array of the parameterized type.
 *
 * @param T   elements of the collection being searched are of this type.
 *            The parameter T must implement Comparable.
 */
public class BinarySearch<T extends Comparable<T>> {

    /* Search for target in collection. Return true on success. */
```

Example 5-5. Binary Search implementation in Java (continued)

```java
public boolean search(T[] collection, T target) {
    // null is never included in the collection
    if (target == null) { return false; }

    int low = 0, high = collection.length - 1;
    while (low <= high) {
        int ix = (low + high)/2;
        int rc = target.compareTo(collection[ix]);

        if (rc < 0) {
            // target is less than collection[i]
            high = ix - 1;
        } else if (rc > 0) {
            // target is greater than collection[i]
            low = ix + 1;
        } else {
            // found the item.
            return true;
        }
    }

    return false;
}
```

Three variables are used in the implementation: low, high, and ix. low is the lowest index of the current subarray being searched, high is the upper index of the same subarray, and ix is the midpoint of the subarray. The performance of this code depends on the number of times the loop executes.

Consequences

BINARY SEARCH adds a small amount of complexity for large performance gains. The complexity can increase when the collection is not stored in a simple in-memory data structure, such as an array. There must be a way to access element $A[i]$ for $0 \leq i < n$ in the collection based upon the natural order of the elements in the collection, as represented by the Comparable interface. A large collection might need to be kept in secondary storage, such as a file on a disk. In such a case, the ith element is accessed by its offset location within the file. Using secondary storage, the time required to search for an element is dominated by the costs to accessing the storage; other solutions related to BINARY SEARCH may be appropriate. See "Variations" for algorithms that address these issues.

Analysis

BINARY SEARCH divides the problem size approximately in half every time it executes the loop. The maximum number of times the collection of size n is cut in half is log (n), if n is a power of 2; otherwise, it is $\lfloor \log (n) \rfloor$. If we use a single operation to determine whether two items are equal, lesser than, or greater than (as is made possible by the Comparable interface), then only $\lfloor \log (n) \rfloor$ comparisons are needed, resulting in a classification of O(log n).

We ran 100 trials of 524,288 searches for an item stored in a collection in memory of size n (ranging in size from 4,096 to 524,288) with probability p (sampled at 1.0, 0.5, and 0.0) of finding each item. After removing the best and worst performers for each trial, Table 5-2 shows the average performance for the remaining 98 trials.

Table 5-2. In-memory execution of 524,288 searches using Binary Search compared to Sequential Search (in seconds)

n	Sequential Search time			Binary Search time		
	p = 1.0	p = 0.5	p = 0.0	p = 1.0	p = 0.5	p = 0.0
4,096	3.8643	5.5672	7.2143	0.0809	0.0773	0.0704
8,192	7.2842	10.7343	14.1308	0.0861	0.0842	0.0755
16,384	14.0036	20.9443	27.7101	0.0928	0.0902	0.0814
32,768	27.8042	40.7164	54.3972	0.0977	0.1065	0.1067
65,536	54.8484	81.1192	107.8211	0.1206	0.1155	0.1015
131,072	107.6957	161.6651	215.1825	0.1246	0.1251	0.1127
262,144	*	*	*	0.1373	0.1346	0.1232
524,288	*	*	*	0.1479	0.1475	0.133

These trials were designed to ensure that for the $p=1.0$ case all elements in the collection are being searched for with equal probability; if this were not the case, the results could be skewed. For both SEQUENTIAL SEARCH and BINARY SEARCH, the input is an array of sorted integers in the range $[0,n)$. To produce 524,288 search items known to be in the collection ($p=1.0$), we cycle through the n numbers $524,288/n$ times.

Table 5-3 shows the times for performing 524,288 searches on a collection stored on a local disk. The searched-for item either always exists in the collection (e.g., $p=1.0$) or it never does (e.g., we search for -1 in the collection $[0,n)$). The data is simply a file of ascending integers, where each integer is packed into four bytes. The dominance of disk access is clear since the results in Table 5-3 are nearly 200 times slower than those in Table 5-2. As n doubles in size, note how the performance of the search increases by a fixed amount, a clear indication that the performance of BINARY SEARCH is O(log n).

Table 5-3. Secondary-storage Binary Search performance for 524,288 searches (in seconds)

n	p = 1.0	p =0.0
4,096	2.8403	2.8025
8,192	3.4829	3.4942
16,384	4.1842	4.0046
32,768	4.9028	4.7532
65,536	5.5598	5.449
131,072	6.4186	6.1808
262,144	7.1226	6.9484
524,288	7.8316	7.4513

Variations

If you wanted to support a "search-or-insert" operation, then the final value of ix at line 10 in Figure 5-2 identifies the index value into which the missing element can be inserted (and all higher indexed values would need to be bumped up).

There are two primary variations on BINARY SEARCH. The first involves dealing with dynamic data where one must tune the implementation to allow efficient insertions and deletions into the collection while maintaining acceptable search performance. If an array is used to store the collection, insertions and deletions are quite inefficient, since every array entry should contain a valid element. Therefore, inserting involves extending the array (physically or logically) and pushing on average half of the elements ahead one slot. Deletion requires shrinking the array and moving half of the elements one index position lower. Neither of these is acceptable.

As long as the collection fits in memory, a good choice is to switch to a hash-based search approach using *collision chaining*. See the later section "Hash-based Search," which describes a straightforward approach to searching dynamic data. An alternate method is to create a binary search tree in memory. This approach can be simple to implement if the insertions and deletions are random enough that the tree does not become too biased. However, experience has shown that this is rarely the case, and a more complex type of search tree—a balanced binary search tree—must be used (Cormen et al., 2001).

The second variation addresses the case in which the data is both dynamic and too large to fit into memory. When this occurs, the search time is dominated by input/output operations to secondary storage. One effective solution is to use an *n*-ary tree called a B-Tree. This is a multilevel tree that is fine-tuned for performance on secondary storage. A complete analysis of B-Trees can be found in (Cormen et al., 2001). A helpful online B-Tree tutorial with examples can be found at *http://www.bluerwhite.org/btree*.

Hash-based Search

The previous sections on searching apply in specific cases that require a small number of elements (SEQUENTIAL SEARCH) or an ordered collection (BINARY SEARCH). We need more powerful techniques for searching larger collections that are not necessarily ordered. One of the most common approaches is to use a *hash function* to transform one or more characteristics of the searched-for item into a value that is used to index into an indexed hash table. Hash-based searching has better average-case performance than the other search algorithms described in this chapter. Many books on algorithms discuss hash-based searching under the topic of *hash tables* (Chapter 11 in Cormen et al., 2001); you may also find this topic in books on data structures that describe hash tables.

In HASH-BASED SEARCH (Figure 5-3), the *n* elements of a collection C are first loaded into a hash table A that has b bins. The concept of a *key* enables this to happen. Each element $e \in C$ can be mapped to a key value k=key(e) such that if $e_i=e_j$ then $key(e_i)=key(e_j)$.* A hash function h=hash(e) uses the key value key(e) to

---

* Note that the reverse is not necessarily true since key values do not have to be unique.

determine the bin $A[h]$ into which to insert e, where $0{\leq}h{<}b$. Once the hash table A is constructed, then searching for an item t is transformed into a search for t within $A[h]$ where $h{=}hash(t)$.

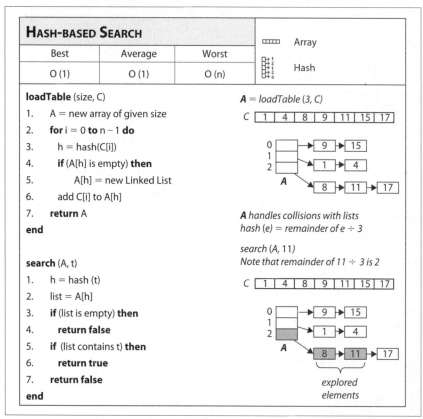

Figure 5-3. Hash-based Search fact sheet

The general pattern for hash-based searching is shown in Figure 5-4 with a small example. The components of HASH-BASED SEARCH are:

- The universe U that defines the set of possible keys. Each element $e{\in}C$ maps to a key $k{\in}U$.

- The hash table, A, which stores the n elements from the original collection C. A may contain just the elements themselves or it may contain the key values of the elements. There are b locations within A.

- The hash function, *hash*, which computes an integer index h into the hash table using $key(e)$, where $0{\leq}h{<}b$.

There are two main concerns when implementing HASH-BASED SEARCH: the design of the hash function, and how to handle *collisions* (when two keys map to the same bin in A). Collisions occur in almost all cases where $b{<}{<}|U|$, that is, when b is much smaller than the number of potential keys that exist in the universe U. Note that if $b{<}n$ there won't be enough space in the hash table A to

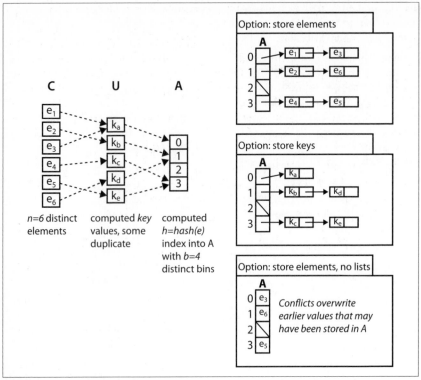

Figure 5-4. General approach to hashing

store all of the *n* elements from the original collection. When this happens, it is common for *A* to store a set of elements (typically in a linked list) in each of its *b* bins, as shown in options "store elements" and "store keys" in Figure 5-4.[*]

Improper hash function design can lead to poor distribution of the keys in the primary storage. A poorly designed hash function has two consequences: many slots in the hash table may be unused—wasting space—and there will be many collisions where the keys map into the same slot, which worsens performance.

There will inevitably be collisions with keys with most input. The collision-handling strategy has a significant impact on a search algorithm's performance, especially as the expected number of collisions increases.

Input/Output

To search for a target item *t*, it must have one or more properties that can be used as a key *k*; these keys determine the universe *U*. Unlike BINARY SEARCH, the original collection *C* does not need to be ordered. Indeed, even if the elements in *C*

---

[*] Alternatively, if the elements themselves are stored directly in *A* (as shown by the "store elements, no lists" option in Figure 5-4), then you need to deal with collisions; otherwise, elements inserted into the hash table may be lost.

were ordered in some way, the hashing method that inserts elements into the hash table A does not attempt to replicate this ordering within A.

The input to HASH-BASED SEARCH is the computed hash table, A, and the target element t being sought. The algorithm returns true if t exists in the linked list stored by $A[h]$ where $h=hash(t)$. If $A[h]$ is empty or t does not exist within the linked list stored by $A[h]$, then false is returned to indicate that t is not present in A (and by implication, it does not exist in C). The pseudocode in Figure 5-3 shows the simplified version where A stores lists containing the elements themselves as key values.

Assumptions

The variable n represents the number of elements in the original collection C and b represents the number of bins in the indexed collection, A.

Context

Suppose we are creating a text editor and want to add a component that will check the spelling of words as the user types. There are several free word lists available that can be downloaded from the Internet (see *http://www.wordlist.com*). Performance is essential for this application. We must be able to search the word list quickly, or the program will be unusable for even the slowest typists. We will probably check word spellings in a separate thread that must keep up with the changes to the document or file.[*]

We must keep the words in memory since disk access will degrade performance too much. A typical English word list contains more than 200,000 words and could be stored in an array that would use about 2.5MB memory (this includes space for the words themselves and a list of pointers to the words, as shown in Figure 5-5). We use pointers because word lengths vary and we want to optimize memory usage.

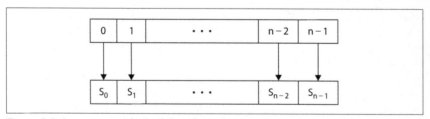

Figure 5-5. Storing strings for hash-based searching

We know from the earlier section "Binary Search" that we can expect about 18 string comparisons[†] on average if we use BINARY SEARCH. String comparisons can be expensive—even when we optimize the code, there is a loop that compares bytes.

---

[*] Hash-based searches require the complete word before the search can begin. With a binary search approach, one may search for the work incrementally as it is being typed, but this introduces additional complexity to the program.

[†] log (200,000) = 17.61

Sometimes we write these loops by hand in an assembly language to ensure that we optimize for the specific architecture, such as making sure that we don't stall the instruction pipeline in the more common cases and unroll the loop to fill the pipeline when possible. One goal, therefore, is to minimize the number of string comparisons.

We first need to define a function to compute the key for a string, s, in the word list. One goal for the key function is to produce as many different values as possible but it is not required for the values to all be unique. A popular technique is to produce a value based on each piece of information from the original string:

$$key(s)=s[0]*31^{(len-1)}+s[1]*31^{(len-2)}+ \ldots +s[len-1]$$

where $s[i]$ is the ith character (as a value between 0 and 255) and len is the length of the string s. Computing this function is simple as shown in the Java code in Example 5-6 (adapted from the Open JDK source code), where chars is the array of characters that defines a string.[*] By our definition, the hashCode() method for the java.lang.String class is the $key()$ function.

Example 5-6. Sample Java hashCode

```java
public int hashCode( ) {
    int h = hash;
    if (h == 0) {
        for (int i = 0; i < chars.length; i++) {
            h = 31*h + chars[i];
        }
        hash = h;
    }
    return h;
}
```

Because this hashCode method tries to be efficient, it caches the value of the computed hash to avoid recomputation (i.e., it computes the value only if hash is 0).

Next, we construct the hash table. We have n strings but what should be the size of the hash table A? In an ideal case, A could be $b=n$ bins where the hash function is a one-to-one function from the set of strings in the word collection onto the integers $[0,n)$. This does not occur in the normal case, so we instead try to have a hash table that has as few empty bins as possible. If our *hash* function distributes the keys evenly, we can achieve reasonable success by selecting an array size approximately as large as the collection. We define $hash(s)=key(s)\%b$, where % is the modulo operator that returns the remainder when dividing $key(s)$ by b.

The advanced reader should, at this point, question the use of a basic hash function and hash table for this problem. Since the word list is static, we can do better by creating a *perfect hash function*. A perfect hash function is one that guarantees no collisions for a specific set of keys. In this case a perfect hash function can be used; this is discussed in the upcming "Variations" section. Let's first try to solve the problem without one.

---

[*] The code can be downloaded from the Open JDK website at *http://openjdk.java.net*.

For our first try at this problem, we choose a primary array A that will hold $b=2^{18}-1=262,143$ elements. Our word list contains 213,557 words. If our hash function perfectly distributes the strings, there will be no collisions and there will be only about 40,000 open slots. This, however, is not the case. Table 5-4 shows the distribution of the hash values* for the Java String class on our word list with a table of 262,143 slots. As you can see, no slot contains more than seven strings; for nonempty slots, the average number of strings per slot is approximately 1.46. Each row shows the number of slots used and how many strings hash to those slots. Almost half of the table slots (116,186) have no strings that hash to them. So, this hashing function wastes about 500KB of memory—assuming that the size of a pointer is four bytes and that we don't fill up the empty entries with our collision-handling strategy. You may be surprised that this is quite a good hashing function and finding one with better distribution will require a more complex scheme. For the record, there were only five pairs of strings with identical key values (for example, both "hypoplankton" and "unheavenly" have a computed key value of 427,589,249)!

Table 5-4. Hash distribution using Java String.hashCode() method as key with b=262,143

Number of hits	Number of slots
0	116,186
1	94,319
2	38,637
3	10,517
4	2,066
5	362
6	53
7	3

Finally, we need to decide on a strategy for handling collisions. One approach is to store a pointer to a list of entries in each slot of the primary hash table, rather than a single object. This approach, shown in Figure 5-6, is called *chaining*.

The overhead with this approach is that you have either a list or the value nil (representing "no list") in each slot. When a slot has only a single search item, it must be accessed using the list capability. For our first approximation of a solution, we start with this approach and refine it if the performance becomes an issue.

Forces

Choosing the hashing function is just the first decision that must be made when implementing HASH-BASED SEARCH. Hashing has been studied for decades, and there are numerous papers that describe effective hash functions, but they are used in much more than searching. For example, special types of hash functions are essential for cryptography. For searching, a hash function should have a good distribution and should be quick to compute with respect to machine cycles.

---

* In this chapter, the hashCode method associated with each Java class represents the *key* function described earlier. Recall that $hash(s)=key(s)\%b$.

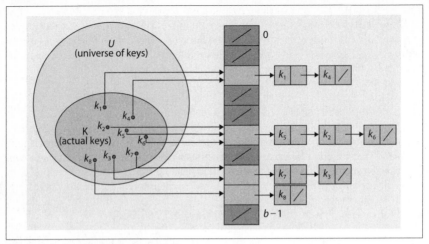

Figure 5-6. Handling collisions with lists

Storage space poses another design issue for HASH-BASED SEARCH. The primary storage, A, must be large enough to hold all of the search keys with enough space left over for storing the collision keys. The size of A is typically chosen to be a prime number. However, we can use any number when we are not using open addressing (see the upcoming "Variations" section). A good choice in practice is 2^k-1, even though this value isn't always prime. The elements stored in the hash table have a direct effect on memory. Consider how Figure 5-3 stores each string element in a linked list, so the elements of the array that serves as A are linked list objects. These are pointers to objects on the heap. Each list has overhead storage that contains pointers to the first and last elements of the list and, if you use the LinkedList class from the Java JDK, a significant amount of additional fields and classes that make the implementation quite flexible. One could write a much simpler linked list class that provides only the necessary capabilities, but this certainly adds additional cost to the implementation of the hash-based searching algorithm.

If you use the LinkedList class, each non-empty element of A will require 12 bytes of memory, assuming that the size of a pointer is four bytes. Each string element is incorporated into a ListElement that requires an additional 12 bytes. For the previous example of 213,557 words, we require 5,005,488 bytes of memory beyond the actual string storage. The breakdown of this is:

- Size of the primary table: 1,048,572 bytes
- Size of 116,186 linked lists: 1,394,232 bytes
- Size of 213,557 list elements: 2,562,684 bytes

Storing the strings also has an overhead if you use the JDK String class. Each string has 12 bytes of overhead. We can therefore add 213,557*12 = 2,562,684 additional bytes to our overhead. So, the algorithm chosen in the example requires 7,568,172 bytes of memory to support it. The actual number of characters in the strings in the word list we used in the example is only 2,099,075.

Our algorithm then requires approximately 4.6 times the space required for the characters in the strings. One might argue that this is the price of using the classes in the JDK. The engineering tradeoff must weigh the simplicity and reuse of the classes compared to a more complex implementation that reduces the memory.

When memory is at a premium, you can use one of several variations discussed later to optimize the memory usage. If, however, you have available memory, a reasonable hash function that does not produce too many collisions, and a ready-to-use linked list implementation, the JDK solution is usually acceptable.

As long as the hash function distributes the elements in the collection fairly evenly, hash-based searching has excellent performance. The average time required to search for an element is constant, or $O(1)$.

There are other forces that affect the implementation. The major ones deal with the static or dynamic nature of the collection. In our example, we know how big our word list is, and we are not going to add or remove words from the list—at least not during a single program execution. If, however, we have a dynamic collection that requires many additions and deletions of elements, we must choose a data structure for the hash table that optimizes these operations. Our collision handling in the example works quite well since inserting into a linked list can be done in constant time and deleting an item is proportional to the length of the list. If the hash function distributes the elements well, the individual lists are relatively short.

Solution

There are two parts to the solution for HASH-BASED SEARCH. The first is to create the hash table. The code in Example 5-7 shows how to use linked lists to hold the elements that hash into a specific table element. The input elements from collection *C* are retrieved using an Iterator.

Example 5-7. Loading the hash table

```
public void load (Iterator<V> it) {
  listTable = (LinkedList<V>[]) new LinkedList[tableSize];

  // Pull each value from the iterator and find desired bin h.
  // Add to existing list or create new one into which value is added.
  while (it.hasNext()) {
    V v = it.next();

    int h = hashMethod.hash(v);
    if (listTable[h] == null) {
      listTable[h] = new LinkedList<V>();
    }

    // Add element into linked list for bin 'h'
    LinkedList<V> list = (LinkedList<V>) listTable[h];
    list.add(v);
  }
}
```

Note how the table is composed of tableSize bins, each of which is of type LinkedList<V>.* Also note how the table stores the actual objects from the collection C in the chained link lists of the hash table rather than just the key values.

Searching the table for elements now becomes trivial. The code in Example 5-8 does the job. Once the hash function returns an index into the hash table, we look to see whether the table bin is empty. If it's empty, we return false, indicating that the searched-for string is not in the collection. Otherwise, we search the linked list at that bin to determine the presence or absence of the searched-for string.

Example 5-8. Searching for an element

```
public boolean search (V v){
  int h = hashMethod.hash(v);
  LinkedList<V> list = (LinkedList<V>) listTable[h];
  if (list == null) { return false; }

  return list.contains(v);
}

// The following is the implementation of the hash method above.
int hash(V v){
  int h = v.hashCode( );
  if (h < 0) { h = 0 - h; }
  return h % tableSize;
}
```

Note that the hash function ensures that the hash index is in the range [0,*table-Size*). With the hashCode function for the String class, the hash function must cover the case when the integer arithmetic in hashCode overflows and returns a negative number. This is necessary because the modulo operator (%) returns a negative number if given a negative value.† For example, using the JDK hashCode method for String objects, the string "aaaaaa" returns the value −1,425,372,064.

Consequences

Perhaps more than any other search method, HASH-BASED SEARCH exhibits the consequences of the design decisions we make when selecting the data structure to store the elements in the collection. It is imperative to understand the dynamic properties of the input and choose the structure accordingly.

Analysis

HASH-BASED SEARCH has excellent performance characteristics. We analyze it in parts. The components to searching for an element in a hash table are:

- Computing the hash value
- Accessing the item in the table indexed by the hash value
- Finding the specified item in the presence of collisions

---

* <V> is the typed parameter for the HashTable to allow it to store any type of element.

† In Java, the expression −5%3 is equal to the value −2.

All HASH-BASED SEARCH algorithms share the first two components; different behaviors come about when variations to collision handling are employed.

The cost of computing the hash value must be bounded by a fixed, constant upper bound. If you consider the example in this section, computing the hash value was proportional to the length of the string. For any finite collection of words, there is a longest string with length k. If t_k is the time it takes to compute the hash value for the longest string, then it will require $\leq t_k$ to compute any hash value. Computing the hash value is therefore considered to be a constant time operation.

The second part of the algorithm also performs in constant time. If the table is stored on secondary storage, there may be a variation that depends upon the position of the element and the time required to position the device, but this has a constant upper bound.

If we can show that the third part of the computation also has a constant upper bound, then we can easily prove that the time performance of hash-based searching is constant. When we use chaining, we use the *load factor*, $\alpha=n/b$, where b is the number of bins in the hash table and n is the number of elements stored in the hash table. The load factor computes the average number of elements in a list in the chain.

The worst-case performance for finding an element by chaining is $O(n)$, which occurs when all elements hash to the same bin in the table. The average number of bins to search is α. For a detailed analysis, see Chapter 11 of (Cormen et al., 2001).

Table 5-5 compares the performance of the code from Example 5-8 with the existing JDK class java.util.Hashtable on hash tables of different sizes. For the tests labeled $p=1.0$, each of the 213,557 words is used as the target item to ensure that the word exists in the hash table. For the tests labeled $p=0.0$, each of these words has its last character replaced with a * to ensure that the word does not exist in the hash table. Note also that we keep the size of the search words for these two cases the same to ensure that the cost for computing the hash is identical. We ran each test 100 times and discarded the best- and worst-performing trials. The average of the remaining 98 trials is shown in Table 5-5. To understand these results we produce statistics on the hash tables we create, shown in Table 5-6. As the load factor goes down, the average length of each element linked list also goes down, leading to improved performance.

As the size of the hash table A approximately doubles, the time to find an item decreases, because the linked lists of elements are shorter. Indeed, by the time $b=1,045,875$ no linked list contains more than five elements. Because a hash table can typically grow large enough to ensure that all linked lists of elements are small, its search performance is considered to be $O(1)$. However, this is contingent (as always) on having sufficient memory and a suitable hash function to disperse the elements throughout the bins of the hash table. About 81% of the 213,557 words are mapped to unique hash table bins when $b=1,045,875$ using the hash function from Example 5-6.

Table 5-5. Search time (in milliseconds) for various hash table sizes

b	Our hashtable shown in Example 5-8		java.util.Hashtable with default capacity	
	p = 1.0	p = 0.0	p = 1.0	p = 0.0
4,095	1143.33	2039.10	104.42	47.85
8,191	673.91	1095.67	99.48	45.26
16,383	433.87	615.63	111.74	48.60
32,767	308.03	364.88	107.11	47.33
65,535	237.07	245.86	98.53	45.14
131,071	194.37	172.81	98.53	44.47
262,143	164.85	118.93	96.62	44.32
524,287	144.97	79.87	94.24	44.97
1,048,575	136.97	62.42	96.77	43.22

Table 5-6 shows the actual load factor in the hash tables we create as b increases. Note how the maximum length of the element linked lists drops consistently while the number of bins containing a unique element rapidly increases once b is sufficiently large. You can see that the performance of hash tables becomes O(1) when the size of the hash table is sufficiently large.

Table 5-6. Statistics of hash tables created by example code

b	Load factor α	Min length of linked list	Max length of linked list	Number Unique
4,095	54.04	27	82	0
8,191	27.5	9	46	0
16,383	15	2	28	0
32,767	9.5	0	19	349
65,535	6.5	0	13	8,190
131,071	5	0	10	41,858
262,143	3.5	0	7	94,319
524,287	3.5	0	7	142,530
1,048,575	2.5	0	5	173,912

The performance of the existing java.util.Hashtable class outperforms our example code, but the savings are reduced as the size of the hash table grows. The reason is that java.util.Hashtable has optimized list classes that efficiently manage the element chains. In addition, java.util.Hashtable automatically "rehashes" the entire hash table when the load factor is too high; the rehash strategy is discussed in the "Variations" section, next. It increases the cost of building the hash table but improves the performance of searching. If we prevent the "rehash" capability, then the performance of search in java.util.Hashtable is nearly consistent with our implementation. Table 5-7 shows the number of times rehash is invoked when building the java.util.Hashtable hash table and the total time (in milliseconds) required to build the hash table. We constructed the hash tables from the word list described earlier; after running 100 trials the best and worst performing timings were discarded and the table contains the average of the remaining 98 trials. The designers of this class perform extra computation while the hash table is being constructed to improve the performance of searches (a common tradeoff to make). In columns 3 and 5 of Table 5-7, there is a noticeable cost penalty when a rehash occurs. Also note that in the last two rows the hash tables do not rehash themselves, so the results in columns 3, 5, and 7 are nearly identical. Rehashing while building the hash table improves the overall performance by reducing the average length of the element chains.

Table 5-7. Comparable times (in milliseconds) to build hash tables

b	Our hash table	JDK hash table (α=.75f)		JDK hash table (α=4.0f)		JDK hash table (α=n/b) no rehash
	Build Time	Build Time	#Rehash	Build Time	#Rehash	Build Time
4,095	1116.08	165.77	7	166.81	4	644.31
8,191	647.32	162.96	6	165.48	3	364.56
16,383	421.57	164.20	5	162.85	2	230.42
32,767	332.82	164.36	4	149.29	1	164.08
65,535	273.77	155.62	3	131.19	0	131.05
13,1071	256.39	147.17	2	118.47	0	116.07
262,143	280.06	127.57	1	90.20	0	91.09
524,287	264.87	89.93	0	89.77	0	89.61
1,048,575	257.83	92.09	0	93.55	0	92.65

Searching

Variations

One main variation of HASH-BASED SEARCH is to modify the way collisions are handled. Instead of placing into a linked list all elements that hash to a slot in the hash table, we can use the technique known as *open addressing*, which stores the colliding items directly in the hash table A. This approach is shown in Figure 5-7. With open addressing the hash table reduces storage overhead, such as pointers to the next element in a list for collisions. To use open addressing, we change the hash function to take two arguments, $h(u,j)=i$, where $u \in U$ and i and j are integers in the range $[0,b)$, in which b is the size of A. In general we let $h(u,0)=i=h'(u)$ where h' is a hash function, such as previously described. If the slot at $A[i]$ is occupied and the item does not match the sought-for item, we calculate the value of $h(u,1)$. If that slot is occupied and does not match the sought-for item, we consider slot $h(u,2)$ and repeat until the item is found, the slot is empty, or the hash function produces an index whose slot we have already visited (which indicates a failure).

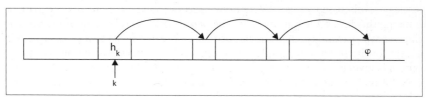

Figure 5-7. Open addressing

Assuming we ensure that we don't revisit a slot, the worst-case performance of this approach is $O(b)$. Open addressing performs well for searching. The expected number of probes in an unsuccessful search is $1/(1-\alpha)$, and the worst-case performance for a successful search is $(1/\alpha)\ln(1/1-\alpha)$;[*] see (Cormen et al., 2001) for details. One finds two common types of *probing* with open addressing. The first is *linear probing*, where our hash function is $h(u,j) = (h'(u)+j) \bmod n$. When we have a collision, we simply look at the next slot in the hash table, using it as a circular structure. This approach is susceptible to clusters of elements forming that lead to long sequences of slots that must be searched—especially if α is close to 1.0. To mitigate this clustering we might use *quadratic probing*, in which our hash function is of the form $h(u,j)=(h'(u)+f(j)) \bmod m$, where f is a quadratic function on j.

In Table 5-5 we saw that there is tremendous savings by enforcing that the hash table does not rehash its contents. A rehash operation is made possible if the hash table can be constructed with a target load factor before any elements are added to it. When the hash table contains more elements than it was designed for, it can resize itself. The typical way to do this is to double the number of bins and add one (since hash tables usually contain an odd number of bins). Once more bins are available, all existing elements in the hash table must be rehashed to be properly placed in the new structure. This is an expensive operation that should reduce the overall cost of future searches, but it must be run infrequently; otherwise, the performance of the hash table will degrade. You should allow a hash table to rehash its contents when you are unsatisfied with the ability of the hash function to assign elements evenly within the hash table. The default target load factor for the java.util.Hashtable class is .75; if you set this value to n/b, then the hash table will never call rehash.

The example shown previously in the "Context" section used a fixed set of strings for the hash table. When confronted with this special case, we can achieve truly optimal performance by using *perfect hashing*. Perfect hashing uses two hash functions. We use a standard hash function to index into the primary table, A. Each slot, $A[i]$, points to a smaller secondary hash table, S_i, that has an associated hash function h_i. If there are k keys that hash to slot $A[i]$, then the S_i will contain k^2 slots. This seems like a lot of wasted memory, but judicious choice of the initial hash function can reduce this to an amount similar to previous variations. The selection of appropriate hash functions guarantees that there are no collisions in the secondary tables. This means we have an algorithm with constant performance—$O(1)$. Details on the analysis of perfect hashing can be found in (Cormen et al., 2001). Doug Schmidt (1990) has written an excellent paper on perfect hashing generation and there are freely available downloads of perfect hash function generators in various programming languages.

In general, although there may be many potential elements e_i associated with a specific key value k, the hash table A might be designed to store just a single one of these. That is, if $e_i \in C$ and $e_j \in C$, then $i=j$ if and only if $key(e_i)=key(e_j)$. The reason for this restriction is to enable lookup for a single element e when

[*] The *ln* function computes the natural logarithm of a number in base e.

given just its key value, $key(e)$. If the original collection C contained two identical elements, then only one of them would be properly stored by the hash table A.*

Binary Tree Search

Binary searching on an array in memory is efficient, as we have already seen. However, the effectiveness of searching on arrays is reduced greatly when the underlying data in the search set changes frequently. With a dynamic search set, one must adopt a different data structure in order to maintain acceptable search performance.

Search trees are the most common data structure used to store dynamic search sets. Search trees perform well in memory and when stored on secondary storage. The most common type of search tree is the *binary search tree*, where each interior node in the tree has at most two child nodes. Another type of search tree, called a *B-Tree*, is an *n*-ary tree designed to be easily stored on disk.

Input/Output

The input and output to algorithms using search trees is the same as for BINARY SEARCH. Each element e from a collection C to be stored in the search tree needs to have one or more properties that can be used as a key k; these keys determine the universe U. The elements must also have properties that distinguish them from other elements in the set. The search tree will store the elements from C.

Context

Memory leaks are serious problems for programmers. When a program will run for an extended period, such as many of the server applications used in today's systems, memory leaks will eventually cause the program to exceed the amount of memory allocated to its process and then crash, often with disastrous consequences.

One might write a program to monitor memory allocations and deallocations and report on a program's memory profile in order to detect the presence of memory leaks. Such a memory profiler can be written quite simply by writing new malloc() and free() functions that record the appropriate information before allocating and freeing memory. We want to record every memory allocation and when that memory is freed, we must remove it from the set of active allocations.

In the context described, we have no *a priori* knowledge of how many elements we need to store. A hash-based search would work, but we may select a hash table size that is much too small for effective resource usage. An alternate search strategy is to use a search tree. When we plan on maintaining our search data set in memory, we typically use a *binary search tree*. Binary search trees perform well with dynamic data where insertions and deletions are frequent.

---

* GPERF for C and C++ can be downloaded from *http://www.gnu.org/software/gperf/*, and JPERF for Java can be downloaded from *http://www.anarres.org/projects/jperf/*.

A binary search tree, T, is a finite set of nodes that are identified by an ordered property, or key. The set of nodes may be empty, or it might contain a root node n_r. Each node n refers to two binary search trees, T_l, and T_r, and obeys the property that if k is the key for node n, then all keys in T_l are $\leq k$ and all the keys in T_r are $\geq k$. This property is called the *binary-search-tree property* (Cormen et al., 2001). Figure 5-8 shows a small example of a binary tree. Each node has an integer key that identifies the node. You can see that finding a key in the tree in Figure 5-8 requires examining at most three nodes, starting with the root node. The tree is perfectly balanced. That is, each node that has any children has exactly two children. A perfectly balanced binary tree has 2^n-1 nodes for some $n \geq 1$ and a height of $n-1$.

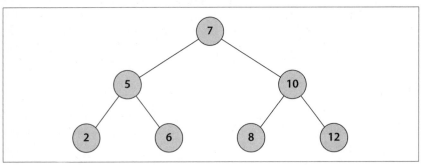

Figure 5-8. A simple binary search tree

Trees may not always be balanced. In the worst case, a tree may be degenerate and have the basic properties of a list. Consider the same nodes for Figure 5-8 arranged in the way shown in Figure 5-9. Here the nodes were added in ascending order and—although the structure fits the strict definition of a binary tree, with the left subtree of each node being an empty tree—the structure is effectively a list.

Forces

If we simply need to locate a search item, the first choice should be a hash-based solution. Some factors that might alter our decision to use a binary search tree are:

- The data set size is unknown, and the implementation must be able to handle any possible size that will fit in memory.
- The data set is highly dynamic, and there will be many insertions and deletions during the data structure's lifetime.
- The application requires traversing the data in ascending or descending order.

Once we decide to use a search tree, we must make the following decisions about the tree's details:

- If we need to be able to traverse the data set in order starting at any specific node, the appropriate pointers to parent nodes must be included in the node structure.
- If the data is dynamic, we must balance the tree.

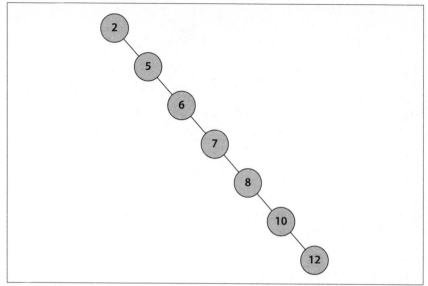

Figure 5-9. A degenerate binary search tree

In most applications we need to balance the tree to avoid a *skewed tree*, where there are a few branches that are much longer or shorter than the other branches—or in the worst case a degenerate tree, as in Figure 5-9. Two popular types of balanced trees can be used for binary search. One is the AVL tree, proposed by Adel'son-Vel'skii and Landis in 1962. An AVL tree obeys the following *balancing* property: no node has subtrees that differ in height by more than 1.

A more recent type of balanced binary tree is called a *red-black tree*. Red-black trees are approximately balanced. Using a red-black tree guarantees that no branch has a height more than two times that of any other. A red-black tree satisfies the following conditions (Cormen et al., 2001):

- Every node is labeled either red or black.
- The root is black.
- Every leaf node contains a null value and is black.
- All red nodes have two black children.
- Every simple path from a node to one of its descendant leaf nodes contains the same number of black nodes.

In the diagrams that follow, we have not shown the null value leaf nodes in the interest of space. When you look at the diagrams, you should imagine that each leaf node in the diagram actually has two black children, and that these have null values.

Figure 5-10 shows a valid red-black tree containing seven different integers inserted in the following order: 13, 26, 43, 17, 25, 15, and 16.

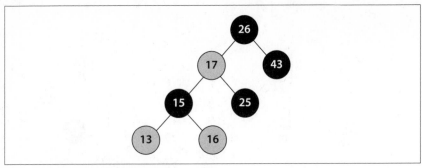

Figure 5-10. Sample red-black tree

Now we want to add a node with a key of 14. Using the standard semantics of binary trees, 14 will be inserted as the right child of the node with value 13. The red-black tree insertion algorithm modifies the tree as shown in Figure 5-11; we describe this process in the "Solution" section, next.

Solution

Searching a red-black tree is no different than searching any binary tree. The code to search for a value stored in a red-black tree is shown in Example 5-9. Starting at the root, we inspect each node for the given key value, traversing to the left child if the key is smaller than the node's key, and traversing to the right child if the key is larger than the node's key.

Example 5-9. Java implementation of search

```java
public V search(K k) {
    BalancedBinaryNode<K,V> p = root;
    while (p != null) {
        int cmp = compare(k, p.key);
        if (cmp == 0) {
            return p.value;
        } else if (cmp < 0) {
            p = p.left;
        } else {
            p = p.right;
        }
    }

    // not found
    return null;
}
```

The key to the red-black tree algorithm is maintaining the red-black conditions when values are inserted and deleted. We describe the insertion process here; the deletion procedure is sufficiently complex that we leave the details for the implementation, which you can find in the `algs.model.tree.BalancedTree` class. Further details can be found in (Cormen et al. 2001).

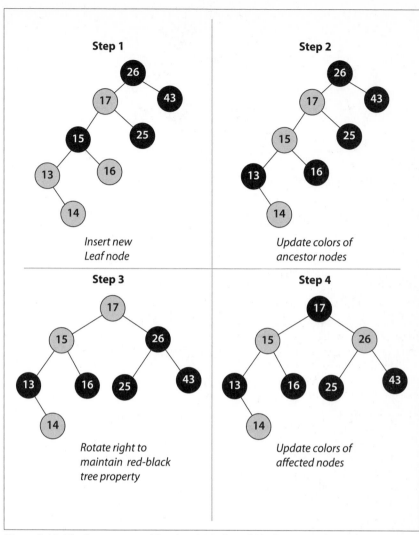

Figure 5-11. The four steps in adding key 14 to the red-black tree

To insert a node into a red-black tree, we need to find the appropriate place in the tree where the new node will be placed. When we add the value of 14 to the tree shown in Figure 5-10, a new node containing 14 will become the right-child of the leaf node containing the value 13 (labeled "Step 1" in Figure 5-11). Once inserted, the properties of the red-black tree are violated so the tree must adjust itself. In Step 2 the colors of the nodes are updated to ensure condition 4 of red-black trees. In Step 3 the tree is rotated to the right to ensure condition 5 of red-black trees. Finally, in Step 4 the colors of the nodes are updated to ensure condition 4 of red-black trees.

The fundamental operation when restructuring the tree is a rotation about a node. We modify the pointers in the tree to effect the rotation. Figure 5-12 shows the results of rotating left or right about a node. The tree on the left can be rotated left about node *a* to get the tree on the right. Similarly, you can perform a right rotation about node *b* to the tree on the right to get the tree on the left.

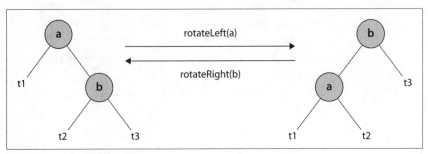

Figure 5-12. Red-black node rotations

You can see that in order to perform rotations, the node structure in red-black trees requires parent pointers. Code to perform a left rotation is shown in Example 5-10; the implementation for right rotation is similar. You can find in (Cormen et al. 2001) the details on why the rotateLeft and rotateRight implementations work.

Example 5-10. Java implementation of rotating a node left

```java
protected void rotateLeft(BalancedBinaryNode<K,V> p) {
    BalancedBinaryNode<K,V> r = p.right;
    p.right = r.left;
    if (r.left != null)
        r.left.parent = p;
    r.parent = p.parent;
    if (p.parent == null)
        root = r;
    else if (p.parent.left == p)
        p.parent.left = r;
    else
        p.parent.right = r;
    r.left = p;
    p.parent = r;
}
```

Notice that the rotations maintain the binary search tree property because the ordering of nodes is unchanged. Once the new value is inserted into the red-black tree, the tree updates itself to restore conditions 4 and 5 of red-black trees.

Consequences

Red-black trees—as well as other balanced binary trees—require more code to implement than simple binary search trees. The tradeoff is usually worth it in terms of runtime performance gains. Red-black trees have two storage requirements as far as the data structures used for nodes:

- Each node requires space to store the node's color. This is a minimum of one bit, but in practice, most implementations use at least a byte.

- Every node must have a parent link, which is not a requirement for a binary search tree.

Red-black trees also require a node with a null value at the root. One can implement this using a single null-valued node and make all leaf pointers point to it.

Analysis

The average-case performance of search in a red-black tree is the same as a BINARY SEARCH, that is O(log n). However, now insertions and deletions can be performed in O(log n) time as well.

Variations

There are other balanced tree structures. The most common one is the AVL tree, mentioned previously. Red-black trees and other balanced binary trees are fine choices for in-memory searching. When the data set becomes too large to be kept in memory, another type of tree is typically used: the n-way tree, where each node has $n>2$ children. A common version of such trees is called the *B-tree*, which performs very well in minimizing the number of disk accesses to find a particular item in large data sets. B-trees are commonly used when implementing relational databases.

References

Adel'son-Vel'skii, G. M., and E. M. Landis, "An algorithm for the organization of information," *Soviet Mathematics Doklady*, 3:1259–1263, 1962.

Cormen, Thomas H., Charles E. Leiserson, Ronald L. Rivest, and Clifford Stein, *Introduction to Algorithms*, Second Edition. McGraw-Hill, 2001.

Hester, J.H. and D.S. Hirschberg, "Self-Organizing Linear Search," *ACM Computing Surveys*, 17 (3): 295–312, 1985.

Knuth, Donald, *The Art of Computer Programming, Volume 3: Sorting and Searching*, Third Edition. Addison-Wesley, 1997.

Schmidt, Douglas C., "GPERF: A Perfect Hash Function Generator," Proceedings of the Second C++ Conference": 87–102, 1990. Available at *http://citeseerx.ist. psu/viewdoc/summary?doi=10.1.1.44.8511*, accessed May 10, 2008.

Searching

6

Graph Algorithms

Overview

Graphs are fundamental structures used in computer science to represent complex structured information. The images in Figure 6-1 are all sample graphs.

In this chapter we investigate common ways to represent graphs and some associated algorithms that occur frequently. Inherently, a graph contains a set of elements, known as *vertices*, and relationships between pairs of these elements, known as *edges*. In this chapter we consider only simple graphs that avoid (a) self-edges from a vertex to itself, and (b) multiple edges between the same pair of vertices.

Graphs

A graph G = (V,E) is defined by a set of vertices, V, and a set of edges, E, over pairs of these vertices. There are distinct types of graphs that occur commonly in algorithms:

Undirected graphs
Model relationships between vertices (u,v) without caring about the direction of the relationship. These graphs are useful for capturing symmetric information. For example, a road from town A to town B can be traversed in either direction.

Directed graphs
Model relationships between vertices (u,v) that are distinct from, say, the relationship between (v,u), which may or may not exist. For example, a program to provide driving directions must store information on one-way streets to avoid giving illegal directions.

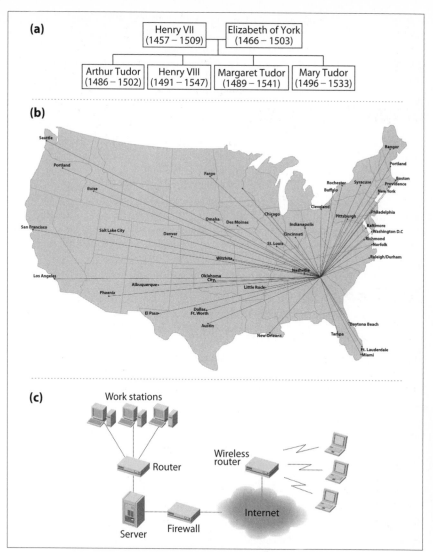

Figure 6-1. (a) House of Tudor, (b) computer network, (c) airline schedule

Weighted graphs

Model relationships where there is a numeric value known as a *weight* associated with the relationship between vertices (*u,v*). Sometimes these values can store arbitrary non-numeric information. For example, the edge between towns A and B could store the mileage between the towns; alternatively, it could store estimated traveling time in minutes.

Hypergraphs

Model multiple relationships that may exist between the same two vertices (*u,v*); in this chapter, however, we will limit our discussion to simple graphs.

If a path exists between any two pairs of vertices in a graph, then that graph is *connected*. A directed, weighted graph defines a nonempty set of vertices $\{v_0, ...,$ $v_{n-1}\}$, a set of directed edges between pairs of distinct vertices (such that every pair has at most one edge between them in each direction), and a positive weight associated with each edge. In many applications, the weight is considered to be a distance or cost. For some applications, we may want to relax the restriction that the weight must be positive (for example, a negative weight could reflect a profit), but we will be careful to declare when this happens.

Consider the directed, weighted graph in Figure 6-2, which is composed of six vertices and four edges. There are two standard data structures to store such a graph; both data structures explicitly store the weights and implicitly store the directed edges. One could store the graph as n adjacency lists, as shown in Figure 6-3, where each vertex v_i maintains a linked list of nodes, each of which stores the weight of the edge leading to an adjacent vertex of v_i. Thus the base structure is a one-dimensional array of vertices in the graph. Adding an edge requires additional processing to ensure that no duplicate edges are added.

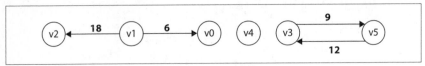

Figure 6-2. Sample directed, weighted graph

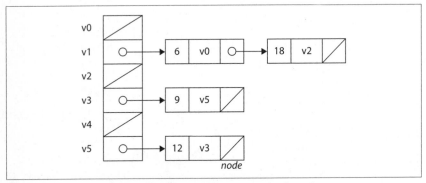

Figure 6-3. Adjacency list representation of directed, weighted graph

Figure 6-4 shows how to store the directed, weighted graph as an n-by-n adjacency matrix A of integers, indexed in both dimensions by the vertices. The entry $A[i][j]$ stores the weight of the edge from v_i to v_j; when $A[i][j] = 0$, there is no edge from v_i to v_j. With the adjacency matrix representation, adding an edge takes constant time.

We can use adjacency lists and matrices to store undirected graphs as well. Consider the undirected graph in Figure 6-5. We use the notation $<v_0, v_1, ..., v_{k-1}>$ to describe a path of k vertices in a graph that traverses $k-1$ edges (v_i, v_{i+1}) for $0 \le i < k-1$; paths in a directed graph honor the direction of the edge. In Figure 6-5, the path $<v_3, v_1, v_5, v_4>$ is valid. In this graph there is a *cycle*, which is a path of vertices that includes the same vertex multiple times. A cycle is typically represented in its most minimal form.

	v0	v1	v2	v3	v4	v5
v0	0	0	0	0	0	0
v1	6	0	18	0	0	0
v2	0	0	0	0	0	0
v3	0	0	0	0	0	⑨—A[3][5]
v4	0	0	0	0	0	0
v5	0	0	0	12	0	0

Figure 6-4. Adjacency matrix representation of directed, weighted graph

In Figure 6-5, a cycle exists in the path $<v_3, v_1, v_5, v_4, v_2, v_1, v_5, v_4, v_2>$, and this cycle is best represented by the notation $<v_1, v_5, v_4, v_2, v_1>$. Note that in the directed, weighted graph in Figure 6-2, there is a cycle $< v_3, v_5, v_3>$.

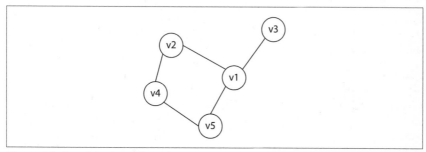

Figure 6-5. Sample undirected graph

When using an adjacency list to store an undirected graph, the same edge (u,v) appears twice—once in the linked list of neighbor vertices for u and once for v. Thus the storage of undirected graphs in an adjacency list is twice as much as for a directed graph with the same number of vertices and edges. When using an adjacency matrix to store an undirected graph, you must ensure that the entry $A[i][j]=A[j][i]$; no additional storage is necessary.

Storage Issues

There are several observations to make when using a two-dimensional matrix to represent potential relationships among n elements in a set. First, the matrix requires n^2 elements of storage, yet there are times when the number of relationships is much smaller. In these cases—known as *sparse* graphs—it may be impossible to store large graphs with more than several thousand vertices because of the limitations of computer memory. For example, using the standard Java virtual machine heap size of 256MB, creating a two-dimensional matrix new int[4096][4096] exceeds the available memory. Although one can execute programs on computers with more available memory, it is a fact that there is a fixed upper size beyond which no matrix can be constructed. Additionally, traversing through large matrices to locate the few edges in sparse graphs becomes costly, and this storage representation prevents efficient algorithms from achieving their true potential. Second, matrices are unsuitable when there may be multiple relationships between a pair of elements. To store these relationships in a matrix, each element would become a list, and the abstraction of $A[i][j]$ being the ijth element breaks.

Each of these adjacency representations contains the same information. Suppose, however, you were writing a program to compute the cheapest flights between any pair of cities in the world that are served by commercial flights. The weight of an edge would correspond to the cost of the cheapest direct flight between that pair of cities (assuming that airlines do not provide incentives by bundling flights). In 2005, Airports Council International (ACI) reported a total of 1,659 airports worldwide, resulting in a two-dimensional matrix with 2,752,281 entries. The question "how many of these entries has a value?" is dependent upon the number of direct flights. ACI reported 71.6 million "aircraft movements" in 2005, roughly translating to a daily average of 196,164 flights. Even if all of these flights represented an actual direct flight between two unique airports (clearly the number of direct flights will be much smaller), this means that the matrix is 93% empty—a good example of a sparse matrix!

When representing an undirected graph using adjacency lists, there are opportunities to reduce the storage space. To demonstrate, assume a vertex u has edges to the following adjacent vertices: 2, 8, 1, 5, 3, 10, 11, and 4. First, the adjacent vertices could be stored in increasing order to enable rapid failure when checking whether an edge (u,v) exists. Under this scheme, checking whether edge $(u,6)$ exists would require only six comparisons, although eight adjacent vertices exist. Of course, adding an edge no longer takes constant time, however, so there is a tradeoff decision to be made. Second, to improve the performance of the check to see whether edge (u,v) exists, the adjacency list could store the ranges of the adjacent vertices; this example requires eight nodes in the adjacency list, which could be reduced to three: 1–5, 8, and 10–11. This scheme also reduces the check to determine whether an edge exists, while slowing down the performance when adding or removing an edge.

Graph Analysis

When applying the algorithms in this chapter, the essential factor that determines whether to use an adjacency list or adjacency matrix is whether the graph is sparse. We compute the performance of each algorithm in terms of the number of vertices in the graph, $|V|$, and the number of edges in the graph, $|E|$. As is common in the literature on algorithms, we simplify the presentation of the formulas that represent best, average, and worst case by using V and E within the big-O notation. Thus $O(V)$ means a computation requires a number of steps that is directly proportional to the number of vertices in the graph. However, the density of the edges in the graph will also be relevant. Thus $O(E)$ for a sparse graph is on the order of $O(V)$, whereas for a dense graph it is closer to $O(V^2)$.

As we will see, some algorithms have two different variations whose performance changes based upon the structure of the graph; one variation might execute in $O((V+E)^*\log V)$ time, while another executes in $O(V^2+E)$ time. Which one is more efficient? Table 6-1 shows that the answer depends on whether the graph G is sparse or dense. For sparse graphs, $O((V+E)^*\log V)$ is more efficient, whereas for dense graphs $O(V^2+E)$ is more efficient. The table entry labeled "Break-even graph" identifies the type of graphs for which the expected performance is the same $O(V^2)$ for both sparse and dense graphs; in these graphs, the number of edges is on the order of $O(V^2/\log V)$.

Table 6-1. Performance comparison of two algorithm variations

Graph type	$O((V+E)*\log V)$	Comparison	$O(V^2+E)$
Sparse graph: E is $O(V)$	$O(V \log V)$	is smaller than	$O(V^2)$
Break-even graph: E is $O(V^2/\log V)$	$O(V^2+V*\log V) = O(V^2)$	is equivalent to	$O(V^2+V^2/\log V) = O(V^2)$
Dense graph: E is $O(V^2)$	$O(V^2 \log V)$	is larger than	$O(V^2)$

Data Structure Design

The UML diagram in Figure 6-6 represents the core functionality we expect for graphs in this chapter; see Chapter 3 for details on UML diagrams. The C++ Graph class stores a (directed or undirected) graph using an adjacency list representation implemented with core classes from the C++ Standard Template Library (STL). Specifically, it stores the information as an array of lists, one list for each vertex. For each vertex u there is a list of IntegerPair objects representing the edge (u,v) of weight w.

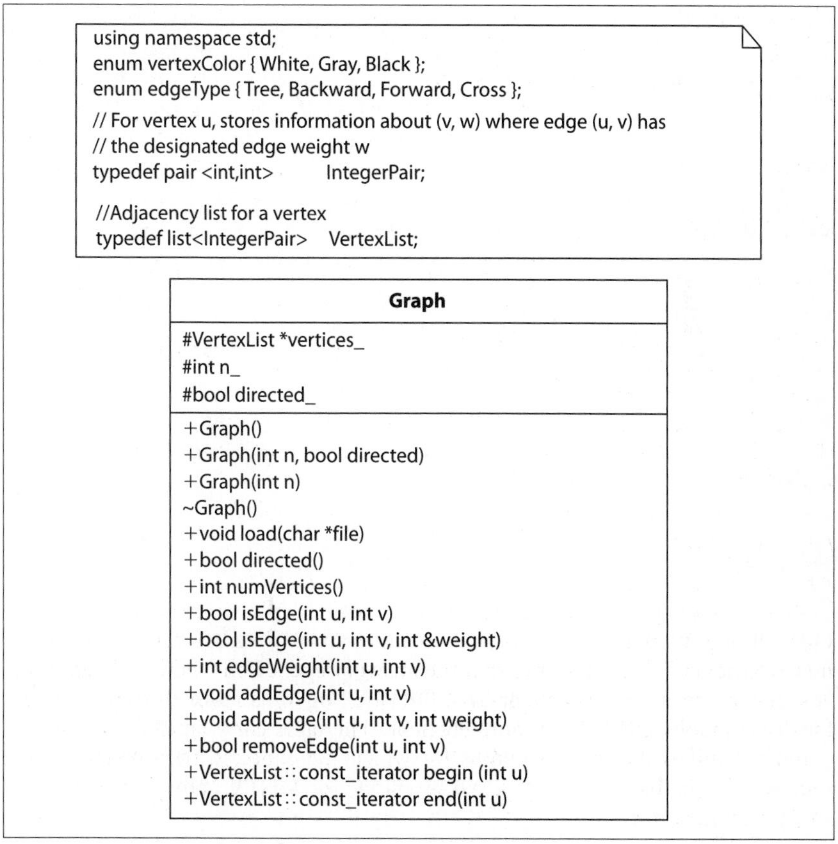

```
using namespace std;
enum vertexColor { White, Gray, Black };
enum edgeType { Tree, Backward, Forward, Cross };

// For vertex u, stores information about (v, w) where edge (u, v) has
// the designated edge weight w
typedef pair <int,int>     IntegerPair;

//Adjacency list for a vertex
typedef list<IntegerPair>   VertexList;
```

Graph
#VertexList *vertices_   #int n_   #bool directed_
+Graph()   +Graph(int n, bool directed)   +Graph(int n)   ~Graph()   +void load(char *file)   +bool directed()   +int numVertices()   +bool isEdge(int u, int v)   +bool isEdge(int u, int v, int &weight)   +int edgeWeight(int u, int v)   +void addEdge(int u, int v)   +void addEdge(int u, int v, int weight)   +bool removeEdge(int u, int v)   +VertexList::const_iterator begin (int u)   +VertexList::const_iterator end(int u)

Figure 6-6. Core graph operations

The operations from Figure 6-6 are subdivided into several categories:

Create
> A graph can be initially constructed from a set of *n* vertices, and it may be directed or undirected. load(char *) updates the graph using the vertex and edge information stored in a data file. When a graph is undirected, adding edge (*u,v*) also adds edge (*v,u*).

Query
> One can determine whether a graph is directed, find all outgoing edges for a given vertex, determine whether an edge exists, and determine the weight associated with an edge. One can construct an iterator that returns the neighboring edges (and their weights) for any vertex in the graph.

Update
> One can add edges to, or remove edges from, the graph.

Problems

There are many problems that can be solved using graph structures. In this chapter we will cover some of the more relevant ones, and you will have opportunities to find many of your own to investigate.

Given the structure defined by the edges in a graph, many problems can be defined in terms of the shortest path that exists between two vertices in the graph, where the length of a path is the sum of the lengths of the edges of that path. In the "single source shortest path" problem (see Example 6-6), one is given a specific vertex, *s*, and asked to compute the shortest path to all other vertices in the graph. The "all pairs shortest path" problem (Example 6-7) requires that the shortest path be computed for all pairs (*u,v*) of vertices in the graph. Some problems seek a deeper understanding of the underlying graph structure. The minimum spanning tree (MST) of an undirected, weighted graph is a subset of that graph's edges such that (a) the original set of vertices is still connected in the MST, and (b) the sum total of the weights of the edges in the MST is minimum. We show how to efficiently solve this problem later in this chapter, in the section "Minimum Spanning Tree Algorithms."

We begin by discussing ways to explore a graph. Two common approaches for carrying out such a search are DEPTH-FIRST SEARCH and BREADTH-FIRST SEARCH.

Depth-First Search

Consider the maze shown on the left in Figure 6-7. After some practice, a child can rapidly find the path that stretches from the start box labeled *s* to the target box labeled *t*. One way to solve this problem is to make as much forward progress as possible and assume that you are not far from the target location. That is, randomly select a direction whenever a choice is possible and stridently set off in that direction, marking where you have come from. If you ever reach a dead end or you can make no further progress without revisiting ground you have already covered, then reverse until a non-traveled branch is found and set off in that direction.

The numbers on the right side of Figure 6-7 reflect the branching points of one such solution; in fact, every square in the maze is visited in this solution.

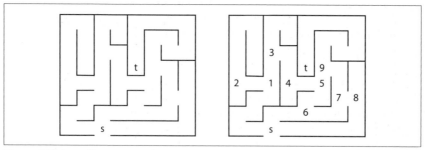

Figure 6-7. A small maze to get from s to t

We can represent the maze in Figure 6-7 by creating a graph consisting of vertices and edges. A vertex is created for each branching point in the maze (labeled by numbers on the right in Figure 6-7), as well as "dead ends." An edge exists only if there is a direct path in the maze between the two vertices where no choice in direction can be made. The undirected graph representation of the maze from Figure 6-7 is shown in Figure 6-8; each vertex has a unique identifier.

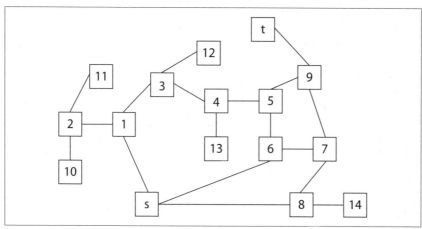

Figure 6-8. Graph representation of maze from Figure 6-7

To solve the maze, we need only ask whether a path exists in the graph $G=(V,E)$ of Figure 6-7 from the vertex s to the target vertex, t. In this example, all edges are undirected, but one could easily consider directed edges if the maze imposed such restrictions.

The fact sheet in Figure 6-9 contains pseudocode describing DEPTH-FIRST SEARCH. The heart of DEPTH-FIRST SEARCH is a recursive dfs_visit(u) operation, which visits a vertex u that previously has not been visited before. dfs_visit(u) records its progress by coloring vertices one of three colors:

White
Vertex has not yet been visited

Gray
Vertex has been visited, but it may have an adjacent vertex that has not yet been visited

Black
Vertex has been visited and so have all of its adjacent vertices

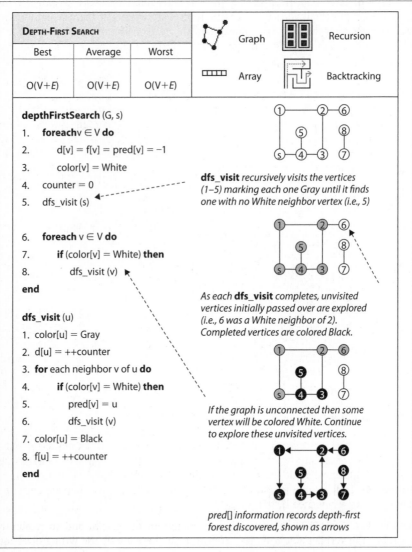

Depth-First Search		
Best	Average	Worst
O(V+E)	O(V+E)	O(V+E)

Graph   Recursion

Array   Backtracking

depthFirstSearch (G, s)

1.   **foreach** v ∈ V **do**
2.   d[v] = f[v] = pred[v] = −1
3.   color[v] = White
4.   counter = 0
5.   dfs_visit (s)

6.   **foreach** v ∈ V **do**
7.   **if** (color[v] = White) **then**
8.   dfs_visit (v)
end

dfs_visit (u)

1. color[u] = Gray
2. d[u] = ++counter
3. **for** each neighbor v of u **do**
4.   **if** (color[v] = White) **then**
5.   pred[v] = u
6.   dfs_visit (v)
7. color[u] = Black
8. f[u] = ++counter
end

dfs_visit recursively visits the vertices (1–5) marking each one Gray until it finds one with no White neighbor vertex (i.e., 5)

*As each **dfs_visit** completes, unvisited vertices initially passed over are explored (i.e., 6 was a White neighbor of 2). Completed vertices are colored Black.*

If the graph is unconnected then some vertex will be colored White. Continue to explore these unvisited vertices.

pred[] information records depth-first forest discovered, shown as arrows

Figure 6-9. Depth-First Search fact sheet

Initially, all vertices are colored white, and DEPTH-FIRST SEARCH invokes dfs_visit on the source vertex, s. dfs_visit(u) colors u gray before recursively invoking dfs_visit on all adjacent vertices of u that have not yet been visited (i.e., they are colored white). Once these recursive calls have completed, u can be colored black, and the function returns. When the recursive dfs_visit function returns, DEPTH-FIRST SEARCH backtracks to an earlier vertex in the search (indeed, to a vertex that is colored gray), which may have an unvisited adjacent vertex that must be explored.

For both directed and undirected graphs, DEPTH-FIRST SEARCH investigates the graph from s until all vertices reachable from s are visited. If there remain unvisited vertices in G that are not reachable from s, DEPTH-FIRST SEARCH randomly selects one of them to be the new source vertex and it repeats. This process continues until all vertices in G are visited.

During its execution, DEPTH-FIRST SEARCH traverses the edges of the graph, computing information that reveals the inherent, complex structure of the graph. DEPTH-FIRST SEARCH maintains a counter that is incremented when a vertex is first visited (and colored gray) and when DEPTH-FIRST SEARCH is done with the vertex (and colored black). For each vertex, DEPTH-FIRST SEARCH records:

pred[v]
> The predecessor vertex that can be used to recover a path from the source vertex s to the vertex v

discovered[v]
> The value of the incrementing counter when DEPTH-FIRST SEARCH first encounters vertex v; abbreviated as $d[v]$

finished[v]
> The value of the incrementing counter when DEPTH-FIRST SEARCH is finished with vertex v; abbreviated as $f[v]$

The order in which vertices are visited will change the value of the counter, and so will the order in which the neighbors of a vertex are listed. This computed information is useful to a variety of algorithms built on DEPTH-FIRST SEARCH, including topological sort, identifying strongly connected components, and identifying potential weak spots in a network. Given the graph in Figure 6-8 and assuming that the neighbors of a vertex are listed in increasing numerical order, the information computed during the search is shown in Figure 6-10. The vertices of the graph show their color when the counter reaches 18, just when vertex 8 is visited (line 2 of dfs_visit in Figure 6-9). Some parts of the graph (i.e., the vertices colored black) have been fully searched and will not be revisited. Note that (a) white vertices have computed d[ ]>18 (since they have not been visited yet); (b) black vertices have computed f[ ]≤18 since they have been fully processed; and (c) gray vertices have d[ ]≤18 and f[ ]≥18 since they are currently being recursively visited by dfs_visit.

DEPTH-FIRST SEARCH has no global awareness of the graph, and so it blindly searches the vertices <5, 6, 7, 8>, even though these are in the wrong direction from the target, t. Once DEPTH-FIRST SEARCH completes, the pred[ ] values can be used to generate a path from each vertex to the original source vertex, s.

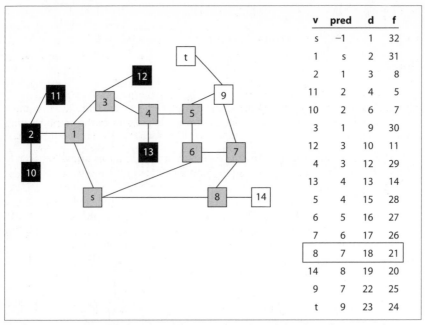

v	pred	d	f
s	−1	1	32
1	s	2	31
2	1	3	8
11	2	4	5
10	2	6	7
3	1	9	30
12	3	10	11
4	3	12	29
13	4	13	14
5	4	15	28
6	5	16	27
7	6	17	26
8	7	18	21
14	8	19	20
9	7	22	25
t	9	23	24

Figure 6-10. Computed d, f, and pred data for a sample undirected graph; vertices are colored when counter reaches 18

Note that this path may not be the shortest possible path—in this case the path has seven vertices <s,1,3,4,5,9,t>, while a shorter path of five vertices exists <s,6,5,9,t>.*

Input/Output

Input

A graph G=(V,E) and a source vertex s∈ V. The quantity n represents the number of vertices in G.

Output

DEPTH-FIRST SEARCH produces three computed arrays. d[v] determines the depth-first numbering of the counter when v is first visited; it is the value of the counter when dfs_visit is invoked. pred[v] determines the predecessor vertex of v based on the depth-first search ordering. f[v] determines the depth-first numbering of the counter when v is determined to be completely visited; it is the value of the counter when control returns from dfs_visit. If the original graph is unconnected, then the pred[] values actually encode a depth-first forest of depth-first tree search results. To find the roots of the trees in this forest, scan pred[] to find vertices r whose pred[r] value is −1.

---

* Here the notion of a "shortest path" refers to the number of decision points between s and t.

Assumptions

The algorithm works for undirected as well as directed graphs.

Context

DEPTH-FIRST SEARCH only needs to store a color (either white, gray, or black) with each vertex as it traverses the graph. Thus DEPTH-FIRST SEARCH requires only minimal overhead in storing information while it explores the graph starting from s.

DEPTH-FIRST SEARCH can store its processing information in arrays separately from the graph. Indeed, the only requirements DEPTH-FIRST SEARCH has on the graph is that one can iterate over the vertices that are adjacent to a given vertex. This feature makes it easy to perform DEPTH-FIRST SEARCH on complex information, since the dfs_visit function accesses the original graph as a read-only structure. DEPTH-FIRST SEARCH is a blind search that relies only on local information, rather than an intelligent plan, to reach the target vertex, t.

Solution

A sample C++ solution is shown in Example 6-1. Note that vertex color information is used only within the dfs_search and dfs_visit methods.

Example 6-1. Depth-First Search implementation

```
#include "dfs.h"

// visit a vertex, u, in the graph and update information
void dfs_visit (Graph const &graph, int u,              /* in */
        vector<int> &d, vector<int> &f,                 /* out */
        vector<int> &pred, vector<vertexColor> &color,  /* out */
        int &ctr, list<EdgeLabel> &labels) {            /* out */
  color[u] = Gray;
  d[u] = ++ctr;

  // process all neighbors of u.
  for (VertexList::const_iterator ci = graph.begin(u);
       ci != graph.end(u); ++ci) {
    int v = ci->first;

    // Compute edgeType and add to labelings. Default to cross
    edgeType type = Cross;
    if (color[v] == White) { type = Tree; }
    else if (color[v] == Gray) { type = Backward; }
    else { if (d[u] < d[v]) type = Forward; }
    labels.push_back(EdgeLabel (u, v, type));

    // Explore unvisited vertices immediately and record pred[].
    // Once recursive call ends, backtrack to adjacent vertices.
    if (color[v] == White) {
      pred[v] = u;
      dfs_visit (graph, v, d, f, pred, color, ctr, labels);
```

Graph
Algorithms

Example 6-1. Depth-First Search implementation (continued)

```
    }
  }

  color[u] = Black;  // our neighbors are complete; now so are we.
  f[u] = ++ctr;
}

/**
 * Perform Depth-First Search starting from vertex s, and compute the
 * values d[u] (when vertex u was first discovered), f[u] (when all
 * vertices adjacent to u have been processed), pred[u] (the predecessor
 * vertex to u in resulting depth-first search forest), and label edges
 * according to their type.
 */
void dfs_search (Graph const &graph, int s,          /* in */
          vector<int> &d, vector<int> &f,            /* out */
          vector<int> &pred, list<EdgeLabel> &labels) /* out */
{
  // initialize d[], f[], and pred[] arrays. Mark all vertices White
  // to signify unvisited. Clear out edge labels.
  int ctr = 0;
  const int n = graph.numVertices();
  vector<vertexColor> color (n, White);
  d.assign(n, -1);
  f.assign(n, -1);
  pred.assign(n, -1);
  labels.clear();

  // Search starting at the source vertex; when done, visit any
  // vertices that remain unvisited.
  dfs_visit (graph, s, d, f, pred, color, ctr, labels);
  for (int u = 0; u < n; u++) {
    if (color[u] == White) {
      dfs_visit (graph, u, d, f, pred, color, ctr, labels);
    }
  }
}
```

If the d[] and f[] information is not needed, then the statements that compute these values (and the parameters to the functions) can be removed from the code solution in Example 6-1. DEPTH-FIRST SEARCH can capture additional information about the edges of the graph. Specifically, in the depth-first forest produced by DEPTH-FIRST SEARCH, there are four types of edges:

Tree edges
> For all vertices *v* whose pred[*v*]=*u*, the edge (*u,v*) was used by dfs_visit(u) to explore the graph. These edges record the progress of DEPTH-FIRST SEARCH. Edge (*s*,1) is an example in Figure 6-10.

Back edges

> When dfs_visit(u) encounters a vertex *v* that is adjacent to *u* and is already colored gray, then DEPTH-FIRST SEARCH detects it is revisiting old ground. The edge (8,*s*) is an example in Figure 6-10.

Forward edges

> When dfs_visit(u) encounters a vertex *v* that is adjacent to *u* and is already marked black, the edge (*u*,*v*) is a forward edge if vertex *u* was visited before *v*. Again, DEPTH-FIRST SEARCH detects it is revisiting old ground. The edge (5,9) is an example in Figure 6-10.

Cross edges

> When dfs_visit(u) encounters a vertex *v* that is adjacent to *u* and is already marked black, the edge (*u*,*v*) is a cross edge if vertex *v* was visited before *u*. Cross edges are possible only in directed graphs.

The code to compute these edge labels is included in Example 6-1. For undirected graphs, the edge (*u*,*v*) may be labeled multiple times; it is common to accept the labeling the first time an edge is encountered, whether as (*u*,*v*) or as (*v*,*u*).

Analysis

The recursive dfs_visit function is called once for each vertex in the graph. The loop in the dfs_search function is executed no more than *n* times. Within dfs_visit, every neighboring vertex must be checked; for directed graphs, each edge is traversed once, whereas in undirected graphs they are traversed once and are seen one other time. In any event, the total performance cost is O(*V*+*E*).

Breadth-First Search

BREADTH-FIRST SEARCH (shown in Figure 6-11) takes a different approach from DEPTH-FIRST SEARCH when searching a graph. BREADTH-FIRST SEARCH systematically visits all vertices in the graph *G*=(*V*,*E*) that are *k* edges away from the source vertex *s* before visiting any vertex that is *k+1* edges away. This process repeats until no more vertices are reachable from *s*. BREADTH-FIRST SEARCH does not visit vertices in *G* that are not reachable from *s*.

BREADTH-FIRST SEARCH makes its progress without requiring any backtracking. It records its progress by coloring vertices white, gray, and black, as DEPTH-FIRST SEARCH did. Indeed, the same colors and definitions apply. To compare directly with DEPTH-FIRST SEARCH, we can construct a similar notion of a counter that increments when a vertex is first visited (and colored gray) and when the vertex is last visited (and colored black). Given the graph used earlier in Figure 6-8, in the same amount of time (i.e., when the counter reaches 18), BREADTH-FIRST SEARCH is able to progress to the state shown in Figure 6-12, where vertex 12 has just been colored gray. Note that BREADTH-FIRST SEARCH is done with vertices {1,6,8}, which are one edge away from *s*, and vertices {2,3}, which are two edges away from *s*.

Graph
Algorithms

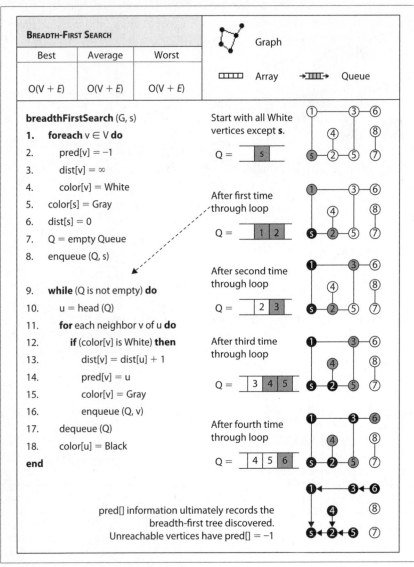

Figure 6-11. Breadth-First Search fact sheet

The remaining vertices two edges away from *s*, vertices {7,14,5}, are all in the queue waiting to be processed. Some vertices three edges away from *s* have been visited—vertices {11,10,12,4}—although BREADTH-FIRST SEARCH is not yet done with them. Note that all vertices within the queue are colored gray, reflecting their active status.

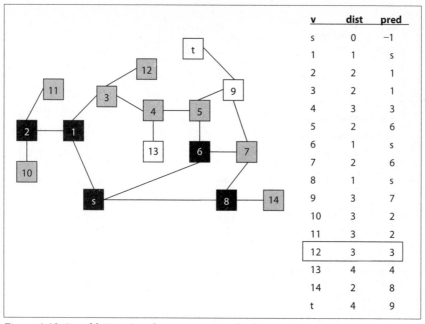

v	dist	pred
s	0	−1
1	1	s
2	2	1
3	2	1
4	3	3
5	2	6
6	1	s
7	2	6
8	1	s
9	3	7
10	3	2
11	3	2
12	3	3
13	4	4
14	2	8
t	4	9

Figure 6-12. Breadth-First Search progress on graph when counter reaches 18

Input/Output

Input

A graph $G=(V,E)$ and a source vertex $s \in V$. The quantity n represents the number of vertices in G.

Output

BREADTH-FIRST SEARCH produces two computed arrays. dist[v] determines the number of edges in a shortest path from s to v. pred[v] determines the predecessor vertex of v based on the breadth-first search ordering. The pred[] values will encode the breadth-first tree search result; if the original graph is unconnected, then all vertices w unreachable from s have a pred[w] value of −1.

Assumptions

The algorithm works for undirected as well as directed graphs.

Context

BREADTH-FIRST SEARCH stores the vertices that are still "at play" within a queue, and thus there may be a non-trivial storage space required for very large graphs. BREADTH-FIRST SEARCH is guaranteed to find a shortest path in graphs whose vertices are generated "on the fly" (as will be seen in Chapter 7). Indeed, all paths in the generated breadth-first tree are shortest paths from s in terms of edge count.

Solution

A sample C++ solution is shown in Example 6-2. BREADTH-FIRST SEARCH stores its state in a stack, and therefore there are no recursive function calls.

Example 6-2. Breadth-First Search implementation

```
#include "bfs.h"

/**
 * Perform breadth-first search on graph from vertex s, and compute BFS
 * distance and pred vertex for all vertices in the graph.
 */
void bfs_search (Graph const &graph, int s,              /* in */
                 vector<int> &dist, vector<int> &pred)   /* out */
{
  // initialize dist and pred to mark vertices as unvisited. Begin at s
  // and mark as Gray since we haven't yet visited its neighbors.
  const int n = graph.numVertices( );
  pred.assign(n, -1);
  dist.assign(n, numeric_limits<int>::max( ));
  vector<vertexColor> color (n, White);

  dist[s] = 0;
  color[s] = Gray;

  queue<int> q;
  q.push(s);
  while (!q.empty( )) {
    int u = q.front( );

    // Explore neighbors of u to expand the search horizon
    for (VertexList::const_iterator ci = graph.begin(u);
         ci != graph.end(u); ++ci) {
      int v = ci->first;
      if (color[v] == White) {
        dist[v] = dist[u]+1;
        pred[v] = u;
        color[v] = Gray;
        q.push(v);
      }
    }

    q.pop( );
    color[u] = Black;
  }
}
```

Analysis

During initialization, BREADTH-FIRST SEARCH updates information for all vertices, and therefore the initialization cost is $O(V)$. When a vertex is first visited (and colored gray), it is inserted into the queue, and no vertex is added twice.

Since the queue can add and remove elements in constant time, the cost of managing the queue is $O(V)$. Finally, each vertex is dequeued exactly once and its adjacent vertices are traversed. The sum total of the edge loops, therefore, is bounded by the total number of edges, or $O(E)$. Thus the total performance is $O(V+E)$.

Single-Source Shortest Path

Suppose you want to fly a private plane on the shortest path from Saint Johnsbury, VT to Waco, TX. Assume you know the distances between the airports for all pairs of cities and towns that are reachable from each other in one nonstop flight of your plane. The best-known algorithm to solve this problem, DIJKSTRA'S ALGORITHM (illustrated in Figure 6-13), finds the shortest path from Saint Johnsbury to all other airports, although the search may be halted once the shortest path to Waco is known. A variation of this search (A*SEARCH, discussed in Chapter 7), directs the search with heuristic information when approximate answers are acceptable.

DIJKSTRA'S ALGORITHM conceptually operates in greedy fashion by expanding a set of vertices, S, for which the shortest path from s to every vertex $v \in S$ is known, *but only using paths that include vertices in S.* Initially, S equals the set $\{s\}$. To expand S, as shown in Figure 6-14, DIJKSTRA'S ALGORITHM finds the vertex $v \in V-S$ (i.e., the vertices outside the shaded region in Figure 6-14) whose distance to s is smallest, and follows v's edges to see whether a shorter path exists to another vertex. After processing v_2, for example, the algorithm determines that the distance from s to v_3 is really 17 through the path $<s,v_2,v_3>$. Once S expands to equal V, the algorithm completes.

Input/Output

Input

A directed, weighted graph $G=(V,E)$ and a source vertex $s \in V$. Each edge $e=(u,v)$ has an associated positive weight in the graph. The quantity n represents the number of vertices in G.

Output

DIJKSTRA'S ALGORITHM produces two computed arrays. The primary result is the array dist[] of values representing the distance from source vertex s to each vertex in the graph. Note that dist[s] is zero. The secondary result is the array pred[], which can be used to rediscover the actual shortest paths from vertex s to each vertex in the graph. You will need to review the solution in Example 6-3 to see how pred is updated.

Assumptions

The edge weights are positive (i.e., greater than zero); if this assumption is not true, then dist[u] may contain invalid results. Even worse, DIJKSTRA'S ALGORITHM will loop forever if a cycle exists whose sum of all weights is less than zero.

Graph
Algorithms

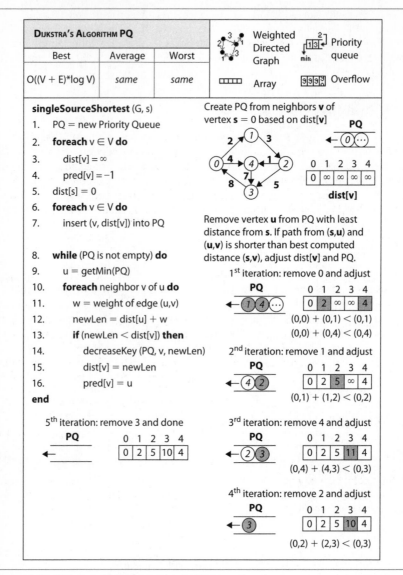

Figure 6-13. *Dijkstra's Algorithm with priority queue fact sheet*

We assume that no arithmetic overflow occurs in line 12 of Figure 6-13; should you be concerned, simply add a check that the computed newLen≥0.

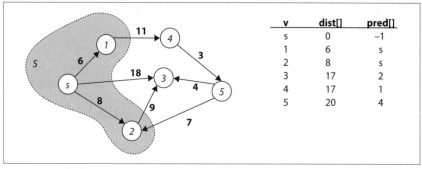

Figure 6-14. Dijkstra's Algorithm expands the set S

Solution

As DIJKSTRA'S ALGORITHM executes, dist[v] represents the maximum length of the shortest path found from the source *s* to *v* using only vertices visited within the set *S*. Also, for each *v* ∈ *S*, dist[v] is correct. Fortunately, DIJKSTRA'S ALGORITHM does not actually compute and store the set *S*. It initially constructs a set containing the vertices in *V*, and then it removes vertices one at a time from the set to compute proper dist[v] values; for convenience, we continue to refer to this ever-shrinking set as *V–S*. DIJKSTRA'S ALGORITHM terminates when all vertices are either visited or are shown to not be reachable from the source vertex *s*.

In the C++ solution shown in Example 6-3, a binary heap stores the vertices in the set *V–S* as a priority queue because, in constant time, one can locate the vertex with smallest priority (where the priority is determined by the vertex's distance from *s*). Additionally, when a shorter path from *s* to *v* is found, dist[v] is decreased, requiring the heap to be modified. Fortunately, the decreaseKey operation on priority queues represented using binary heaps can be performed on average in O(log *q*) time, where *q* is the number of vertices in the binary heap, which will always be less than or equal to the number of vertices, *n*.

Example 6-3. Dijkstra's Algorithm with priority queue implementation

```
#include "BinaryHeap.h"
#include "Graph.h"

/** Given directed, weighted graph, compute shortest distance to vertices
 * (dist) and record predecessor links (pred) for all vertices. */
void singleSourceShortest(Graph const &g, int s,              /* in */
                          vector<int> &dist, vector<int> &pred) { /* out */
  // initialize dist[] and pred[] arrays. Start with vertex s by setting
  // dist[] to 0. Priority Queue PQ contains all v in G.
  const int n = g.numVertices();
  pred.assign(n, -1);
  dist.assign(n, numeric_limits<int>::max());
  dist[s] = 0;
  BinaryHeap pq(n);
  for (int u = 0; u < n; u++) { pq.insert (u, dist[u]); }
```

Example 6-3. Dijkstra's Algorithm with priority queue implementation (continued)

```
// find vertex in ever-shrinking set, V-S, whose dist[] is smallest.
// Recompute potential new paths to update all shortest paths
while (!pq.isEmpty()) {
  int u = pq.smallest();

  // For neighbors of u, see if newLen (best path from s->u + weight
  // of edge u->v) is better than best path from s->v. If so, update
  // in dist[v] and re-adjust binary heap accordingly. Compute in
  // long to avoid overflow error.
  for (VertexList::const_iterator ci = g.begin(u); ci != g.end(u); ++ci) {
    int v = ci->first;
    long newLen = dist[u];
    newLen += ci->second;
    if (newLen < dist[v]) {
      pq.decreaseKey (v, newLen);
      dist[v] = newLen;
      pred[v] = u;
    }
  }
}
}
```

Consequences

Arithmetic error also may occur if the sum of the individual edge weights exceeds numeric_limits<int>::max( ) (although the individual values do not). To avoid this situation, the computed newLen uses a long data type.

Analysis

In the implementation of DIJKSTRA'S ALGORITHM in Example 6-3, the loop that constructs the initial priority queue performs the insert operation V times, resulting in performance $O(V \log V)$. In the remaining while loop, each edge is visited once, and thus decreaseKey is called no more than E times, which contributes $O(E \log V)$ time. Thus, the overall performance is $O((V + E) \log V)$.

The fact sheet in Figure 6-15 describes a version of DIJKSTRA'S ALGORITHM suitable for dense graphs represented using an adjacency matrix. The C++ implementation found in Example 6-4 is simpler since it avoids the use of a binary heap. The efficiency of this version is determined by considering how fast the smallest dist[] value in $V–S$ can be retrieved. The while loop is executed n times, since S grows one vertex at a time. Finding the smallest dist[u] in $V–S$ inspects all n vertices. Note that each edge is inspected exactly once in the inner loop within the while loop. Thus, the total running time of this version is $O(V^2+E)$.

Example 6-4. Implementation of Dijkstra's Algorithm for dense graphs

```
#include "Graph.h"
void singleSourceShortest(Graph const &graph, int s,              /* in */
                          vector<int> &dist, vector<int> &pred) { /* out */

  // initialize dist[] and pred[] arrays. Start with vertex s by setting
  // dist[] to 0.
  const int n = graph.numVertices( );
  pred.assign(n, -1);
  dist.assign(n, numeric_limits<int>::max( ));
  vector<bool> visited(n);
  dist[s] = 0;

  // find vertex in ever-shrinking set, V-S, whose dist value is smallest
  // Recompute potential new paths to update all shortest paths
  while (true) {
    // find shortest distance so far in unvisited vertices
    int u = -1;
    int sd = numeric_limits<int>::max( );   // assume not reachable
    for (int i = 0; i < n; i++) {
      if (!visited[i] && dist[i] < sd) {
        sd = dist[i];
        u = i;
      }
    }
    if (u == -1) { break; }    // no more progress to be made

    // For neighbors of u, see if length of best path from s->u + weight
    // of edge u->v is better than best path from s->v.
    visited[u] = true;
    for (VertexList::const_iterator ci = graph.begin(u);
         ci != graph.end(u); ++ci) {
      int v = ci->first;                // the neighbor v
      long newLen = dist[u];            // compute as long
      newLen += ci->second;             // sum with (u,v) weight
      if (newLen < dist[v]) {
        dist[v] = newLen;
        pred[v] = u;
      }
    }
  }
}
```

We can further optimize Example 6-4 to remove all of the C++ standard template library objects, as shown in Example 6-5. By reducing the overhead of the supporting classes, we realize impressive performance benefits, as discussed in the "Comparison" section.

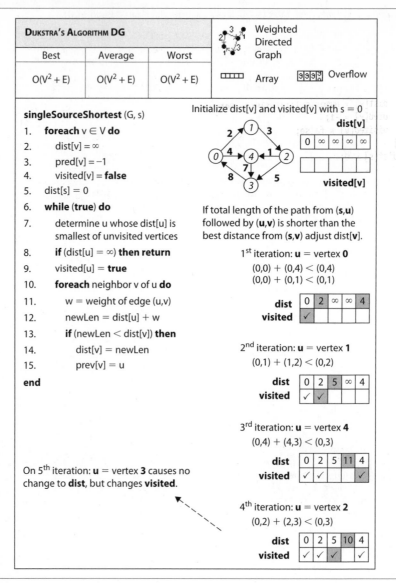

Figure 6-15. Dijkstra's Algorithm for dense graphs fact sheet

Example 6-5. Optimized Dijkstra's Algorithm for dense graphs

```
/**
 * Given int[][] of edge weights in raw form, compute shortest distance to
 * all vertices in graph (dist) and record predecessor links for all
 * vertices (pred) to be able to recreate these paths. An edge weight of
 * INF means no edge. Suitable for Dense Graphs Only.
 */
void singleSourceShortestDense(int n, int ** const weight, int s,  /* in */
```

Example 6-5. Optimized Dijkstra's Algorithm for dense graphs (continued)

```
                            int *dist, int *pred) {              /* out */
// initialize dist[] and pred[] arrays. Start with vertex s by setting
// dist[] to 0. All vertices are unvisited.
bool *visited = new bool[n];
for (int v = 0; v < n; v++) {
  dist[v] = numeric_limits<int>::max( );
  pred[v] = -1;
  visited[v] = false;
}
dist[s] = 0;

// find shortest distance from s to all unvisited vertices.  Recompute
// potential new paths to update all shortest paths. Exit if u remains -1.
while (true) {
  int u = -1;
  int sd = numeric_limits<int>::max( );
  for (int i = 0; i < n; i++) {
    if (!visited[i] && dist[i] < sd) {
      sd = dist[i];
      u = i;
    }
  }
  if (u == -1) { break; }

  // For neighbors of u, see if length of best path from s->u + weight
  // of edge u->v is better than best path from s->v. Compute using longs.
  visited[u] = true;
  for (int v = 0; v < n; v++) {
    int w = weight[u][v];
    if (v == u) continue;

    long newLen = dist[u];
    newLen += w;
    if (newLen < dist[v]) {
      dist[v] = newLen;
      pred[v] = u;
    }
  }
}
delete [] visited;
}
```

Variations

If a shortest flight path has many hops, you might be solving the wrong problem. For example, if the intent was to reduce gas consumption, an initial hypothesis is that the shortest path would be the way to go. However, one must factor in the gas consumed in landing and taking off. You'd figure out the extra fuel consumption in a landing and take-off and convert this to the equivalent distance (say, D) you'd have to fly in order to consume this much fuel. You then add D to the distance between each pair of airports and find the shortest path in the modified problem.

In this presentation we tried to minimize the distance traversed. In other applications we might replace distance with time (e.g., deliver a packet over a network as quickly as possible) or with cost (e.g., given the costs of legs of commercial flights, find the cheapest way to fly from St. Johnsbury to Waco). Solutions to these problems also correspond to shortest paths.

We may seek the most reliable path to send a message from one point to another through a network where we know the probability that any leg of a transmission delivers the message correctly. The probability of any path (sequence of legs) delivering a message correctly is the product of all the probabilities along the path. Using the same technique that made multiplication possible on a slide rule, we can replace the probability on each edge with minus the logarithm of the probability. The shortest path in this new graph corresponds to the most reliable path in the original graph.

DIJKSTRA'S ALGORITHM cannot be used when edge weights are negative. However, BELLMAN-FORD (shown in Example 6-6 and Figure 6-16) can be used as long as there is no cycle of negative weight—that is, a cycle in the graph whose edge weights sum to a value less than zero. The concept of a "shortest path" is meaningless when such a cycle exists. Although the sample graph in Figure 6-13 contains a cycle involving vertices {1,3,2}, the edge weights are positive, so BELLMAN-FORD and DIJKSTRA'S ALGORITHM continue to work.

Example 6-6. Bellman-Ford algorithm for single source shortest path

```
#include "Graph.h"
/**
 * Given directed, weighted graph, compute shortest distance to all vertices
 * in graph (dist) and record predecessor links for all vertices (pred) to
 * be able to recreate these paths. Graph weights can be negative so long
 * as there are no negative cycles.
 */
void singleSourceShortest(Graph const &graph, int s,            /* in */
                          vector<int> &dist, vector<int> &pred){  /* out */
  // initialize dist[] and pred[] arrays.
  const int n = graph.numVertices();
  pred.assign(n, -1);
  dist.assign(n, numeric_limits<int>::max());
  dist[s] = 0;

  // After n-1 times we can be guaranteed distances from s to all
  // vertices are properly computed to be shortest. So on the nth
  // pass, a change to any value guarantees there is negative cycle.
  // Leave early if no changes are made.
  for (int i = 1; i <= n; i++) {
    bool failOnUpdate = (i == n);
    bool leaveEarly = true;

    // Process each vertex, u, and its respective edges to see if
    // some edge (u,v) realizes a shorter distance from s->v by going
    // through s->u->v. Use longs to prevent overflow.
```

```
for (int u = 0; u < n; u++) {
  for (VertexList::const_iterator ci = graph.begin(u);
       ci != graph.end(u); ++ci) {
    int v = ci->first;
    long newLen = dist[u];
    newLen += ci->second;
    if (newLen < dist[v]) {
      if (failOnUpdate) { throw "Graph has negative cycle"; }
      dist[v] = newLen;
      pred[v] = u;
      leaveEarly = false;
    }
  }
}
if (leaveEarly) { break; }
}
}
```

Intuitively BELLMAN-FORD operates by making n sweeps over a graph that check to see if any edge (u,v) is able to improve on the computation for dist[v] given dist[u] and the weight of the edge over (u,v). At least $n–1$ sweeps are needed, for example, in the extreme case that the shortest path from s to some vertex v goes through all vertices in the graph. Another reason to use $n–1$ sweeps is that the edges can be visited in an arbitrary order, and this ensures that all reduced paths have been found. Indeed, visiting edges in a different order leads to a different set of computations that reduce the dist[] values. Figure 6-17 shows two executions of BELLMAN-FORD on two graphs whose only difference is the labeling of vertices v_1 and v_4. Both executions nonetheless arrive at the same result, if you consider the relabeling.

BELLMAN-FORD is thwarted only when there exists a negative cycle of directed edges whose total sum is less than zero. To detect such a negative cycle, we execute the primary processing loop n times (one more than necessary), and if there is an adjustment to some dist[] value, a negative cycle exists. The performance of BELLMAN-FORD is $O(V^*E)$, as clearly seen by the nested loops.

Comparison

The following list compares the expected performance of the three algorithms by computing a rough cost estimate:

- BELLMAN-FORD: $O(V^*E)$
- DIJKSTRA'S ALGORITHM for dense graphs: $O(V^2+E)$
- DIJKSTRA'S ALGORITHM with priority queue: $O((V+E)^*\log V)$

We compare these algorithms under different scenarios. Naturally, to select the one that best fits your data, you should benchmark the implementations as we have done. In the following tables, we execute the algorithms 10 times and discard the best and worst performing runs; the tables show the average of the remaining eight runs.

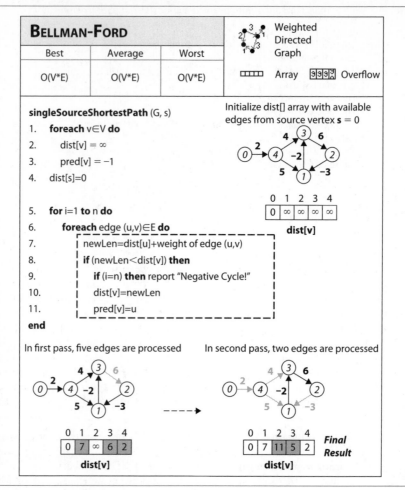

Figure 6-16. Bellman-Ford fact sheet

Benchmark data

It is difficult to generate "random graphs." In Table 6-2, we show the performance on graphs with $V=k^2+2$ vertices and $E=k^3-k^2+2k$ edges in a highly stylized graph construction (for details, see the code implementation in the repository). Note that the number of edges is roughly $n^{1.5}$ where n is the number of vertices in V. The best performance comes from using the priority queue implementation of DIJSKTRA'S ALGORITHM but BELLMAN-FORD is not far behind. Note how the variations optimized for dense graphs perform poorly.

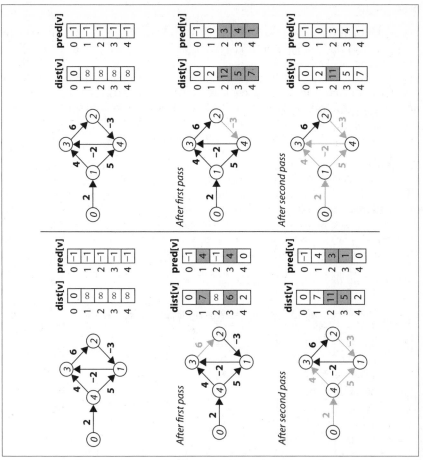

Figure 6-17. *Different executions of Bellman-Ford have the same result*

Table 6-2. *Time (in seconds) to compute single source shortest path on benchmark graphs*

V	E	Dijkstra's Algorithm with PQ	Dijkstra's Algorithm for DG	Optimized Dijkstra's Algorithm for DG	Bellman-Ford
6	8	0.01	0.008	0.005	0.005
18	56	0.015	0.016	0.009	0.006
66	464	0.036	0.08	0.042	0.017
258	3,872	0.114	0.71	0.372	0.102
1,026	31,808	1	15.8	9.8	1.8
4,098	258,176	10.5	260.4	155.7	14.3
16,386	2,081,024	51.5	2113.7	1215.6	80.3

Dense graphs

For dense graphs, E is on the order of $O(V^2)$; for example, in a complete graph of $n=|V|$ vertices that contains an edge for every pair of vertices, there are $n(n-1)/2$ edges. Using BELLMAN-FORD on such dense graphs is not recommended, since its performance degenerates to $O(V^3)$. The set of dense graphs reported in Table 6-3 is taken from a set of publicly available data sets used by researchers investigating the Traveling Salesman Problem (TSP).* We executed 100 trials and discarded the best and worst performances; the table contains the average of the remaining 98 trials. Although there is little difference between the priority queue and dense versions of DIJSKTRA'S ALGORITHM, there is a vast improvement in the optimized DIJSKTRA'S ALGORITHM, as shown in the fifth column of the table. In the final column we show the performance time for BELLMAN-FORD on the same problems, but these results are the averages of only five executions because the performance degrades so sharply. The lesson to draw from the last column is that the absolute performance of BELLMAN-FORD on small graphs seems to be quite reasonable, but when compared relatively to its peers on dense graphs, one sees clearly that it is the wrong algorithm to use on these graphs.

Table 6-3. Time (in seconds) to compute single source shortest path on dense graphs

V	E	Dijkstra's Algorithm with PQ	Dijkstra's Algorithm for DG	Optimized Dijkstra's Algorithm for DG	Bellman-Ford
980	479,710	0.0918	0.1147	0.0128	0.2444
1,621	1,313,010	0.2194	0.2601	0.0329	0.7978
6,117	18,705,786	3.6256	4.0361	0.2301	66.0659
7,663	29,356,953	8.3147	8.8592	0.3644	222.3107
9,847	48,476,781	15.2602	16.2169	0.6116	431.2807
9,882	48,822,021	14.7536	16.5594	0.6224	277.8776

Sparse graphs

Large graphs are frequently sparse, and the results in Table 6-4 confirm that one should use the DIJSKTRA'S ALGORITHM with a priority queue rather than the implementation crafted for dense graphs; note how the implementation for dense graphs is 10 times slower. The rows in the table are sorted by the number of edges in the sparse graphs, since that appears to be the determining cost factor in the results.

Table 6-4. Time (in seconds) to compute single source shortest path on large sparse graphs

V	E	Density	Dijkstra's Algorithm with PQ	Dijkstra's Algorithm for DG	Optimized Dijkstra's Algorithm for DG
3,403	137,845	2.8 %	0.0453	0.2038	0.098
3,243	294,276	1.2 %	0.017	0.1922	0.1074
19,780	674,195	0.17 %	0.1002	2.9697	1.805

---

* http://www.iwr.uni-heidelberg.de/groups/comopt/software/TSPLIB95/

All Pairs Shortest Path

Instead of finding the shortest path from a single source, we often want to find a shortest path* between any two vertices (v_i, v_j). The fastest solution to this problem uses a powerful problem-solving technique called *dynamic programming*.

There are two interesting features of dynamic programming:

- It solves small, constrained versions of the problem. When the constraints are tight, the function is simple to compute, and then the constraints are systematically relaxed until finally they yield the value of the desired answer.

- Although one seeks an optimum answer to a problem, it is easier to compute the *value* of an optimum answer rather than the answer itself. In our case, we compute, for each pair of vertices (v_i, v_j), the length of a shortest path from v_i to v_j and perform additional computation to recover the actual path.

The goal is to compute an *n*-by-*n* matrix dist such that for all pairs of vertices (v_i, v_j), dist[i][j] contains the length of a shortest path from v_i to v_j. The pseudocode for FLOYD-WARSHALL is shown in Figure 6-18, together with its execution on a small example.

Input

A directed, weighted graph $G=(V,E)$. Each edge $e=(u,v)$ has an associated positive weight in the graph. The quantity *n* represents the number of vertices in *G*.

Output

FLOYD-WARSHALL produces the matrix dist[][] of values representing the shortest distance from each vertex *u* to every vertex in the graph (including itself). Note that if dist[u][v] is ∞, then there is no path from *u* to *v*. The actual shortest path between any two vertices can be computed from a second matrix, pred[][], also computed by the algorithm.

Assumptions

The edge weights must be positive (i.e., greater than zero).

Solution

A dynamic programming approach will compute, in order, a series of matrices $dist_k$ for $0 \le k \le n$ such that $dist_k[i][j]$ will be the length of a shortest path from v_i to v_j that may only pass through vertices $v_1, v_2, ..., v_k$ in addition to v_i and v_j.† When $k=0$, for instance, $dist_0[i][j]$ is the weight of the edge (v_i, v_j), or ∞ if no such edge exists. To continue this example, when $k=1$, we can determine for all *i* and *j* whether the path of two edges (v_i, v_1) and (v_1, v_j) is shorter than the direct edge (v_i, v_j). If we continue this logic until $k=n$, then we can compute $dist_n[i][j]$, which represents the shortest distance from v_i to v_j passing through vertices $v_1, v_2, ..., v_n$.

---

* There may be several paths with the same total distance.

† These vertices are not necessarily distinct; that is, *i* may equal *j* or $1 \le i \le k$ or $1 \le j \le k$.

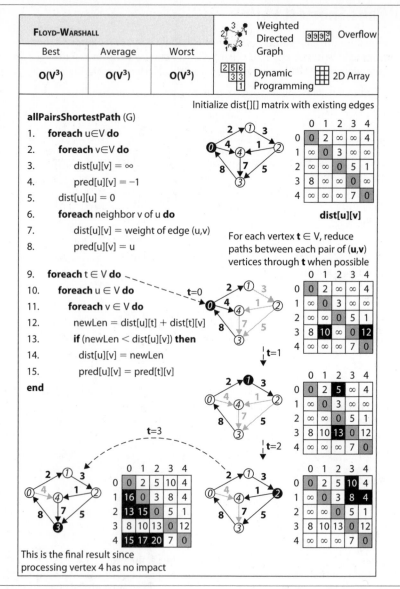

Figure 6-18. Floyd-Warshall fact sheet

For values of $k>0$, we assume when computing $dist_k$ that we have already computed $dist_{k-1}$ (in dynamic programming, one must solve the subproblems in an appropriate order).

FLOYD-WARSHALL proceeds by incrementing k from 0 to n until $dist_n[][]$ is computed. When computing $dist_k[i][j]$, we need to know whether a shortest path from v_i to v_j (which may only pass through vertices $v_1, v_2, ..., v_k$ in addition to v_i and v_j) passes through vertex v_k:

- If it does not, the result of our previous computation, $dist_{k-1}[i][j]$, is still our best result.

- If it does, such a shortest path can be split into two subpaths: a shortest path from v_i to v_k of length $dist_{k-1}[i][k]$ plus a shortest path from v_k to v_j of length $dist_{k-1}[k][j]$. The computed shortest path from v_i to v_j is then $dist_{k-1}[i][k]+dist_{k-1}[k][j]$.

Instead of trying to distinguish between these two cases, we compute both values and take the smaller. When the smaller value is the second case, FLOYD-WARSHALL determines that a shorter path exists between vertex i and j than its previous calculation. It may seem surprising that we don't need to record what that path is. Even more surprising is that we only need a single matrix *dist* rather than $n+1$ matrices $dist_k$ because we are only concerned with the total distance, not the path that involves the fewest number of vertices. The surprisingly brief solution is shown in Example 6-7.

Example 6-7. Floyd-Warshall algorithm for computing all pairs shortest path

```
#include "Graph.h"

void allPairsShortest(Graph const &graph,            /* in */
                  vector< vector<int> > &dist,     /* out */
                  vector< vector<int> > &pred) {   /* out */
  int n = graph.numVertices();

  // Initialize dist[][] with 0 on diagonals, INFINITY where no edge
  // exists, and the weight of edge (u,v) placed in dist[u][v]. pred
  // initialized in corresponding way.
  for (int u = 0; u < n; u++) {
    dist[u].assign(n, numeric_limits<int>::max());
    pred[u].assign(n, -1);
    dist[u][u] = 0;
    for (VertexList::const_iterator ci = graph.begin(u);
         ci != graph.end(u); ++ci) {
      int v = ci->first;
      dist[u][v] = ci->second;
      pred[u][v] = u;
    }
  }

  for (int k = 0; k < n; k++) {
    for (int i = 0; i < n; i++) {
      if (dist[i][k] == numeric_limits<int>::max()) { continue; }

      // If an edge is found to reduce distance, update dist[][].
      // Compute using longs to avoid overflow of Infinity-distance.
      for (int j = 0; j < n; j++) {
        long newLen = dist[i][k];
        newLen += dist[k][j];

        if (newLen < dist[i][j]) {
          dist[i][j] = newLen;
          pred[i][j] = pred[k][j];
```

Example 6-7. Floyd-Warshall algorithm for computing all pairs shortest path (continued)

```
            }
        }
      }
    }
}
```

FLOYD-WARSHALL computes a dist[i][j] matrix that stores the resulting computations of the shortest path from v_i to v_j in the weighted, directed graph; along the way, it computes a pred[i][j] matrix to be used to reconstruct an actual shortest path between two vertices. The simple function shown in Example 6-8 constructs an actual shortest path (there may be more than one) from a given v_s to v_t. It works by recovering predecessor information from the pred matrix.

Example 6-8. Code to recover shortest path from the computed pred[][]

```
/**
 * Output path as vector of vertices from s to t given the pred results
 * from an allPairsShortest execution. Note that s and t must be valid
 * integer vertex identifiers. If no path is found between s and t, then an
 * empty path is returned.
 */
void constructShortestPath(int s, int t,                    /* in */
                           vector< vector<int> > const &pred, /* in */
                           list<int> &path) {                 /* out */
  path.clear();
  if (t < 0 || t >= (int) pred.size() || s < 0 || s >= (int) pred.size()) {
    return;
  }

  // construct path until we hit source 's' or -1 if there is no path.
  path.push_front(t);
  while (t != s) {
    t = pred[s][t];
    if (t == -1) { path.clear(); return; }

    path.push_front(t);
  }
}
```

Analysis

The time taken by FLOYD-WARSHALL is dictated by the number of times the minimization function is computed, which is $O(V^3)$, as can be seen from the three nested loops. The constructShortestPath function in Example 6-8 executes in $O(E)$ since the shortest path might include every edge in the graph.

Minimum Spanning Tree Algorithms

Given an undirected, connected graph $G=(V,E)$, one might be concerned with finding a subset ST of edges from E that "span" the graph by ensuring that the graph remains connected. If we further require that the total weights of the edges in ST are minimized, then we are interested in finding a minimum spanning tree (MST).

PRIM'S ALGORITHM, illustrated in Figure 6-19, shows how to construct an MST from such a graph by using a greedy approach in which each step of the algorithm makes forward progress toward a solution without reversing earlier decisions. PRIM'S ALGORITHM grows a spanning tree T one edge at a time until an MST results (and the resulting spanning tree is provably minimum). It randomly selects a start vertex $s \in V$ to belong to a growing set S, and it ensures that T forms a tree of edges rooted at s. PRIM'S ALGORITHM is greedy in that it incrementally adds edges to T until an MST is computed. The intuition behind the algorithm is that the edge (u,v) with lowest weight between $u \in S$ and $v \in V-S$ must belong to the MST. When such an edge (u,v) with lowest weight is found, it is added to T and the vertex v is added to S.

The algorithm uses a priority queue to store the vertices $v \in V-S$ with an associated priority equal to the lowest weight of some edge (u,v) where $u \in S$. This carefully designed approach ensures the efficiency of the resulting implementation.

Solution

The C++ solution shown in Example 6-9 relies on a binary heap to provide the implementation of the priority queue that is central to PRIM'S ALGORITHM. Ordinarily, using a binary heap would be inefficient because of the check in the main loop for whether a particular vertex is a member of the priority queue (an operation not supported by binary heaps). However, the algorithm ensures that vertices are only removed from the priority queue as it processes, so we need only maintain a status array inQueue[] that is updated whenever a vertex is extracted from the priority queue. In another implementation optimization, we maintain an external array key[] that records the current priority key for each vertex in the queue, which again eliminates the need to search the priority queue for a given vertex identifier.

Example 6-9. Prim's Algorithm implementation with binary heap

```
/**
 * Given undirected graph, compute MST starting from a randomly
 * selected vertex. Encoding of MST is done using 'pred' entries.
 */
void mst_prim (Graph const &graph, vector<int> &pred) {
  // initialize pred[] and key[] arrays. Start with arbitrary
  // vertex s=0. Priority Queue PQ contains all v in G.
  const int n = graph.numVertices();
  pred.assign(n, -1);
  vector<int> key(n, numeric_limits<int>::max());
  key[0] = 0;
```

Graph Algorithms

Example 6-9. Prim's Algorithm implementation with binary heap (continued)

```
BinaryHeap pq(n);
vector<bool> inQueue(n, true);
for (int v = 0; v < n; v++) {
  pq.insert(v, key[v]);
}

while (!pq.isEmpty()) {
  int u = pq.smallest();
  inQueue[u] = false;

  // Process all neighbors of u to find if any edge beats best distance
  for (VertexList::const_iterator ci = graph.begin(u);
       ci != graph.end(u); ++ci) {
    int v = ci->first;
    if (inQueue[v]) {
      int w = ci->second;
      if (w < key[v]) {
        pred[v] = u;
        key[v] = w;
        pq.decreaseKey(v, w);
      }
    }
  }
}
```

Consequences

For dense graphs, the priority queue can be implemented instead with a Fibonacci heap. This improves the performance to $O(E+V^*\log V)$, a significant speedup over the binary heap implementation.

Analysis

The initialization phase of PRIM'S ALGORITHM inserts each vertex into the priority queue (implemented by a binary heap) for a total cost of $O(V \log V)$. The decreaseKey operation in PRIM'S ALGORITHM requires $O(\log q)$ performance, where q is the number of elements in the queue, which will always be less than $|V|$. It can be called at most $2^*|E|$ times since each vertex is removed once from the priority queue and each undirected edge in the graph is visited exactly twice. Thus the total performance is $O((V+2^*E)^*\log n)$ or $O((V+E)^*\log V)$.

Variations

KRUSKAL'S ALGORITHM is an alternative to PRIM'S ALGORITHM. It uses a "disjoint-set" data structure to build up the minimum spanning tree by processing all edges in the graph in order of weight, starting with the edge with smallest weight and ending with the edge with largest weight. KRUSKAL'S ALGORITHM can be implemented in $O(E \log E)$; with a sophisticated implementation of the disjoint-set data structure, this can be reduced to $O(E \log V)$. Details on this algorithm can be found in (Cormen et al., 2001).

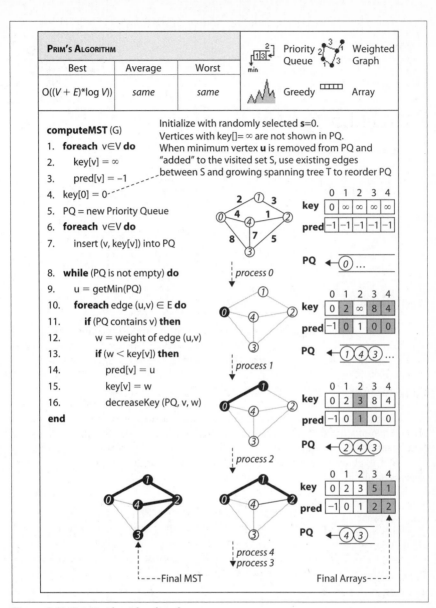

Figure 6-19. Prim's Algorithm fact sheet

References

Cormen, Thomas H., Charles E. Leiserson, Ronald L. Rivest, and Clifford Stein. *Introduction to Algorithms*, Second Edition. McGraw-Hill, 2001.

7

Path Finding in AI

Overview

To solve a problem when there is no clear algorithm for computing a valid solution, we turn to path finding. In this chapter we will cover two related path-finding approaches, one for *game trees* and the other for *search trees*. These approaches rely on a common structure, namely a state tree where the root node represents the initial state and edges represent potential moves that transform the state into a new state. The searches are challenging because the underlying structure is not computed in its entirety, due to the explosion of the number of states. In a game of checkers, for example, there are roughly $5*10^{20}$ different board configurations (Schaeffer, 2007). Thus the trees over which the search proceeds are constructed on demand as needed. The two path-finding approaches are characterized as follows:

Game tree

> Two players take alternating turns in making moves that modify the game state from its initial state. There are potentially many states in which either player can win the game. There also may be some states that are "draws," in which case no one wins. A path-finding algorithm maximizes the chances that a player will win the game (or force a draw).

Search tree

> A single agent is given a task to accomplish, starting from an initial board state, with a series of allowed move types. In most cases, there is exactly one goal state that is desired. A path-finding algorithm identifies the exact sequence of moves that will transform the initial state into the goal state.

Game Trees

The game of tic-tac-toe is played on a three-by-three board where players take turns placing X and O marks on the board. The first player to place three of his marks in a row wins; the game is a draw if no spaces remain and no player has won. Any 10-year-old child knows that the player making the first move can never lose, even against a player who makes no mistakes. A computer program that plays tic-tac-toe can be written to deliver the same result based on artificial intelligence (AI) algorithms developed for *combinatorial games* such as checkers and chess (but not poker, which relies on chance). In a combinatorial game, there is an initial game position, and each player makes alternating moves that update the game state until some winning condition is achieved (or the game is drawn, with no player winning).

In tic-tac-toe there are only 765 unique positions (ignoring reflections and rotations of the board state) and a calculated 26,830 possible games that can be played (Schaeffer, 2002). The first player can always force a win or a draw, and quite often undergraduate computer science students are asked to write tic-tac-toe programs in an AI class. One need only construct the *game tree*, as shown partially in Figure 7-1, and find a path from the current game state (represented as the top node in this tree) to some future game state that ensures either a victory or a draw for the player faced with the current game state.

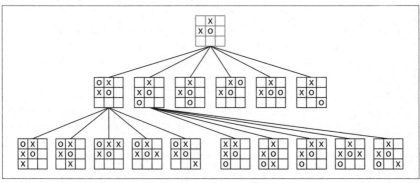

Figure 7-1. Partial game tree given an initial tic-tac-toe game state

A game tree is also known as an AND/OR tree since it is formed by two different types of nodes. The game tree in Figure 7-1 is constructed for player O. The top node is an OR node, since the goal is to select just one of the six available moves in the middle tier. The middle-tier nodes are AND nodes, since the goal (from O's perspective) is to ensure that all countermoves by X (as shown as children nodes in the bottom tier) will still lead to either a victory or a draw for O. The game tree in Figure 7-1 is only partially expanded since there are actually 30 different game states in the bottom tier. The top game state is particularly interesting because neither X nor O has won by the bottom tier (i.e., after two moves). Intuitively, this means that a tic-tac-toe program must look at least three moves ahead to determine how O should best respond in this circumstance.

The game tree represents the full set of potential game states that result from sequences of valid moves from the initial state; due to its size, it may never be computed fully. The goal of a path-finding algorithm is to determine from a game state the player's move that maximizes (or even guarantees) his chance of winning the game. We thus transform an intelligent set of player decisions into a *path-finding problem* over the game tree. This approach works for games with small game trees, but it also can be scaled to solve more complex problems.

The American game of checkers is played on an eight-by-eight board with an initial set of 24 pieces (12 red and 12 black). For decades researchers attempted to determine whether the opening player could force a draw or a win. Although it is difficult to compute exactly, there are roughly $5*10^{20}$ possible board positions in checkers. The size of the game tree must therefore be incredibly large. After nearly 18 years of computations (sometimes on as many as 200 computers), researchers at the University of Alberta, Canada claim they have demonstrated that perfect play by both players leads to a draw (Schaeffer, 2007).

Path finding in AI provides specific algorithms that can be used to tackle incredibly complex problems that can be translated into a combinatorial game of alternating players. Early researchers in artificial intelligence (Shannon, 1950) considered the challenge of building a chess-playing machine and developed two types of approaches for search problems that continue to define the state of the practice today:

Type A

Consider the various allowed moves for both players a fixed set of turns into the future, and determine the most favorable position that results for the original player. Then, select the initial move that makes progress in that direction.

Type B

Add some adaptive decision based upon knowledge of the game rather than static evaluation functions. More explicitly, (a) evaluate promising positions as far as necessary to find a stable position where the board evaluation truly reflects the strength of the resulting position, and (b) select appropriate available moves so pointless possibilities do not consume precious time.

In this chapter, we describe the most popular and powerful approaches to reduce the size of the search space for combinatorial game problems. We first describe the family of Type A algorithms, which provide a general-purpose approach for searching a game tree to find the best move for a player in a two-player game. These algorithms include MINIMAX, ALPHABETA, and NEGMAX. More advanced Type B algorithms are described as well (such as ITERATIVEDEEPENING).

The algorithms discussed in this chapter become unnecessarily complicated if the underlying information is poorly modeled. Many of the examples in textbooks or on the Internet naturally describe these algorithms in the context of a particular game. However, it may be difficult to separate the arbitrary way in which the game is represented from the essential elements of these algorithms. For this reason, we intentionally designed a set of object-oriented interfaces to maintain a clean separation between the algorithms and the games. We'll now briefly summarize the core concepts of game tree algorithms, which are illustrated in Figure 7-2.

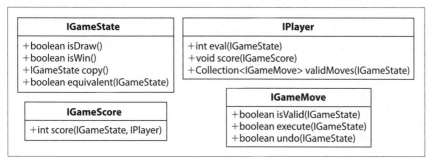

Figure 7-2. Core concepts for game tree algorithms

The IGameState interface abstracts the essential concepts needed to conduct searches over a game state. It defines the interface for:

Interpreting the game state
> isDraw( ) determines whether the game concludes with neither player winning; isWin( ) determines whether the game is won.

Managing the game state
> copy( ) returns an identical copy of the game state so moves can be applied without updating the original game state; equivalent(IGameState) determines whether two game state positions are equal.

The IPlayer interface abstracts the abilities of a player to manipulate the game state:

Evaluating a board
> eval(IGameState) returns an integer evaluating the game state from the player's perspective; score(IGameScore) sets the scoring computation the player uses to evaluate a game state.

Generating valid moves
> validMoves(IGameState) returns a collection of available moves given the game state.

The IGameMove interface defines how moves can manipulate the game state. The move classes are problem-specific, and the search algorithm need not be aware of their specific implementation. IGameScore defines the interface for scoring computations. In this chapter, we use the BoardEvaluation scoring function for tic-tac-toe, which was defined by Nil Nilsson (1971). Let $nc(gs,p)$ be the number of rows, columns, or diagonals on a tic-tac-toe game state, gs, in which player p may still get three in a row. We then define score(IGameState gs, IPlayer player) to be:

- $+\infty$ if player has won the game in game state gs
- $-\infty$ if the opponent of player has won the game in game state gs
- $nc(gs, player)-nc(gs, opponent)$ if neither player has won the game in game state gs

From a programming perspective, the heart of the path-finding algorithm for a game tree is an implementation of the IEvaluation interface shown in Example 7-1.

Example 7-1. Common interface for game tree path finding

```
public interface IEvaluation {
  IGameMove bestMove(IGameState state, IPlayer player, IPlayer opponent);
}
```

Given a node representing the current game state, the algorithm computes the best move for player assuming that opponent will play a perfect game in return. Later we will investigate how MINIMAX, NEGMAX, and ALPHABETA can be used to search game trees.

Search Trees

The 8-puzzle is formed using a three-by-three grid containing eight square tiles numbered 1 to 8 and an empty space that contains no tile. A tile adjacent (either horizontally or vertically) to the empty space can be moved by sliding it into the empty space. The aim is to start from a shuffled initial state and move tiles to achieve the goal state, as shown in Figure 7-3. There are no competing players taking alternate turns for these problems, but the behavior is quite similar to game trees. There is an initial state (the top node in the search tree), and a sequence of moves transforms the board state until a goal state is reached (labeled "GOAL"). The eight-move solution in Figure 7-3 is recorded as the bold path from the initial node to the goal node.

We use the term *search tree* to refer to the tree representing the set of intermediate board states as the path-finding algorithm progresses. The computed structure is a tree because the algorithm ensures that it does not visit a board state twice. The algorithm decides the order of board states to visit as it attempts to reach the goal.

Often, the search tree rapidly explodes to contain (potentially) millions of states. The algorithms in this chapter describe how to efficiently search through these trees more rapidly than using a blind search. To describe the inherent complexity of the problem, we introduce DEPTH-FIRST SEARCH and BREADTH-FIRST SEARCH as two potential approaches to path-finding algorithms. We then present the powerful A*SEARCH algorithm for finding a minimal-cost solution (under certain conditions). We'll now briefly summarize the core concepts, illustrated in Figure 7-4, that will be used when discussing search tree algorithms.

The INode interface abstracts the essential concepts needed to conduct searches over a board state. This interface groups together code for:

Generating valid moves
    validMoves( ) returns a list of available moves for a board state.

Evaluating the board state
    score(int) associates an integer score with the board state, representing the result of an evaluation function; score( ) returns the evaluation result previously associated with the board state.

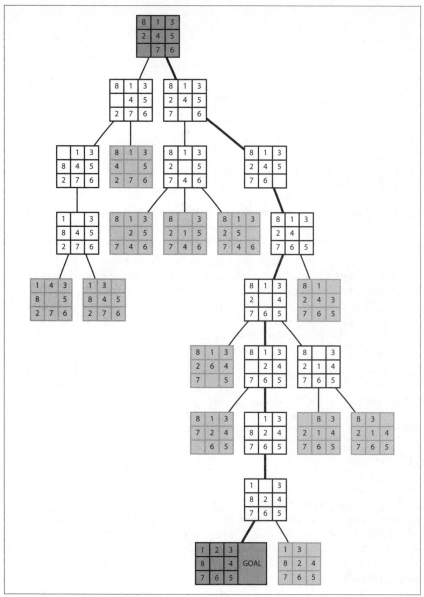

Figure 7-3. Sample 8-puzzle search

Managing the board state

copy( ) returns an identical copy of the board state (except for the optional stored data); equivalent (INode) determines whether two board states are equal (sophisticated implementations may detect rotational symmetries in the board state or other means for equivalence). key( ) returns an object such that if two board states have the same key( ) result, then the board states are equivalent.

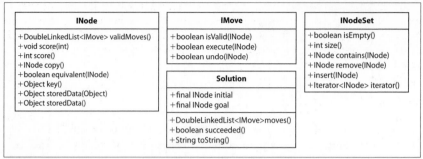

INode	IMove	INodeSet
+DoubleLinkedList<IMove> validMoves() +void score(int) +int score() +INode copy() +boolean equivalent(INode) +Object key() +Object storedData(Object) +Object storedData()	+boolean isValid(INode) +boolean execute(INode) +boolean undo(INode)	+boolean isEmpty() +int size() +INode contains(INode) +INode remove(INode) +insert(INode) +Iterator<INode> iterator()

Solution
+final INode initial +final INode goal
+DoubleLinkedList<IMove>moves() +boolean succeeded() +String toString()

Figure 7-4. Core concepts for search tree algorithms

Managing optional board state data

> storedData(Object o) associates the given object with the board state to be used by search algorithms; storedData( ) returns the optionally stored data that may be associated with the board state.

The INodeSet interface abstracts the underlying implementation of a set of INodes. Some algorithms require a queue of INodes, some a stack, and others a balanced binary tree. Once properly constructed (using the StateStorageFactory class), the provided operations enable the algorithm to manipulate the state of the INode set. The IMove interface defines how moves can manipulate the board state; the specific move classes are problem-specific, and the search algorithm need not be aware of their specific implementation.

From a programming perspective, the heart of the path-finding algorithm for a search tree is the implementation of the ISearch interface shown in Example 7-2. Given such a solution, the moves that produced the solution can be extracted.

Example 7-2. Common interface for search tree path finding

```
public interface ISearch {
  Solution search (INode initial, INode goal);
}
```

Given a node representing the initial board state and a desired goal node, an ISearch implementation will compute a path representing a solution, or return null if no solution was found. To differentiate from game trees, we use the term "board state" when discussing search tree nodes.

Key Concepts

Given a problem that seems like a game, can it be solved using the path-finding algorithms in this chapter? We'll now describe the key concepts that must be true to use the algorithms described.

Representing state

Typically, the game state captures all state information known at that position in the game. For example, in chess, the King can "castle" with the Rook only if

(a) neither piece has yet moved, (b) the intervening two squares are empty and not currently attacked by an enemy piece, and (c) the King is not currently in check. Note that (b) and (c) can be computed directly from the board state and therefore do not need to be stored; however, the game state must separately store which King and Rook have moved.

The game state stores information about the game at each node in the search tree. For games with exponentially large game trees, the state must be stored as compactly as possible. If symmetries exist in the state, such as with Connect Four®, Othello, or the 15-puzzle, then the search tree can be greatly reduced by detecting and eliminating identical states that may simply be rotated or reflected. More complex representations called *bitboards* have been used for chess, checkers, or Othello to manage the incredibly large number of states with impressive efficiency gains (Pepicelli, 2005).

Calculating available moves

At each game state, it must be possible to compute the available moves allowed to the player making the move. The term *branching factor* refers to the total number of moves that are allowed at any individual game state. For games such as tic-tac-toe, the branching factor constantly decreases from its high of nine (at the start of the game) as each mark is made. The original three-by-three Rubik's cube has (on average) a branching factor of 13.5 (Korf, 1985), whereas Connect Four has a branching factor of 7 for most of the game. Checkers is more complicated because of the rule that a player must capture a piece if that move is available. Based on the analysis of a large number of checkers databases, the branching factor for capture positions is 1.20, whereas for non-capture positions it is 7.94; Schaeffer computes the average branching factor during a game to be 6.14 (Schaeffer, 2008). The game of Go has an initial branching factor of over 360 (Berlekamp and Wolfe, 1997).

Many of the algorithms are sensitive to the order by which the available moves are attempted. Indeed, if the branching factor for a game is high and the moves are not properly ordered based upon some evaluative measure of success, then blindly searching a game tree is unlikely to lead to a solution.

Using heuristic information

An algorithm that performs a blind search does not take any advantage of the game state, but rather applies a fixed strategy. A *depth-first* blind search simply iterates through all available moves, recursively applying each one until a solution is found, backtracking to reverse bad decisions as it inexorably computes to the finish. A *breadth-first* blind search methodically explores all possible solutions with k moves before first attempting any solution with $k+1$ moves.

There are several ways to add intelligence to the search (Barr and Feigenbaum, 1981):

Select board state to expand rather than using a fixed decision
> Instead of always imposing a depth-first or a breadth-first structure, a search algorithm might alternate between these two strategies.

Select the order and number of allowed moves to be applied

When considering available moves at a board state, one should evaluate the moves that are likely to lead to a successful outcome before other moves that do not. In addition, one might want to discard out of hand specific moves that do not seem to lead to a successful outcome.

Select board states to "prune" from the search tree

As the search progresses, new knowledge may be discovered that can be used to eliminate board states that had (at one time) been selected to be part of the search.

The most common approach is to define *static evaluation functions* to evaluate the game state at intermediate points in the computation, to order the set of available moves so that moves with a higher probability of leading to a solution are tried first. Path-finding algorithms are extremely sensitive to the evaluation functions used. Indeed, poor evaluation functions can prevent these path-finding algorithms from selecting the best moves to make. As the saying goes, "garbage in, garbage out."

Instead of restricting the evaluation to the current game state, an evaluation function could temporarily expand the game tree a fixed number of moves and select the move that may ultimately lead to a game state with maximum benefit to the player. This is frowned upon in practice because of (a) the cost in performing the operations, and (b) the sharing of code logic, which should otherwise be kept separate.

In the discussion of A*SEARCH we will show sample searches over the 8-puzzle using different evaluation functions, so you can appreciate the subtle art of crafting effective functions.

A static function must take into account various features of the game tree position to return an integer score that reflects the relative strength of the position from a player's perspective. For example, the first successful program to play checkers, developed by Arthur Samuel (1959), evaluated board positions by considering two dozen features of a game, such as the "piece advantage feature" (comparing the number of pieces a player has versus her opponent) and a "winning trade feature" (trading pieces when winning but not when losing). Clearly, a game-solving engine can be a better player if its evaluation function is more accurate than a weaker one.

Maximum expansion depth

Because of limited memory resources, some search algorithms choose to selectively limit the extent to which they expand the search and game trees. This approach has its limits in games where a sequence of moves is intended to coordinate a strategy against an opponent. In chess, for example, a piece is often sacrificed for a potential advantage; if the sacrifice occurs at the edge of the maximum expansion, the advantageous game state would not be found. With a fixed expansion depth, there is a "horizon" created beyond which the search cannot see, often to the detriment of the success of the search.

Assumptions

We assume that the problems all have game states that can be represented effectively, and that there are a finite number of possible moves at each game tree or search tree node. The search space may actually be a graph, rather than a tree, because there may be multiple move sequences that reach the same state. Even so, the resulting path-finding algorithms impose a tree-like structure over the graph by evaluating linear chains of moves.

We use a made-up puzzle, which we call Tiny-Puzzle, as an example within the pseudocode descriptions of DEPTH-FIRST SEARCH, BREADTH-FIRST SEARCH, and A*SEARCH. In Tiny-Puzzle, a board state consists of two non-negative numbers, s_0 and s_1. There are two moves available at each board state—(1) increment s_0, and (2) increment s_1—thus the branching factor is 2 for this game. For example, given the initial state $<s_0=0,s_1=0>$, the goal state $<s_0=1,s_1=2>$ can be reached in three moves: increment s_1, increment s_0, and increment s_1.

Depth-First Search

DEPTH-FIRST SEARCH (Figure 7-5) attempts to locate a path to the goal state by making as much forward progress as possible without visiting the same state twice. Because some search trees explore a high number of board states, DEPTH-FIRST SEARCH is practical only if a maximum search depth is fixed in advance. DEPTH-FIRST SEARCH maintains a stack of *open* board states that have yet to be visited and a set of *closed* board states that have been visited. At each iteration, DEPTH-FIRST SEARCH pops from the stack an unvisited board state and expands it to compute the set of successor board states given the available valid moves. If the goal state is reached, then the search terminates. Any successor board states that already exist within the *closed* set are discarded. The remaining unvisited board states are pushed onto the stack of *open* board states and the search continues.

Figure 7-6 shows the computed search tree for an initial 8-puzzle board state using a depth limit of 9. Note how a path of eight moves is found to the solution (marked as GOAL) after some exploration to depth 9 in other areas of the tree. In all, 50 board states were processed and 4 remain to be explored (shown in light gray).

Input/Output

Input

The algorithm starts from an initial board state and seeks a goal state that must be reached. The algorithm assumes it can iterate through all valid moves given a board state.

Path Finding in AI

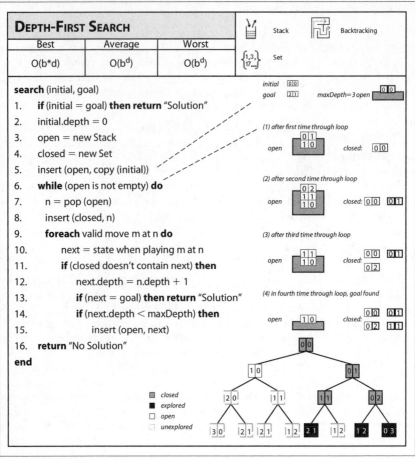

Figure 7-5. Depth-First Search fact sheet

Output

Return a sequence of moves that represents a path from the initial state to the goal state (or declare that no such solution was found given existing resources).

Assumption

For the purposes of analysis, we assume that d is the maximum depth bound for the DEPTH-FIRST SEARCH. We define b to be the branching factor for the underlying search tree.

Context

DEPTH-FIRST SEARCH is a blind search that is practical only if the predicted search space is within the memory space of the computer. One can restrict the search to stop after a fixed depth bound is reached, which enables some control over the resources used.

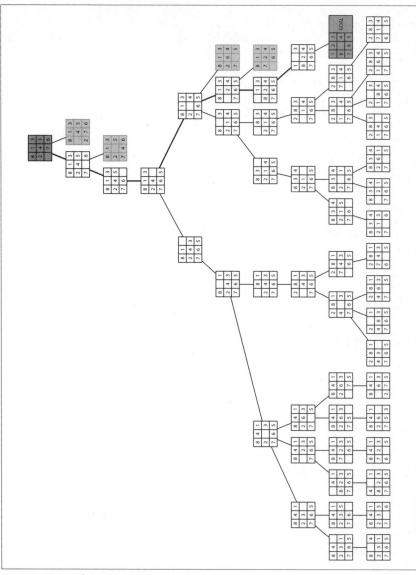

Figure 7-6. Sample Depth-First Search tree for 8-puzzle

Solution

DEPTH-FIRST SEARCH stores the set of *open* (i.e., yet to be visited) board states in a stack, and retrieves them one at a time for processing. In the implementation shown in Example 7-3, the *closed* set is stored in a hash table to efficiently determine when not to revisit a board state previously encountered within the search tree; the hash function used is based on the key computed for each INode object.

Each board state stores a reference, called a DepthTransition, that records (a) the move that generated it, (b) the previous state, and (c) the depth from the initial position. The algorithm generates copies of each board state since the moves are applied directly to the boards and not undone.

Example 7-3. Depth-First Search implementation

```
public Solution search(INode initial, INode goal) {
    // If initial is the goal, return now.
    if (initial.equals(goal)) { return new Solution (initial, goal); }

    INodeSet open = StateStorageFactory.create(OpenStateFactory.STACK);
    open.insert(initial.copy( ));

    // states we have already visited.
    INodeSet closed = StateStorageFactory.create(OpenStateFactory.HASH);
    while (!open.isEmpty( )) {
      INode n = open.remove( );
      closed.insert(n);

      DepthTransition trans = (DepthTransition) n.storedData( );

      // All successor moves translate into appended OPEN states.
      DoubleLinkedList<IMove> moves = n.validMoves( );
      for (Iterator<IMove> it = moves.iterator( ); it.hasNext( ); ) {
        IMove move = it.next( );

        // Execute move on a copy since we maintain sets of board states
        INode successor = n.copy( );
        move.execute(successor);

        // If already visited, try another state
        if (closed.contains(successor) != null) { continue; }

        int depth = 1;
        if (trans != null) { depth = trans.depth+1; }

        // Record previous move for solution trace. If solution, leave now,
        // otherwise add to the OPEN set if still within depth bound
        successor.storedData(new DepthTransition(move, n, depth));
        if (successor.equals(goal)) {
          return new Solution (initial, successor);
        }
        if (depth < depthBound) { open.insert (successor); }
      }
    }

    return new Solution (initial, goal, false);  // No solution
}
```

The implementation in Example 7-3 must be careful to store the *closed* set using a structure that efficiently determines whether a board state is already contained within that set. If, for example, a simple linked list were used, then the accumulated search times in locating an element in the closed set would begin to dominate the performance of this algorithm. Note that as soon as a successor is identified as the goal node, the search algorithm terminates (this is true for BREADTH-FIRST SEARCH as well).

Consequences

One difference between game trees and search trees is that search trees must store copies of board states during the search (witness the *open* and *closed* sets). Search algorithms over game trees typically execute and undo moves as the search progresses.

Unbridled DEPTH-FIRST SEARCH will blindly search through the search tree, potentially visiting a tremendous number of nodes without attempting potentially viable alternative paths. Ironically, using a fixed limit that is too small may result in very large search trees and fail to arrive at a solution that exists just past the depth limit of the tree.

Board states are stored to avoid visiting the same state twice. To increase performance of the algorithm, we assume there is an efficient function for the board state to generate a unique key, such that if two board states compute to the same key, then the board states are equivalent. This notion of equivalence can include board state characteristics such as symmetry. For example, the board state:

8	1	3
2	4	5
	7	6

is a 90-degree rotation of the board state:

3	5	6
1	4	7
8	2	

and could be considered to be equivalent.

DEPTH-FIRST SEARCH stores less information in its *open* set than BREADTH-FIRST SEARCH and therefore requires less space.

Analysis

The performance of the algorithm is governed by problem-specific and generic characteristics. In general, the core operations provided by the *open* and *closed* sets may unexpectedly slow the algorithm down, since naïve implementations would require $O(n)$ performance to locate a board state within the set. The key operations include:

```
open.remove( )
```
    Remove the "next" board state to evaluate

```
closed.insert(INode state)
```
    Add board state to the *closed* set

```
closed.contains(INode state)
```
    Determine whether board state already exists in *closed*

```
open.insert(INode state)
```
    Add board state into the *open* set, to be visited later

Since DEPTH-FIRST SEARCH uses a stack to store the *open* set, the remove and insert operations are performed in constant time. However, if *closed* is simply a linked list, then the execution of closed.contains(INode) may require O(*n*) performance, where *n* is the number of states in the closed set. This overhead can be eliminated by using either a tree or hash structure to store the board states; in both cases, a key value must be used (as provided by the board state class implementing INode).

The problem-specific characteristics that affect the performance are the (a) number of successor board states for an individual board state, and (b) the ordering of the valid moves. Some games have a large number of potential moves at each board state, which means that many depth-first paths may be ill-advised. Also, the way that moves are ordered will affect the overall search. If any heuristic information is available, make sure that moves most likely leading to a solution appear earlier in the ordered list of valid moves. We can also take advantage of symmetries within the board state during the search. Specifically, one can compute a key from a board state that is the same regardless of the rotation of the board (either 90, 180, or 270 degrees); additional symmetries exist (horizontal-flip or vertical-flip). Now, we can't affect the *open* state set, since for DEPTH-FIRST SEARCH this must be a stack-based data structure; however, nothing prevents us from using such space-saving measures for the *closed* state set.

We discuss the performance of DEPTH-FIRST SEARCH using a set of three examples to show how capricious the search is with seemingly slight differences in state. In each example, 10 tiles are moved from the goal state; Table 7-1 shows the results of conducting a depth-first search using varying depth bounds. Occasionally DEPTH-FIRST SEARCH penetrates quickly to locate a solution, as shown in Table 7-2; with a depth bound of 8 it finds an eight-move solution for initial state N1 after searching 25 board states (which is 2 moves better than the 10 moves we used to create N1 in the first place). Figure 7-7 illustrates the search tree size for depth-first search as depth increases. In general, the size of the search tree grows exponentially based upon the branching factor b. For the 8-puzzle, the *branching factor* is between 1.6 and 3.81, based upon where the empty tile is located (Reinefeld, 1993). The three approximation functions for the size of the search tree with depth bound of d for each of the three initial positions are:

N1: $size(n) = 0.3429 * d^{2.6978}$

N2: $size(n) = .2403 * d^{3.2554}$

N3: $size(n) = 0.2814 * d^{3.044}$

Table 7-1. Size of search tree (open + closed) for three initial positions

Depth bound d	8 1 3 / 2 4 5 / 7 6	8 1 3 / 7 2 5 / 4 6	1 4 / 7 3 2 / 6 8 5
1	1	1	1
2	3	3	3
3	7	7	7
4	15	15	15
5	31	31	31
6	51	51	51
7	90	90	90
8	25	149	150
9	37	254	259
10	54	345	113
11	81	421	195
12	105	518	293
13	168	728	401
14	216	678	400
15	328	1,133	652
16	1,374	1,991	886
17	2,121	2,786	1,443
18	729	1,954	1,897
19	1,218	3,240	3,575
20	1,601	4,350	2,211
21	1,198	5,496	7,437
22	2,634	6,315	1,740
23	4,993	11,053	6,267
24	3,881	8,031	4,214
25	6,723	20,441	11,494
26	2,071	15,074	15,681
27	5,401	10,796	26,151
28	1,206	16,233	2,081
29	1,958	33,526	22,471
UNBOUNDED	53	1,962	67,808

Table 7-2. Solutions for depth-first search tree by ply depth for three initial positions

d	N1 moves	N2 moves	N3 moves
1	0	0	0
2	0	0	0
3	0	0	0

d	N1 moves	N2 moves	N3 moves
4	0	0	0
5	0	0	0
6	0	0	0
7	0	0	0
8	8	8	0
9	8	8	0
10	8	8	10
11	8	8	10
12	12	12	10
13	12	0	10
14	8	14	14
15	8	14	14
16	10	0	14
17	10	0	10
18	12	18	10
19	12	18	10
20	20	18	10
21	20	0	14
22	20	18	22
23	20	18	10
24	24	14	22
25	8	0	18
26	26	14	26
27	20	24	0
28	28	14	28
29	28	26	18
UNBOUNDED	30	1,029	37,980

Given the size of the search trees in Figure 7-7, one wonders about the quality of the solutions produced by this effort. We make the following two observations:

An ill-chosen depth level may prevent a solution from being found

For initial position N2 and a depth of 25, no solution was found after searching 20,441 board states. How is this even possible? Because DEPTH-FIRST SEARCH will not visit the same board state twice. Specifically, the closest this particular search comes to finding the solution is on the 3,451st board state:

1	2	3
7	8	4
6		5

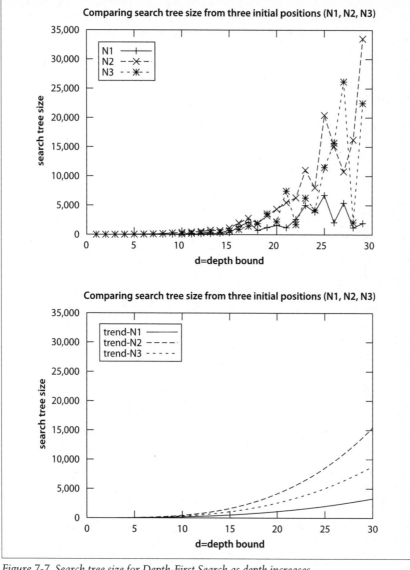

Figure 7-7. Search tree size for Depth-First Search as depth increases

which is inspected in the 25th level. This board is only three moves away from the solution! Since it was visited and not expanded upon, it was added to the *closed* set. Since the depth limit is reached, no further exploration from this state is made, and if DEPTH-FIRST SEARCH were to encounter this node at an earlier level, it would not explore further since the node exists in the *closed* set.

As the depth level increases, the solution found may be suboptimal
Note how the discovered solutions grow as the depth limit increases, sometimes to be two or three times larger than necessary.

Interestingly, given the initial board state N1, an unbounded DEPTH-FIRST SEARCH will actually find a 30-move solution after processing only 30 board states, with 23 left in its *open* set to be processed. However, this fortunate series of events is unlikely to be repeated, as you can see from the solutions that unbounded DEPTH-FIRST SEARCH found for initial board states N2 and N3.

Breadth-First Search

BREADTH-FIRST SEARCH (Figure 7-8) attempts to locate a path by methodically evaluating board states closest to the initial board state without visiting the same state twice. BREADTH-FIRST SEARCH is guaranteed to find the shortest path to the goal state, if such a path exists.

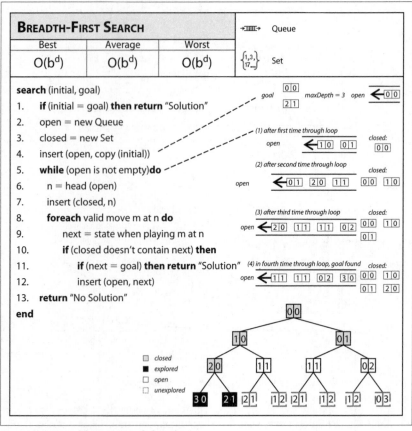

Figure 7-8. Breadth-First Search fact sheet

In truth, the only difference from DEPTH-FIRST SEARCH is that BREADTH-FIRST SEARCH maintains a queue of *open* states that have yet to be visited, whereas DEPTH-FIRST SEARCH uses a stack. At each iteration, BREADTH-FIRST SEARCH removes from the front of the queue an unvisited board state and expands it to compute the set of successor board states given the valid moves. If the goal state is reached, then the search terminates. Any successor board states that already exist within the *closed* set are discarded. The remaining unvisited board states are appended to the end of the queue of *open* board states, and the search continues.

Using the example from the 8-puzzle starting at:

2	8	3
1	6	4
7		5

the computed search tree is shown in Figure 7-9. Note how a solution is found with five moves after all paths with four moves are explored (and nearly all five-move solutions were inspected). The 20 dark-gray board states in the figure are board states in the *open* queue waiting to be inspected. In total, 25 board states were processed.

Input/Output

Input

The algorithm starts from an initial board state and seeks a goal state that must be reached. The algorithm assumes it can iterate through all valid moves given a board state.

Output

Return a sequence of moves that represents a minimal-cost solution from the initial state to the goal state (or declare that no such solution was found given existing resources).

Context

This blind search is practical only if the predicted search space is within the memory space of the computer. Since BREADTH-FIRST SEARCH methodically checks all shortest paths first, it may take quite a long time to locate paths that require a large number of moves. This algorithm may not be suitable if all that is needed is some path from its initial state to the goal (i.e., if there is no need for it to be the absolute shortest path).

Solution

BREADTH-FIRST SEARCH stores the set of *open* (i.e., yet to be visited) board states in a queue, and retrieves them one at a time from the front for processing. The *closed* set is stored using a hash table. Each board state stores a back link, called a Transition, that records the move that generated it and a reference to the previous state. BREADTH-FIRST SEARCH generates copies of each board state, since the moves are applied directly to the boards and not undone. Example 7-4 shows the implementation.

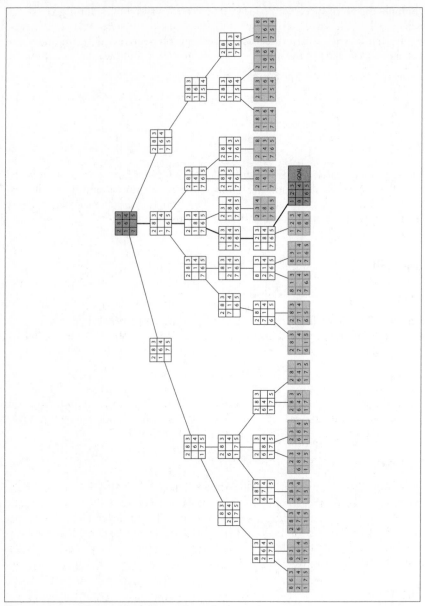

Figure 7-9. Sample Breadth-First Search tree for 8-puzzle

Example 7-4. Breadth-First Search implementation

```
public Solution search(INode initial, INode goal) {
    // Return now if initial is the goal
    if (initial.equals(goal)) { return new Solution (initial, goal); }
```

Example 7-4. Breadth-First Search implementation (continued)

```
// Start from the initial state
INodeSet open = StateStorageFactory.create(StateStorageFactory.QUEUE);
open.insert(initial.copy());

// states we have already visited.
INodeSet closed = StateStorageFactory.create(StateStorageFactory.HASH);
while (!open.isEmpty()) {
  INode n = open.remove();
  closed.insert(n);

  // All successor moves translate into appended OPEN states.
  DoubleLinkedList<IMove> moves = n.validMoves();
  for (Iterator<IMove> it = moves.iterator(); it.hasNext(); ) {
    IMove move = it.next();

    // make move on a copy
    INode successor = n.copy();
    move.execute(successor);

    // If already visited, search this state no more
    if (closed.contains(successor) != null) {
      continue;
    }

    // Record previous move for solution trace. If solution, leave
    // now, otherwise add to the OPEN set.
    successor.storedData(new Transition(move, n));
    if (successor.equals(goal)) {
      return new Solution (initial, successor);
    }
    open.insert(successor);
  }
}

return new Solution (initial, goal, false);  // No solution.
}
```

Consequences

BREADTH-FIRST SEARCH will blindly search through the search tree, potentially visiting a tremendous number of nodes while attempting all alternative paths. It is guaranteed to locate the shortest path to the solution, but to do so it maintains a large set of *open* board states. Fortunately, the *open* board states are accessed as a queue, so the removal and insertion can be performed in constant time.

Analysis

As with DEPTH-FIRST SEARCH, the performance behavior of the algorithm is governed by problem-specific and generic characteristics. The same analysis regarding the generic characteristics of DEPTH-FIRST SEARCH applies here, and the only difference is the size of the set of *open* board states. BREADTH-FIRST

SEARCH must store on the order of b^d board states in *open*, where b is the branching factor for the board states and d is the depth of the solution found. This is much higher than DEPTH-FIRST SEARCH, which only needs to store about $b*d$ board states in *open* at any one time, based upon the actively pursued board state at depth d. BREADTH-FIRST SEARCH is guaranteed to find the solution with the least number of moves that transform the initial board state to the goal board state.

A*Search

BREADTH-FIRST SEARCH finds an optimal solution (if one exists), but it may explore a tremendous number of nodes since it makes no attempt to intelligently select the order of moves to investigate. In contrast, DEPTH-FIRST SEARCH tries to rapidly find a path by making as much progress as possible when investigating moves; however, it must be bounded because otherwise it may fruitlessly search unproductive areas of the search tree. A*SEARCH adds heuristic intelligence to guide its search rather than blindly following either of these fixed strategies.

A*SEARCH, shown in Figure 7-10, is an iterative, ordered search that maintains a set of *open* board states to explore in an attempt to reach the goal state. At each search iteration, A*SEARCH uses an evaluation function $f^*(n)$ to select a board state n from *open* whose $f^*(n)$ has the smallest value. $f^*(n)$ has the distinctive structure $f^*(n)=g^*(n)+h^*(n)$, where:

$g^*(n)$ estimates shortest sequence of moves from the initial state to n

$h^*(n)$ estimates shortest sequence of moves from n to the goal state

$f^*(n)$ estimates shortest sequence of moves from initial state to goal state through n

The asterisk (*) refers to the use of heuristic information (an historical convention from when the algorithm was first defined in 1968), thus $f^*(n)$, $g^*(n)$, and $h^*(n)$ are estimates of the actual costs $f(n)$, $g(n)$, and $h(n)$, which are unknown until a solution is found. In short, having a low $f^*(n)$ score suggests that the board state n is close to the final goal state.

The most critical component of $f^*(n)$ is the heuristic evaluation that computes $h^*(n)$, since $g^*(n)$ can be computed on the fly by recording with each board state its depth from the initial state.* If $h^*(n)$ is unable to accurately separate promising board states from unpromising board states, A*SEARCH will perform no better than the blind searches already described. If, however, $h^*(n)$ can provide an accurate estimate such that $0 \le h^*(n) \le h(n)$, then $f^*(n)$ can be used to locate a minimal-cost solution.

---

* Note that $g^*(n) \ge g(n)$ because there may, in fact, be a shorter move sequence that achieves the same board state.

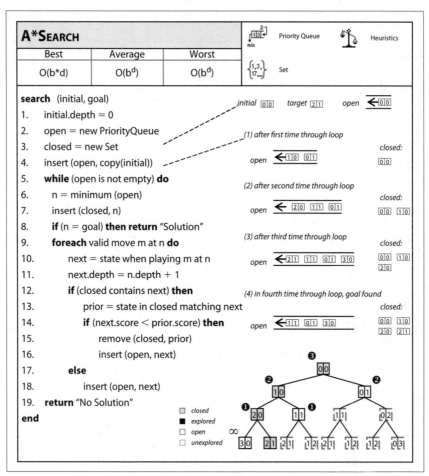

Figure 7-10. A*Search fact sheet

Input/Output

Input

The algorithm starts from an initial board state in a search tree and a goal state that must be reached. It assumes that it can (a) iterate through all valid moves for a given board state, and (b) compute the evaluation function $f^*(n)$ on a board state n.

Output

Return a sequence of moves that represents the solution that most closely approximates the minimal-cost solution from the initial state to the goal state (or declare that no such solution was found given existing resources).

Assumptions

If $0 \leq h^*(n) \leq h(n)$ and $g^*(n) \geq g(n)$, then A*SEARCH will find the minimal-cost solution, if it exists.

Context

Using the example from the 8-puzzle starting at:

8	1	3
	4	5
2	7	6

two computed search trees are shown in Figures 7-11 and 7-12. Figure 7-11 uses the GoodEvaluator $f^*(n)$ function proposed by Nilsson (1971). Figure 7-12 uses the WeakEvaluator $f^*(n)$ function also proposed by Nilsson. The light-gray board states depict the *open* set when the goal is found. Both GoodEvaluator and WeakEvaluator locate the same eight-move solution to the goal node (labeled "GOAL") but GoodEvaluator is more efficient in its search. Let's review the $f^*(n)$ values associated with the nodes in both search trees to see why the WeakEvaluator search tree explores more nodes. Observe that just two moves away from the initial state in the GoodEvaluator search tree, there is a clear path of nodes with ever-decreasing $f^*(n)$ values that lead to the goal node. In contrast, the WeakEvaluator search tree explores four moves away from the initial state before narrowing its search direction. WeakEvaluator fails to differentiate board states; indeed, note how the $f^*(n)$ value of the goal node is actually higher than the $f^*(n)$ values of the initial node and all three of its children nodes.

The $h^*(n)$ component of $f^*(n)$ must be carefully designed, and this effort is more of a craft than a science. $h^*(n)$ must be efficient to compute; otherwise, the search time becomes onerous. Much of the available A*SEARCH literature describes highly specialized $h^*(n)$ functions for different domains, such as route finding on digital terrains (Wichmann and Wuensche, 2004) or project scheduling under limited resources (Hartmann, 1999). Pearl (1984) has written an extensive (and unfortunately out-of-print) reference for designing effective heuristics. Korf (2000) discusses further strategies for designing admissible $h^*(n)$ functions. Michalewicz and Fogel (2004) provide a recent perspective on the use of heuristics in problem solving, not just for A*SEARCH.

Solution

A*SEARCH stores the *open* board states so it can efficiently remove the board state whose evaluation function is smallest. When compared with BREADTH-FIRST SEARCH and DEPTH-FIRST SEARCH, there is a subtle difference in when A*SEARCH determines that it reaches the goal. Recall that BREADTH-FIRST SEARCH and DEPTH-FIRST SEARCH check when the successor board states are generated.

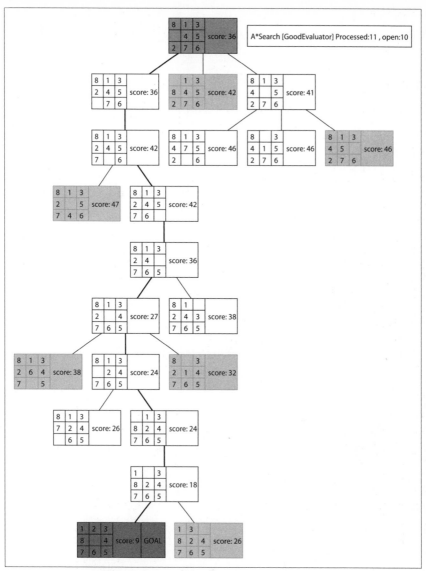

Figure 7-11. Sample A*Search tree in 8-puzzle using GoodEvaluator f*(n)

Specifically, A*SEARCH checks whether the goal state is reached only when a board state is removed from the set of *open* board states; this is done to ensure that the solution represents the shortest number of moves from the initial board state. Example 7-5 contains a sample Java implementation.

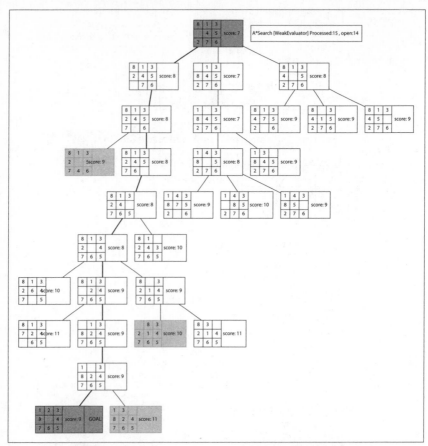

*Figure 7-12. Sample A*Search tree in 8-puzzle using WeakEvaluator f*(n)*

*Example 7-5. A*Search implementation*

```
public Solution search(INode initial, INode goal) {
  // Start from the initial state
  INodeSet open = StateStorageFactory.create(StateStorageFactory.TREE);
  INode copy = initial.copy();
  scoringFunction.score(copy);
  open.insert(copy);

  // Use Hashtable to store states we have already visited.
  INodeSet closed = StateStorageFactory.create(StateStorageFactory.HASH);
  while (!open.isEmpty()) {
```

*Example 7-5. A*Search implementation (continued)*

```
  // Remove node with smallest evaluation function and mark closed.
  INode n = open.remove();
  closed.insert(n);

  // Return if goal state reached.
  if (n.equals(goal)) { return new Solution (initial, n); }

  // Compute successor moves and update OPEN/CLOSED lists.
  DepthTransition trans = (DepthTransition) n.storedData();
  int depth = 1;
  if (trans != null) { depth = trans.depth+1; }
  DoubleLinkedList<IMove> moves = n.validMoves();
  for (Iterator<IMove> it = moves.iterator(); it.hasNext(); ) {
    IMove move = it.next();

    // Make move and score the new board state.
    INode successor = n.copy();
    move.execute(successor);

    // Record previous move for solution trace and compute
    // evaluation function to see if we have improved upon
    // a state already closed
    successor.storedData(new DepthTransition(move, n, depth));
    scoringFunction.score(successor);

    // If already visited, see if we are revisiting with lower
    // cost. If not, just continue; otherwise, pull out of closed
    // and process
    INode past = closed.contains(successor);
    if (past != null) {
      if (successor.score() >= past.score()) {
        continue;
      }

      // we revisit with our lower cost.
      closed.remove(past);
    }

    // place into open.
    open.insert (successor);
  }
}

// No solution.
return new Solution (initial, goal, false);
}
```

Path Finding in AI

As with BREADTH-FIRST SEARCH and DEPTH-FIRST SEARCH, board states are entered into the *closed* set when processed. Because A*SEARCH incorporates heuristic information that includes a $g^*(n)$ computational component, there is one situation when A*SEARCH may review a past decision on boards already visited. A board state to be inserted into the *open* set may have a lower evaluation score than an identical state that has already been visited. If so, A*SEARCH removes the past board state in *closed* so it can locate a minimum-cost solution.

Each board state stores a back link, called a `DepthTransition`, to record (a) the move that generated it, (b) a reference to the previous board state, and (c) the depth from the initial position. In A*SEARCH, the depth value is frequently used as the $g^*(n)$ component within the evaluation function. The algorithm generates copies of each board state, since the moves are applied directly to the boards and not undone.

Consequences

The success of A*SEARCH is directly dependent upon its heuristic function. If $h^*(n)$ is always zero, A*SEARCH is nothing more than BREADTH-FIRST SEARCH. However, if $h^*(n)>h(n)$, A*SEARCH may not be able to find the optimal solution, although it may be possible to return some solution, assuming that $h^*(n)$ is not wildly off the mark.

One should use A*SEARCH only if a heuristic function $h^*(n)$ is found that is *admissible*. A heuristic function is admissible if $0 \leq h^*(n) \leq h(n)$. There are two sides to this constraint. If $h^*(n)$ ever returns a negative number (stating, somehow, that the board state n is "past" the goal state), then the contribution of $g^*(n)$ is negated when computing $f^*(n)$. If $h^*(n)>h(n)$, the estimate is too high and A*SEARCH may not find the optimal solution. However, it is difficult to determine an effective $h^*(n)$ that is admissible and that can be computed effectively. There are numerous examples of inadmissible $h^*(n)$ that still lead to solutions that are practical without necessarily being optimal.

A*SEARCH will find an optimal solution if its heuristic function $h^*(n)$ is admissible. For the 8-puzzle, Table 7-3 shows the evaluation of three heuristic functions over the sample board state:

1	4	8
7	3	
6	5	2

Table 7-3. Comparing three evaluation $h^*(n)$ functions

Measure name	Description of h*(n)	Evaluation of h*(n)	Statistics
GoodEvaluator	P(n) + 3*S(n), where P(n) is the sum of the Manhattan distances that each tile is from "home." S(n) is a sequence score that checks the non-central squares in turn, allotting 2 for every tile not followed by its proper successor and 0 for every other tile, except that a piece in the center scores 1.	13+3*11=46	13-move solution closed:14 open: 12

Table 7-3. Comparing three evaluation h*(n) functions (continued)

Measure name	Description of h*(n)	Evaluation of h*(n)	Statistics
WeakEvaluator	Count number of misplaced tiles.	7	13-move solution closed:145 open:110
BadEvaluator	Take differences of opposite cells (across from the center square) and compare against the ideal of 16. Ignore blank cell.	$(7-0) + (6-8) +$ $(5-4) + (2-1) = 7$ Score is $\|16-7\|=9$	421-move solution closed: 2499 open: 1583

Forces

BREADTH-FIRST SEARCH and DEPTH-FIRST SEARCH inspect the *closed* set to see whether it contains a board state, so we used a hash table for efficiency. However, for A*SEARCH we may need to reevaluate a board state that had previously been visited if its evaluated score function is lower. Why would this happen? Recall the situation in DEPTH-FIRST SEARCH where board states at the depth limit were found to be (as it turned out) only three moves away from the goal state. These board states were placed into the *closed* set, never to be processed again. In A*SEARCH, if these same board states are revisited with a lower evaluated score, they become available again.

A*SEARCH must be able to rapidly locate the board state in the *open* set with the lowest evaluation score. Note that both BREADTH-FIRST SEARCH and DEPTH-FIRST SEARCH were able to use a constant time operation to retrieve the next board state from the open set because they were using a queue and a stack, respectively. If we stored the *open* set as an ordered list, the performance suffers because inserting a board state into the *open* set takes O(*n*); we can't use a binary heap to store the *open* set, since we don't know in advance how many board states are to be evaluated. Thus we use a balanced binary tree, which offers O(log *n*) performance for retrieving the lowest-cost board state and for inserting nodes into the *open* set.

Analysis

The computational behavior of A*SEARCH is entirely dependent upon the heuristic function. One recent result (Russel and Norvig, 2003) shows that if $|h(x)-h^*(x)|\leq log\ h^*(x)$, then the performance is O(*d*), where *d* reflects the distance to the computed solution, rather than O(b^d), where *b* represents the branching factor for the search tree. However, this condition is rather hard to satisfy; GoodEvaluator, which works so well for the 8-puzzle, for example, does not meet this criteria.

As the board states become more complex, heuristic functions become more important than ever—and more complicated to design. They must remain efficient to compute, or the entire search process is affected. However, even rough heuristic functions are capable of pruning the search space dramatically. For example, the 15-puzzle, the natural extension of the 8-puzzle, includes 15 tiles in a four-by-four board. It requires but a few minutes of work to create a 15-puzzle

GoodEvaluator based upon the logic of the 8-puzzle GoodEvaluator. With the goal state of:

1	2	3	4
5	6	7	8
9	10	11	12
13	14	15	

and an initial state of:

2	10	8	3
1	6		4
5	9	7	11
13	14	15	12

A*SEARCH rapidly locates a 15-move solution after processing 39 board states with 43 board states in the *open* set waiting to be explored, as shown in Figure 7-13.

With a 15-move limit, DEPTH-FIRST SEARCH fails to locate a solution after exploring 22,136 board states. After 172,567 board states (85,213 in the *closed* set and 87,354 remain in the *open* set), BREADTH-FIRST SEARCH ran out of memory with 64MB of RAM trying to accomplish the same task. Of course you could add more memory or increase the depth limit, but you should not expect those to be the reasons why you are able to solve these problems.

But do not be fooled by how easily A*SEARCH solved this sample 15-puzzle; when attempted on a more complicated initial board, such as:

5	1	2	4
14	9	3	7
13	10	12	6
15	11	8	

A*SEARCH runs out of memory. Clearly the rough evaluation function for the 15-puzzle is ineffective for the 15-puzzle, which has over 10^{25} possible states (Korf, 2000).

Variations

Instead of only searching forward from the initial state, some have proposed a bidirectional search algorithm using forward and backward ordered searches (Kaindl and Kainz, 1997). Initially discarded by early AI researchers as being unworkable, Kaindl and Kainz have presented powerful arguments that the approach should be reconsidered.

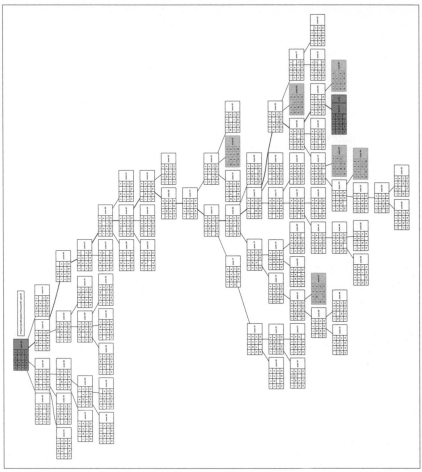

Figure 7-13. Sample A*Search tree for 15-puzzle

A common powerful alternative to A*SEARCH is known as ITERATIVEDEEPENINGA* (or IDA*), developed by Korf (1985). It relies on a series of expanding depth-first searches with a fixed cost-bound. For each successive iteration, the bound is increased based upon the results of the prior iteration. IDA* is more efficient than BREADTH-FIRST SEARCH or DEPTH-FIRST SEARCH alone since each computed cost value is based on actual move sequences rather than a heuristic estimate. Korf (2000) has described how powerful heuristics, coupled with IDA*, have been used to solve random instances of the 15-puzzle, evaluating more than 400 million board states during the search process.

Barr and Feigenbaum (1981) present several alternatives to consider when one cannot efficiently compute an admissible $h^*(n)$ function.

Related Algorithms

Although A*SEARCH produces minimal-cost solutions, the search space may be too large for A*SEARCH to complete. The major ideas that augment A*SEARCH and address these very large problems include:

Iterative deepening
> This state search strategy uses repeated iterations of limited depth-first search, with each iteration increasing the depth limit. This approach can prioritize the nodes to be searched in successive iterations, thus reducing non-productive searching and increasing the likelihood of rapidly converging on winning moves. Also, because the search space is fragmented into discrete intervals, real-time algorithms can search as much space as allowed within a time period and return a "best effort" result. First applied to A*SEARCH by (Korf, 1985) to create IDA*.

Transposition tables
> To avoid repeating computations that have already proved fruitless, one can hash game states and store in a transposition table the length of the path (from the source state) needed to reach that state. If the state appears later in the search, and its current depth is greater than what was discovered earlier, the search can be terminated. This approach can avoid searching entire subtrees that will ultimately prove to be unproductive.

Hierarchy
> If the game state can be represented as a hierarchy, rather than as a flat model, techniques can be applied to restructure large search spaces into clusters, over which A*SEARCH can be run. Hierarchical Path-Finding A* (HPA*) is an example of this approach (Botea et al., 2004).

Memory-bounded
> Instead of restricting the search space by computation time, one could perform a "lossy" search and choose to throw away various nodes as the search progresses, focusing on searches within areas that are deemed relevant. SIMPLIFIED MEMORY BOUNDED A* (SMA*) is an example (Russel, 1992).

Reinefeld and Marsland (1994) summarize a variety of interesting extensions to A*SEARCH. Much information on the use of A*SEARCH in AI systems is available in textbooks and various online sources (Barr and Feigenbaum, 1981).

Comparison

BREADTH-FIRST SEARCH is guaranteed to find the solution with the least number of moves from the initial state, although it may evaluate a rather large number of potential move sequences as it operates. DEPTH-FIRST SEARCH tries to make as much progress as possible each time it searches, and may locate a solution rather quickly, but it also may waste a lot of time on searching parts of the search tree that seem to offer no hope for success.

It is thus worthwhile to compare DEPTH-FIRST SEARCH, BREADTH-FIRST SEARCH, and A*SEARCH directly with one another. Using the 8-puzzle as our sample game, we created an initial state by randomly moving n tiles (ranging from 2, 4, 8, and 16); note that the same tile will not be moved twice in a row, since that would "undo" the move. Once n reached 32, the searches ran out of memory. For each board state, we execute BREADTH-FIRST SEARCH, DEPTH-FIRST SEARCH(n), DEPTH-FIRST SEARCH($2*n$), and A*SEARCH. For each move size n:

- We total the number of board states in the *open* and *closed* lists—this reveals the efficiency of the algorithm in locating the solution. The columns marked with # contain the average of these totals over all runs.

- We total the number of moves in the solution once found—this reveals the efficiency of the found solution paths. The columns marked with s contain the average of these totals over all runs. The number in parentheses records the number of trials that failed to locate a solution within the given ply depth.

Table 7-4 contains the aggregate results of 1,000 trials, where n random moves were made ($n=2$ through 14). Table 7-4 shows two statistics: (a) the average number of states of the generated search trees, (b) the average number of moves of the identified solutions.

Table 7-4. Comparing search algorithms

n	#A*	#BFS	#DFS(n)	#DFS (2n)	sA*	sBFS	sDFS(n)	sDFS2(n)
2	5.0	4.5	3.0	6.4	2	2	2	2
3	7.0	13.4	7.0	26.8	3	3	3	3
4	9.0	25.6	12.3	66.1	4	4	4	5.0
5	11.1	46.3	21.2	182.5	5	5	5	5.9
6	12.5	77.2	31.7	317.8	6	6	6	9.5 (45)
7	14.9	136.5	57.4	751.4	6.8	6.8	6.92	9.6 (279)
8	17.1	220.5	85.6	1095.2	7.7	7.7	7.9 (40)	13 (209)
9	22.0	367.9	147.2	2621.7	8.8	8.7	8.8 (75)	13.1 (355)
10	25.5	578.8	211.7	3152.9	9.8	9.6	9.8 (236)	16.5 (316)
11	33.1	926.4	296.6	6723.3	10.6	10.4	10.6 (431)	17.1 (369)
12	42.3	1445.7	440.8	5860.5	11.9	11.3	11.6 (350)	20.7 (402)
13	56.6	2351.3	558.9	12483.1	13.2	12.2	12.3 (615)	21.7 (313)
14	60.7	3579.7	900.3	14328.1	14.5	13.0	13.3 (593)	25.1 (259)

Note that as n increases by one, the size of the search tree grows exponentially for all blind approaches, but the A*SEARCH tree remains manageable. To be precise, the growth rates of these blind searches are estimated by the following functions:

$$DFS2(n) \cong 0.2867*n^{4.0722}$$

$$DFS(n) \cong 0.2405*n^{2.9517}$$

$$BFS(n) \cong 0.2585*n^{3.4041}$$

BREADTH-FIRST SEARCH always finds the shortest path to the solution, but note that A*SEARCH is not far behind (because of the GoodEvaluator heuristic) even though it explores significantly fewer board states. In separate trials of A*SEARCH with up to 30 random moves, the growth rate of the search tree was $O(n^{1.5147})$; although not linear, this size is significantly smaller than for the blind searches. The actual exponent in each of these growth rate functions is dependent upon the branching factor for the problem being solved. The results of Table 7-4 are shown graphically in Figure 7-14.

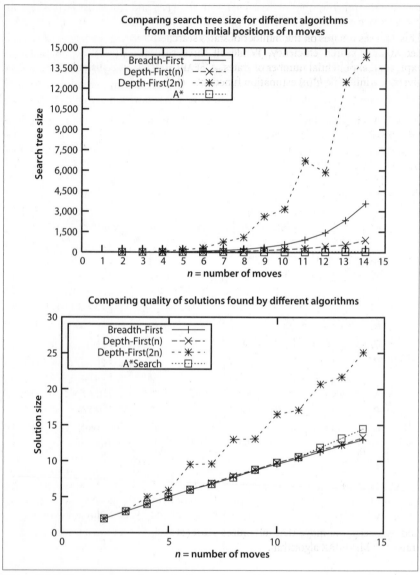

Figure 7-14. Comparing search tree size for random positions

BREADTH-FIRST SEARCH finds the shortest path to the solution, though the resulting solutions for A*SEARCH are nearly identical. Finally, note how the horizon effect prevents DEPTH-FIRST SEARCH from solving numerous cases (recall this happens when a board state node that is only a step or two away from the goal is added to the *closed* set). In fact, in this example run of 1,000 trials, DEPTH-FIRST SEARCH failed more than 60% of the time when using a maximum depth bound of 13.

This analysis focuses on the number of states searched as being the prime factor in determining search efficiency. While all three searches have the potential to explore an exponential number of states, A*SEARCH explores the smallest number given an admissible $h^*(n)$ estimation function.

There are other known ways to solve n^2-1 sliding tile puzzles besides relying on path finding. One ingenious approach proposed by Parberry (1995) is to use divide and conquer. That is, given an n-by-n puzzle, where $n>3$, first complete the leftmost column and topmost row and then recursively solve the resulting $(n-1)^2-1$ puzzle. When the inner problem to be solved is the three-by-three square, then simply use brute force. This approach is guaranteed to find a solution that uses at most 5^*n^3 moves.

We have now completed our discussion of search trees. The remaining algorithms in this chapter operate on game trees.

Minimax

Given a specific position in a game tree from the perspective of an initial player, a search program must find a move that leads to the greatest chance of victory (or at least a draw). Instead of considering only the current game state and the available moves at that state, the program must consider any countermoves that its opponent will make after it makes each move. The program must assume that the opponent will select its best move choice and make no mistakes. The program assumes there is an evaluation function score(state, player) that returns an integer representing the score of the game state from player's perspective; smaller integer numbers (which may be negative) reflect weaker positions.

The game tree is expanded by considering future game states after a sequence of n moves have been made. Each level of the tree alternates between *MAX* levels (where the goal is to benefit the player by maximizing the evaluated score of a game state) and *MIN* levels (where the goal is to benefit the opponent by minimizing the evaluated score of a game state). At alternating levels, then, the program selects a move that maximizes score(state, initial), but when the opponent is making its move, the program assumes the opponent is intelligent and so selects the move that minimizes score(state, initial). Figure 7-15 illustrates the MINIMAX algorithm.

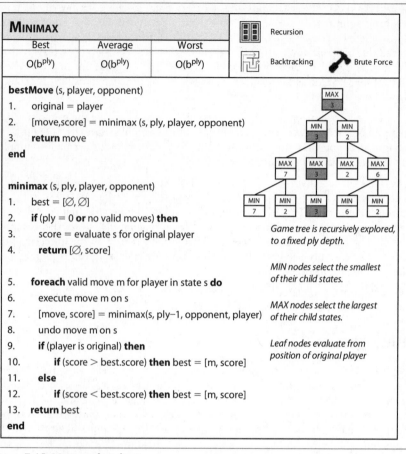

MINIMAX			
Best	Average	Worst	
$O(b^{ply})$	$O(b^{ply})$	$O(b^{ply})$	

Recursion

Backtracking   Brute Force

bestMove (s, player, opponent)
1.   original = player
2.   [move,score] = minimax (s, ply, player, opponent)
3.   **return** move
end

minimax (s, ply, player, opponent)
1.   best = [∅, ∅]
2.   **if** (ply = 0 **or** no valid moves) **then**
3.   score = evaluate s for original player
4.   **return** [∅, score]

5.   **foreach** valid move m for player in state s **do**
6.   execute move m on s
7.   [move, score] = minimax(s, ply–1, opponent, player)
8.   undo move m on s
9.   **if** (player is original) **then**
10.   **if** (score > best.score) **then** best = [m, score]
11.   **else**
12.   **if** (score < best.score) **then** best = [m, score]
13.   **return** best
end

Game tree is recursively explored, to a fixed ply depth.

MIN nodes select the smallest of their child states.

MAX nodes select the largest of their child states.

Leaf nodes evaluate from position of original player

Figure 7-15. Minimax fact sheet

Input/Output

Input

The algorithm starts from an initial position in a game tree and assumes that it can (a) iterate through all valid moves for a given player at a game state, and (b) evaluate the game state to compute an integer representing the strength of the game from a player's perspective. Smaller integer numbers reflect weaker positions. The algorithm looks ahead a fixed number of moves, called the *ply depth*.

Output

Return a move from among the valid moves that leads to the best future game state for a specific player, as determined by the evaluation function.

Assumptions

Evaluating the game state is complex, and one must resort to heuristic evaluations to determine the better game state. Indeed, developing accurate evaluation functions for games such as chess, checkers, or reversi (also known as Othello) is the greatest challenge in designing intelligent programs. We assume these evaluation functions are available.

Context

MINIMAX requires no additional bookkeeping other than the individual game state. One need only define a score(state, player) method that evaluates the game state from the perspective of a given player, where a negative number represents a weak game state for the player and a positive number represents a strong game state.

The size of the game tree is determined by the number of available moves at each game state. Assume there are b moves valid at the initial game state and that each move takes away a potential move from the opponent. If the ply depth is d, the total number of game states checked is

$$\sum_{i=1}^{d} \frac{b!}{(b-i)!}$$

where $b!$ is the factorial of b. To give an example of the scale involved, when $b=10$ and $d=6$, the total number of game states that must be evaluated is 187,300.

MINIMAX depends on the accuracy of the state evaluation function, score(state, player). During the recursive invocation within MINIMAX, this evaluation function must be consistently applied to use the *original player* for whom a move is being calculated; it must not be invoked with alternating player and opponent, or the minimum and maximum recursive evaluations will not coordinate their efforts.

Solution

The helper class MoveEvaluation pairs together an IMove and the int evaluation to be associated with that move. MINIMAX explores to a fixed ply depth, or when a game state has no valid moves for a player. The Java code in Example 7-6 returns the best move for a player in a given game state.

Example 7-6. Minimax Java implementation

```java
public class MinimaxEvaluation implements IEvaluation {
    IGameState state;      /** State to be modified during search. */
    int ply;               /** Ply depth. How far to continue search. */
    IPlayer original;      /** Evaluate all states from this perspective. */

    public MinimaxEvaluation (int ply) {
        this.ply = ply;
    }
```

Example 7-6. Minimax Java implementation (continued)

```java
    public IGameMove bestMove (IGameState s,
                               IPlayer player, IPlayer opponent) {
      this.original = player;
      this.state = s.copy( );

      MoveEvaluation me = minimax(ply, IComparator.MAX,
                                  player, opponent);
      return me.move;
    }

    private MoveEvaluation minimax (int ply, IComparator comp,
                                    IPlayer player, IPlayer opponent) {

      // If no allowed moves or a leaf node, return game state score.
      Iterator<IGameMove> it = player.validMoves(state).iterator( );
      if (ply == 0 || !it.hasNext( )) {
        return new MoveEvaluation (original.eval(state));
      }

      // Try to improve on this lower bound (based on selector).
      MoveEvaluation best = new MoveEvaluation (comp.initialValue( ));

      // Generate game states that result from all valid moves
      // for this player.
      while (it.hasNext( )) {
        IGameMove move = it.next( );
        move.execute(state);

        // Recursively evaluate position. Compute Minimax and swap
        // player and opponent, synchronously with MIN and MAX.
        MoveEvaluation me = minimax (ply-1, comp.opposite( ),
                                     opponent, player);
        move.undo(state);

        // Select maximum (minimum) of children if we are MAX (MIN)
        if (comp.compare(best.score, me.score) < 0) {
          best = new MoveEvaluation (move, me.score);
        }
      }
      return best;
    }
}
```

The *MAX* and *MIN* selectors simply evaluate scores to properly select the minimum or maximum score as desired. This implementation is simplified by defining an IComparator interface, shown in Figure 7-16, which defines *MAX* and *MIN* and consolidates how they select the best move from their perspective. Switching between the *MAX* and *MIN* selector is done using the opposite( ) method. The worst score for each of these comparators is returned by initialValue( ); the actual value is different for *MAX* and *MIN*.

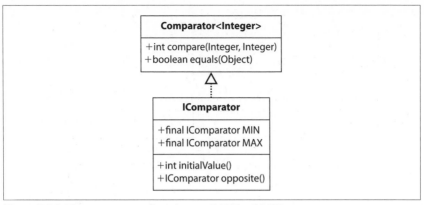

Figure 7-16. IComparator interface abstracts MAX and MIN operators

Consequences

This algorithm can rapidly become overwhelmed by the sheer number of game states generated during the recursive search. In chess, where the average number of moves on a board is often considered to be 30 (Laramée, 2000), to look ahead only five moves (i.e., $b=30$, $d=5$) requires evaluating up to 25,137,931 board positions. This value is determined by the expression:

$$\sum_{i=0}^{d} b^i$$

MINIMAX can take advantage of symmetries in the game state (such as rotations of the board or reflections) by caching past states viewed (and their respective scores), but the savings are game-specific.

Analysis

Figure 7-17 contains a two-ply exploration of an initial tic-tac-toe game state for player O using MINIMAX. The alternating levels of *MAX* and *MIN* show how the first move from the left—placing an O in the upper-left corner—is the only move that averts an immediate loss. Note that all possible game states are expanded, even when it becomes clear that the opponent X can secure a win if O makes a poor move choice.

The depth of the game tree is fixed, and each potential game state in the ply-depth sequence of moves is generated for evaluation. When there is a fixed number b of moves at each game state (or even when the number of available moves reduces by one with each level), then the total number of game states searched in a d-ply MINIMAX is on the order of $O(b^d)$, which demonstrates exponential growth.

Given the results of Figure 7-17, there must be some way to eliminate the exploration of useless game states. *MAX* tries to maximize the evaluated game state given a set of potential moves; as each move is evaluated, *MAX* computes a *maxValue* that determines the highest achievable score that player *MAX* can ensure.

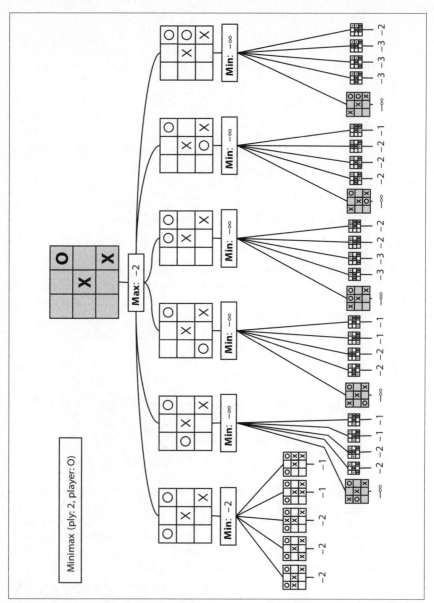

Figure 7-17. Sample Minimax exploration

Because we assume the opponent makes no mistakes, *MAX* can stop searching a *MIN* subtree once player *MIN* is able to counter with a move whose resulting game state evaluates to less than this *maxValue*. Similarly, *MIN* tries to minimize the evaluated game state given a set of potential moves; as each move is evaluated,

MIN computes a *minValue* that determines the lowest achievable score that player *MIN* can ensure. *MIN* can stop searching a *MAX* subtree once player *MAX* is able to counter with a move whose resulting game state evaluates to greater than this *minValue*. Instead of trying to deal with both of these cases (one for *MIN* and one for *MAX*), we first discuss an alternate arrangement for evaluating the game tree that uses a consistent approach, regardless of level in the game tree.

Variations

The ply depth can be eliminated if the game tree is small enough to be represented completely in memory.

NegMax

The NEGMAX algorithm replaces the alternative *MAX* and *MIN* levels of MINIMAX with a single approach used at each level of the game tree. It also forms the basis for the ALPHABETA algorithm presented next. In MINIMAX, the game state is always evaluated from the perspective of the player making the initial move (which requires that this piece of information is stored for use within the evaluation function).

Instead of viewing a game tree as alternating levels where the original player must maximize its score or minimize its opponent's score, NEGMAX consistently seeks the move that produces the maximum of the negative values of a state's children nodes. Intuitively, after a player has made its move, the opponent will try to make its best move; thus, to find the best move for a player, select the one that restricts the opponent from scoring too highly. If you compare the pseudocode examples in Figures 7-15 and 7-18, you will see two identical game trees in MINIMAX and in NEGMAX; the only difference is how the game states are scored. Note that the first of the two available moves for the original player is the best choice, since the opponent is restricted the most.

Input/Output

Input and output are the same as for MINIMAX.

Context

Context is the same as for MINIMAX.

Solution

In Example 7-7, note that the score for each MoveEvaluation is simply the evaluation of the game state from the perspective of the player making that move. Reorienting each evaluation toward the player making the move simplifies the algorithm implementation.

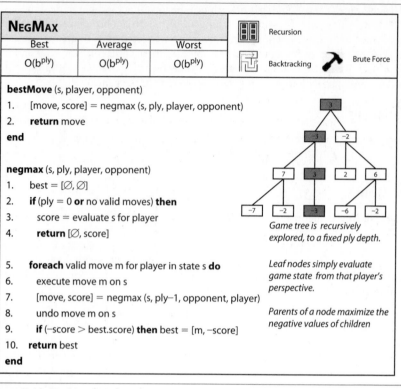

NEGMAX			Recursion
Best	Average	Worst	
$O(b^{ply})$	$O(b^{ply})$	$O(b^{ply})$	Backtracking Brute Force

bestMove (s, player, opponent)
1.   [move, score] = negmax (s, ply, player, opponent)
2.   **return** move
end

negmax (s, ply, player, opponent)
1.   best = [∅, ∅]
2.   **if** (ply = 0 **or** no valid moves) **then**
3.   score = evaluate s for player
4.   **return** [∅, score]

5.   **foreach** valid move m for player in state s **do**
6.   execute move m on s
7.   [move, score] = negmax (s, ply–1, opponent, player)
8.   undo move m on s
9.   **if** (–score > best.score) **then** best = [m, –score]
10. **return** best
end

Game tree is recursively explored, to a fixed ply depth.

Leaf nodes simply evaluate game state from that player's perspective.

Parents of a node maximize the negative values of children

Figure 7-18. NegMax fact sheet

Example 7-7. NegMax implementation

```java
public class NegMaxEvaluation implements IEvaluation {

    IGameState state;      /** State to be modified during search. */
    int ply;               /** Ply depth. How far to continue search. */

    public NegMaxEvaluation (int ply) {
        this.ply = ply;
    }

    public IGameMove bestMove (IGameState s,
                               IPlayer player, IPlayer opponent) {
        this.state = s.copy();
        MoveEvaluation me = negmax(ply, player, opponent);
        return me.move;
    }

    public MoveEvaluation negmax (int ply, IPlayer player, IPlayer opponent) {

        // If no allowed moves or a leaf node, return board state score.
        Iterator<IGameMove> it = player.validMoves(state).iterator();
        if (ply == 0 || !it.hasNext()) {
```

Example 7-7. NegMax implementation (continued)

```
            return new MoveEvaluation(player.eval(state));
        }

        // Try to improve on this lower-bound move.
        MoveEvaluation best = new MoveEvaluation (MoveEvaluation.minimum( ));

        // get moves for this player and generate the boards that result from
        // making these moves. Select maximum of the negative scores of children.
        while (it.hasNext( )) {
            IGameMove move = it.next( );
            move.execute(state);

            // Recursively evaluate position using consistent negmax.
            // Treat score as negative value.
            MoveEvaluation me = negmax (ply-1, opponent, player);
            move.undo(state);

            if (-me.score > best.score) {
                best = new MoveEvaluation (move, -me.score);
            }
        }

        return best;
    }
}
```

Consequences

NEGMAX is useful because it prepares a simple foundation on which to extend to ALPHABETA if required. Because board scores are routinely negated in this algorithm, we must be careful to choose values for the evaluation of winning and losing states. Specifically, the minimum value must be the negated value of the maximum value. Note that Integer.MIN_VALUE (in Java this is defined as 0x80000000 or −2,147,483,648) is not the negated value of Integer.MAX_VALUE (in Java, defined as 0x7fffffff or 2,147,483,647). For this reason, we use Integer.MIN_VALUE+1 as the minimum value, which is retrieved by the static function MoveEvaluation.minimum( ). For completeness, we provide MoveEvaluation.maximum( ) as well.

Analysis

Figure 7-19 contains a two-ply exploration of an initial tic-tac-toe game state for player O using NEGMAX. Note that all possible game states are expanded, even when it becomes clear that the opponent X can secure a win if O makes a poor move choice. The scores associated with each of the leaf game states are evaluated from that player's perspective (in this case, the original player O). Note how the score for the initial game state is −2, because that is the "maximum of the negative scores of its children."

The number of states explored by NEGMAX is the same as MINIMAX, or on the order of b^d for a d-ply search with a fixed number b of moves at each game state.

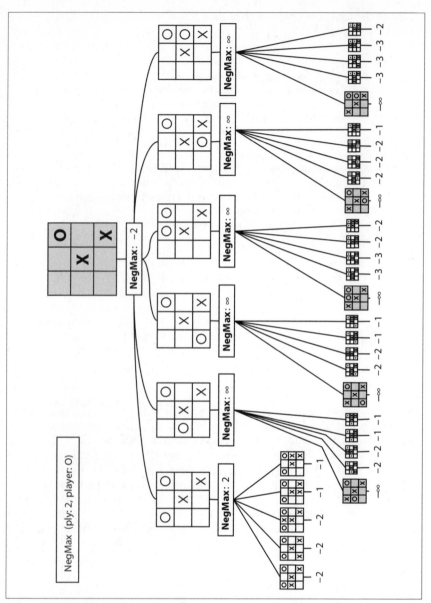

Figure 7-19. Sample NegMax exploration

One last observation is how NEGMAX handles the leaf nodes in the game tree (e.g., when the decreasing value of ply finally hits zero). As you can see from the code in Example 7-7, these leaf node game states are all evaluated from that final player's perspective, which means the selected MoveEvaluation for the parent nodes of these leaf nodes is simply the maximum over these leaf nodes.

NEGMAX streamlines the algorithm since there is no longer a need to alternate between *MAX* and *MIN* nodes evaluating the common state function. Recall how MINIMAX required the scoring function to always be evaluated from the perspective of the player for whom the initial move is desired? In NEGMAX, it is imperative that the game state is evaluated based upon the player making the move. The reason is that the search algorithm selects the child node that is "the maximum of the negative value of all children."

AlphaBeta

The MINIMAX algorithm properly evaluates a player's best move when considering the opponent's countermoves. However, this information is not used while the game tree is generated! Consider the BoardEvaluation scoring function introduced earlier. Recall Figure 7-17, which shows the partial expansion of the game tree from an initial game state after X has made two moves and O has made just one move.

Note how MINIMAX plods along even though each of the subsequent searches reveals a losing board if X is able to complete the diagonal. A total of 36 nodes is evaluated. MINIMAX takes no advantage of the fact that the original decision for O to play in the upper-left corner prevented X from scoring an immediate victory. Instead of seeking ad-hoc strategies to use past information found during the search, ALPHABETA (Figure 7-20) defines a consistent strategy to prune unproductive searches from the search tree. Using ALPHABETA, the equivalent expansion of the game tree is shown in Figure 7-21.

As ALPHABETA searches for the best move, it remembers that X can score no higher than 2 if O plays in the upper-left corner. For each subsequent other move for O, ALPHABETA determines that X has at least one countermove that outperforms the first move for O (indeed, in all cases X can win). Thus, the game tree expands only 16 nodes (a savings of more than 50% from MINIMAX). More importantly, there is no need to compute potential moves and modify state when the end result is not going to matter.

ALPHABETA selects the same move that MINIMAX would have selected, with potentially significant performance savings. As with the other path-finding algorithms already described in this chapter, ALPHABETA assumes that players make no mistakes, and it avoids exploring parts of the game tree that will have no impact on the game under this assumption.

ALPHABETA recursively searches through the game tree and maintains two values, α and β, that define a "window of opportunity" for a player as long as $\alpha<\beta$. The value α represents the lower bound of the game states found for the player so far (or $-\infty$ if none have been found) and declares that the player has found a move to ensure it can score at least that value. Higher values of α mean the player is doing well; when $\alpha=+\infty$, the player has found a winning move and the search can terminate. The value β represents the upper bound of game states so far (or $+\infty$ if none have been found) and declares the maximum board that the player can achieve. When β drops lower and lower, it means that the opponent is doing better at restricting the player's options. Since ALPHABETA has a maximum ply depth beyond which it will not search, any decisions that it makes are limited to this scope.

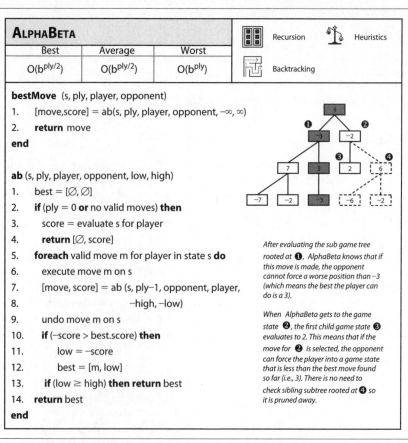

AlphaBeta

Best	Average	Worst
$O(b^{ply/2})$	$O(b^{ply/2})$	$O(b^{ply})$

Recursion   Heuristics

Backtracking

bestMove (s, ply, player, opponent)
1.   [move,score] = ab(s, ply, player, opponent, −∞, ∞)
2.   **return** move
end

ab (s, ply, player, opponent, low, high)
1.   best = [∅, ∅]
2.   **if** (ply = 0 **or** no valid moves) **then**
3.   score = evaluate s for player
4.   **return** [∅, score]
5.   **foreach** valid move m for player in state s **do**
6.   execute move m on s
7.   [move, score] = ab (s, ply−1, opponent, player,
8.   −high, −low)
9.   undo move m on s
10.   **if** (−score > best.score) **then**
11.   low = −score
12.   best = [m, low]
13.   **if** (low ≥ high) **then return** best
14. **return** best
end

After evaluating the sub game tree rooted at ❶, AlphaBeta knows that if this move is made, the opponent cannot force a worse position than −3 (which means the best the player can do is a 3).

When AlphaBeta gets to the game state ❷, the first child game state ❸ evaluates to 2. This means that if the move for ❷ is selected, the opponent can force the player into a game state that is less than the best move found so far (i.e., 3). There is no need to check sibling subtree rooted at ❹ so it is pruned away.

Figure 7-20. AlphaBeta fact sheet

The game tree in Figure 7-21 shows the [α,β] values as ALPHABETA executes; initially they are [−∞,∞]. With a two-ply search, ALPHABETA is trying to find the best move for O when considering just the immediate countermove for X. Since ALPHABETA is recursive, we can retrace its progress by considering a traversal of the game tree. The first move ALPHABETA considers is for O to play in the upper-left corner. After all five of X's countermoves are evaluated, it is evident that X can only ensure a score of −2 for itself (using the static evaluation BoardEvaluation for tic-tac-toe). When ALPHABETA considers the second move for O (playing in the middle of the left column), its [α,β] values are now [−2,∞], which means "the worst that O can end up with so far is a state whose score is −2, and the best that O can do is still win the game." When the first countermove for X is evaluated, ALPHABETA detects that X has won, which falls outside of this "window of opportunity," so further countermoves by X no longer need to be considered.

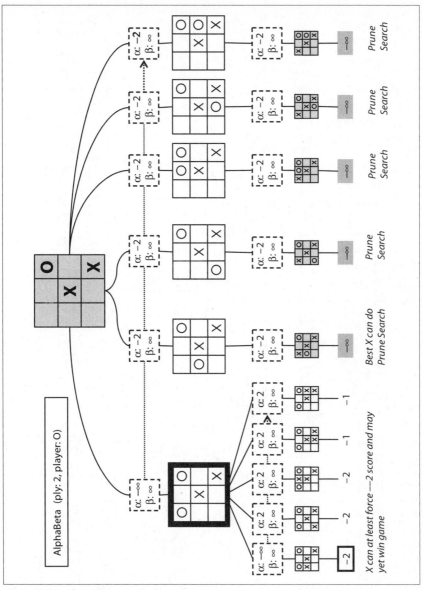

Figure 7-21. AlphaBeta two-ply search

Recall that ALPHABETA is based on NEGMAX, the MINIMAX variant that seeks to maximize the negative score of the opposing player at each level. ALPHABETA ensures that non-productive nodes are not searched. To explain the way ALPHA-BETA prunes the game tree, Figure 7-22 presents a three-ply search of Figure 7-17 that expands 66 nodes (whereas the corresponding MINIMAX game tree would require 156 nodes).

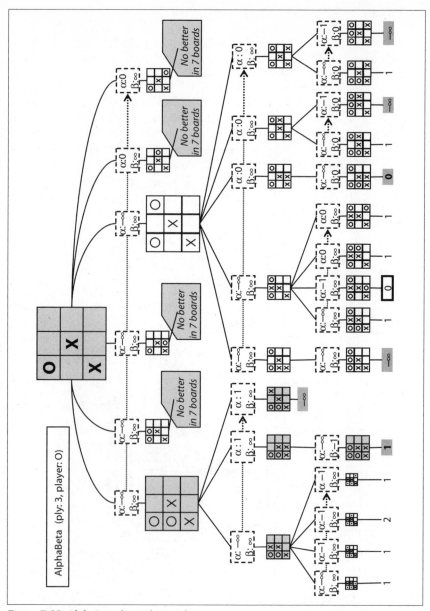

Figure 7-22. AlphaBeta three-ply search

At the initial node *n* in the game tree, player O must consider one of six potential moves. Pruning can occur either on the player's turn or the opponent's turn. In the search shown in Figure 7-22, there are two such examples:

Player's turn

Assume O plays in the middle of the left column and X responds by playing in the middle of the top row (this is the leftmost grandchild of the root node in the search tree). Now, from O's perspective, the best score that O can force is −1 (note that in the diagram the scores are shown as 1 since ALPHA-BETA uses NEGMAX to score its children). This value is remembered when we try to determine what O can achieve if X had instead countered by playing in the middle of the bottom row. Note that [α,β] is now [−∞ ,−1]. ALPHABETA evaluates the result when O plays in the middle of the top row and computes the score 1. Since this value is greater than or equal to the −1 value, the remaining three potential moves for O in this level are ignored.

Opponent's turn

Assume O plays in the middle of the left column and X responds by playing in the upper-right corner, immediately winning the game. ALPHABETA does not have to consider X's two other potential moves, since O will prune the remaining search nodes in the search subtree "rooted" in the decision to play in the middle of the left column.

The pruning of the search occurs when α≥β, or in other words, when the "window of opportunity" closes. When ALPHABETA is based on MINIMAX, there are two ways to prune the search, known as α-prune and β-prune; in the simpler ALPHABETA based on NEGMAX, these two cases are combined into the one discussed here. Because ALPHABETA is recursive, the range [α,β] represents the window of opportunity for the player, and the window of opportunity for the opponent is [−β,−α]. Within the recursive invocation of ALPHABETA the player and opponent are swapped, and the window is similarly swapped. ALPHABETA always returns the same move that MINIMAX (or NEGMAX, for that matter) would have returned; it just requires less expansion of the game tree. ALPHABETA still seeks to expand a tree to a fixed depth, and so in this regard it behaves similarly to DEPTH-FIRST SEARCH.

Input/Output

Input and output are the same as for MINIMAX. The primary distinction is that ALPHABETA takes advantage of the calculated states when determining whether to continue searching a particular subtree.

Solution

The ALPHABETA implementation shown in Example 7-8 augments NEGMAX by terminating early the evaluation of a set of game states once it becomes clear that either the player can't guarantee a better position (the α-prune) or the opponent can't force a worse position (the β-prune).

Example 7-8. AlphaBeta implementation

```
public class AlphaBetaEvaluation implements IEvaluation {
    IGameState state;    /** State to be modified during search. */
    int ply;             /** Ply depth. How far to continue search. */

    public AlphaBetaEvaluation (int ply) { this.ply = ply; }
```

Example 7-8. AlphaBeta implementation (continued)

```
    public IGameMove bestMove (IGameState s,
                               IPlayer player, IPlayer opponent) {
      this.state = s.copy( );
      MoveEvaluation move = alphabeta(ply, player, opponent,
              MoveEvaluation.minimum( ), MoveEvaluation.maximum( ));
      return move.move;
    }

    private MoveEvaluation alphabeta (int ply, IPlayer player, IPlayer opponent,
                                      int alpha, int beta) {
      // If no moves, return evaluation of board from player's perspective.
      Iterator<IGameMove> it = player.validMoves(state).iterator( );
      if (ply == 0 || !it.hasNext( )) {
        return new MoveEvaluation (player.eval(state));
      }

      // Select "maximum of negative value of children" that improves alpha
      MoveEvaluation best = new MoveEvaluation (alpha);
      while (it.hasNext( )) {
        IGameMove move = it.next( );

        // Recursively evaluate position.
        move.execute(state);
        MoveEvaluation me = alphabeta (ply-1, opponent, player, -beta, -alpha);
        move.undo(state);

        // If improved upon alpha, keep track of this move.
        if (-me.score > alpha) {
          alpha = -me.score;
          best = new MoveEvaluation (move, alpha);
        }
        if (alpha >= beta) { return best; } // search no longer productive.
      }
      return best;
    }
}
```

Consequences

Since the resulting moves will be exactly the same as if MINIMAX had executed, the primary consequence is reduced execution time, since a number of states are going to be removed from the expanded game tree.

Analysis

Because ALPHABETA returns the same computed move as MINIMAX and NEGMAX, one way to measure the benefit of ALPHABETA is to determine the savings from the size of the game tree. This task is complicated because ALPHA-BETA will show its most impressive savings if the opponent's best move is evaluated first whenever ALPHABETA executes. When there is a fixed number b of moves at each game state, the total number of potential game states to search in a d-ply ALPHABETA is on the order of b^d. If the moves are ordered by decreasing favorability (i.e., the best move first), then we still have to evaluate all b children for the initiating player (since we are to choose his best move); however, in the best case we only need to evaluate the first move by the opponent. Note in Figure 7-21 that, because of move ordering, the prune occurs after several moves have been evaluated, so the move ordering for that game tree is not optimal.

In the best case, therefore, ALPHABETA evaluates b game states for the initial player on each level, but only one game state for the opponent. So, instead of expanding $b*b*b*...*b*b$ (a total of d times) game states on the dth level of the game tree, ALPHABETA may require only $b*1*b*...*b*1$ (a total of d times). The resulting number of game states is $b^{d/2}$, an impressive savings.

Instead of simply trying to minimize the number of game states, ALPHABETA could explore the same total number of game states as MINIMAX, but instead this would extend the depth of the game tree to $2*d$, thus doubling how far ahead the algorithm can look.

To empirically evaluate MINIMAX and ALPHABETA, we construct a set of initial tic-tac-toe board states that are possible after k moves have been made. We then compute MINIMAX and ALPHABETA with a ply of $d=9-k$, which ensures all possible moves are explored. The results are shown in Table 7-5. Observe the significant reduction of explored states using ALPHABETA.

Table 7-5. Statistics comparing Minimax versus AlphaBeta

k	Minimax states	AlphaBeta states	Aggregate reduction	Individual variation
1	549,945	27,565	95%	±1.3%
2	549,936	47,508	91%	±6.8%
3	549,864	112,086	80%	±10.2%

Individual comparisons show the dramatic improvement of ALPHABETA and some of these cases explain why ALPHABETA is so powerful. On the game state:

ALPHABETA explores only 47 game states (instead of 8,232 for MINIMAX, a 99.4% reduction) to determine that player X should select the center square, after which a win is assured. However, the only way to achieve such deep reductions is if the available moves are ordered such that the best move appears first. Since our tic-tac-toe solution does not order moves, some anomalies will result. For example, given the same board state rotated 180 degrees:

ALPHABETA will explore 960 game states (an 88.3% reduction).

References

Barr, Avron and Edward A. Feigenbaum, *The Handbook of Artificial Intelligence*. William Kaufmann, Inc., 1981.

Berlekamp, Elwyn and David Wolfe, *Mathematical Go: Chilling Gets the Last Point*. A. K. Peters Ltd., May 1997.

Botea, A., M. Müller, and J. Schaeffer, "Near Optimal Hierarchical Path-finding," Journal of Game Development, 1(1), 2004, *http://www.jogd.com/Vol1issue1.html*.

Hartmann, Sonke, *Project Scheduling Under Limited Resources: Models, Methods, and Applications*. Springer, 1999.

Kaindl, Hermann and Gerhard Kainz, "Bidirectional Heuristic Search Reconsidered," *Journal of Artificial Intelligence Research*, Volume 7: 283–317, 1997.

Korf, Richard E., "Depth-First Iterative-Deepening: An Optimal Admissible Tree Search," *Artificial Intelligence*, Volume 27: 97–109, 1985, *http://citeseerx.ist.psu.edu/viewdoc/summary?doi=10.1.1.91.288*.

Korf, Richard E., "Recent Progress in the Design and Analysis of Admissible Heuristic Functions," Proceedings, Abstraction, Reformulation, and Approximation: 4th International Symposium (SARA), Lecture notes in Computer Science #1864: 45–51, 2000.

Laramée, François Dominic, "Chess Programming Part IV: Basic Search," GameDev.net, August 26, 2000, *http://www.gamedev.net/reference/articles/article1171.asp*.

Michalewicz, Zbigniew and David B. Fogel, *How to Solve It: Modern Heuristics*, Second Edition. Springer, 2004.

Nilsson, Nils, *Problem-Solving Methods in Artificial Intelligence*. McGraw-Hill, 1971.

Parberry, Ian, "A Real-Time Algorithm for the (n^2-1)-Puzzle," *Information Processing Letters*, Volume 56: 23–28, 1995, *http://www.eng.unt.edu/ian/pubs/saml.pdf*.

Pearl, Judea, *Heuristics: Intelligent Search Strategies for Computer Problem Solving*. Addison-Wesley, 1984.

Pepicelli, Glen, "Bitwise Optimization in Java: Bitfields, Bitboards, and Beyond," O'Reilly on Java.com, February 2, 2005, *http://www.onjava.com/pub/a/onjava/2005/02/02/bitsets.html*.

Reinefeld, Alexander, "Complete Solution of the Eight-Puzzle and the Benefit of Node Ordering in IDA*," Proceedings of the 13th International Joint Conference on Artificial Intelligence (IJCAI), Volume 1, 1993, *http://citeseerx.ist.psu.edu/viewdoc/summary?doi=10.1.1.40.9889*.

Reinefeld, Alexander and T. Anthony Marsland, "Enhanced Iterative-Deepening Search," *IEEE Transactions on Pattern Analysis and Machine Intelligence*, 16(7): 701–710, 1994. *http://citeseer.ist.psu.edu/article/reinefeld94enhanced.html*.

Russel, Stuart, "Efficient memory-bounded search methods," Proceedings, 10th European Conference on Artificial Intelligence (ECAI): 1–5, 1992.

Russell, S. J. and P. Norvig, *Artificial Intelligence: A Modern Approach*. Prentice Hall, 2003.

Samuel, Arthur, "Some Studies in Machine Learning Using the Game of Checkers," *IBM Journal* 3(3): 210–229, *http://www.research.ibm.com/journal/rd/033/ibmrd0303B.pdf*.

Schaeffer, Jonathan, "Game Over: Black to Play and Draw in Checkers," *Journal of the International Computer Games Association* (ICGA), *http://www.cs.unimaas.nl/icga/journal/contents/Schaeffer07-01-08.pdf*.

Schaeffer, Jonathan, Neil Burch, Yngvi Björnsson, Akihiro Kishimoto, Martin Müller, Robert Lake, Paul Lu, and Steve Sutphen, "Checkers is Solved," *Science Magazine*, September 14, 2007, 317(5844): 1518–1522, *http://www.sciencemag.org/cgi/content/abstract/317/5844/1518*.

Shannon, Claude, "Programming a Computer for Playing Chess," *Philosophical Magazine*, 41(314), 1950, *http://tinyurl.com/ChessShannon-pdf*.

Wichmann, Daniel R. and Burkhard C. Wuensche, "Automated Route Finding on Digital Terrains," Proceedings of IVCNZ, Akaroa, New Zealand, pp. 107–112, November 2004, *http://www.cs.auckland.ac.nz/~burkhard/Publications/IVCNZ04_WichmannWuensche.pdf*.

Path Finding in AI

8

Network Flow Algorithms

Overview

There are numerous problems that can be viewed as a network of vertices and edges, with a capacity associated with each edge over which commodities flow. The algorithms found in this chapter are, in many ways, the direct product of the need to solve these specific classes of problems. Ahuja (1993) contains an extensive discussion on numerous applications of network flow algorithms:

Assignment
> Given a set of tasks to be carried out by a set of employees, find an assignment that minimizes the overall expense when different employees may cost different amounts based upon the task to which they are assigned.

Bipartite Matching
> Given a set of applicants who have been interviewed for a set of job openings, find a matching that maximizes the number of applicants selected for jobs for which they are qualified.

Transportation
> Determine the most cost-effective way to ship goods from a set of supplying factories to a set of retail stores selling these goods.

Transshipment
> Determine the most cost-effective way to ship goods from a set of supplying factories to a set of retail stores selling these goods, while potentially using a set of warehouses as intermediate stations.

Maximum Flow
> Given a network that shows the potential capacity over which goods can be shipped between two locations, compute the maximum flow supported by the network.

One way to explain how these specialized problems are solved is to describe the relationship between network flow problems. Figure 8-1 shows the relationships between these problems in thin, labeled rectangles, with brief descriptions in the larger boxes. A more general instance of a problem is related to a more specific instance of the problem by a directed edge. For example, the Transportation problem is a specialized instance of the Transshipment problem because transportation graphs do not contain intermediate transshipment nodes. Thus a program that solves the Transshipment problem can be immediately applied to solve Transportation problems.

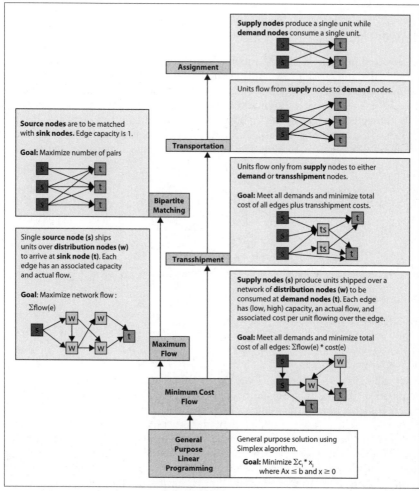

Figure 8-1. Relationship between network flow problems

In this chapter we present the FORD-FULKERSON algorithm, which solves the Maximum Flow problem. FORD-FULKERSON can be immediately applied to solve Bipartite Matching problems, as shown in Figure 8-1. Upon further reflection, the approach outlined in FORD-FULKERSON can be generalized to solve the more powerful Minimal Cost Flow problem, which enables us to immediately solve the Transshipment, Transportation, and Assignment problems.

In principle, you could apply Linear Programming (LP) to all of the problems shown in Figure 8-1, but then you would have to convert these problems into the proper LP form, whose solution would then have to be recast into the original problem. We'll show an example using LP to solve a flow network problem at the end of the chapter. In practice, however, the specialized algorithms described in this chapter outperform LP by several orders of magnitude for the problems shown in Figure 8-1.

Network Flow

As depicted in Figure 8-2, the common abstraction that models a flow network is a directed graph $G=(V,E)$, where V is the set of vertices and E is the set of edges over these vertices. The graph itself is typically connected (though not every edge need be present). A special source vertex $s \in V$ produces units of a commodity that flow through the edges of the graph to be consumed by a sink vertex $t \in V$ (also known as the *target* or *terminus*). A flow network assumes that the supply of units produced is infinite and that the sink vertex can consume all units it receives.

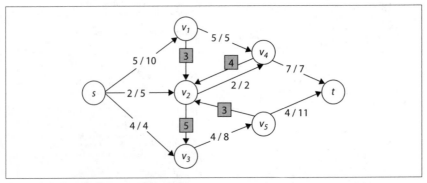

Figure 8-2. Sample flow network graph

Each edge (u,v) has a flow $f(u,v)$ that defines the number of units of the commodity that flows from u to v. An edge also has a capacity $c(u,v)$ that constrains the maximum number of units that can flow over that edge. In Figure 8-2, each vertex is numbered (with vertices s and t clearly marked) and each edge is labeled as f/c, showing the flow over that edge and the maximum possible flow. The edge between s and v_1, for example, is labeled 5/10, meaning that 5 units flow over that edge, which can sustain a capacity of up to 10. When no units are flowing over an edge (as is the case with the edge between v_5 and v_2), only the capacity is shown, outlined in a gray box.

The following criteria must be satisfied for any feasible flow f through a network:

Capacity constraint

The flow $f(u,v)$ through an edge cannot be negative and cannot exceed the capacity of the edge $c(u,v)$, $0 \le f(u,v) \le c(u,v)$. If an edge (u,v) doesn't exist in the network, then $c(u,v)=0$.

Flow conservation

Aside from the source vertex s and sink vertex t, each vertex $u \in V$ must satisfy the property that the sum of $f(v,u)$ for all edges (v,u) in E (the flow into u) must equal the sum of $f(u,w)$ for all edges $(u,w) \in E$ (the flow out of u). This property ensures that flow is neither produced nor consumed in the network, except at s and t.

Skew symmetry

For consistency, the quantity $f(v,u)$ represents the net flow from vertex u to v. This means that it must be the case that $f(u,v)=-f(v,u)$; this holds even if both edges (u,v) and (v,u) exist in a directed graph (as they do in Figure 8-2).

In the ensuing algorithms we refer to a network path that is a non-cyclic path of unique vertices $<v_1,v_2,...,v_n>$ involving $n-1$ consecutive edges (v_i,v_j) in E. In the directed graph shown in Figure 8-2, one possible network path is $<v_3,v_5,v_2,v_4>$. In a network path, the direction of the edges can be ignored. In Figure 8-3, a possible network path is $<s,v_1,v_4,v_2,v_3,t>$.

Maximum Flow

Given a flow network, it is possible to compute the maximum flow (*mf*) between vertices s and t given the capacity constraints $c(u,v) \ge 0$ for all directed edges $e=(u,v)$ in E. That is, compute the largest amount that can flow out of source s, through the network, and into sink t given specific capacity limits on individual edges. Starting with a feasible flow (a flow of 0 through every edge is feasible), FORD-FULKERSON (Figure 8-3) successively locates an *augmenting path* through the network from s to t to which more flow can be added. The algorithm terminates when no augmenting paths can be found. The Max-flow Min-cut theorem (Ford-Fulkerson, 1962) guarantees that with non-negative flows and capacities, FORD-FULKERSON always terminates and identifies the maximum flow in a network.

Input/Output

In this presentation, we describe FORD-FULKERSON using linked lists to store edges. Each vertex u maintains two separate lists: forward edges for the edges emanating from u and backward edges for the edges coming into u; thus each edge appears in two lists, doubling the total storage. The code repository provided with this book contains an implementation using a two-dimensional matrix to store edges, a more appropriate data structure to use for dense flow network graphs.

FORD-FULKERSON			Weighted Directed Graph	Greedy
Best	Average	Worst		
O(E*mf)	O(E*mf)	O(E*mf)	Array	

compute (G)

1. **while** (find augmenting path in G) **do**
2.   processPath (path)

end

processPath (path)

1. v = sink
2. delta = ∞
3. **while** (v ≠ source) do
4.   u = vertex previous to v in path
5.   **if** (edge (u,v) is forward) **then**
6.   t = (u,v).capacity − (u,v).flow
7.   **else** t = (v,u).flow
8.   **if** (t < delta) **then** delta = t
9.   v = u

10. v = sink
11. **while** (v ≠ source) **do**
12.   u = vertex previous to v in path
13.   **if** (edge (u,v) is forward) **then**
14.   (u,v).flow += delta
15.   **else** (v,u).flow −= delta
16.   v = u

end

Augment path <s,2,4,t> with 2 units.

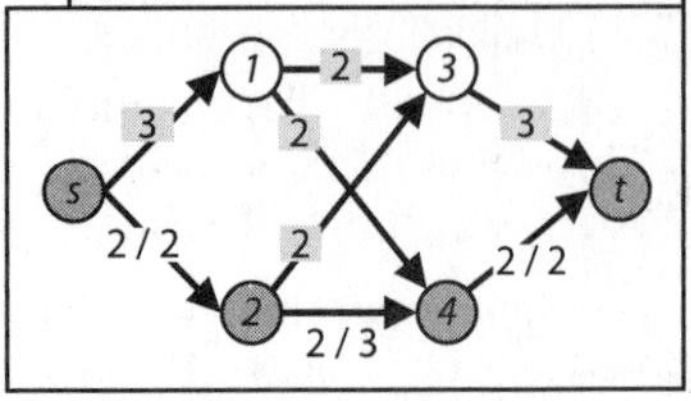

Augment <s,1,3,t> with 2 units. See how edge (3,t) is under-used.

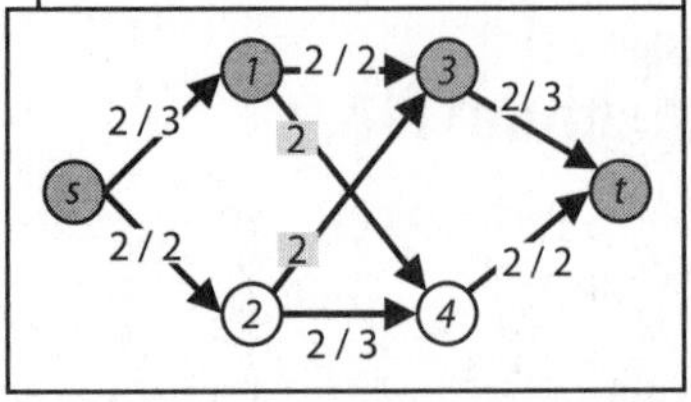

Augment <s,1,4,2,3,t> with 1 unit. Flow from (2,4) is redirected over (2,3).

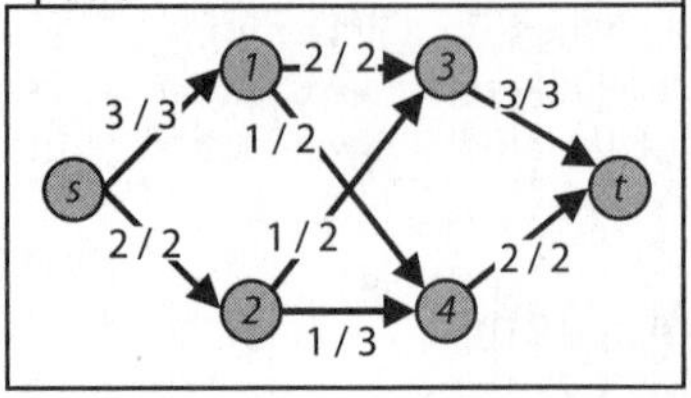

Figure 8-3. Ford-Fulkerson fact sheet

Input

The flow network is defined by a graph $G=(V,E)$ with designated start vertex s and sink vertex t. Each directed edge $e=(u,v)$ in E has a defined integer capacity $c(u,v)$ and actual flow $f(u,v)$.

Output

FORD-FULKERSON computes for each edge (*u*,*v*) in *E*, an integer flow *f*(*u*,*v*) representing the units flowing through edge (*u*,*v*). The resulting flow is the maximum allowed from *s* to *t* given capacity constraints. As a side effect of its termination, FORD-FULKERSON computes the *min cut* of the network—in other words, the set of edges that form a bottleneck, preventing further units from flowing across the network from *s* to *t*.

Solution

FORD-FULKERSON relies on the following structures:

FlowNetwork
> Represents the network flow problem. This is an abstract class for two implementations, one based on adjacency lists and the other using arrays. The getEdgeStructure( ) method returns the underlying storage used for the edges.

VertexStructure
> Maintains two linked lists (forward and backward) for the edges leaving and entering a vertex.

EdgeInfo
> Records information about edges in the network flow.

VertexInfo
> Records in an array the augmenting path found by the search method. It records the previous vertex in the augmenting path and whether it was reached through a forward or backward edge.

FORD-FULKERSON is implemented in Example 8-1 and illustrated in Figure 8-4. A configurable Search object computes the augmented path in the network to which additional flow can be added without violating the flow network criteria. FORD-FULKERSON makes continual progress because suboptimal decisions made in earlier iterations of the algorithm can be fixed without having to undo all past history.

Example 8-1. Sample Java Ford-Fulkerson implementation

```java
public class FordFulkerson {
    FlowNetwork network;    /** Represents the FlowNetwork problem. */
    Search searchMethod;    /** Search method. */

    // Construct instance to compute maximum flow across given
    // network using given search method to find augmenting path.
    public FordFulkerson (FlowNetwork network, Search method) {
        this.network = network;
        this.searchMethod = method;
    }
```

Example 8-1. Sample Java Ford-Fulkerson implementation (continued)

```java
// Compute maximal flow for the flow network. Results of the
// computation are stored within the flow network object.
public boolean compute () {
  boolean augmented = false;
  while (searchMethod.findAugmentingPath(network.vertices)) {
    processPath(network.vertices);
    augmented = true;
  }
  return augmented;
}

// Find edge in augmenting path with lowest potential to be increased
// and augment flows within path from source to sink by that amount
protected void processPath(VertexInfo []vertices) {
  int v = network.sinkIndex;
  int delta = Integer.MAX_VALUE;        // goal is to find smallest
  while (v != network.sourceIndex) {
    int u = vertices[v].previous;
    int flow;
    if (vertices[v].forward) {
      // Forward edges can be adjusted by remaining capacity on edge
      flow = network.edge(u, v).capacity - network.edge(u, v).flow;
    } else {
      // Backward edges can only be reduced by their existing flow
      flow = network.edge(v, u).flow;
    }
    if (flow < delta) { delta = flow; }   // smaller candidate flow
    v = u;  // follow reverse path to source
  }

  // Adjust path (forward is added, backward is reduced) with delta.
  v = network.sinkIndex;
  while (v != network.sourceIndex) {
    int u = vertices[v].previous;
    if (vertices[v].forward) {
      network.edge(u, v).flow += delta;
    } else {
      network.edge(v, u).flow -= delta;
    }
    v = u;  // follow reverse path to source
  }
  Arrays.fill(network.vertices, null);   // reset for next iteration
  }
}
```

Any search method that extends the abstract Search class in Figure 8-5 can be used to locate an augmenting path. The original description of FORD-FULKERSON uses DEPTH-FIRST SEARCH while EDMONDS-KARP uses BREADTH-FIRST SEARCH (see Chapter 6).

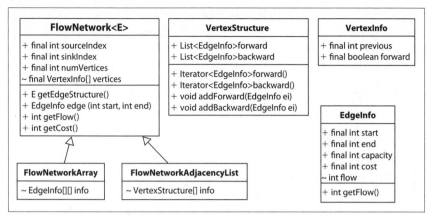

Figure 8-4. Modeling information for Ford-Fulkerson

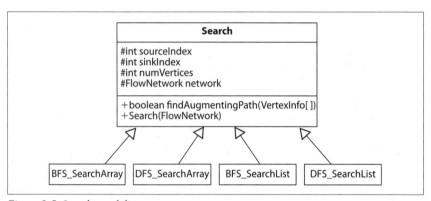

Figure 8-5. Search capability

The flow network example in Figure 8-3 shows the results of using DEPTH-FIRST SEARCH to locate an augmenting path; the implementation is listed in Example 8-2. The path structure contains a stack of vertices during its search. A potential augmenting path is expanded by popping a vertex u from the stack and expanding to an adjacent unvisited vertex v that satisfies one of two constraints: (i) edge (u,v) is a forward edge with unfilled capacity; (ii) edge (v,u) is a forward edge with flow that can be reduced. Eventually, the sink vertex t is visited or path becomes empty, in which case no augmenting path is possible.

Example 8-2. Using Depth-First Search to locate augmenting path

```
public boolean findAugmentingPath (VertexInfo[] vertices) {
    // Begin potential augmenting path at source.
    vertices[sourceIndex] = new VertexInfo (-1);
    Stack<Integer> path = new Stack<Integer>();
    path.push (sourceIndex);

    // Process forward edges from u; then try backward edges
    VertexStructure struct[] = network.getEdgeStructure();
```

Example 8-2. Using Depth-First Search to locate augmenting path (continued)

```
while (!path.isEmpty( )) {
    int u = path.pop( );

    // try to make forward progress first...
    Iterator<EdgeInfo> it = struct[u].forward( );
    while (it.hasNext( )) {
        EdgeInfo ei = it.next( );
        int v = ei.end;

        // not yet visited AND has unused capacity? Plan to increase.
        if (vertices[v] == null && ei.capacity > ei.flow) {
            vertices[v] = new VertexInfo (u, FORWARD);

            if (v == sinkIndex) { return true; }  // we have found one!
            path.push (v);
        }
    }

    // try backward edges
    it = struct[u].backward( );
    while (it.hasNext( )) {
        // try to find an incoming edge into u whose flow can be reduced.
        EdgeInfo rei = it.next( );
        int v = rei.start;

        // now try backward edge not yet visited (can't be sink!)
        if (vertices[v] == null && rei.flow > 0) {
            vertices[v] = new VertexInfo (u, BACKWARD);
            path.push(v);
        }
    }
}

// nothing
return false;
}
```

As the path is expanded, back-pointers between vertices are maintained by the VertexInfo[] structure to enable the augmenting path to be traversed within FordFulkerson.processPath.

The implementation of the BREADTH-FIRST SEARCH alternative, known as EDMONDS-KARP, is shown in Example 8-3. Here the path structure contains a queue of vertices during its search. The potential augmenting path is expanded by removing a vertex *u* from the head of the queue and appending to the end of the queue adjacent unvisited vertices through which the augmented path may exist. Again, either the sink vertex *t* will be visited or path becomes empty (in which case no augmenting path is possible). Given the same example flow network from Figure 8-3, the four augmenting paths located using BREADTH-FIRST SEARCH are <*s*,1,3,*t*>, <*s*,1,4,*t*>, <*s*,2,3,*t*>, and <*s*,2,4,*t*>. The resulting maximum flow will be the same.

Example 8-3. Using Breadth-First Search to locate augmenting path

```java
public boolean findAugmentingPath (VertexInfo []vertices) {
    // Begin potential augmenting path at source with maximum flow.
    vertices[sourceIndex] = new VertexInfo (-1);
    DoubleLinkedList<Integer> path = new DoubleLinkedList<Integer>( );
    path.insert (sourceIndex);

    // Process forward edges out of u; then try backward edges into u
    VertexStructure struct[] = network.getEdgeStructure( );
    while (!path.isEmpty( )) {
      int u = path.removeFirst( );

      Iterator<EdgeInfo> it = struct[u].forward( );     // edges out from u
      while (it.hasNext( )) {
        EdgeInfo ei = it.next( );
        int v = ei.end;

        // if not yet visited AND has unused capacity? Plan to increase.
        if (vertices[v] == null && ei.capacity > ei.flow) {
          vertices[v] = new VertexInfo (u, FORWARD);
          if (v == sinkIndex) { return true; }  // path is complete.
          path.insert (v);                      // otherwise append to queue
        }
      }

      it = struct[u].backward( );               // edges into u
      while (it.hasNext( )) {
        // try to find an incoming edge into u whose flow can be reduced.
        EdgeInfo rei = it.next( );
        int v = rei.start;

        // Not yet visited (can't be sink!) AND has flow to be decreased?
        if (vertices[v] == null && rei.flow > 0) {
          vertices[v] = new VertexInfo (u, BACKWARD);
          path.insert (v);                      // append to queue
        }
      }
    }

    return false;     // no augmented path located.
}
```

Consequences

When FORD-FULKERSON terminates, the vertices in V can be split into two disjoint sets, S and T (where T is defined to be $V–S$). Note that $s \in S$, whereas $t \in T$. S is computed to be the set of vertices from V that were visited in the final failed attempt to locate an augmenting path. The importance of these sets is that the forward edges between S and T comprise a "min-cut" of the flow network. That is, these edges form the "bottleneck" in the flow network because (a) the flow network is separated into two sets of vertices, S and T, where the capacity that can flow from S to T is minimized, and (b) the available flow between S and T is already at full capacity.

Analysis

FORD-FULKERSON terminates because the units of flow are non-negative integers (Ford-Fulkerson, 1962). The performance of FORD-FULKERSON using DEPTH-FIRST SEARCH is $O(E^*mf)$ and is based on the final value of the maximum flow, mf. Briefly, it is possible that in each iteration only one unit of flow is added to the augmenting path, and thus networks with very large capacities might require a great number of iterations. It is striking that the running time is based not on the problem size (i.e., the number of vertices or edges) but on the capacities of the edges themselves. When using BREADTH-FIRST SEARCH (identified by name as the EDMONDS-KARP variation), the performance becomes $O(V^*E^2)$. BREADTH-FIRST SEARCH finds the shortest augmented path in $O(V+E)$, which is really $O(E)$ since the number of vertices is smaller than the number of edges in the connected flow network graph. Cormen et al. (2001) prove that the number of flow augmentations performed is on the order of $O(V^*E)$, leading to the final result that EDMONDS-KARP has $O(V^*E^2)$ performance. EDMONDS-KARP often outperforms FORD-FULKERSON by relying on BREADTH-FIRST SEARCH to pursue all potential paths in order of length, rather than potentially wasting much effort in a depth-first "race" to the sink.

Optimization

Typical implementations of flow network problems use arrays to store information. We choose instead to present each algorithm with readable code so readers can understand how the algorithm works. It is worth considering, however, how much performance speedup can be achieved by optimizing the resulting code; in Chapter 2 we showed a nearly 40% performance improvement in multiplying n-digit numbers. It is clear that faster code can be written, yet it may not be easy to understand the code or maintain it if the problem changes. With this caution in mind, Example 8-4 contains an optimized Java implementation of FORD-FULKERSON.

Example 8-4. Optimized Ford-Fulkerson implementation

```java
public class Optimized extends FlowNetwork {
    int[][] capacity;      // Contains all capacities.
    int[][] flow;          // Contains all flows.
    int[] previous;        // Contains predecessor information of path.
    int[] visited;         // Visited during augmenting path search.

    final int QUEUE_SIZE;  // Size of queue will never be greater than n
    final int queue[];     // Use circular queue in implementation

    // Load up the information
    public Optimized (int n, int s, int t, Iterator<EdgeInfo> edges) {
        // Have superclass initialize first.
        super (n, s, t);

        queue = new int[n];
        QUEUE_SIZE = n;
        capacity = new int[n][n];
```

Example 8-4. Optimized Ford-Fulkerson implementation (continued)

```
    flow = new int[n][n];
    previous = new int[n];
    visited = new int [n];

    // Initially, the flow is set to zero. Pull info from input.
    while (edges.hasNext( )) {
      EdgeInfo ei = edges.next( );
      capacity[ei.start][ei.end] = ei.capacity;
    }
  }

  // Compute and return the maxFlow.
  public int compute (int source, int sink) {
    int maxFlow = 0;
    while (search(source, sink)) { maxFlow += processPath(source, sink); }
    return maxFlow;
  }

  // Augment flow within network along path found from source to sink.
  protected int processPath(int source, int sink) {
    // Determine amount by which to increment the flow. Equal to
    // minimum over the computed path from sink to source.
    int increment = Integer.MAX_VALUE;
    int v = sink;
    while (previous[v] != -1) {
      int unit = capacity[previous[v]][v] - flow[previous[v]][v];
      if (unit < increment) { increment = unit; }
      v = previous[v];
    }

    // push minimal increment over the path
    v = sink;
    while (previous[v] != -1) {
      flow[previous[v]][v] += increment;  // forward edges.
      flow[v][previous[v]] -= increment;  // don't forget back edges
      v = previous[v];
    }

    return increment;
  }

  // Locate augmenting path in the Flow Network from source to sink
  public boolean search (int source, int sink) {
    // clear visiting status. 0=clear, 1=actively in queue, 2=visited
    for (int i = 0 ; i < numVertices; i++) { visited[i] = 0; }

    // create circular queue to process search elements
    queue[0] = source;
    int head = 0, tail = 1;
    previous[source] = -1;      // make sure we terminate here.
    visited[source] = 1;        // actively in queue.
    while (head != tail) {
```

Example 8-4. Optimized Ford-Fulkerson implementation (continued)

```
      int u = queue[head];  head = (head + 1) % QUEUE_SIZE;
      visited[u] = 2;

      // add to queue unvisited neighboring vertices of u with enough capacity.
      for (int v = 0; v < numVertices; v++) {
        if (visited[v] == 0 && capacity[u][v] > flow[u][v]) {
          queue[tail] = v;  tail = (tail + 1) % QUEUE_SIZE;
          visited[v] = 1;        // actively in queue.
          previous[v] = u;
        }
      }
    }

    return visited[sink] != 0;  // did we make it to the sink?
  }
}
```

Related Algorithms

The PUSH/RELABEL algorithm introduced by Goldberg and Tarjan (1986) improves the performance to $O(V^*E^*\log(V^2/E))$ and also provides an algorithm that can be parallelized for greater gains. A variant of the problem, known as the Multi-Commodity Flow problem, generalizes the Maximum Flow problem stated here. Briefly, instead of having a single source and sink, consider a shared network used by multiple sources s_i and sinks t_i to transmit different commodities. The capacity of the edges is fixed, but the usage demands for each source and sink may vary. Practical applications of algorithms that solve this problem include routing in wireless networks (Fragouli and Tabet, 2006). Leighton and Rao (1999) have written a widely cited reference for multi-commodity problems.

There are several slight variations to the Maximum Flow problem:

Vertex capacities
 What if a flow network places a maximum capacity $k(v)$ flowing through a vertex v in the graph? Construct a modified flow network G' as follows. For each vertex v in the network, create two vertices v' and v''. Create edge (v'',v') with a flow capacity of $k(v)$. For each edge (x,v) in the original graph with capacity $c(x,v)$, create new edge (x,v'') with capacity $c(x,v)$ from original graph G. For each edge (v,w) in the original graph G, create edge (v',w) in G' with capacity $k(v)$. A solution in G' determines the solution to G.

Undirected edges
 What if the flow network G has undirected edges? Construct a modified flow network G' as follows. In a new graph, all vertices are the same. For each edge (u,v) in the original graph with capacity $c(u,v)$, construct a pair of edges (u,v) and (v,u) each with the same capacity $c(u,v)$. A solution in G' determines the solution to G.

Bipartite Matching

Matching problems exist in numerous forms. Consider the following scenario. Five applicants have been interviewed for five job openings. The applicants have listed the jobs for which they are qualified. The task is to match applicants to jobs such that each job opening is assigned to exactly one qualified applicant. It may be surprising to discover that we can use FORD-FULKERSON to solve the Bipartite Matching problem. This technique is known in computer science as "problem reduction." We reduce the Bipartite Matching problem to a Maximum Flow problem in a flow network by showing (a) how to map the Bipartite Matching problem input into the input for a Maximum Flow problem, and (b) how to map the output of the Maximum Flow problem into the output of the Bipartite Matching problem.

Input/Output

Input

A Bipartite Matching problem consists of a set of $1 \leq i \leq n$ elements, $s_i \in S$; a set of $1 \leq j \leq m$ partners, $t_j \in T$; and a set of $1 \leq k \leq p$ acceptable pairs, $p_k \in P$, that associate an element $s_i \in S$ with a partner $t_j \in T$. The sets S and T are disjoint, which gives this problem its name.

Output

A set of pairs (s_i, t_j) selected from the original set of acceptable pairs, P. These pairs represent a maximum number of pairs allowed by the matching. The algorithm guarantees that no greater number of pairs is possible to be matched (although there may be other arrangements that lead to the same number of pairs).

Solution

Instead of devising a new algorithm to solve this problem, we reduce a Bipartite Matching problem instance into a Maximum Flow instance. In Bipartite Matching, selecting the match (s_i, t_j) for element $s_i \in S$ with partner $t_j \in T$ prevents either s_i or t_j from being selected again in another pairing. To produce this same behavior in a flow network graph $G=(V,E)$, construct G as follows:

V contains n+m+2 vertices
 Each element s_i maps to a vertex numbered i. Each partner t_j maps to a vertex numbered $n+j$. Create a new source vertex *src* (labeled 0) and a new target vertex *tgt* (labeled $n+m+1$).

E contains n+m+k edges
 There are n edges connecting the new *src* vertex to the vertices mapped from S. There are m edges connecting the new *tgt* vertex to the vertices mapped from T. For each of the k pairs, $p_k=(s_i,t_j)$, add the edge $(i,n+j)$. Set the flow capacity for each of these edges to 1.

We claim that computing the Maximum Flow in the flow network graph G produces a maximal matching set for the original Bipartite Matching problem; proofs are available (Cormen et al., 2001). For an example, consider Figure 8-6(a) where it is suggested that the two pairs (a,z) and (b,y) form the maximum number of pairs; the corresponding flow network using this construction is shown in Figure 8-6(b). Upon reflection we can improve this solution to select three pairs, (a,z), (c,y), and (b,x). The corresponding adjustment to the flow network is made by finding the augmenting path <0,3,5,2,4,7>.

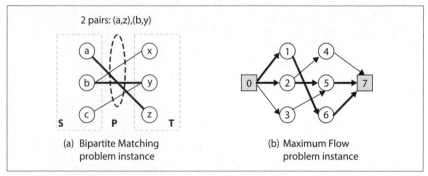

(a) Bipartite Matching
problem instance

(b) Maximum Flow
problem instance

Figure 8-6. Small Bipartite Matching instance reduced to Maximum Flow instance

Once the maximum flow is determined, we convert the output of the Maximum Flow problem into the appropriate output for the Bipartite Matching problem. That is, for every edge (s_i,t_j) whose flow is 1, output that the pairing $(s_i,t_j) \in P$ is selected. In the code shown in Example 8-5, error checking has been removed to simplify the presentation.*

Example 8-5. Bipartite Matching using Ford-Fulkerson

```
public class BipartiteMatching {

    ArrayList<EdgeInfo> edges;  /* Edges for S and T. */
    int ctr = 0;                /* Unique id counter. */

    /* Maps that convert between problem instances. */
    Hashtable<Object,Integer> map = new Hashtable<Object,Integer>();
    Hashtable<Integer,Object> reverse = new Hashtable<Integer,Object>();

    int srcIndex;   /* Source index of flow network problem. */
    int tgtIndex;   /* Target index of flow network problem. */
    int numVertices; /* Number of vertices in flow network problem. */

    public BipartiteMatching (Object[] setS, Object[] setT, Object[][] pairs)
        throws RuntimeException {

        edges = new ArrayList<EdgeInfo>();
```

---

* To find full details, see class `algs.model.network.matching.BipartiteMatching` in the repository.

Example 8-5. Bipartite Matching using Ford-Fulkerson (continued)

```
  // convert pairs into appropriate input for FlowNetwork. All edges
  // will have capacity of 1.
  for (int i = 0; i < pairs.length; i++) {
    Integer src = map.get(pairs[i][0]);
    Integer tgt = map.get(pairs[i][1]);
    if (src == null) {
      map.put(pairs[i][0], src = ++ctr);
      reverse.put(src, pairs[i][0]);
    }
    if (tgt == null) {
      map.put(pairs[i][1], tgt = ++ctr);
      reverse.put(tgt, pairs[i][1]);
    }

    edges.add(new EdgeInfo(src, tgt, 1));
  }

  // add extra "source" and extra "target" vertices
  srcIndex = 0;
  tgtIndex = setS.length + setT.length+1;
  numVertices = tgtIndex+1;
  for (Object o : setS) {
    edges.add(new EdgeInfo(0, map.get(o), 1));
  }
  for (Object o : setT) {
    edges.add(new EdgeInfo(map.get(o), ctr+1, 1));
  }
}

public Iterator<Pair> compute() {
  FlowNetworkArray network = new FlowNetworkArray(numVertices,
                  srcIndex, tgtIndex, edges.iterator());
  FordFulkerson solver = new FordFulkerson (network,
                  new DFS_SearchArray(network));
  solver.compute();

  // retrieve from original edgeInfo set; ignore created edges to the
  // added 'source' and 'target'. Only include in solution if flow == 1
  ArrayList<Pair> pairs = new ArrayList<Pair>();
  for (EdgeInfo ei : edges) {
    if (ei.start != srcIndex && ei.end != tgtIndex) {
      if (ei.getFlow() == 1) {
        pairs.add(new Pair(reverse.get(ei.start), reverse.get(ei.end)));
      }
    }
  }

  return pairs.iterator();
}
}
```

Analysis

For a problem reduction to be efficient, it must be possible to efficiently map both the problem instance and the computed solutions. The Bipartite Matching problem $M=(S,T,P)$ is converted into a graph $G=(V,E)$ in $n+m+k$ steps. The resulting graph G has $n+m+2$ vertices and $n+m+k$ edges, and thus the size of the graph is only a constant size larger than the original Bipartite Matching problem size. This important feature of the construction ensures that we have an efficient solution to the Bipartite Matching problem. Once a maximum flow has been computed by FORD-FULKERSON, the edges in the network with a flow of 1 correspond to pairs in the Bipartite Matching problem that belong to the computed matching. To determine these edges requires k steps, so there is only an extra $O(k)$ processing required to "read" the solution to Bipartite Matching.

Reflections on Augmenting Paths

Solving the Maximum Flow problem does not help us to immediately solve any of the remaining problems discussed earlier in this chapter. However, by solving the Maximum Flow problem we are inspired to consider a class of similar problems that seek to maximize the flow through a flow network while at the same time minimizing the cost of that flow. If we associate with each edge (u,v) in the network a cost $d(u,v)$ that reflects the per-unit cost of shipping a unit over edge (u,v), then the goal is to minimize:

$$\Sigma\, f(u,v)^*d(u,v)$$

for all edges in the flow network. Now, for FORD-FULKERSON, we stressed the importance of finding an augmenting path that could increase the maximum flow through the network. What if we modify the search routine to find the least costly augmentation, if one exists? We have already seen greedy algorithms (such as PRIM'S ALGORITHM for building a Minimum Spanning Tree in Chapter 6) that iteratively select the least costly extension; perhaps such an approach will work here.

To find the least costly augmentation path, we cannot rely strictly on a breadth-first or a depth-first approach. As we saw with PRIM'S ALGORITHM, we must use a priority queue to store and compute the distance of each vertex in the flow network from the source vertex. We essentially compute the costs of shipping an additional unit from the source vertex to each vertex in the network, and we maintain a priority queue based on the ongoing computation. As the search proceeds, the priority queue stores the ordered set of nodes that define the active searching focus. To expand the search, retrieve from the priority queue the vertex u whose distance (in terms of cost) from the source is the smallest. We then locate a neighboring vertex v that has not yet been visited and that meets one of two conditions: either (a) the forward edge (u,v) still has remaining capacity to be increased, or (b) the backward edge (v,u) has flow that can be reduced. If the sink index is encountered during the exploration, the search can terminate successfully with an augmenting path; otherwise, no such augmenting path exists. The Java implementation of ShortestPathArray is shown in Example 8-6.

Example 8-6. Shortest path (in costs) search for Ford-Fulkerson

```java
public boolean findAugmentingPath (VertexInfo[] vertices) {
    Arrays.fill(vertices, null);    // reset for iteration

    // Construct queue using BinaryHeap. The inqueue[] array avoids
    // an O(n) search to determine if an element is in the queue.
    int n = vertices.length;
    BinaryHeap<Integer> pq = new BinaryHeap<Integer> (n);
    boolean inqueue[] = new boolean [n];

    // initialize dist[] array. Use INT_MAX when edge doesn't exist.
    for (int u = 0; u < n; u++) {
        if (u == sourceIndex) {
            dist[u] = 0;
            pq.insert(sourceIndex, 0);
            inqueue[u] = true;
        } else {
            dist[u] = Integer.MAX_VALUE;
        }
    }

    while (!pq.isEmpty()) {
        int u = pq.smallestID();
        inqueue[u] = false;

        /** When reach sinkIndex we are done. */
        if (u == sinkIndex) { break; }

        for (int v = 0; v < n; v++) {
            if (v == sourceIndex || v == u) continue;

            // forward edge with remaining capacity if cost is better.
            EdgeInfo cei = info[u][v];
            if (cei != null && cei.flow < cei.capacity) {
                int newDist = dist[u] + cei.cost;
                if (0 <= newDist && newDist < dist[v]) {
                    vertices[v] = new VertexInfo (u, Search.FORWARD);
                    dist[v] = newDist;
                    if (inqueue[v]) {
                        pq.decreaseKey(v, newDist);
                    } else {
                        pq.insert(v, newDist);
                        inqueue[v] = true;
                    }
                }
            }

            // backward edge with at least some flow if cost is better.
            cei = info[v][u];
            if (cei != null && cei.flow > 0) {
                int newDist = dist[u] - cei.cost;
                if (0 <= newDist && newDist < dist[v]) {
                    vertices[v] = new VertexInfo (u, Search.BACKWARD);
```

```
                    dist[v] = newDist;
                    if (inqueue[v]) {
                        pq.decreaseKey(v, newDist);
                    } else {
                        pq.insert(v, newDist);
                        inqueue[v] = true;
                    }
                }
            }
        }
    }

    return dist[sinkIndex] != Integer.MAX_VALUE;
}
```

Armed with this strategy for locating the lowest-cost augmenting path, we can solve the remaining problems shown in Figure 8-1. To show the effect of this low-cost search strategy, we show in Figure 8-7 the side-by-side computation on a small example comparing a straightforward Maximum Flow computation with a Minimum Cost Flow computation. Each iteration moving vertically down the figure is another pass through the while loop within the compute( ) method of FORD-FULKERSON (as seen in Example 8-1). The result, at the bottom of the figure, is the maximum flow found by each approach.

In this example, you are the shipping manager in charge of two factories in Chicago (v_1) and Washington, D.C. (v_2) that can each produce 300 widgets daily. You must ensure that two customers in Houston (v_3) and Boston (v_4) each receive 300 widgets a day. You have several options for shipping, as shown in the figure. For example, between Washington, D.C. and Houston, you may ship up to 280 widgets daily at $4 per widget, but the cost increases to $6 per widget if you ship from Washington, D.C. to Boston (although you can then send up to 350 widgets per day along that route).

It may not even be clear that FORD-FULKERSON can be used to solve this problem, but note that we can create a graph G with a new source vertex s_0 that connects to the two factory nodes (v_1 and v_2) and the two customers (v_3 and v_4) connect to a new sink vertex t_5. On the lefthand side of Figure 8-7 we execute the EDMONDS-KARP variation to demonstrate that we can meet all of our customer needs as requested, at the total daily shipping cost of $3,600. To save space, the source and sink vertices s_0 and t_5 are omitted. During each of the four iterations by FORD-FULKERSON, the impact of the augmented path is shown (when an iteration updates the flow for an edge, the flow value is shaded gray).

Is this the lowest cost we can achieve? On the righthand side of Figure 8-7 we show the execution of FORD-FULKERSON using ShortestPathArray as the search strategy, as described in Example 8-6. Note how the first augmented path found takes advantage of the lowest-cost shipping rate. Also ShortestPathArray only uses the costliest shipping route from Chicago (v_1) to Houston (v_3) when there is no other way to meet the customer needs; indeed, when this happens, note how the augmented path reduces the existing flows between Washington, D.C. (v_2) and Houston (v_3), as well as between Washington, D.C. (v_2) and Boston (v_4).

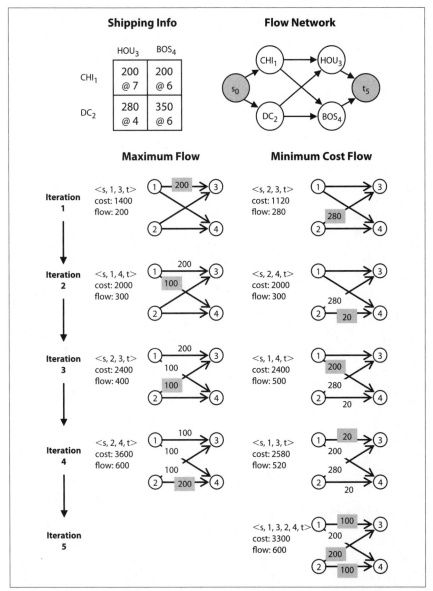

Figure 8-7. Side-by-side computation showing difference when considering the minimum cost flow

Minimum Cost Flow

To solve a Minimum Cost Flow problem we need only construct a flow network graph and ensure that it satisfies the criteria discussed earlier—capacity constraint, flow conservation, and skew symmetry—as well as two additional criteria:

Supply satisfaction
> For each source vertex $s_i \in S$, the sum of $f(s_i, v)$ for all edges $(s_i, v) \in E$ (the flow out of s_i) minus the sum of $f(u, s_i)$ for all edges $(u, s_i) \in E$ (the flow into s_i) must be less than or equal to $sup(s_i)$. That is, the supply $sup(s_i)$ at each source vertex is a firm upper bound on the net flow from that vertex.

Demand satisfaction
> For each sink vertex $t_j \in T$, the sum of $f(u, t_j)$ for all edges $(u, t_j) \in E$ (the flow into t_j) minus the sum of $f(t_j, v)$ for all edges $(t_j, v) \in E$ (the flow out of t_j) must be less than or equal to $dem(t_j)$. That is, the $dem(t_j)$ at each target vertex is a firm upper bound on the net flow into that vertex.

To simplify the algorithmic solution, we further constrain the flow network graph to have a single source vertex and sink vertex. This can be easily accomplished by taking an existing flow network graph with any number of source and sink vertices and adding two new vertices. First, add a new vertex (which we refer to as s_0) to be the source vertex for the flow network graph, and add edges (s_0, s_i) for all $s_i \in S$ whose capacity $c(s_0, s_i) = sup(s_i)$ and whose cost $d(s_0, s_i) = 0$. Second, add a new vertex (which we often refer to as *tgt*, for target) to be the sink vertex for the flow network graph, and add edges (t_j, tgt) for all $t_j \in T$ whose capacity $c(t_j, tgt) = dem(t_j)$ and whose cost $d(t_0, t_j) = 0$. As you can see, adding these vertices and edges does not increase the cost of the network flow, nor do they reduce or increase the final computed flow over the network.

The supplies $sup(s_i)$, demands $dem(t_j)$, and capacities $c(u, v)$ are all greater than 0. The shipping cost $d(u, v)$ associated with each edge may be greater than or equal to zero. When the resulting flow is computed, all $f(u, v)$ values will be greater than or equal to zero.

We are now ready to present the constructions that allow us to solve each of the remaining flow network problems listed in Figure 8-1. For each problem we describe how to reduce the problem to Minimum Cost Flow.

Transshipment

There exists m supply stations s_i, each capable of producing $sup(s_i)$ units of a commodity. There are n demand stations t_j, each demanding $dem(t_j)$ units of the commodity. There are w warehouse stations w_k, each capable of receiving and reshipping (known as "transshipping") a maximum max_k units of the commodity at the fixed warehouse processing cost of wp_k per unit. There is a fixed shipping cost of $d(i, j)$ for each unit shipping from supply station s_i to demand stations t_j, a fixed transshipping cost of $ts(i, k)$ for each unit shipped from supply station s_i to warehouse station w_k, and a fixed transshipping cost of $ts(k,j)$ for each unit shipped from warehouse station w_k to demand station t_j. The goal is to determine the flow $f(i,j)$ of units from supply station s_i to demand station t_j that minimizes the overall total cost, which can be concisely defined as:

Total Cost (TC) = Total Shipping Cost (TSC) + Total Transshipping Cost (TTC)

$TSC = \Sigma_i \Sigma_j\, d(i,j)^*f(i,j)$

$TTC = \Sigma_i \Sigma_k\, ts(i,k)^*f(i,k) + \Sigma_j \Sigma_k\, ts(j,k)^*f(j,k)$

The goal is to find integer values for $f(i,j) \geq 0$ that ensure that TC is a minimum while meeting all of the supply and demand constraints. Finally, the net flow of units through a warehouse must be zero, to ensure that no units are lost (or added!). The supplies $sup(s_i)$ and demands $dem(t_i)$ are all greater than 0. The shipping costs $d(i,j)$, $ts(i,k)$, and $ts(k,j)$ may be greater than or equal to zero.

Solution

We convert the Transshipment problem instance into a Minimum Cost Flow problem instance (as illustrated in Figure 8-8) by constructing a graph $G=(V,E)$ such that:

V contains $n+m+2^*w+2$ vertices
> Each supply station s_i maps to a vertex numbered i. Each warehouse w_k maps to two different vertices, one numbered $m+2^*k-1$ and one numbered $m+2^*k$. Each demand station t_j maps to $1+m+2^*w+j$. Create a new source vertex src (labeled 0) and a new target vertex tgt (labeled $n+m+2^*w+1$).

E contains $(w+1)^*(m+n)+m^*n+w$ edges
> The process for constructing edges from the Transshipment problem instance can be found in the Transshipment class in the code repository.

Once the Minimum Cost Flow solution is available, the transshipment schedule can be constructed by locating those edges $(u,v) \in E$ whose $f(u,v) > 0$. The cost of the schedule is the sum total of $f(u,v)^*d(u,v)$ for these edges.

Transportation

The Transportation problem is simpler than the Transshipment problem because there are no intermediate warehouse nodes. There exists m supply stations s_i, each capable of producing $sup(s_i)$ units of a commodity. There are n demand stations t_j, each demanding $dem(t_j)$ units of the commodity. There is a fixed per-unit cost $d(i,j) \geq 0$ associated with transporting a unit over the edge (i,j). The goal is to determine the flow $f(i,j)$ of units from supply stations s_i to demand stations t_j that minimizes the overall transportation cost, TSC, which can be concisely defined as:

Total Shipping Cost $(TSC) = \Sigma_i \Sigma_j\, d(i,j)^*f(i,j)$

The solution must also satisfy both the total demand for each demand station t_j and the supply capabilities for supply stations s_i.

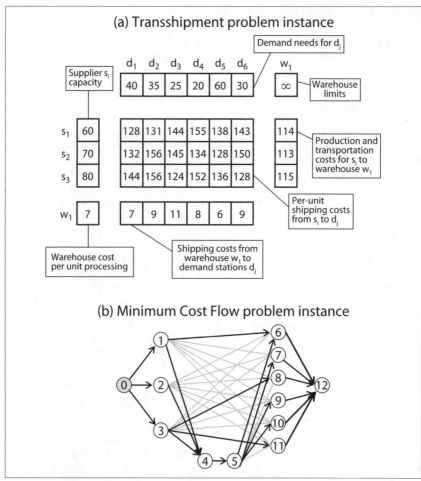

Figure 8-8. Sample Transshipment problem instance converted to Minimum Cost Flow problem instance

Solution

We convert the Transportation problem instance into a Transshipment problem instance with no intermediate warehouse nodes.

Assignment

The Assignment problem is simply a more restricted version of the Transportation problem: each supply node must supply only a single unit, and the demand for each demand node is also one.

Solution

We convert the Assignment problem instance into a Transportation problem instance, with the restriction that the supply nodes provide a single unit and the demand nodes require a single unit.

Linear Programming

The different problems described in this chapter can all be solved using Linear Programming (LP), a powerful technique that optimizes a linear objective function, subject to linear equality and inequality constraints (Bazarra and Jarvis, 1977).

To show LP in action, we convert the Transportation problem depicted in Figure 8-7 into a series of linear equations to be solved by an LP solver. We use a general-purpose commercial mathematics software package known as Maple (*http://www.maplesoft.com*) to carry out the computations. As you recall, the goal is to maximize the flow over the network while minimizing the cost. We associate a variable with the flow over each edge in the network; thus the variable e13 represents $f(1,3)$. The function to be minimized is Cost, which is defined to be the sum total of the shipping costs over each of the four edges in the network. This cost equation has the same constraints we described earlier for network flows:

Flow conservation
    The sum total of the edges emanating from a source vertex must equal its supply. The sum total of the edges entering a demand vertex must be equal to its demand.

Capacity constraint
    The flow over an edge $f(i,j)$ must be greater than or equal to zero. Also, $f(i,j) \leq c(i,j)$.

When executing the Maple solver, the computed result is {e13=100, e24=100, e23=200, e14=200}, which corresponds exactly to the minimum cost solution of 3,300 found earlier (see Example 8-7).

Example 8-7. Maple commands to apply minimization to Transportation problem

```
with(simplex);

Constraints := [
  # conservation of units at each node
  e13+e14   = 300,  # CHI
  e23+e24   = 300,  # DC

  e13+e23   = 300,  # HOU
  e14+e24   = 300,  # BOS

  # maximum flow on individual edges
  0 <= e13, e13 <= 200,
  0 <= e14, e14 <= 200,
```

Example 8-7. Maple commands to apply minimization to Transportation problem (continued)

```
  0 <= e23, e23 <= 280,
  0 <= e24, e24 <= 350
];

Cost := 7*e13 + 6*e14 + 4*e23 + 6*e24;

# Invoke linear programming to solve problem
minimize (Cost, Constraints, NONNEGATIVE);
```

The SIMPLEX algorithm designed by George Dantzig in 1947 makes it possible to solve problems such as those shown in Example 8-7, which involve hundreds or thousands of variables (McCall, 1982). SIMPLEX has repeatedly been shown to be efficient in practice, although the approach can, under the right circumstances, lead to an exponential number of computations. It is not recommended to implement the SIMPLEX algorithm yourself, both because of its complexity and because there are commercially available software libraries that do the job for you.

References

Ahuja, Ravindra K., Thomas L. Magnanti, and James B. Orlin, *Network Flows: Theory, Algorithms, and Applications*. Prentice Hall, 1993.

Bazarra, M. and J. Jarvis, *Linear Programming and Network Flows*. John Wiley & Sons, 1977.

Cormen, Thomas H., Charles E. Leiserson, Ronald L. Rivest, and Clifford Stein, *Introduction to Algorithms*, Second Edition. McGraw Hill, 2001.

Ford, L. R. Jr. and D. R. Fulkerson, *Flows in Networks*. Princeton University Press, 1962.

Fragouli, Christina and Tarik Tabet, "On conditions for constant throughput in wireless networks," ACM Transactions on Sensor Networks (TOSN), 2 (3): 359–379, 2006, *http://portal.acm.org/citation.cfm?id=1167938*.

Goldberg, A. V. and R. E. Tarjan, "A new approach to the maximum flow problem," Proceedings of the eighteenth annual ACM symposium on Theory of computing, pp. 136–146, 1986. *http://portal.acm.org/citation.cfm?doid=12130. 12144*.

Leighton, Tom and Satish Rao, "Multicommodity max-flow min-cut theorems and their use in designing approximation algorithms," *Journal of the ACM*, 46 (6): 787–832, 1999, *http://portal.acm.org/citation.cfm?doid=331524.331526*.

McCall, Edward H., "Performance results of the simplex algorithm for a set of real-world linear programming models," *Communications of the ACM*, 25(3): 207–212, March 1982, *http://portal.acm.org/citation.cfm?id=358461*.

Orden, Alex, "The Transhipment Problem," *Management Science*, 2(3), 1956.

9

Computational Geometry

Overview

This overview introduces a set of problems from the field of computational geometry. Many of these problems were first investigated by mathematicians over the past few centuries. Since the 1970s, computational geometry has been recognized as the systematic study of geometric algorithms and data structures that enable their efficient execution. These algorithms solve numerous real-world problems, some of which we will present in this chapter. Too often, the data structures and algorithms presented in this chapter have been considered "too advanced" for the undergraduate curriculum. Software professionals, however, will readily be able to learn these structures and the principles behind the algorithms and apply them to the challenging problems they must face.

Classifying Problems

A computational geometry problem inherently involves geometric objects, such as points, lines, and polygons. More precisely, a computational geometry problem is defined by (a) the type of input data to be processed, (b) the computation to be performed, and (c) whether the task is static or dynamic. These classifications help identify the techniques that can improve efficiency across families of related problems.

Input data

A computational geometry problem must define the input data. The following are the most common types of input data to be processed:

- A set of points in the two-dimensional plane
- A set of line segments in the plane
- A set of rectangles in the plane
- A set of arbitrary polygons in the plane

Two-dimensional structures (lines, rectangles, and circles) have three-dimensional counterparts (planes, cubes, and spheres) and even *n*-dimensional counterparts (such as hyperplanes, hypercubes, and hyperspheres). For advanced computational geometry problems, the type of input data can expand to higher dimensions.

Do We Need More Than Three Dimensions?

Computational geometry problem: Given a set of 14 million points in a 29-dimensional plane, find the closest neighbor for each point.

Real-world service: The eHarmony matchmaking service (*http://www.eharmony.com*) claims it is "the first relationship service on the Web to use a scientific approach to match highly compatible singles." Using their patented (U.S. Patent No. 6,735,568) Compatibility Matching System™, eHarmony predicts the long-term compatibility between two people. All users of the system (estimated to be 14 million by February 2007) fill out a 436-question Relationship Questionnaire. eHarmony then determines closeness of match between two people based on 29 dimensions. eHarmony reported in November 2003 that 91% of its users received 10 or more potential matches.

Data imputation problem: An input file contains 14 million records, where each record has 29 fields with text or numeric values. Some of these values are suspected to be wrong or missing. We can infer/impute "corrections" for the suspicious values by finding other records "close to" the suspicious records.

We first describe a set of core interfaces for the computational geometry domain and then introduce a set of classes that realize these interfaces. All algorithms are coded against these interfaces to enable maximum portability.

The algorithms in this chapter depend upon a set of core concepts, shown in Figure 9-1:

IPoint
> Represents the basic Cartesian point (*x*,*y*) using double floating-point accuracy. Provides a default comparator that sorts by *x*, from left to right, and breaks ties by sorting *y*, from bottom to top.

IRectangle
> Represents a rectangle in Cartesian space; can determine whether it intersects an IPoint or contains an IRectangle.

ILineSegment
> Represents a finite segment in Cartesian space with a fixed start and end point. In "normal position," the start point will have a higher *y* coordinate than the end point, except for horizontal lines (in which case the leftmost end point is designated as the start point). It can determine intersections with other ILineSegment or IPoint objects; it can determine whether an IPoint object is on its left or right when considering the direction of the line from its end point to its start point.

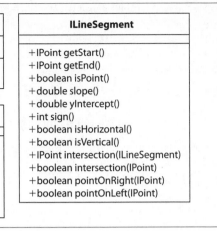

IPoint	
+Comparator<IPoint> xy_sorter	
+double getX() +double getY()	

ILineSegment
+IPoint getStart() +IPoint getEnd() +boolean isPoint() +double slope() +double yIntercept() +int sign() +boolean isHorizontal() +boolean isVertical() +IPoint intersection(ILineSegment) +boolean intersection(IPoint) +boolean pointOnRight(IPoint) +boolean pointOnLeft(IPoint)

IRectangle
+double getLeft() +double getBottom() +double getRight() +double getTop() +boolean intersects(IPoint) +boolean contains(IRectangle)

Figure 9-1. Core interfaces for computational geometry

These concepts naturally extend into multiple dimensions, as shown in Figure 9-2:

IMultiPoint

> Represents an *n*-dimensional Cartesian point with a fixed number of dimensions, with each coordinate value using double floating-point accuracy; can determine distance to another IMultiPoint with same dimensionality. Can return array of coordinate values to optimize performance by some algorithms.

IHypercube

> Represents an *n*-dimensional solid shape with [*left*, *right*] bounding values for a fixed number of dimensions; can determine whether it intersects an IMultiPoint or contains an IHypercube with the same dimensionality.

IMultiLineSegment

> Represents a finite segment in *n*-dimensional Cartesian space.

IMultiPoint	IHypercube	IMultiLineSegment
+int dimensionality() +double getCoordinate(int) +double distance(IMultiPoint) +double[] raw()	+int dimensionality() +double getLeft(int) +double getRight(int) +boolean intersects(IMultiPoint) +boolean contains(IHypercube) +boolean intersects(double[])	+int dimensionality() +IMultiPoint getStartPoint() +IMultiPoint getEndPoint()

Figure 9-2. Interfaces to represent multiple dimensional data

The allowed point values are traditionally real numbers, which forces an implementation to use floating-point primitive types to store data. In the 1970s, computations over floating-point values were relatively costly compared to integer arithmetic.

Today's computers are sufficiently advanced that this no longer is an obstacle to performance. However, Chapter 2 discusses important issues, such as round-off error, relating to floating-point computations that impact the algorithms in this chapter.

Finally, some computational geometry algorithms require the concept of an interval over integer values, shown in Figure 9-3:

IInterval

> Represents the semi-closed range [*left*, *right*) over integer values; that is, it includes the value *left* but not the value *right*. It can determine its relationship to a given integer value (whether to the left, to the right, or intersecting).

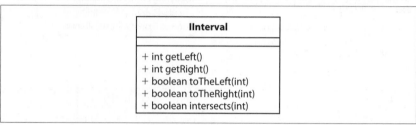

Figure 9-3. Interface to represent interval [left, right)

Each of these interface types is realized by a set of concrete classes used to instantiate the actual objects (for example, the class TwoDPoint realizes both the IPoint and IMultiPoint interfaces).

Computation

Computations in computational geometry are typically related to spatial questions, such as those shown in Table 9-1. There are three general task types:

Query

> Select existing elements within the input set based upon a set of desired constraints (e.g., closest, furthest); these tasks are most directly related to the search algorithms discussed in Chapter 5.

Computation

> Perform a series of calculations over the input set (e.g., line segments) to produce a number of specific geometric structures that incorporate the elements from the input set (e.g., intersections over these line segments). The result of the computation task is the answer to the problem.

Preprocessing

> Embed the input set in a rich data structure to be used to answer a set of questions. In other words, the result of the preprocessing task is used as input for a set of other questions.

Table 9-1. Computational geometry problems and their application

Computational geometry problem(s)	Real-world application(s)
Find the closest point to a given point. Find the furthest point from a given point.	Given a car's location, find the closest gasoline station. Given an ambulance station, find the furthest hospital from a given set of facilities to determine worst-case travel time.
Determine whether a polygon is simple (i.e., two non-consecutive edges cannot share a point).	An animal from an endangered species has been tagged with a radio transmitter that emits the animal's location. Scientists would like to know when the animal crosses its own path to find commonly used trails.
Compute the smallest circle enclosing a set of points. Compute the largest interior circle of a set of points that *doesn't* contain a point.	Statisticians use various techniques when analyzing data. Enclosing circles can identify clusters, whereas large gaps in data suggest anomalous or missing data.
Determine the full set of intersections within a set of line segments, or within a set of circles, rectangles, or arbitrary polygons.	Very Large Scale Integration (VLSI) design rule checking.

In the sections of this chapter, we present the various computational abstractions used to solve computational geometry problems. These techniques are by no means limited to geometry problems and have many real-world applications. For example, the sweep technique shows how to organize objects into a complete ordering for processing when those objects (such as points, line segments, or polygons) have no immediate ordering available.

Nature of the task

A static task requires only that an answer be delivered on demand for a specific input data set. However, there are two important dynamic considerations that alter the way that a problem may be approached:

- Is the task to be requested multiple times over the same input data set? If so, then one should preprocess the input set to improve the efficiency of future task requests.
- Might the input data set change after the task has been requested? If so, then one should investigate data structures that gracefully enable such alterations.

Dynamic tasks require data structures that can grow and shrink as demanded by changes to the input set. Arrays of fixed length might be suitable for static tasks, but dynamic tasks require one to assemble linked lists or stacks of information together to serve a common purpose. Refer to Chapter 6 for the benefits and limitations of the two ways to store graphs, namely adjacency lists and adjacency matrices.

Assumptions

The most effective approach to develop or understand an efficient solution to a problem is to analyze the assumptions and invariants about the input set (or the task to be performed). For example:

- Given an input set of line segments, can there be horizontal or vertical segments?
- Given a set of points, is it possible that three points are collinear (that is, can be found on the same mathematical line in the plane)? If not, the points are said to be in general position, which simplifies many algorithms.
- Does the input set contain a uniform distribution of points? Or is it skewed or clustered in a way that could force an algorithm into its worst-case behavior?

Most of the algorithms presented in this chapter have unusual boundary cases that are challenging to compute properly; we describe these situations in the code examples.

Classic Problems in Computational Geometry

We motivate the algorithms described in this chapter by presenting several of the classic problems that, in a sense, define the field of computational geometry. To solve these problems efficiently, one must know several key data structures and algorithmic techniques that will prove useful in other domains as well. We describe each problem and briefly describe and analyze an initial intuitive algorithm to determine the expected running time to solve the problem. In the remaining sections of this chapter, we present more elegant and efficient algorithms for solving these problems. As we have repeatedly said in this book, the obvious solution can usually be improved by: (a) taking advantage of the unique aspects of the problem, and (b) storing information using an appropriate data structure that supports the algorithm.

Convex hull

Given a set of points P in a two-dimensional plane, the convex hull is the smallest convex shape that fully encloses all points in P; a line segment drawn between any two points within the hull lies totally within it. The hull is formed by a clockwise ordering of h points $L_0 \ldots L_{h-1}$. The first point L_0 is typically the leftmost point* in the set P (although any point can be the start). Each sequence of three hull points L_i, L_{i+1}, L_{i+2} creates a right turn; note that this property holds for L_{h-2}, L_{h-1}, L_0 as well.

Given n points, there are $C(n,3)$, or:

$$\binom{n}{3} = \frac{n(n-1)(n-2)}{6}$$

different possible triangles. Point $p_i \in P$ cannot be part of the convex hull if it is contained within a triangle formed by three other distinct points in P (for example, in Figure 9-4 point p_6 can be eliminated by the triangle formed by points p_4, p_7, and p_8). For each of these triangles t_i, a brute-force algorithm could eliminate from the convex hull any of the $n-3$ remaining points if they exist within t_i. Once the hull points are known, a clockwise ordering is determined by selecting the leftmost point as the "base" (in this case p_0) and sorting all remaining points

---

* If multiple points exist in P with the same x coordinate, then L_0 is the one with the smallest y coordinate.

by the angle formed with a vertical line. One must be careful when processing collinear points.

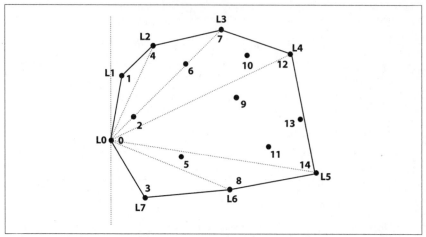

Figure 9-4. Sample set of points in plane with its convex hull drawn

The inefficiency of this approach is clear since it will require $O(n^4)$ individual executions of the triangle detection step. This chapter presents an efficient CONVEX HULL SCAN algorithm that computes the convex hull in $O(n \log n)$.

Computing intersections from a set of line segments

Given a set of line segments S in a two-dimensional plane, determine the full set of intersection points between all segments. One may also want to know if there is at least one intersection (i.e., stop after reporting the first intersection). In the example in Figure 9-5 there are two intersections (shown as small black circles) found in this set of four line segments. The brute-force algorithm shown in Figure 9-6 computes the intersections of the line segments in S using $O(n^2)$ time.

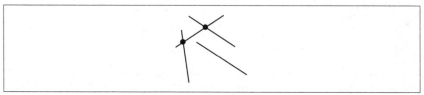

Figure 9-5. Three line segments with two intersections

Example 9-1 shows the implementation of BRUTE FORCE INTERSECTION. There are $C(n,2)$ segment pairs, or:

$$\binom{n}{2} = \frac{n(n-1)}{2}$$

possible pairings. For each pair, the implementation outputs the intersection, if it exists.

Computational
Geometry

BRUTE FORCE INTERSECTION			Brute Force
Best	Average	Worst	
$O(n^2)$	$O(n^2)$	$O(n^2)$	

intersections (S)
1. **foreach** $s_1 \in S$ **do**
2.   **foreach** $s_2 \in S - \{s_1\}$ **do**
3.   p = intersection point of s_1 and s_2
4.   **if** (p exists) **then** record (p, s_1, s_2)
end

Figure 9-6. Brute Force Intersection fact sheet

Example 9-1. Brute Force Intersection implementation

```
public class BruteForceAlgorithm extends IntersectionDetection {

    public Hashtable<IPoint, ILineSegment[]> intersections
            (ILineSegment[] segments) {

        startTime();
        initialize();
        for (int i = 0; i < segments.length-1; i++) {
            for (int j = i+1; j < segments.length; j++) {
                IPoint p = segments[i].intersection(segments[j]);
                if (p != null) {
                    record (p, segments[i], segments[j]);
                }
            }
        }
        computeTime();
        return report;
    }
}
```

This computation requires $O(n^2)$ individual executions of its core step. Determining the intersection between two line segments may involve trigonometric functions or division, both computationally expensive operations; additionally, as described in Chapter 3, such operations often introduce round-off error into the resulting computation. We implement a more efficient technique that detects intersections using only addition, subtraction, multiplication, and comparison (Cormen et al., 2001).

It is not immediately clear that any improvement over $O(n^2)$ is possible, yet this chapter presents the innovative LINE SWEEP algorithm, which on average shows how to compute the results in $O((n+k) \log n)$ where k represents the number of reported intersection points.

Answering nearest neighbor queries

Given a set of points P in a two-dimensional plane, answer nearest neighbor queries of the form, "What point in P is closest to point x using Euclidean distance?" Note that point x does not have to already exist in P.

Given query point x, compare its distance to all other points in P to find the closest one. This requires $O(n)$ linear steps. As we saw in Chapter 5, binary trees helped to reduce the search by eliminating from consideration groups of points that could not be part of the solution. We use trees to partition the points in the two-dimensional plane to reduce the search time as well. The extra cost of preprocessing all points in P into an efficient structure is recouped later by savings of the query computations, which becomes $O(\log n)$. If the number of searches is going to be small, then perhaps the obvious $O(n)$ comparison is best.

Answering range queries

Instead of searching for a specific target point, a query could instead request all points found within a given rectangular region of the two-dimensional plane. The obvious solution requires one to determine whether the target rectangular region contains each point in the set, resulting in $O(n)$ performance.

The same data structure developed for nearest-neighbor queries also supports these queries, known as "orthogonal range" because the rectangular query region is aligned with the x and y axes of the plane. The only way to produce better than $O(n)$ performance is to find a way to both (a) discard from consideration a group of points, and (b) include in the query result a group of points. Using a kd-tree, the query is performed using a recursive traversal, and the performance can be

$$O(\sqrt{n} + r)$$

where r is the number of points reported by the query.

Summary

The code solutions we present for these problems will conform to the API definitions shown in Table 9-2. For each problem, this table also summarizes the performance of the algorithms discussed in this chapter.

Table 9-2. API definition of problems discussed in this chapter

Problem	API description

Convex Hull	`public interface IConvexHull {`
	  `/** Compute ordered array of hull points. */`
	  `IPoint[] compute (IPoint[] points);`
	`}`
	Obvious solution: $O(n^4)$
	Average-case CONVEX HULL SCAN: $O(n \log n)$

Intersecting Line Segments	`public abstract class IntersectionDetection {`
	  `/** Determine all intersections. */`
	  `public abstract Hashtable<IPoint,ILineSegment[]>`
	    `intersections (ILineSegment[] segments);`
	`}`
	Obvious solution: $O(n^2)$
	Average-case LINE SWEEP: $O((n+k) \log n)$ with k=number of intersections found

Problem	API description

Nearest Neighbor	```public class KDTree {```
	 ```/** Return closest point to target. */```
	 ```public IMultiPoint nearest (IMultiPoint target);```
	 ```}```
	 Obvious solution: O(n)
	 Average-case kd-tree NEAREST NEIGHBOR: O(log n)

Range Queries	```public class KDTree {```
	 ```/** Return points within region. */```
	 ```public ArrayList<IMultiPoint> search (```
	 ``` IHypercube space);```
	 ```}```
	 Obvious solution: O(n)
	 Average-case kd-tree RANGE QUERY: O($\sqrt{n} + r$) with r=number of reported points

Convex Hull Scan

To develop an efficient algorithm for computing the convex hull (whose fact sheet appears in Figure 9-7) for a set of points P, we could choose an iterative approach, as shown in Figure 9-8. To determine the next point in the hull, compute the smallest angular difference formed by all non-hull points with an infinite ray determined by the last two discovered hull points. When the partial convex hull contains h points, the angles must be computed for $n-h$ points to determine the next point; this approach is unable to prune away wasted computations that will clearly not be needed.

Andrew's CONVEX HULL SCAN divides the problem into two parts—constructing the partial upper hull and the partial lower hull. First, all points are sorted by their x coordinate (breaking ties by considering the y). Note that the points in Figure 9-8 are already numbered from left to right along the x axis. The partial upper hull starts with the leftmost two points in P. CONVEX HULL SCAN extends the partial upper hull by finding the point p in P whose x coordinate comes next in sorted order after the partial upper hull's last point L_i.

If the three points L_{i-1}, L_i and the candidate point p form a right turn, then CONVEX HULL SCAN extends the partial hull to include p. This decision is equivalent to computing the determinant of the three-by-three matrix shown in Figure 9-9, which represents the cross product $cp=(L_i.x-L_{i-1}.x)(p.y-L_{i-1}.y)-(L_i.y-L_{i-1}.y)(p.x-L_{i-1}.x)$. If cp is negative, then the three points determine a right turn and CONVEX HULL SCAN continues on. If $cp=0$ (the three points are collinear) or if $cp>0$ (the three points determine a left turn), then the middle point L_i must be removed from the partial hull to retain its convex property. CONVEX HULL SCAN computes the convex upper hull by processing all points up to the rightmost point. The lower hull is similarly computed (this time by choosing points in decreasing x coordinate value), and the two partial hulls are joined together.

Figure 9-7 shows CONVEX HULL SCAN in action as it computes the partial upper hall. Note that the overall approach makes numerous mistakes as it visits every point in P from left to right, yet all of these are corrected by dropping—sometimes repeatedly—the middle of the last three points.

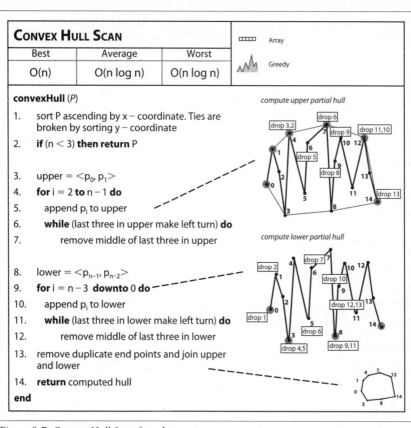

CONVEX HULL SCAN

Best	Average	Worst
O(n)	O(n log n)	O(n log n)

▭▭▭ Array

⋀⋀⋀ Greedy

convexHull (P)

1. sort P ascending by x − coordinate. Ties are broken by sorting y − coordinate
2. **if** (n < 3) **then return** P

3. upper = <p_0, p_1>
4. **for** i = 2 **to** n − 1 **do**
5.   append p_i to upper
6.   **while** (last three in upper make left turn) **do**
7.   remove middle of last three in upper

8. lower = <p_{n-1}, p_{n-2}>
9. **for** i = n − 3 **downto** 0 **do**
10.   append p_i to lower
11.   **while** (last three in lower make left turn) **do**
12.   remove middle of last three in lower
13. remove duplicate end points and join upper and lower
14. **return** computed hull

end

compute upper partial hull

compute lower partial hull

Figure 9-7. Convex Hull Scan fact sheet

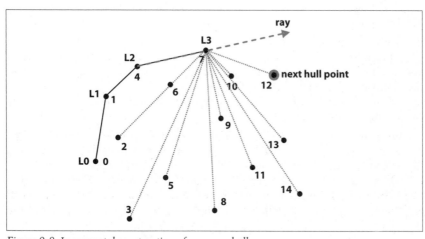

Figure 9-8. Incremental construction of a convex hull

Computational Geometry

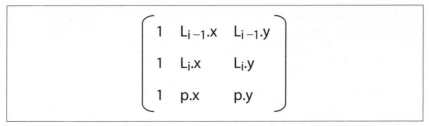

Figure 9-9. Computing the determinant of an array of three points to decide right turn

Input/Output

Input

A set of two-dimensional points P in a plane.

Output

An ordered list L containing the h vertices of the convex hull of P in clockwise order. The convex hull is a polygon defined by the points $L_0, L_1, ..., L_{h-1}$, where h is the number of points in L. Note that the polygon is formed from the h line segments $<L_0, L_1>, <L_1, L_2>, ..., < L_{h-1}, L_0>$.

Assumptions

To avoid trivial solutions, we assume $|P| \geq 3$. No two points are "too close" to each other (as determined by the implementation). If two points are too close to each other and one of those points is on the convex hull, CONVEX HULL SCAN might incorrectly select an invalid convex hull point (or discard a valid convex hull point); however, the difference would be negligible.

Context

The Akl-Toussaint heuristic (1978) can noticeably improve performance of the overall algorithm by discarding all points that exist within the extreme quadrilateral (the minimum and maximum points along both x and y axes) computed from the initial set P. Figure 9-10 shows the extreme quadrilateral for the sample points from Figure 9-4, and the discarded points are shown in gray; none of these points can belong to the convex hull.

To determine whether a point p is within the extreme quadrilateral, imagine a line segment s from p to an extreme point at $(p.x, -\infty)$, and count the number of times that s intersects the four line segments of the quadrilateral;[*] if the count is 1, then p is inside and can be eliminated. This computation requires a fixed number of steps, so it is O(1), which means applying the Akl-Toussaint heuristic to all points is O(n). For large random samples, this heuristic can remove nearly half of the

---

[*] The implementation handles special cases, such as when line segment s exactly intersects one of the end points of the extreme quadrilateral.

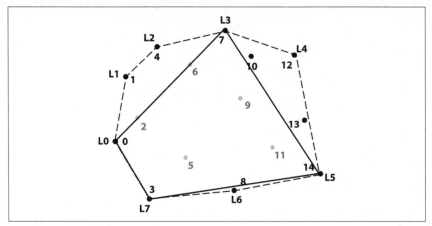

Figure 9-10. The Akl-Toussaint heuristic at work

initial points, and since these points are discarded before the sort operation, the costly sorting step in the algorithm is reduced.

Forces

CONVEX HULL SCAN requires only primitive operations (such as multiply and divide), making it easier to implement than GRAHAMSCAN (Graham, 1972), which requires using trigonometric identities. If CONVEX HULL SCAN uses QUICKSORT to initially sort the points, its performance suffers because of the well-documented problems that QUICKSORT has with nearly sorted data (see "Quicksort" in Chapter 4). CONVEX HULL SCAN can support a large number of points since it is not recursive. The implementation in Example 9-2 uses arrays; if it used linked lists, then it would use INSERTION SORT, which would worsen the performance to $O(n^2)$. Using balanced binary trees to store the input points instead of arrays would eliminate the sorting step, yet add extra complication to the code requesting the convex hull. The fastest implementation occurs if the input set is uniformly distributed and so it can be sorted in $O(n)$ using BUCKET SORT, since the resulting performance would also be $O(n)$. The supporting code repository contains each of the described implementations that we benchmark for performance later in the "Analysis" section.

Solution

Example 9-2 shows how CONVEX HULL SCAN first computes the partial upper hull before reversing direction and computing the partial lower hull. The final convex hull is the combination of the two partial hulls. Figure 9-11 summarizes the `PartialHull` class.

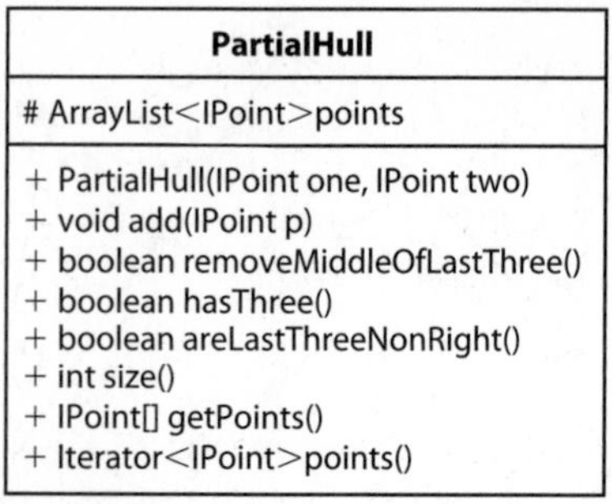

PartialHull
ArrayList<IPoint>points
+ PartialHull(IPoint one, IPoint two) + void add(IPoint p) + boolean removeMiddleOfLastThree() + boolean hasThree() + boolean areLastThreeNonRight() + int size() + IPoint[] getPoints() + Iterator<IPoint>points()

Figure 9-11. PartialHull supporting class

Example 9-2. Convex Hull Scan solution to convex hull

```
public class ConvexHullScan implements IConvexHull {

  public IPoint [] compute (IPoint[] points) {
    // sort by x-coordinate (and if ==, by y-coordinate).
    int n = points.length;
    new HeapSort<IPoint>().sort(points, 0, n-1, IPoint.xy_sorter);
    if (n < 3) { return points; }

    // Compute upper hull by starting with leftmost two points
    PartialHull upper = new PartialHull(points[0], points[1]);
    for (int i = 2; i < n; i++) {
        upper.add(points[i]);
        while (upper.hasThree() && upper.areLastThreeNonRight()) {
            upper.removeMiddleOfLastThree();
        }
    }

    // Compute lower hull by starting with rightmost two points
    PartialHull lower = new PartialHull(points[n-1], points[n-2]);
    for (int i = n-3; i >= 0; i--) {
        lower.add(points[i]);
        while (lower.hasThree() && lower.areLastThreeNonRight()) {
            lower.removeMiddleOfLastThree();
        }
    }

    // remove duplicate end points when combining.
    IPoint[] hull = new IPoint[upper.size()+lower.size()-2];
    System.arraycopy(upper.getPoints(), 0, hull, 0, upper.size());
    System.arraycopy(lower.getPoints(), 1, hull,
                        upper.size(), lower.size()-2);
    return hull;
  }
}
```

Consequences

Because the first step of this algorithm must sort the points, we rely on HEAP-SORT to achieve the best average performance without suffering from the worst-case behavior of QUICKSORT as described in Chapter 4. However, in the average case, QUICKSORT will outperform HEAPSORT, so you should consider the likelihood that the worst case for QUICKSORT will occur.

Analysis

We ran a set of 100 trials on randomly generated two-dimensional points from the unit square; the best and worst trials were discarded, and Table 9-3 shows the average performance results of the remaining 98 trials. The table also shows the breakdown of average times to perform the heuristic plus some information about the solution.

Given a uniform distribution of n random points within the [0,1] unit square, Table 9-3 describes statistics that reveal some of the underlying reasons for why CONVEX HULL SCAN is so efficient.

Table 9-3. Example showing running times (in milliseconds) and applied Akl-Toussaint heuristic

n	Average number of points on hull	Average time to compute	Average number of points removed by heuristic	Average time to compute heuristic	Average time to compute with heuristic
4,096	21.65	8.95	2,023	1.59	4.46
8,192	24.1	18.98	4,145	2.39	8.59
16,384	25.82	41.44	8,216	6.88	21.71
32,768	27.64	93.46	15,687	14.47	48.92
65,536	28.9	218.24	33,112	33.31	109.74
131,072	32.02	513.03	65,289	76.36	254.92
262,144	33.08	1168.77	129,724	162.94	558.47
524,288	35.09	2617.53	265,982	331.78	1159.72
1,048,576	36.25	5802.36	512,244	694	2524.30

As the size of the input set increases, nearly half of its points can be removed by the Akl-Toussaint heuristic. More surprising, perhaps, is the low number of points on the convex hull. The second column in Table 9-3 validates the claim by Preparata and Shamos (1985) that the number of points should be O(log n), which may be surprising given the large number of points. One insight behind this low number is that in a large random set, each individual point has a small probability of being on the convex hull.

The first step in CONVEX HULL SCAN explains the cost of O(n log n) when the points are sorted using one of the standard comparison-based sorting techniques described in Chapter 4. As previously mentioned, if the points are already sorted, then this step can be skipped and the resulting steps require just O(n) processing.

The loop that computes the upper partial hull (lines 4–7 in Figure 9-7) processes $n-2$ points; the inner while loop (lines 6–7) cannot execute more than $n-2$ times, and the same logic applies to the loop that computes the lower partial hull (lines 9–12). The total time for the remaining steps of CONVEX HULL SCAN is thus $O(n)$.

Problems with floating-point arithmetic appear when CONVEX HULL SCAN computes the cross product calculation. Instead of strictly comparing whether the cross product $cp<0$, PartialHull determines whether $cp<\delta$, where δ is 10^{-9}.

Variations

The sorting step of CONVEX HULL SCAN can be eliminated if the points are already known to be in sorted order; in this case, CONVEX HULL SCAN can perform in $O(n)$. Alternatively, if the input points are drawn from a uniform distribution, then one can use BUCKET SORT (see "Bucket Sort" in Chapter 4) to also achieve $O(n)$ performance. Another convex hull variation known as QUICKHULL (Preparata and Shamos, 1985) uses the "divide and conquer" technique inspired by QUICKSORT to compute the convex hull.

There is one final variation to consider. CONVEX HULL SCAN doesn't actually need a sorted array when it constructs the partial upper hull; it just needs to iterate over all points in P in order, from smallest x coordinate to highest x coordinate. This behavior is exactly what occurs if one constructs a binary heap from the points in P and repeatedly removes the smallest element from the heap. If the removed points are stored in a linked list, then the points can be simply "read off" the linked list to process the points in reverse order from right to left. The code for this variation (identified as Heap in Figure 9-12) is available in the code repository accompanying this book.

The performance results shown in Figure 9-12 were generated from three data set distribution types:

Circle data
> n points distributed evenly over the unit circle. Note that all of these points will belong to the convex hull, so this is an extreme case.

Uniform data
> n points distributed evenly over the unit square. As n increases, the majority of these points will not be part of the convex hull, so this represents another extreme case.

Slice data
> n points distributed unevenly; $n-2$ points are clustered in thin slices just to the left of .502. The data set also contains the point (0,0) and (1,0). This set is constructed to defeat BUCKET SORT.

We ran a series of trials using data sets of size $n = 512$ to 131,072 points,* the two data set distributions, and the different implementations described in Example 9-2

---

* We limited the slice data set size to 2,048 because BUCKET SORT rapidly degenerated to $O(n^2)$ performance.

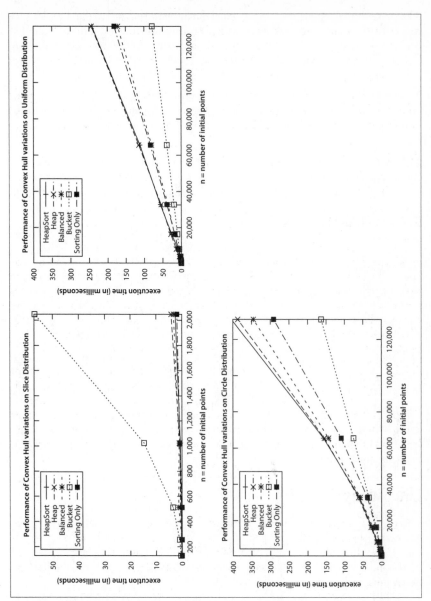

Figure 9-12. Performance of convex hull variations

and the code repository. As a baseline for comparison, we include performance results for using HEAPSORT simply to sort the points. We did not employ the Akl-Toussaint heuristic. For each data set size, we ran 100 trials and discarded the best- and worst-performing runs. The resulting average time (in milliseconds) of the remaining 98 trials is depicted in Figure 9-12. One can clearly see the direct correlation between the sort time and the times to compute the convex hull.

Computational
Geometry

Also, the implementation using balanced binary trees shows the best performance of the approaches that use comparison-based sorting techniques. Note that the implementation using BUCKETSORT offers the most efficient implementation, but only because the input set is drawn from a uniform distribution. In the general case, computing a convex hull can be performed in $O(n \log n)$.

The convex hull problem can be extended to three dimensions and higher where the goal is to compute the bounding polyhedron surrounding the three-dimensional point space. Unfortunately, in higher dimensions, more complex implementations are required.

Melkman (1987) has developed an algorithm that produces the convex hull for a simple polyline or polygon in $O(n)$. Quite simply, it avoids the need to sort the initial points by taking advantage of the ordered arrangement of points in the polygon itself.

Related Algorithms

Once a convex hull has been created, it can be maintained efficiently using an approach proposed by Overmars and van Leeuwen (1981). Instead of storing the convex hull simply as an array of points, the points are stored in a tree structure that supports both deletion and insertion of points. The cost of either an insert or delete is known to be $O(\log^2 n)$, and so the overall cost of constructing the hull becomes $O(n \log^2 n)$ while still requiring only $O(n)$ space. This result reinforces the principle that every performance benefit comes with its own tradeoff.

One of the earliest algorithms to compute the convex hull is GRAHAMSCAN, developed in 1972 using simple trigonometric identities. Using the determinant computation shown earlier in Figure 9-9, an appropriate implementation needs only simple data structures and basic mathematical operations. GRAHAMSCAN computes the convex hull in $O(n \log n)$ since it first sorts points by the angles they make with the point $s \in P$ with the smallest y coordinate and the x-axis. One challenge in completing this sort is that points with the same angle must be ordered by the distance from s.

LineSweep

There are numerous situations where one must detect intersections between geometric shapes. In VLSI chip design, precise circuits are laid out on a circuit board, and there must be no unplanned intersections. For travel planning, a set of roads could be stored in a database as line segments whose street intersections are determined by line segment intersections.

Figure 9-13 shows an example with seven intersections found between six line segments. Perhaps we don't have to compare all possible $C(n,2)$ or $n^*(n-1)/2$ line segments. After all, line segments that are clearly apart from one another (in this example, S1 and S4) cannot intersect. LINESWEEP is a proven approach that improves efficiency by focusing on a subset of the input elements as it progresses. Imagine sweeping a horizontal line L across the input set of line segments from the top to the bottom and reporting the intersections when they are found by L. Figure 9-13 shows the state of line L as the sweep occurs from top to bottom (at nine distinct and specific locations).

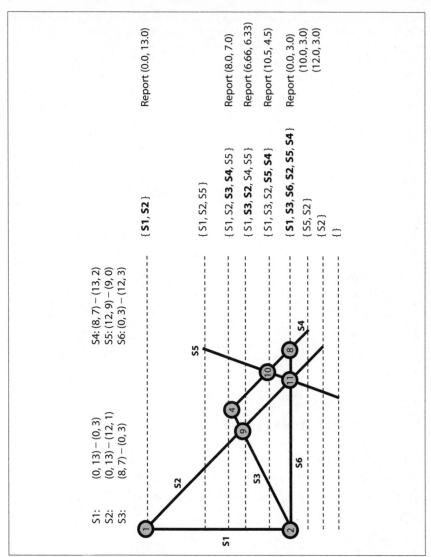

Figure 9-13. Detecting seven intersections for six line segments

The innovation of LINESWEEP is recognizing that line segments can be ordered from left to right at a specific *y* coordinate.* Line segment intersections can then occur only between neighboring segments in the state of the sweep line. Specifically, for two line segments S_i and S_j to intersect, there must be some time during the line sweep when they are neighbors. Indeed, LINESWEEP can efficiently locate intersections because it maintains this line state efficiently.

---

* Horizontal segments are addressed by considering the left end point to be "higher" than the right end point.

Looking closer at the nine selected locations of the horizontal sweep line in Figure 9-13, you will see that each occurs at (i) the start or end of a line segment, or (ii) an intersection. LINESWEEP doesn't actually "sweep" a line across the Cartesian plane; rather, it inserts the 2*n segment end points into an event queue, which is a modified priority queue, as shown in Figure 9-14. All intersections involving start and end points of existing line segments can be detected when processing these points. LINESWEEP processes the queue to build up the state of the sweep line L to determine when neighboring line segments intersect; the logic is shown in Figure 9-15.

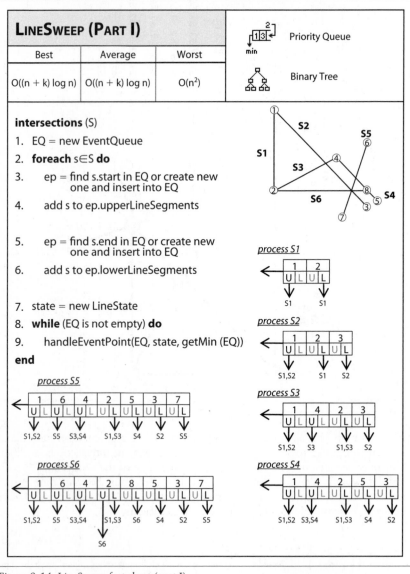

Figure 9-14. LineSweep fact sheet (part I)

LINESWEEP (PART II)			

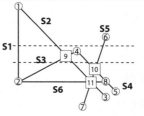

Priority Queue

Binary Tree

Best	Average	Worst
O((n + k) log n)	O((n + k) log n)	O(n²)

handleEventPoint (EQ, state, ep)

1. left = segment in state to left of ep
2. right = segment in state to right of ep
3. compute intersections in state from (left to right)
4. report intersections (if any) at ep

5. remove segments in state between (but not including) left and right. Left and right are now guaranteed to be neighbors
6. advance the state sweep point down to ep
7. update = **false**
8. **if** (new segments start at ep) **then**
9.   insert into state new segments
10.   update = **true**
11. **if** (intersections associated with ep) **then**
12.   insert into state intersections
13.   update = **true**
14. **if** (update) **then**
15.   updateQueue (EQ, left, left's successor)
16.   updateQueue (EQ, right, right's predecessor)
17. **else**
18.   update (EQ, left, right)
end

updateQueue (EQ, left, right)

1. **if** (neighboring left and right segments intersect below sweep point) **then**
2.   insert their intersection point into EQ
end

Before handling point 4
EQ = < 4, 2, 8, 5, 3, 7 >
state = < S1,S2,S5 >

After handling point 4
EQ = < 9, 2, 8, 5, 3, 7 >
*state = {S1,S2,**S3**,**S4**,S5 }*
Report (4) as intersection.

After handling point 9
EQ = < 10, 2, 8, 5, 3, 7 >
*state = {S1,**S3**,**S2**,S4,S5 }*
Report (9) as intersection.

Figure 9-15. LineSweep fact sheet (part II)

Input/Output

Input

A set of n line segments S in the Cartesian plane.

Output

The full set of k points representing the intersections (if any exist) between these line segments and, for each of these k points, p_i, the actual line segments from S that intersect at p_i.

Assumptions

There can be no duplicate segments in S. No two line segments in S are collinear (that is, overlap each other and have the same slope). The algorithm supports both horizontal and vertical line segments by carefully performing computations and ordering segments appropriately. No line segment should be a single point (i.e., a line segment whose start and end point are the same).

Context

When the expected number of intersections is much smaller than the number of line segments, this algorithm will handily outperform a brute-force approach. When there are a significant number of intersections, the bookkeeping of the algorithm may outweigh the benefits.

Forces

A sweep-based approach is useful when you can (a) efficiently construct the line state, and (b) manage the event queue that defines when the sweep line is interpreted. There are numerous special cases to consider within the LINESWEEP implementation, and the resulting code is much more complex than the brute force approach, whose worst-case performance is $O(n^2)$. You would only choose this algorithm for the expected performance savings.

LINESWEEP produces partial results intermittently until the entire input set has been processed and all output results are produced. In the example here, the line state is a balanced binary tree of line segments, which is possible because we can impose an ordering on the segments at the sweep line point. The event queue can also simply be a balanced binary tree of event points, sorted lexicographically.

To simplify the coding of the algorithm, the binary tree used to store the line state is an augmented balanced binary tree in which only the leaf nodes contain real information. Interior nodes store min and max information about the leftmost segment in the left subtree and rightmost segment in the right subtree. The ordering of segments within the tree is made based upon the sweep point, the current EventPoint being processed from the priority queue.

Solution

The solution described in Example 9-3 depends upon the EventPoint, EventQueue, and LineState classes depicted in Figures 9-16 and 9-17.

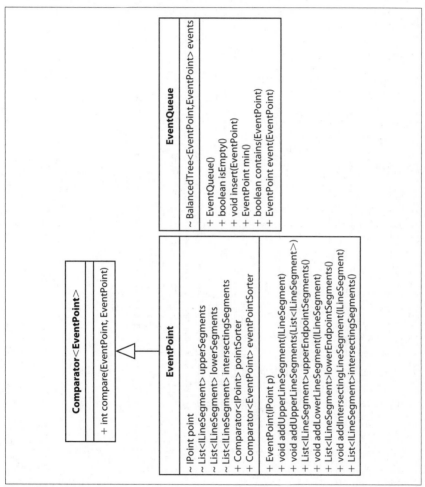

Figure 9-16. EventPoint class

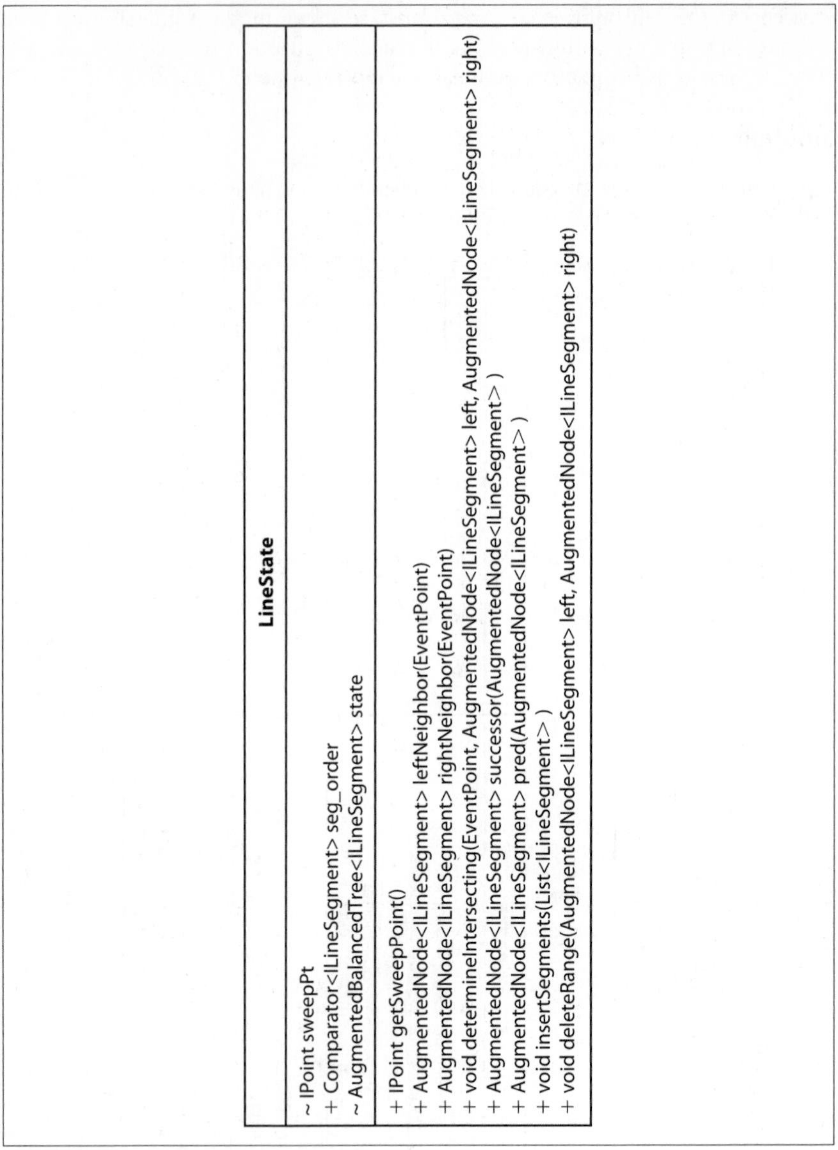

LineState

~ IPoint sweepPt
+ Comparator<ILineSegment> seg_order
~ AugmentedBalancedTree<ILineSegment> state

+ IPoint getSweepPoint()
+ AugmentedNode<ILineSegment> leftNeighbor(EventPoint)
+ AugmentedNode<ILineSegment> rightNeighbor(EventPoint)
+ void determineIntersecting(EventPoint, AugmentedNode<ILineSegment> left, AugmentedNode<ILineSegment> right)
+ AugmentedNode<ILineSegment> successor(AugmentedNode<ILineSegment>)
+ AugmentedNode<ILineSegment> pred(AugmentedNode<ILineSegment>)
+ void insertSegments(List<ILineSegment>)
+ void deleteRange(AugmentedNode<ILineSegment> left, AugmentedNode<ILineSegment> right)

Figure 9-17. LineState class

Example 9-3. LineSweep Java implementation

```java
public class LineSweep extends IntersectionDetection {
    // Store line sweep state and event queue
    LineState lineState = new LineState();
    EventQueue eq = new EventQueue();

    // Compute the intersection of all segments from array of segments.
    public Hashtable<IPoint,ILineSegment[]>
```

Example 9-3. LineSweep Java implementation (continued)

```
intersections (ILineSegment[] segs){
// construct Event Queue from segments. Ensure that only unique
// points appear by combining all information as it is discovered
for (ILineSegment ils : segs) {
  EventPoint ep = new EventPoint(ils.getStart( ));
  EventPoint old = eq.event(ep);
  if (old == null) { eq.insert(ep); } else { ep = old; }

  // add upper line segments to ep (the object in the queue)
  ep.addUpperLineSegment(ils);

  ep = new EventPoint(ils.getEnd( ));
  old = eq.event(ep);
  if (old == null) { eq.insert(ep); } else { ep = old; }

  // add lower line segments to ep (the object in the queue)
  ep.addLowerLineSegment(ils);
}

// Sweep top to bottom, processing each Event Point in the queue
while (!eq.isEmpty( )) {
  EventPoint p = eq.min( );
  handleEventPoint(p);
}

// return report of all computed intersections
return report;
}

// Process events by updating line state and reporting intersections.
private void handleEventPoint (EventPoint ep) {
// Find segments, if they exist, to left (and right) of ep in
// linestate Intersections can only happen between neighboring
// segments. Start with nearest ones because as line sweeps down
// we will find any other intersections that (for now) we put off.
AugmentedNode<ILineSegment> left = lineState.leftNeighbor(ep);
AugmentedNode<ILineSegment> right = lineState.rightNeighbor(ep);

// determine intersections 'ints' from neighboring line segments and
// get upper segments 'ups' and lower segments 'lows' for this event
// point. An intersection exists if > 1 segment is associated with
// event point
lineState.determineIntersecting(ep, left, right);
List<ILineSegment> ints = ep.intersectingSegments( );
List<ILineSegment> ups = ep.upperEndpointSegments( );
List<ILineSegment> lows = ep.lowerEndpointSegments( );
if (lows.size() + ups.size() + ints.size() > 1) {
  record (ep.p, new List[]{lows,ups,ints});
}

// Delete everything after left until left's successor is right.
// Then update the sweep point, so insertions will be ordered. Only
// ups and ints are inserted because they are still active.
```

Example 9-3. LineSweep Java implementation (continued)

```java
      lineState.deleteRange(left, right);
      lineState.setSweepPoint(ep.p);
      boolean update = false;
      if (!ups.isEmpty()) {
        lineState.insertSegments (ups);
        update = true;
      }
      if (!ints.isEmpty()) {
        lineState.insertSegments (ints);
        update = true;
      }

      // If state shows no intersections at this event point, see if left
      // and right segments intersect below sweep line, and update event
      // queue properly. Otherwise, if there was an intersection, the order
      // of segments between left & right have switched so we check two
      // specific ranges, namely, left and its (new) successor, and right
      // and its (new) predecessor.
      if (!update) {
        if (left != null && right != null) { updateQueue (left, right); }
      } else {
        if (left != null) { updateQueue (left, lineState.successor(left)); }
        if (right != null) { updateQueue (lineState.pred(right), right); }
      }
    }

    // Any intersections below sweep line are inserted as event points.
    private void updateQueue (AugmentedNode<ILineSegment> left,
                              AugmentedNode<ILineSegment> right) {
      // Determine if the two neighboring line segments intersect. Make
      // sure that new intersection point is *below* the sweep line and
      // not added twice.
      IPoint p = left.key().intersection(right.key());
      if (p == null) { return; }
      if (EventPoint.pointSorter.compare(p,lineState.sweepPt) > 0) {
        EventPoint new_ep = new EventPoint(p);
        if (!eq.contains(new_ep)) { eq.insert(new_ep); }
      }
    }
}
```

When the initial EventQueue is initialized with 2*n EventPoint objects, each stores the ILineSegment objects that start (known as *upper segments*) and end (known as *lower segments*) at the stored IPoint object. When LINESWEEP discovers an intersection between line segments, an EventPoint representing that intersection is inserted into the EventQueue as long as it occurs below the sweep line. In this way, no intersections are missed and none are duplicated. For proper functioning, if this intersecting event point already exists within the EventQueue, then the intersecting information is updated within the queue rather than being inserted twice.[*]

---

[*] It is for this reason that LINESWEEP must be able to determine whether the priority queue contains a specific EventPoint object.

In Figure 9-14, when the event point representing the lower point[*] for segment S6 was inserted into the priority queue, LINESWEEP only stored S6 as a lower segment; once it is processed, it will additionally store S4 as an intersecting segment. For a more complex example, when the event point representing the intersection of segments S2 and S5 is inserted into the priority queue, it stores no additional information. Once this event point is processed, it will store segments S6, S2, and S5 as intersecting segments.

The computational engine behind LINESWEEP is contained within the LineState class depicted in Figure 9-17. LineState maintains the current sweep point as it sweeps from the top of the Cartesian plane downward. When the minimum entry is extracted from the EventQueue, the provided pointSorter comparator properly returns the EventPoint objects from top to bottom. The true work of LINESWEEP occurs in the determineIntersecting method of LineState: the intersections are determined by iterating over those segments between *left* and *right*. Full details on these supporting classes are found in the code repository accompanying this book.

Consequences

LINESWEEP achieves $O((n+k) \log n)$ performance because it can reorder the active line segments when the sweep point is advanced. If this step requires more than $O(\log s)$ for its operations, where s is the number of segments in the state, then the entire performance of the overall algorithm will degenerate to $O(n^2)$. For example, if the line state were stored simply as a doubly linked list (a useful structure to rapidly find predecessor and successor segments), the insert operation would increase to require $O(s)$ time to properly locate the segment in the list, and as the set S of line segments increases, the performance degradation will soon become noticeable.

Similarly, the event queue must support an efficient operation to determine whether an event point is already present in the queue. Using a heap-based priority queue implementation—as provided by java.util.PriorityQueue, for example—also forces the algorithm to degenerate to $O(n^2)$. Beware of code implementations that claim to implement an $O(n \log n)$ algorithm but instead produce an $O(n^2)$ implementation!

Analysis

LINESWEEP inserts the 2^*n segment end points into an event queue, a modified priority queue that supports the following operations in time $O(\log q)$, where q is the number of elements in the queue:

min
> Remove the minimum element from the queue.

insert (e)
> Insert the element into its proper location within the ordered queue.

---

[*] Actually the *rightmost* end point, since S6 is horizontal.

member (e)

Determine whether the given element is a member of the queue. Note that this operation is not strictly required of a generic priority queue type.

Only unique points appear in the event queue; that is, if the same event point is inserted, its information is combined with the event point already in the queue. Thus when the points from Figure 9-13 are initially inserted, the event queue contains only eight event points.

LINESWEEP sweeps from top to bottom and updates the line state by adding and deleting segments in their proper order. In Figure 9-13, the ordered line state reflects the line segments that intersect the sweep line, from left to right after processing the event point. To properly compute intersections, LINESWEEP must determine the segment in the state to the left of (or right of) a given segment S_i. LINESWEEP uses an augmented balanced binary tree to process all of the following operations in time $O(\log t)$, where t is the number of elements in the tree:

insert (s)

Insert the line segment s into the tree.

delete (s)

Delete segment s from the tree.

previous (s)

Return the segment immediately before s in the ordering (if one exists).

successor (s)

Return the segment immediately after s in the ordering (if one exists).

To properly maintain the ordering of segments, LINESWEEP swaps the order of segments when a sweep detects an intersection between segments S_i and S_j; fortunately, this too can be performed in $O(\log t)$ time simply by updating the sweep line point and then deleting and reinserting the line segments S_i and S_j. In Figure 9-13, for example, this swap occurs when the third intersection (6.66, 6.33) is found.

The initialization phase of the algorithm constructs a priority queue from the 2^*n points (start and end) in the input set of n lines. The event queue must additionally be able to determine whether a new point p already exists within the queue; for this reason, we cannot simply use a heap to store the event queue, as is commonly done with priority queues. Since the queue is ordered, we must define an ordering of two-dimensional points. Point p1<p2 if p1.y>p2.y; however, if p1.y=p2.y, then p1<p2 if p1.x<p2.x. The size of the queue will never be larger than $2n+k$, where k is the number of intersections and n is the number of input line segments.

All intersection points detected by LINESWEEP below the sweep line are added to the event queue, where they will be processed to swap the order of intersecting segments when the sweep line finally reaches the intersection point. Note that all intersections between neighboring segments will be found below the sweep line, and no intersection point will be missed.

As LINESWEEP processes each event point, line segments are added to the state when an upper end point is visited, and removed when a lower end point is visited.

Thus the line state will never store more than n line segments. The operations that probe the line state can be performed in O(log n) time, and since there are never more than O($n+k$) operations over the state, our cost is O(($n+k$) log ($n+k$)). Because k is no larger than C(n,2) or $n^*(n-1)/2$, the inner equation can be simplified as follows:

$$O((n+k) \log (n+k)) = O((n+k) \log (n^*(n+1)/2))$$

Now, using the properties of logarithms, the following is true:

$$\log (n^*(n+1)/2) = \log n + \log (n+1) - \log 2 \le \log n + \log (2n) - 1 \le 2 \log n$$

which results in the following:

$$O((n+k) \log (n^*(n+1)/2)) = O(2^*(n+k) \log n)$$

therefore the overall performance is demonstrably still O(($n+k$) log n).

Because the performance of LINESWEEP is dependent upon complex properties of the input (i.e., the total number of intersections, the average number of line segments maintained by the sweep line at any given moment), we can only benchmark its performance given a specific problem and input data. We'll discuss two such problems now.

An interesting problem from mathematics is how to compute an approximate value of π using just a set of toothpicks and a piece of paper (known as Buffon's needle problem). If the toothpicks all are *len* units long, then draw a set of vertical lines on the paper, d units apart from one another where $d{\ge}len$. Randomly toss n toothpicks on the paper and let k be the number of intersections with the vertical lines. It turns out that the probability that a toothpick intersects a line (which can be computed as k/n) is equal to $(2^*len)/(\pi^*d)$.[*]

When the number of intersections is much less than n^2, the BRUTE FORCE INTERSECTION algorithm will waste time checking lines that don't intersect (as we see in Table 9-4). When there are many intersections, the determining factor will be the average number of line segments maintained by LineState during the duration of LINESWEEP. When it is low (as might be expected with random line segments in the plane), LINESWEEP will be the winner.

Table 9-4. *Timing comparison (in milliseconds) between algorithms on Buffon's needle problem*

n	LineSweep	Brute Force	Average number of intersections	Estimate for π
16	479.5918	0	1.02	3.147541
32	153.0612	0	2.14	3.047619
64	469.3878	0	3.99	3.324675
128	316.3265	795.9184	8.53	3.213389
256	1255.102	3346.939	17.83	3.237092
512	4448.98	10357.14	40.48	3.191688
1,024	8448.98	44408.16	97.15	3.223505

[*] *http://mathworld.wolfram.com/BuffonsNeedleProblem.html*

n	LineSweep	Brute Force	Average number of intersections	Estimate for π
2,048	22122.45	172234.7	263.07	3.086274
4,096	61632.65	685438.8	789.46	3.152588

In the worst case—that is, when there are $O(n^2)$ intersections among the line segments—LINESWEEP will seriously underperform because of the overhead in maintaining the line state in the face of so many intersections. Table 9-5 shows how the BRUTE FORCE algorithm handily outperforms LINESWEEP, where n is the number of line segments whose intersection creates the maximum of $n^*(n-1)/2$ intersection points.

Table 9-5. Worst-case comparison of LineSweep versus BruteForce (in ms)

n	LineSweep (avg)	BruteForce (avg)
2	0	0
4	0.1531	0
8	0.6429	0
16	0.6327	0
32	6.4082	0.6327
64	36.7959	0.6429
128	218.2551	3.2245
256	1566.4898	34.5918
512	9791.4592	209.0102

Variations

One interesting variation requires only that the algorithm report one of the intersection points, rather than all points; it would be useful to detect whether two polygons intersect. This algorithm requires only $O(n \log n)$ time, and may more rapidly locate the first intersection in the average case. Another variation considers an input set of red and blue lines where the only desired intersections are those between different colored line segments (Palazzi and Snoeyink, 1994).

Nearest Neighbor Queries

Given a set of points P in a two-dimensional Cartesian plane, answer nearest neighbor queries of the form, "What point in P is closest to point x?" Note that x does not have to be a preexisting point in P. These queries also extend to input sets whose points are found in n-dimensional space. The naïve implementation is to inspect all points in P, resulting in a linear $O(n)$ algorithm. Since P is known in advance, perhaps there is some way to structure its information to speed up queries by discarding from consideration large groups of points in P.

Perhaps we could partition the plane into k^2 bins of some fixed size m by m, as shown in Figure 9-18(a). Here 10 input points in P (shown as circles) are placed into nine enclosing bins (the large shaded number reflects the number of points in the respective bin). When searching for the closest neighbor for a point x (shown as a small black square), find its enclosing bin. If that bin is not empty, then we only need to search the bins that intersect the focus circle whose radius is

$$\sqrt{2}m$$

In this example, however, there are no points in the target bin, and the three neighboring bins will need to be examined. This approach may lead to gross inefficiencies because (a) most of the bins may in fact be empty, and (b) the algorithm would still have to search multiple neighboring bins. In brief, partitioning P into fixed bins is ineffective for resolving nearest neighbor queries.

An alternate solution is to construct the Voronoi diagram (Preparata and Shamos, 1985) of the set P, which partitions the plane into a set of n regions R_i ($0 \le i < n$), each of which is defined as "the set of points closer to p_i than to any other point in P." Thus the regions self-adapt to be as large as required.[*] In a two-dimensional plane, each region is a polygon (for higher dimensions, each region is an n-dimensional polyhedron). The image in Figure 9-18(b) shows the Voronoi diagram for the same points used earlier in Figure 9-18(a). Once the structure is computed, the result of a nearest neighbor query is immediate once the enclosing region R_i is found. The algorithm for constructing Voronoi diagrams takes $O(n \log n)$ in the average case, but it is complicated to implement. With a Voronoi diagram, nearest neighbor queries can be answered in $O(\log n)$.

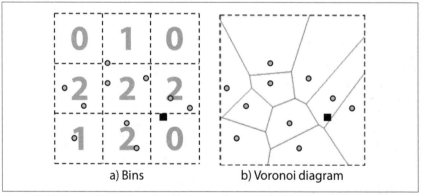

| a) Bins | b) Voronoi diagram |

Figure 9-18. Bin and Voronoi approaches toward nearest neighbor

In Figure 9-19(a), the same 10 points from Figure 9-18 are shown in a kd-tree, so named because it can subdivide a k-dimensional plane along the perpendicular axes of the coordinate system. The structure of the kd-tree from Figure 9-19(a) is depicted as a binary tree in Figure 9-19(b). For the remainder of this discussion we assume a two-dimensional tree, but the approach can be used for arbitrary dimensions.

[*] Note that in the Voronoi diagram, points on the convex hull have "open-ended" regions that extend outward to the edge of the diagram, whereas internal nodes have finite regions.

A kd-tree is a recursive binary tree structure whose nodes contain points and a coordinate label (i.e., either x or y) that determines the partitioning line. The root node represents the rectangular region [x_{low}=–∞, y_{low}=–∞, x_{high}=+∞, y_{high}=+∞] in the plane partitioned along the vertical line V through point p_1. The left subtree further partitions the region to the left of V, whereas the right subtree further partitions the region to the right of the V. The left child of the root represents a partition along the horizontal line H through p_2 that subdivides the region to the left of V into a region above the line H and a region below the line H. The region [–∞,–∞, $p_1.x$,+∞] is associated with the left child of the root, whereas the region [$p_1.x$,–∞, +∞,+∞] is associated with the right child of the root. These regions are effectively nested, and one can see that the region of an ancestor node wholly contains the regions of any of its descendant nodes.

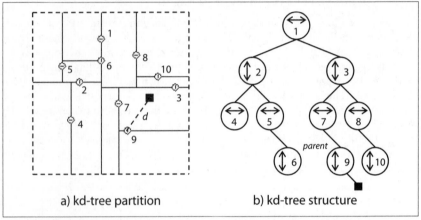

a) kd-tree partition   b) kd-tree structure

Figure 9-19. Division of two-dimensional plane using kd-tree

When these kd-trees are properly constructed, nodes on level i reflect rectangles that are roughly twice as large as the rectangles on level $i+1$. This property will enable the NEAREST NEIGHBOR algorithm (depicted in Figure 9-20) to efficiently search for a target point in O(log n) performance because it will be able to discard entire subtrees containing points that are demonstrably too far to be the closest point. In the upcoming section "Range Queries," we will see how the structure improves the performance of range queries over the points.

Input/Output

Input

A set of two-dimensional points P in a plane. A set of nearest neighbor queries (not known in advance) is issued one at a time to find the nearest point in P to a point x.

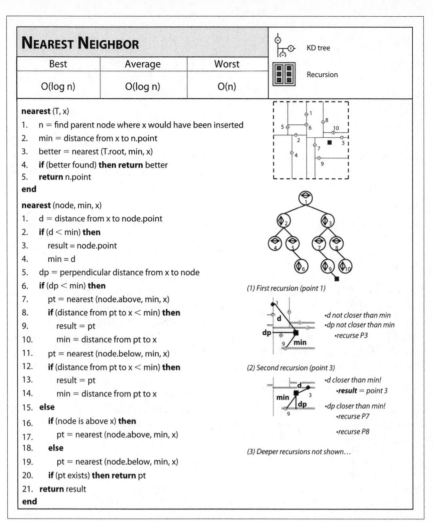

NEAREST NEIGHBOR

Best	Average	Worst
O(log n)	O(log n)	O(n)

KD tree

Recursion

nearest (T, x)
1.　n = find parent node where x would have been inserted
2.　min = distance from x to n.point
3.　better = nearest (T.root, min, x)
4.　**if** (better found) **then return** better
5.　**return** n.point
end

nearest (node, min, x)
1.　d = distance from x to node.point
2.　**if** (d < min) **then**
3.　　result = node.point
4.　　min = d
5.　dp = perpendicular distance from x to node
6.　**if** (dp < min) **then**
7.　　pt = nearest (node.above, min, x)
8.　　**if** (distance from pt to x < min) **then**
9.　　　result = pt
10.　　min = distance from pt to x
11.　　pt = nearest (node.below, min, x)
12.　　**if** (distance from pt to x < min) **then**
13.　　　result = pt
14.　　min = distance from pt to x
15.　**else**
16.　　**if** (node is above x) **then**
17.　　　pt = nearest (node.above, min, x)
18.　　**else**
19.　　　pt = nearest (node.below, min, x)
20.　　**if** (pt exists) **then return** pt
21.　**return** result
end

(1) First recursion (point 1)

• d not closer than min
• dp not closer than min
• recurse P3

(2) Second recursion (point 3)

• d closer than min!
• **result** = point 3
• dp closer than min!
• recurse P7
• recurse P8

(3) Deeper recursions not shown…

Figure 9-20. Nearest Neighbor Query fact sheet

Output

Given the points P, a kd-tree is computed. For each query point x, a point in P is output as being the closest neighbor to x.

Assumptions

If two points are "too close" to each other through floating-point error, the algorithm may incorrectly select the wrong point; however, the distance to the actual closest point would be so close that there should be no impact by this faulty response.

Context

When comparing this approach against a brute-force approach that compares the distances between query point x and each point $p \in P$, there are two important costs to consider: (1) the cost of constructing the kd-tree, and (2) the cost of locating the query point x within the tree structure. The tradeoffs that impact these costs are:

Number of dimensions
> As the number of dimensions increases, the cost of constructing the kd-tree overwhelms its utility. Some authorities believe that for above 20 dimensions, this approach is less efficient than a straight comparison against all points.

Number of points in the input set
> When the number of points is small, the cost of constructing the structure may outweigh the improved performance.

Forces

Binary trees can remain efficient search structures because they can be balanced as nodes are inserted into and deleted from the tree. Unfortunately, kd-trees cannot be balanced so easily, because of the deep structural information about the dimensional plane that they represent. The ideal solution is to construct the initial kd-tree so that either (a) the leaf nodes are at the same level in the tree, or (b) all leaf nodes are within one level of all other leaf nodes. Example 9-4 contains the implementation of the well-known technique that uses recursion to iterate over each of the coordinate dimensions. Simply put, it selects the median element from a set of points to represent the node; and the elements "below" the median are inserted into the left subtree, whereas elements "above" the median are inserted into the right subtree. The code works for arbitrary dimensions.

Example 9-4. Recursively construct a balanced kd-tree

```
public class KDFactory {
  // Known comparators for partitioning points along dimensional axes.
  private static Comparator<IMultiPoint> comparators[];

  // Recursively construct KDTree using median method on input points.
  public static KDTree generate (IMultiPoint []points) {
    if (points.length == 0) { return null; }

    // median will be the root.
    int maxD = points[0].dimensionality();
    KDTree tree = new KDTree(maxD);

    // Make dimensional comparators that compare points by ith dimension
    comparators = new Comparator[maxD+1];
    for (int i = 1; i <= maxD; i++) {
      comparators[i] = new DimensionalComparator(i);
    }
```

Example 9-4. Recursively construct a balanced kd-tree (continued)

```
    tree.setRoot(generate (1, maxD, points, 0, points.length-1));
    return tree;
  }

  // generate the node for the d-th dimension (1 <= d <= maxD)
  // for points[left, right]
  private static DimensionalNode generate (int d, int maxD,
                                      IMultiPoint points[],
                                      int left, int right) {
    // Handle the easy cases first
    if (right < left) { return null; }
    if (right == left) { return new DimensionalNode (d, points[left]); }

    // Order the array[left,right] so the mth element will be the median
    // and the elements prior to it will all be <=, though they won't
    // necessarily be sorted; similarly, the elements after will all be >=
    int m = 1+(right-left)/2;
    Selection.select(points, m, left, right, comparators[d]);

    // Median point on this dimension becomes the parent
    DimensionalNode dm = new DimensionalNode (d, points[left+m-1]);

    // update to the next dimension, or reset back to 1
    if (++d > maxD) { d = 1; }

    // recursively compute left and right sub-trees, which translate
    // into 'below' and 'above' for n-dimensions.
    dm.setBelow(maxD, generate (d, maxD, points, left, left+m-2));
    dm.setAbove(maxD, generate (d, maxD, points, left+m, right));
    return dm;
  }
}
```

The select operation was described in the solution section of "Quicksort" in Chapter 4. It can select the kth smallest number recursively in $O(n)$ time in the average case; however, it does degrade to $O(n^2)$ in the worst case. To avoid such an occurrence, use the BFPRT selection algorithm, also discussed in Chapter 4, whose worst case is guaranteed to be $O(n)$, although it will be outperformed in the average case by the standard select operation.

Solution

Figure 9-21 shows the UML design of the classes that implement kd-trees. The structure is based extensively on binary trees, the primary difference being the extra information maintained by each DimensionalNode object, namely, the Hypercube region for which the node is responsible and its below and above children.

Given an existing kd-tree, the nearest neighbor for a target point x can be found using the NEAREST NEIGHBOR algorithm coded in Example 9-5. The pseudocode described earlier in Figure 9-20 shows the first few steps of a sample invocation of the algorithm.

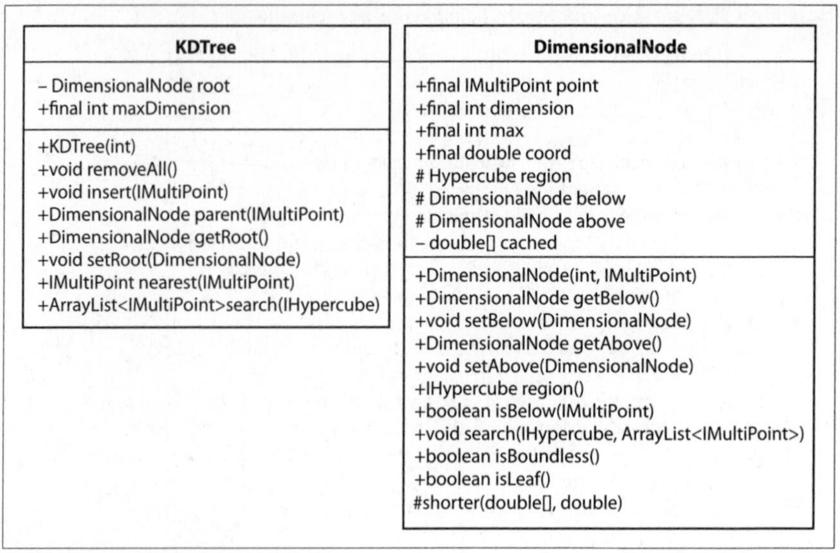

KDTree	DimensionalNode
– DimensionalNode root +final int maxDimension	+final IMultiPoint point +final int dimension +final int max +final double coord # Hypercube region # DimensionalNode below # DimensionalNode above – double[] cached
+KDTree(int) +void removeAll() +void insert(IMultiPoint) +DimensionalNode parent(IMultiPoint) +DimensionalNode getRoot() +void setRoot(DimensionalNode) +IMultiPoint nearest(IMultiPoint) +ArrayList<IMultiPoint>search(IHypercube)	+DimensionalNode(int, IMultiPoint) +DimensionalNode getBelow() +void setBelow(DimensionalNode) +DimensionalNode getAbove() +void setAbove(DimensionalNode) +IHypercube region() +boolean isBelow(IMultiPoint) +void search(IHypercube, ArrayList<IMultiPoint>) +boolean isBoundless() +boolean isLeaf() #shorter(double[], double)

Figure 9-21. kd-tree core concepts

Example 9-5. Nearest Neighbor Queries implemented with kd-tree

```
// method in KDTree
public IMultiPoint nearest (IMultiPoint target) {
  if (root == null) return null;

  // find parent node to which target would have been inserted. This is our
  // best shot at locating closest point; compute best distance guess so far
  DimensionalNode parent = parent(target);
  IMultiPoint result = parent.point;
  double smallest = target.distance(result);

  // now start back at the root, and check all rectangles that potentially
  // overlap this smallest distance. If better one is found, return it.
  double best[] = new double[] { smallest };

  double raw[] = target.raw();
  IMultiPoint betterOne = root.nearest (raw, best);
  if (betterOne != null) { return betterOne; }
  return result;
}

// method in DimensionalNode. min[0] contains best computed shortest distance.
IMultiPoint nearest (double[] rawTarget, double min[]) {
    // Update minimum if we are closer.
    IMultiPoint result = null;

    // If shorter, update minimum
    double d = shorter(rawTarget, min[0]);
    if (d >= 0 && d < min[0]) {
      min[0] = d;
```

```
      result = point;
    }

    // determine if we must dive into the subtrees by computing direct
    // perpendicular distance to the axis along which node separates
    // the plane. If d is smaller than the current smallest distance,
    // we could "bleed" over the plane so we must check both.
    double dp = Math.abs(coord - rawTarget[dimension-1]);
    IMultiPoint newResult = null;

    if (dp < min[0]) {
      // must dive into both. Return closest one.
      if (above != null) {
        newResult = above.nearest (rawTarget, min);
        if (newResult != null) { result = newResult; }
      }

      if (below != null) {
        newResult = below.nearest(rawTarget, min);
        if (newResult != null) {  result = newResult; }
      }
    } else {
      // only need to go in one! Determine which one now.
      if (rawTarget[dimension-1] < coord) {
        if (below != null) {
          newResult = below.nearest (rawTarget, min);
        }
      } else {
        if (above != null) {
          newResult = above.nearest (rawTarget, min);
        }
      }
    }

    // Use smaller result, if found.
    if (newResult != null) { return newResult; }
  }
  return result;
}
```

The key to understanding NEAREST NEIGHBOR is that we first locate the region where the target point would have been inserted, since this will likely contain the closest point. We then validate this assumption by recursively checking from the root back down to this region to see whether some other point is actually closer (this could easily happen because the rectangular regions of the kd-tree were created based upon the arbitrary input set). In unbalanced kd-trees, this checking process might incur an $O(n)$ total cost, reinforcing the notion that the input set must be properly processed.

The example solution has two improvements to speed up its performance. First, the comparisons are made on the "raw" double[] array representing each point. Second, a shorter method in DimensionalNode is used to determine when the distance between two d-dimensional points is smaller than the minimum distance computed so far; this method (found in this book's code repository) exits immediately when a partial computation of the Euclidean distance exceeds the minimum found.

Consequences

Assuming the initial kd-tree is balanced, the search can advantageously discard up to half of the points in the tree during the recursive invocations. Note that there will be times that two recursive invocations are required, but only in the case where the computed minimum distance is just large enough to cross over the dividing line for a node, in which case both sides need to be explored to find the closest point.

Analysis

The kd-tree is initially constructed as a balanced kd-tree, where the dividing line on each level is derived from the median of the points remaining at that level. Locating the parent node of the target query can be found in $O(\log n)$ by traversing the kd-tree as if the point were to be inserted. However, note that the algorithm at times makes two recursive invocations: one for the above child and one for the below child. If the double recursion occurs frequently, the algorithm degrades to be $O(n)$, so it is worth understanding how often it can occur. The multiple invocations only occur when the perpendicular distance, dp, from the target point to the node's point is less than the best computed minimum. As the number of dimensions increases, there are more potential points that satisfy these criteria. Table 9-6 provides some empirical evidence to describe how often this occurs. A balanced kd-tree is created from $n=4$ to 131,072 random two-dimensional points generated within the unit square. A set of 50 nearest point queries is issued for a random point within the unit square, and Table 9-6 records the average number of times two recursive invocations occurred (that is, when $dp<min[0]$ and the node in question has both an above and a below child), as compared to single recursive invocations.

Table 9-6. Ratio of double recursion invocations to single

n	d=2 #Recursions	d=2 #Double recursion	d=10 #Recursion	d=10 #Double recursion
4	1.54	0.54	1.02	1
8	2.8	1.08	1.04	3
16	4.3	1.36	1.48	6.84
32	5.66	2.14	1.86	14.58
64	8.08	2.58	3.54	30.42
128	9.24	2.58	8.64	60.06
256	10.36	2.42	25.42	109.9
512	11.76	2.8	52.44	222.44
1,024	13.2	3.06	122.32	421.68
2,048	15.48	3.22	244.54	730.84

Table 9-6. Ratio of double recursion invocations to single (continued)

n	d=2 #Recursions	d=2 #Double recursion	d=10 #Recursion	d=10 #Double recursion
4,096	15.96	2.72	466.1	1183.1
8,192	17.18	3.3	925.22	1876.66
16,384	19.9	3.38	1552.98	2939.08
32,768	18.78	3.14	2769.72	5118.76
65,536	20.88	3.16	3272.24	4788.3
131,072	23.32	3.98	5376.06	7703.72

From this random data, the number of double recursions appears to be on the order of .3*log(n) for two dimensions, but this jumps to 342*log(n) for 10 dimensions (a 1,000-fold increase). The important observation is that both of these estimation functions conform to O(log n). But what happens when d increases to be "sufficiently close" to n in some way? The data graphed in Figure 9-22 shows that as d increases, the number of double recursions actually approaches $n/2$. In fact, as d increases, the number of single recursions conforms to a normal distribution whose mean is very close to log(n), which tells us that eventually all recursive invocations are of the double variety. The impact this fact has on the performance of nearest neighbor queries is that as d approaches log(n), the investment in using kd-trees begins to diminish until the resulting performance is no better than O(n) since the number of double recursions plateaus at $n/2$.

Certain input set data sets force NEAREST NEIGHBOR to work hard even in two dimensions. For example, let's change the input for Table 9-6 such that the n unique two-dimensional points are found on a unit circle of radius $r>1$, but the nearest query points still lie within the unit square. When n=131,072 points, the number of single recursions has jumped 10-fold to 235.8 while the number of double recursions has exploded to 932.78 (a 200-fold increase!). Thus the nearest neighbor query will degenerate in the worst case to O(n) given specifically tailored queries for a given input set.

We can also evaluate the performance of the NEAREST NEIGHBOR algorithm by comparing its performance against a straight brute force O(n) comparison. Given a data set of size n=4,096 points where 128 searches random are to be executed, how large must the dimensionality d of the input set be before the brute-force NEAREST NEIGHBOR implementation outperforms the kd-tree implementation? We ran 100 trials and discarded the best and worst trials, computing the average of the remaining 98 trials. The results are graphed in Figure 9-23 and show that for d=10 dimensions and higher, the brute-force nearest neighbor implementation outperforms the NEAREST NEIGHBOR kd-tree algorithm. If we increase the number of points to n=131,072, the crossover occurs at d=12, so the specific crossover point depends upon the machine hardware on which the code executes the specific values of n and d, and the distribution of points in the input set. We do not include in this crossover analysis the cost of constructing the kd-tree since that cost can be amortized across all searches; when done in this case the results shown in Figure 9-23 still hold.

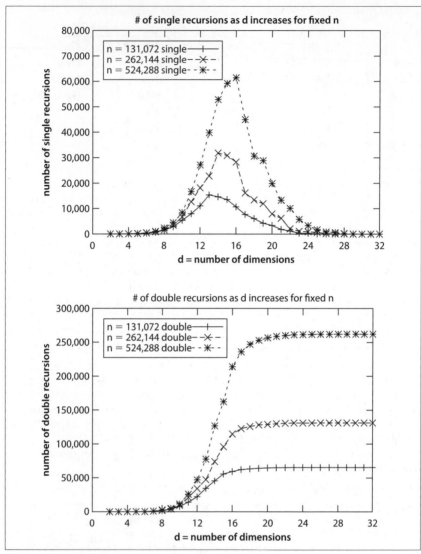

Figure 9-22. Number of double recursions as n and d increase

The results in Figure 9-23 confirm that as the number of dimensions increases, the benefit of using NEAREST NEIGHBOR over brute force decreases. The cost of constructing the kd-trees is not a driving factor in the equation, since that is driven primarily by the number of data points to be inserted into the kd-tree, not by the number of dimensions. On larger data set sizes, the savings is more pronounced. Another reason for the worsening performance as d increases is that computing the Euclidean distance between two d-dimensional points is an $O(d)$ operation: as d increases, each computation simply takes more time.

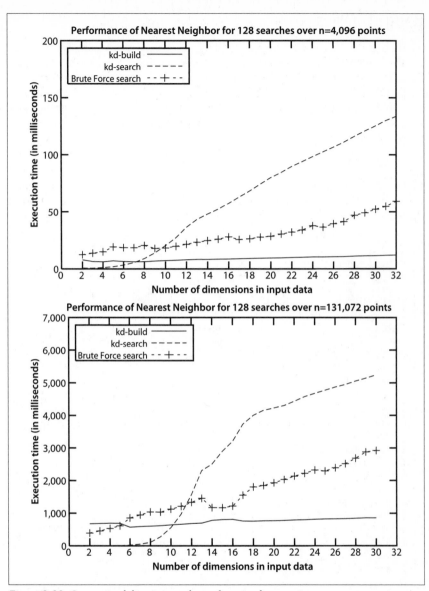

Figure 9-23. Comparing kd-tree versus brute-force implementation

Variations

In the described implementation, the method nearest traverses from the root back down to the computed parent; alternate implementations start from the parent and traverse back to the root, in bottom-up fashion.[*]

---

[*] See *http://www.codeproject.com/KB/architecture/KDTree.aspx*.

Computational Geometry

Range Queries

Given a rectangular range R defined by $[x_{low}, y_{low}, x_{high}, y_{high}]$ and a set of points P, which points in P are contained within the rectangle R? A brute-force algorithm that inspects all points in P can determine the enclosed points in $O(n)$—can we do better? For the NEAREST NEIGHBOR problem, we organized the points into a kd-tree to process nearest neighbor queries in $O(\log n)$ time. Using the same data structure, we now show how to process RANGE QUERY problems over the Cartesian plane in

$$O(\sqrt{n} + r)$$

where r is the number of points reported by the query. Indeed, when the input set contains d-dimensional data points, the solution scales to solve d-dimensional RANGE QUERY problems in $O(n^{1-1/d}+r)$. Figure 9-24 illustrates.

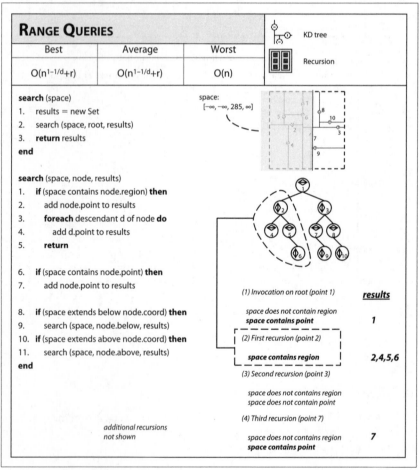

Figure 9-24. Range Queries fact sheet

Input/Output

Input

A set of n points P in d-dimensional space and a d-dimensional hypercube that specifies the desired range query.

Output

The full set of points enclosed by the range query. The points do not appear in any specific order.

Assumptions

The range queries are aligned properly with the axes in the d-dimensional data set since they are specified by d individual ranges, for each dimension of the input set.

Context

Because kd-trees become unwieldy for a large number of dimensions, this algorithm and overall approach is likely to degrade accordingly.

Forces

Because of the versatility of kd-trees, this approach is likely to afford other efficient algorithms. Note that both NEAREST NEIGHBOR and RANGE QUERY problems operate more efficiently because of the kd-trees.

Solution

The Java solution shown in Example 9-6 is a method of the DimensionalNode class, which is simply delegated by the search(IHypercube) method found in KDTree. The key efficiency gain of this algorithm occurs when the region for a DimensionalNode is wholly contained within the desired range query. In this circumstance, all descendant nodes of the DimensionalNode can be added to the results collection because of the kd-tree property that the children for a node are wholly contained within the region of any of its ancestor nodes.

Example 9-6. Range Query implementation

```java
public void search (IHypercube space, ArrayList<IMultiPoint> results) {
  // Wholly contained? Take all descendant points
  if (space.contains (region)) {
    this.drain(results);
    return;
  }

  // Is our point at least contained?
  if (space.intersects (cached)) {
    results.add(point);
  }
```

Example 9-6. Range Query implementation (continued)

```
// recursively progress along both ancestral trees, if demanded.
// The cost in manipulating space to be "cropped" to the proper
// structure is excessive. Leave alone, with no impact on computation.
if (space.getLeft(dimension) < coord) {
  if (below != null) { below.search(space, results); }
}
if (coord < space.getRight(dimension)) {
  if (above != null) { above.search(space, results); }
}
}

/** Visit all descendant nodes in the tree rooted at given node. */
private void drain(ArrayList<IMultiPoint> results) {
  if (below != null) { below.drain (results); }
  results.add(this.point);
  if (above != null) { above.drain (results); }
}
```

The code shown in Example 9-6 is a modified tree traversal that potentially visits every node in the tree. Because the kd-tree partitions the *d*-dimensional data set in hierarchical fashion, there are three decisions RANGE QUERY makes at each node *n*:

Is the region associated with node n fully contained within the query region?
> When this happens, the search traversal can stop because all descendant points belong to the query result. The helper method drain executes a full traversal of the subtree rooted at *n* to add all of these points to the result set.

Does the query region contain the point associated with node n?
> If so, add the point associated with *n* to the result set.

Along the dimension d represented by node n, does query region intersect n?
> It can do so in two ways: if the query region seeks points to the left of *d*, then traverse the *below* subtree of *n*. If the query region seeks points to the right of *d*, then traverse the *above* subtree.

Analysis

It is possible that the query region contains all points in the tree, in which case all nodes are visited by the drain method; this leads to $O(n)$ performance. However, when RANGE QUERY detects that the query region does not intersect an individual node within the kd-tree, it can prune the traversal. The cost savings depends upon the number of dimensions and the specific nature of the input set. It has been shown (Preparata and Shamos, 1985) that RANGE QUERY using kd-trees performs in $O(n^{1-1/d}+r)$ where *r* is the number of results found. As the number of dimensions increases, the benefit decreases. Figure 9-25 graphs the expected performance of an $O(n^{1-1/d})$ algorithm; the distinctive feature of the graph is fast performance for small values of *d* that over time inexorably approaches $O(n)$. Because of the addition of *r* (the number of points returned by the query), the actual performance will deviate from the ideal curve shown in Figure 9-25.

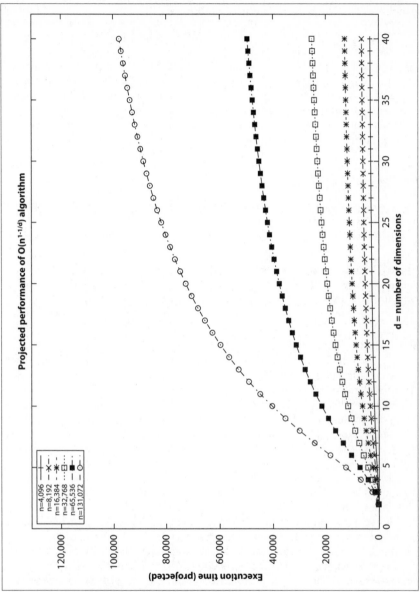

Figure 9-25. Expected performance for $O(n^{1-1/d})$ algorithm

It is difficult to produce sample data sets to show the performance of RANGE QUERY. We demonstrate the effectiveness of RANGE QUERY on a kd-tree by comparing its performance to a brute-force implementation that inspects each point against the desired query region. The *d*-dimensional input set for each of these situations contains *n* points whose coordinate values are drawn uniformly from the range [0,*s*], where *s*=4,096. There are three situations we evaluate:

Computational Geometry

We construct a query region that contains all of the points in the kd-tree. This example provides the maximum speedup supported by the algorithm; its performance is independent of the number of dimensions d in the kd-tree. The kd-tree approach takes about 5–7 times as long to complete; this represents the overhead inherent in the kd-tree structure. In Table 9-7, the performance cost for the brute-force region query increases as d increases because computing whether a d-dimensional point is within a d-dimensional space is an $O(d)$ operation, not constant. The brute force implementation handily outperforms the kd-tree implementation.

Table 9-7. Comparing Range Query execution times in milliseconds (kd-tree versus brute force) for situation 1

n	d=2 RQ	d=3 RQ	d=4 RQ	d=5 RQ	d=2 BF	d=3 BF	d=4 BF	d=5 BF
4,096	51.4	73.9	94.3	124.5	10.5	13.0	12.7	13.6
8,192	199.6	204.3	215.6	228.8	17.8	20.8	25.4	26.0
16,384	354.3	375.1	401.7	422.9	33.7	44.4	55.7	66.1
32,768	678.5	765.8	780.7	827.0	90.8	116.3	129.9	145.3
65,536	1397.3	1482.2	1612.6	1817.8	189.7	226.6	266.4	315.0
131,072	2924.5	3146.4	3305.6	3738.9	378.3	458.9	534.5	638.9

Situation 2: Fractional regions

Because the number of results found, r, plays a prominent role in determining the performance of the algorithm, we construct a set of scenarios to isolate this variable as the number of dimensions increases. Because of the uniformity of the input set, we cannot simply construct a query region $[.5^*s,s]$ for each dimension of input. If we did this, the total volume of the input set queried is $(1/2)^d$, which implies that as d increases the number of expected points, r, returned by the query region decreases. Instead, we construct query regions whose size increases as d increases. For example, in two dimensions the query region with $[.5204^*s,s]$ on each dimension should return $.23^*n$ points since $(1-.5204)^2=.23$. However, for three dimensions the query region must expand to $[.3873^*s, s]$ on each dimension since $(1-.3873)^3=.23$. Using this construction, we fix in advance the desired ratio k such that our constructed query will return k^*n points (where k ranges from .23, .115, 0.0575, 0.02875 and 0.014375). We compare the kd-tree implementation against a brute force implementation as n varies from 4,096 to 131,072 and d varies from 2 to 15, as shown in Figure 9-26. The charts on the left side show the distinctive behavior of the $O(n^{1-1/d})$ kd-tree algorithm while the right side shows the linear performance of brute force. For a 0.23 ratio, the kd-tree implementation only outperforms for $d=2$ and $n \leq 8,192$; however, for a ratio of 0.014375, the kd-tree implementation wins for $d \leq 6$ and $n \leq 131,072$.

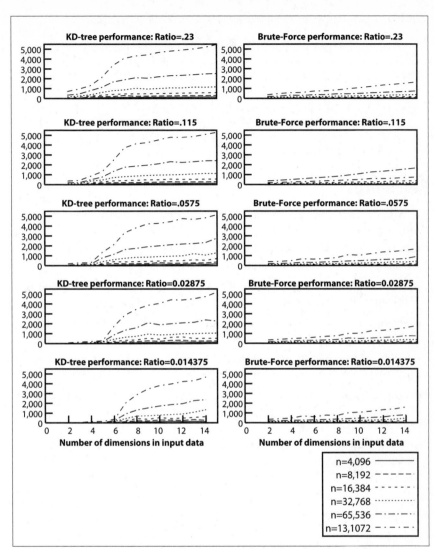

Figure 9-26. Comparing kd-tree versus brute force for situation 2

Situation 3: Empty region

We construct a query region from a single random point drawn uniformly from the same values for the input set. Performance results are shown in Table 9-8. The kd-tree executes nearly instantaneously; all recorded execution times are less than a fraction of a millisecond.

Table 9-8. Brute force Range Query execution times in milliseconds for situation 3

n	d=2 BF	d=3 BF	d=4 BF	d=5 BF
4,096	9.625	10.5	10.125	10.25
8,192	20.75	20.875	21.875	23.875
16,384	41.375	46.125	46.375	51
32,768	90.75	97.25	97.875	105
65,536	201.875	187.125	198.375	217.25
131,072	400.5	386.375	400.375	411.375

References

Akl, Selim G. and Godfried Toussaint, "A Fast Convex Hull Algorithm," *Information Processing Letters*, 7(5), 1978.

Cormen, Thomas H., Charles E. Leiserson, Ronald L. Rivest, and Cliffort Stein, *Introduction to Algorithms*, Second Edition. McGraw Hill, 2001.

Graham, R. L., "An Efficient Algorithm for Determining the Convex Hull of a Finite Planar Set," *Information Processing Letters* 1: 132–133, 1972.

Melkman, A., "On-line construction of the convex hull of a simple polygon," *Information Processing Letters* 25: 11–12, 1987.

Overmars, Mark and Jan van Leeuwen, "Maintenance of Configurations in the Plane," *Journal of Computer and System Sciences*, 23(2): 166–204, 1981.

Palazzi, Larry and Jack Snoeyink, "Counting and Reporting Red/Blue Segment Intersections," *CVGIP: Graphical Models and Image Processing*, 56(4): 304–310, 1994.

Preparata, Franco and Michael Shamos, *Computational Geometry: An Introduction*. Springer-Verlag, 1985.

Chapter 10, *When All Else Fails*
Chapter 11, *Epilogue*

10

When All Else Fails

This chapter is different from the others chapters in this book. While the other chapters provide algorithms that solve common problems, here we present problems that can be solved by algorithms that are interesting in their own right. Knowledge of these algorithms should help designers determine how to apply them to solve seemingly very different problems.

Another difference is that randomness and probability were used in previous chapters when analyzing the average-case behavior of algorithms. Here the randomness is an essential part of the algorithms. Indeed, the probabilistic algorithms we describe here are interesting alternatives to deterministic algorithms. Running the same algorithm on the same input at two different times may provide very different answers. Sometimes we will tolerate wrong answers, and sometimes we will tolerate an algorithm's throwing up its (figurative) hands and saying it can't solve the problem.

One strong assumption is that the algorithms have access to a stream of random bits. It is hard to define randomness, though we have several tests that a sequence of random bits must satisfy. And it is hard to generate a sequence of bits that satisfy these tests.

Variations on a Theme

All the algorithms we considered in this book were expected to give exact answers to an instance of a problem on a sequential, deterministic computer. Much interesting research has been done by relaxing each of these four assumptions:

- Answers must be exact
- Only one instance is being solved
- The platform is sequential
- The platform is deterministic

Relaxing these assumptions permits us to consider various other types of algorithms.

Approximation Algorithms

An approximation algorithm seeks answers that are close to, but not necessarily as good as, the true answer. The general tradeoff is to decrease the time by which the answer is returned at the expense of accuracy.

As an example of the speed improvement of solving problems when exact answers aren't necessary but good answers are acceptable, we consider the Traveling Salesman Problem (TSP). In TSP, we are given a set of cities to visit and the set of distances between each pair of cities. We must determine the least-cost *tour* that starts at a city, visits each city exactly once, and returns to the originating city of the tour. This problem is one of the most heavily researched of all problems in computer science, and it is highly unlikely that there exists a polynomial time algorithm that solves TSP; that is, no algorithm can solve TSP in $O(n^k)$ for fixed integer k. It belongs to a large class of problems (the *NP-hard problems*) for which it is strongly believed that finding an exact answer is inherently very difficult.

But assuming it is known that the distances between locations satisfy the triangular inequality (i.e., for all triples of locations a, b, c, the distance from a to b is never longer than the distance from a to c plus the distance from c to b), Christofides (1976) designed an efficient algorithm to solve the problem that constructs a tour that is never more than 50% longer than a shortest tour.

Offline Algorithms

We may batch instances of a problem to be solved all at once, as opposed to the more usual assumption of online algorithms, in which each instance must be solved as soon as it is presented.

As an example of the improvements in allowing offline algorithms, assume we intend to implement a dictionary in which we insert a set of n numbers $y_1 \ldots y_n$ into an initially empty dictionary and then perform $n/2$ membership queries contains(x_i) for numbers $x_1 \ldots x_{n/2}$. An optimal data structure to perform n insert operations followed by a single contains(x_i) operation is to insert each y_j into an unordered array Y, at a total cost $O(n)$, and then implement the contains(x_i) query with a SEQUENTIAL SEARCH of x_i in array Y at a worst-case cost of $O(n)$. The total worst-case cost of the $n+1$ operations is $O(n)$.

Performing a sequence of $n/2$ executions of SEQUENTIAL SEARCH incurs a total cost of $O(n^2)$. Since there is no way to predict the queries that are to be performed, an online algorithm cannot proactively take steps to minimize the costs of a specific future query (note that an adversary can always thwart such speedup attempts). However, if we batch the sequence of $n/2$ contains queries for offline processing, then we could sort the array Y containing $y_1 \ldots y_n$ and sort an array X containing $x_1 \ldots x_{n/2}$, each at a worst-case cost of $O(n \log n)$, and then scan the two sorted arrays to seek duplicates, at a worst-case cost of $O(n)$. By permitting an offline algorithm to batch the $n/2$ searches, we can solve the sequence of problems in worst-case time $O(n \log n)$; our costs are $O(n^2)$ if we insist upon the online version in which each query must be processed before the next query is read.

Parallel Algorithms

A computational process may spawn several computational processes to work simultaneously on subinstances of a problem. Using the same example from the previous section, "Offline Algorithms," it is possible to speed up the performance of $n/2$ SEQUENTIAL SEARCH executions by executing these searches in parallel on n processors. The resulting worst-case cost of the parallel $n/2$ searches is $O(n)$. If you are interested in pursuing this idea further, you should read the book by Berman and Paul (2004) on the subject. You may also find it worthwhile to read about actual systems that take advantage of parallelism afforded by multicore processors; see Armstrong's *Programming Erlang: Software for a Concurrent World* (2007).

Randomized Algorithms

An algorithm may use a stream of random bits (numbers) in solving a problem. Often we may find fast algorithms to solve a problem when we assume access to a stream of random bits. For practical purposes, one should be aware that streams of random bits are very difficult to generate on deterministic computers. Though we may generate streams of quasi-random bits that are virtually indistinguishable from streams of truly random bits, the cost of generating these streams should not be ignored.

Estimating the Size of a Set

As an example of the speedups that can be obtained in allowing probabilistic algorithms, assume we want to estimate the size of a set of n objects, $\{x_1, ..., x_n\}$, with distinct labels. That is, we want to estimate the value n. It would be straightforward to count all the objects, at a cost of $O(n)$. Clearly this process is guaranteed to yield an exact answer. But if an incorrect estimate of the value of n is tolerable, assuming it could be computed more quickly, the algorithm described in Example 10-1 is a faster alternative.

Example 10-1. Implementation of probabilistic counting algorithm

```
public static double computeK (int n) {
  // Make sure we use data structure with efficient lookup.
  Hashtable<Integer,Boolean> setS = new Hashtable<Integer,Boolean>();

  // Repeatedly probe to see if already located
  int y = 1+((int)(Math.random()*n));
  while (!setS.containsKey(y)) {
    setS.put(y, Boolean.TRUE);
    y = 1+((int)(Math.random()*n));
  }

  // return estimate of original size
  int k = setS.size();
  return 2.0*k*k/Math.PI;
}
```

The expected execution time of this algorithm is

$$O(\sqrt{n})$$

That is, the expected number of executions of the while loop is

$$\sqrt{\frac{\pi n}{2}}$$

This algorithm is similar to the mark-and-release experiments biologists use to estimate the size of a spatially limited population of organisms. Clearly the algorithm can never give the exact value of n, since $2^*k^2/\pi$ can never be an integer. But the value $2^*k^2/\pi$ is an unbiased estimate of n; that is, the expected value of $2^*k^2/\pi$ equals n.

In Table 10-1 we show a sample run of the algorithm that records the results of the computations of a number of separate trials. The probabilistic algorithm generated an estimate for n with t trials (32, 64, 128, and 256). From these trials, the lowest and highest estimates were discarded, and the average of the remaining $t-2$ trials is shown in the respective column. The final three rows show the accuracy of these "average of estimations" by computing (a) the minimum ratio of estimation/target, (b) the maximum ratio of estimation/target, and (c) the range from minimum to maximum. For example, for 32 trials, the estimate of 353,998 for the target 524,288 exhibited the lowest ratio (.68), whereas the estimate 1,527,380 for 1,048,576 exhibited the highest ratio (1.46).

Table 10-1. Sample execution of probabilistic counting algorithm

n	Average for 32	Average for 64	Average for 128	Average for 256
256	314	210	296	362
512	511	684	643	664
1,024	941	905	1,150	1,314
2,048	2,611	3,038	2,405	2,532
4,096	3,779	6,068	4,812	5,378
8,192	7,858	10,656	8,435	10,860
16,384	22,786	21,617	19,169	19,809
32,768	33,509	40,549	36,395	38,863
65,536	85,421	77,335	80,119	93,807
131,072	131,728	172,175	148,549	160,750
262,144	270,187	421,345	375,442	299,551
524,288	353,998	463,923	736,396	642,986
1,048,576	1,527,380	1,417,047	1,299,312	1,334,487
2,097,152	2,291,903	2,106,072	2,615,379	2,445,086
4,194,304	5,348,730	4,565,833	5,653,524	5,132,245
8,388,608	8,017,734	9,791,002	12,220,879	10,064,671
16,777,216	23,006,070	28,363,383	20,316,904	19,470,289
Accuracy	Low: .68	Low: .82	Low: 1.03	Low: 1.14
	High: 1.46	High: 1.69	High: 1.46	High: 1.43
	Range: .78	Range: 0.87	Range: 0.43	Range: 0.29

Because of the random nature of the trials, it is not at all guaranteed that the final accurate result can be achieved simply by averaging over an increasing number of independent random trials. Indeed, you may need an inordinately large number of trials to achieve the desired estimate; instead of trying to use randomization to determine an exact result, one should try to discover algorithms that seek an exact answer.

Estimating the Size of a Search Tree

Two queens on a chess board threaten each other if they're on the same row, column, or diagonal. We say that a set of queens on a chessboard is non-threatening if no two of them threaten each other. Clearly we can't place $n+1$ non-threatening queens on an n-by-n board since two queens can't share the same row. Can we always place n non-threatening queens? This question is known as the n-Queens Problem. Let's generalize this question a bit and count the number of ways to place n non-threatening queens on an n-by-n board. The randomized technique we introduce has a number of applications beyond the game version we discuss here; it can be used whenever we want to estimate the shape of a search tree.

There is no known efficient technique to count the number of solutions to the n-Queens Problem. Table 10-2 contains early computed values taken from Sloane's On-Line Encyclopedia of Integer Sequences.*

Table 10-2. Known count of solutions for n-Queens Problem with our computed estimates

n	Actual number of solutions	Estimation with T=1,024 trials	Estimation with T=8,192 trials	Estimation with T=65,536 trials
1	1	1	1	1
2	0	0	0	0
3	0	0	0	0
4	2	2	2	2
5	10	10	10	10
6	4	5	4	4
7	40	41	39	40
8	92	88	87	93
9	352	357	338	351
10	724	729	694	718
11	2,680	2,473	2,499	2,600
12	14,200	12,606	14,656	13,905
13	73,712	68,580	62,140	71,678
14	365,596	266,618	391,392	372,699
15	2,279,184	1,786,570	2,168,273	2,289,607
16	14,772,512	12,600,153	13,210,175	15,020,881
17	95,815,104	79,531,007	75,677,252	101,664,299
18	666,090,624	713,470,160	582,980,339	623,574,560

* http://www.research.att.com/~njas/sequences/A000170

n	Actual number of solutions	Estimation with T=1,024 trials	Estimation with T=8,192 trials	Estimation with T=65,536 trials
19	4,968,057,848	4,931,587,745	4,642,673,268	4,931,598,683
20	39,029,188,884	17,864,106,169	38,470,127,712	37,861,260,851

To count the number of exact solutions to the 4-Queens Problem, we expand a search tree based upon the fact that each solution will have one queen on each row. Starting with a partial solution of having 0 queens placed, Figure 10-1 shows how there will be a direct extension corresponding to each of the four placements of a queen on the first row.

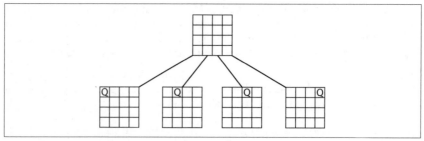

Figure 10-1. Initial search tree for 4-Queens Problem

Extending each of these partial solutions by all non-threatening placements of a queen on the second row yields Figure 10-2.

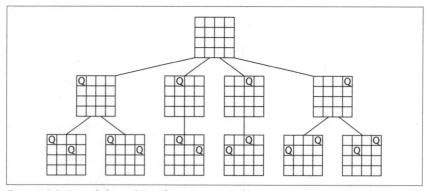

Figure 10-2. Extended search tree for 4-Queens Problem with two queens placed

The first and last partial solutions cannot be extended by placing a queen on the third row. The middle four can be extended to the third row, and of these, the middle two can each be extended to a solution that includes all four rows. (See Figure 10-3.)

Such an exhaustive elaboration of the search tree permits us to see that there are two solutions to the 4-Queens Problem. Trying to compute the number of solutions to

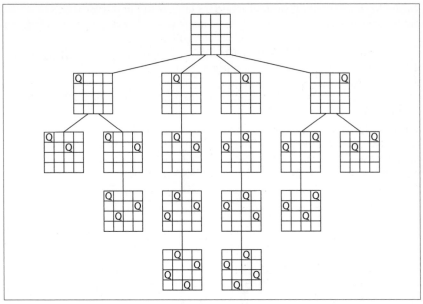

Figure 10-3. Final solution for 4-Queens Problem with four rows extended

the 19-Queens Problem is much harder. Since there are 4,968,057,848 nodes at level 19 of the search tree, and the entire tree has many more nodes, we'd expect to spend a really long time to compute the answer.

Donald Knuth (1975) developed a novel alternative approach to estimate the size and shape of a search tree. His method corresponds to taking a random walk down the tree. For the sake of brevity, we illustrate his technique for the 4-Queens Problem, but clearly it could just as easily be applied to approximate the number of solutions to the 19-Queens Problem. Starting with the root of the search tree (no queens placed), we estimate that there is one node at that level 0. The one operation we must do at any node is to determine the number of children of that node (the number of direct extensions of the partial solution at that node) and then randomly choose one of them. We see that the root node has four children, so we estimate (correctly) that there are four nodes at that level (level1). We then randomly choose one of those four children, let's say the first. This corresponds to the path in Figure 10-4.

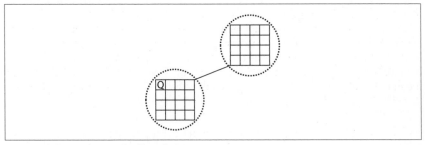

Figure 10-4. Random path of length 2

To the lower node of the current random path, we apply the operation of determining how many children it has (in how many ways can a non-threatening queen be placed on the second row?), and then randomly choose one of them. Noting that there are two children, we estimate that the number of nodes at the next level is two times the estimate of the number of nodes at level 1. That is, we estimate that there are eight nodes at level 2, and we extend our current path by randomly choosing one of the two children at the bottom of the current path, as shown in Figure 10-5.

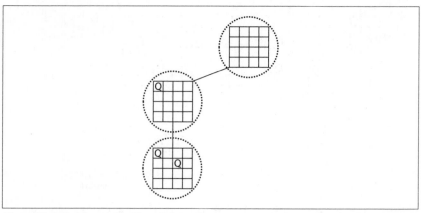

Figure 10-5. Random path of length 3

Now, to the lowest node of the current random path, we apply the operation of determining how many children it has: in how many ways can a non-threatening queen be placed on the third row? Noting that there are 0 ways, we estimate that the number of nodes at the next level is 0 times the estimate of the number of nodes at level 2. That is, we estimate that there are $0*8$ nodes at level 3, and hence 0 nodes at level 4. This implies that we estimate that there are 0 solutions to the 4-Queens Problem. In fact some of the random walks will lead to overestimates, and if we do many random walks and average the estimates, we expect to get closer and closer to the true value. And since each estimate can be computed quickly, this refined (averaged) estimate can also be computed quickly. The expected value of each estimate is the correct value, but the likelihood of the average of a number of estimates being close to the true answer increases as the number of trials being averaged increases. If you refer back to Table 10-2, we show the computed results from our implementation for 1,024, 8,192, and 65,536 trials. No timing information is included, because all results were computed in less than a minute. The final estimate for the 19-Queens problem with T=65,536 trials is within 3% of the actual answer. Indeed, all of the estimations for T=65,536 are within 5.8% of the actual answer. This algorithm has the desirable property that the computed value is more accurate as more random trials are run. Example 10-2 shows the implementation in Java for a single computation of the *n*-Queens estimation. The full code that generated Table 10-2 is available in the repository.

Example 10-2. Implementation of Knuth's randomized estimation of n-Queens problem

```java
/**
 * For an n-by-n board, store up to n non-threatening queens and support
 * search along the lines of Knuth's random walk. It is assumed the
 * queens are being added row by row starting from 0.
 */
public class Board {
  boolean [][] board;    /** The board. */
  final int n;           /** board size. */

  /** Temporary store for last valid positions. */
  ArrayList<Integer> nextValidRowPositions = new ArrayList<Integer>();

  public Board (int n) {
    board = new boolean[n][n];
    this.n = n;
  }

  /** Start with row and work upwards to see if still valid. */
  private boolean valid (int row, int col) {
    // another queen in same column, left diagonal, or right diagonal?
    int d = 0;
    while (++d <= row) {
      if (board[row-d][col]) { return false; } // column
      if (col >= d && board[row-d][col-d]) { return false; } // left-d
      if (col+d < n && board[row-d][col+d]) { return false; } // right-d
    }
    return true; // OK
  }

  /**
   * Find out how many valid children states are found by trying to add
   * a queen to the given row. Returns a number from 0 to n.
   */
  public int numChildren(int row) {
    int count = 0;
    nextValidRowPositions.clear();
    for (int i = 0; i < n; i++) {
      board[row][i] = true;
      if (valid(row, i)) {
        count++;
        nextValidRowPositions.add(i);
      }
      board[row][i] = false;
    }

    return count;
  }
```

Example 10-2. Implementation of Knuth's randomized estimation of n-Queens problem (continued)

```java
  /** If no board is available at this row then return false. */
  public boolean randomNextBoard(int r) {
    int sz = nextValidRowPositions.size();
    if (sz == 0) { return false; }

    // select one randomly
    int c = ((int)(Math.random()*sz));
    board[r][nextValidRowPositions.get(c)] = true;
    return true;
  }
}

public class SingleQuery {

  public static void main (String []args) {
    for (int i = 0; i < 100; i++) {
      System.out.println(i + ": " + estimate(19));
    }
  }

  public static long estimate(int n) {
    Board b = new Board(n);

    int r = 0;
    long lastEstimate = 1;
    while (r < n) {
      int numChildren = b.numChildren(r);

      // no more to go, so no solution found.
      if (!b.randomNextBoard(r)) {
        lastEstimate = 0;
        break;
      }

      // compute estimate based on ongoing tally and advance
      lastEstimate = lastEstimate*numChildren;
      r++;
    }

    return lastEstimate;
  }
}
```

Algorithms That Can Be Wrong, but with Diminishing Probability

In this section we study algorithms that may be wrong, but with diminishing probability. With a modest computation, we can assure that the likelihood of producing a wrong answer can be made arbitrarily small.

Testing Inequality of Databases

Suppose a company keeps multiple distributed copies of a very large database to permit efficient queries from many sites. Queries of the database are much more frequent than updates, and updates are applied at every copy. Also, an adversary with access to the updates may change them. One approach to assuring coherence of the multiple copies in spite of potential adversaries is to send a copy of the database from any site to every other site and test for inequality. But the size of the database makes this transmission prohibitively expensive.

Another approach is to transmit a fingerprint of any copy to every other site and then test whether the fingerprint at every other site is equal to the transmitted fingerprint. More explicitly, we consider a database to be a (large) sequence of bits $(b_0, \ldots b_{n-1})$. The fingerprint of $(b_0, \ldots b_{n-1})$ is $(b_0 + b_1{}^*2^1 + b_2{}^*2^2 + \ldots \ldots b_{n-1}{}^*2^{n-1})$ mod p for some randomly chosen prime number p. We only need to transmit on the order of log (p) bits. If the transmitted fingerprint is different than the fingerprint of the local database, then one can say with certainty that the databases are different. If the fingerprints are the same, however, one can't be certain that the corresponding databases are identical. But the probability that two different databases have the same fingerprint is $1/p$. In order to decrease the probability of incoherent databases passing the fingerprint test, we can repeat the process for several primes. Example 10-3 contains the pseudocode for the COHERENCE TEST algorithm.

Example 10-3. Pseudocode for coherence test algorithm

```
Sub Fingerprint Generation
    Generate a sequence of k primes p1, ..., pk
    for each prime pk
        transmit pk
        transmit (b0 + b1*2 + b2*2^2 + b3*2^3 + ... bn-1*2^n-1) mod pk

Sub Coherence Test
    for each prime pk and fingerprint fk
        if (fk != (a0 + a1*2 + a2*2^2 + ... an-1*2^n-1) mod pk) then
            return "database incoherent"
    return "database coherent"
end sub
```

The probability that different databases slip through this test is $1/(p_1{}^*p_2{}^*\ldots{}^*p_k)$, which can be made diminishingly small by increasing the number of primes.

Zero-Knowledge Proofs

Assume that Patti the Prover wants to convince Victor the Verifier of her identity, but they are communicating over an insecure channel. They assume that Albert the Analyst is listening and wants to be able to convince people that he is Patti. If Patti and Victor know a secret password, "Rosebud," and she identifies herself by transmitting the password, then in the future Albert will be able to identify himself as Patti to Victor. Patti wants a more secure protocol.

The following protocol assumes that the two problems of Graph Isomorphism and Hamiltonian Cycle are too difficult to solve for large graphs:

Hamiltonian Cycle
Given a graph, is there a cycle to visit all the vertices exactly one time by following edges, then returning to the starting vertex?

Graph Isomorphism
Given graphs $G_1=(V_1,E_1)$ and $G_2=(V_2,E_2)$, is there a relabeling of the vertices of V_1 that corresponds to the labels of V_2 such that the graphs become identical?

Figure 10-6 contains an example of two graphs that are isomorphic (i.e., identical) with the given relabeling.

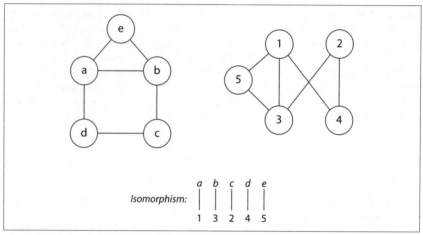

Figure 10-6. Graph Isomorphism example

It is highly unlikely that either of these problems admits an efficient solution for all large instances. We use the difficulty of these problems to develop a protocol for Patti to convince Victor of her identity over an insecure line, while being confident that Albert cannot pose as Patti in the future. Before starting the identification process, Patti constructs a large graph G with a Hamiltonian cycle that she knows. She can do this by starting with a cycle on every vertex, and then adding edges until it would be hard for another person to construct a Hamiltonian cycle. She then publishes this graph, G_{patti}, in a public directory under her name. Both Victor and Albert can read G_{patti}, but only she can construct a Hamiltonian cycle in G_{patti}.

She could prove her identity to Victor by showing him the order of vertices of a Hamiltonian cycle, but then Albert or Victor could pretend to be Patti in the future (her proof is not a zero-knowledge proof). She wants to convince Victor that she knows the secret cycle, without Victor or Albert sharing her knowledge. Example 10-4 contains her protocol.

Example 10-4. Protocol that does not reveal any information

```
Patti constructs graph H by randomly relabeling the vertices of G-patti
Patti transmits H to Victor
Victor flips a coin with two sides (ShowIsomorphism, ShowHamiltonianCycle)
Victor then transmits the results of the flip to Patti.
if Patti receives ShowIsomorphism
    she transmits the re-labeling used to construct H
else
    she transmits the Hamiltonian Cycle in H
```

No matter which question Victor asks Patti (for any flip of his coin), she can answer his question easily, and Victor can verify her answer easily. In case Albert wants to pose as Patti, he has two possibilities: he can construct and transmit his own graph *H*, which somewhat resembles G_{patti} (it could, for example have the same numbers of vertices and edges) and for which he knows a Hamiltonian cycle. But then if Victor the Verifier says "ShowIsomorphism," he can't answer. Or Albert could relabel and transmit the vertices of G_{patti}. But then if Victor the Verifier says "ShowHamiltonianCycle," Albert can't answer. So Albert could fake the protocol one half of the time. In order to be more confident, Victor could play the protocol 100 times (it is efficient, after all). Patti would succeed easily, but the probability that Albert could fake the protocol 100 times is $0.788*10^{-30}$.

Even if Albert observes Patti and Victor playing the game 100 times, he learns nothing that would help him play the game in the future.

References

Armstrong, Joe, *Programming Erlang: Software for a Concurrent World*. Pragmatic Bookshelf, 2007.

Berman, Kenneth and Jerome Paul, *Algorithms: Sequential, Parallel, and Distributed*. Course Technology, 2004.

Christofides, Nicos, "Worst-case analysis of a new heuristic for the travelling salesman problem," Report 388, Graduate School of Industrial Administration, CMU, 1976.

Knuth, Donald, "Estimating the efficiency of backtrack programs," *Mathematics of Computation* 29: 121–136, 1975.

11

Epilogue

Overview

While we have reached the end of this book, there is almost no limit to how much information you can find on algorithms in which you are interested. Indeed, there is no end to the kind of problems to which you can apply the techniques presented in this book.

We finally have the opportunity to step back and review the nearly three dozen algorithms that we described in detail and by example. We hope you are satisfied that we have accomplished what we set out to do. To show the breadth of material that we've covered, we'll now summarize the principles behind the algorithms presented in this book. In doing so, we can demonstrate the similarities of different algorithms that were designed to solve different problems. Instead of simply summarizing each of the previous chapters, we'll end this book by focusing on key principles that were instrumental in designing these algorithms in the first place. We also take this opportunity to summarize the concepts used by each algorithm; recall that these were listed in the algorithm fact sheets in the upper-right corner of those figures. In doing so, we provide a quick summary and make it possible to cross-index this book in terms of shared concepts across different algorithms.

Principle: Know Your Data

We discussed a variety of common actions you might need to perform on some data. You might need to sort data to produce a specific ordering. You might need to search through data to locate a specific piece of information. Your data may be accessible in random access (where you can fetch any piece of information at any time) or sequentially using an Iterator (where each element is generated one at a time). Without specific knowledge about your data, it is only possible to recommend algorithms in the most general way.

If you are sorting data, there is no "one size fits all" approach that consistently delivers the best performance. Table 11-1 summarizes the results of the sorting algorithms presented in Chapter 4. Do you have a set of integers from a limited range to be sorted? No sorting algorithm will be faster than COUNTING SORT, although it requires more storage than other sorting algorithms. Do you have a set of complex data that is already mostly sorted? INSERTION SORT will typically outperform any other approach. Does relative ordering of equal elements matter to you? If so, then a stable sorting algorithm is needed. Are you sure that your input data is drawn from a uniform distribution? You must investigate using BUCKET SORT because of its ability to take advantage of this property to provide exceptional sorting performance. You will be able to select the most appropriate algorithm based upon your data as you become more familiar with the available options.

Table 11-1. Chapter 4: Sorting algorithms

Algorithm	Best	Average	Worst	Concepts	Page
INSERTION SORT	n	n^2	n^2	Array	64
MEDIAN SORT	$n \log n$	$n \log n$	n^2	Array, Recursion, Divide and Conquer	68
SELECT KTH	n	n	n^2	Divide and Conquer	
BLUM-FLOYD-PRATT-RIVEST-TARJAN (BFPRT) Select K[th]	n	n	n	Recursion, Divide and Conquer	
QUICKSORT	$n \log n$	$n \log n$	n^2	Array, Recursion, Divide and Conquer	79
SELECTION SORT	n^2	n^2	n^2	Array, Greedy	
HEAP SORT	$n \log n$	$n \log n$	$n \log n$	Array, Recursion, Binary Heap	87
COUNTING SORT	n	n	n	Array	92
BUCKET SORT	n	n	n	Array, Hash	94

Principle: Decompose the Problem into Smaller Problems

When designing an efficient algorithm to solve a problem, it is helpful if the problem can be decomposed into two (or more) smaller subproblems. It is no mistake that QUICKSORT remains one of the most popular sorting algorithms. Even with the well-documented special cases that cause problems, QUICKSORT offers the best average-case for sorting large collections of information. Indeed, the very concept of an O($n \log n$) algorithm is based on the ability to (a) decompose a problem of size n into two subproblems of about $n/2$ in size, and (b) recombine the solution of the two subproblems into a solution for the original problem. To properly produce an O($n \log n$) algorithm, it must be possible for both of these steps to execute in O(n) time.

QUICKSORT was the first in-place sorting algorithm to demonstrate O($n \log n$) performance. It succeeds by the novel (almost counterintuitive) approach for dividing the problem into two halves, each of which can be solved recursively by applying QUICKSORT to the smaller subproblems.

Problems often can be simply cut in half, leading to impressive performance savings. Consider how BINARY SEARCH converts a problem of size n into a problem of size $n/2$. BINARY SEARCH takes advantage of the repetitive nature of the search task to develop a recursive solution to the problem.

Sometimes a problem can be solved by dividing it into two subproblems without resorting to recursion. CONVEX HULL SCAN produces the final convex hull by constructing and merging together two partial hulls (the upper and lower).

Sometimes a problem can be decomposed into the repeated iteration of a different (seemingly unconnected) smaller problem over the same input data. FORD-FULKERSON computes the maximum flow in a flow network by repeatedly locating an augmenting path to which flow can be added. Eventually, no augmenting paths are possible and the original solution is solved. SELECTION SORT repeatedly locates the maximum value in an array and swaps it with the rightmost element in the array; upon completing n iterations, the array is sorted. Similarly, HEAP SORT repeatedly swaps the largest element in the heap with its proper location in the array.

Table 11-2 contains a comparison of the searching algorithms discussed in Chapter 5.

Table 11-2. Chapter 5: Searching algorithms

Algorithm	Best	Average	Worst	Concepts	Page
SEQUENTIAL SEARCH	1	n	n	Array, Brute Force	107
BINARY SEARCH	1	$\log n$	$\log n$	Array, Divide and Conquer	112
HASH-BASED SEARCH	1	1	n	Array, Hash	117
BINARY TREE SEARCH	1	$\log n$	n	Binary Tree	

Principle: Choose the Right Data Structure

The famed algorithm designer Robert Tarjan was once quoted as saying that any problem can be solved in $O(n \log n)$ time with the right data structure. Many algorithms need to use a priority queue to store partial progress and direct future computations. One of the most common means of implementing a priority queue is through a binary heap, which allows for $O(\log n)$ behavior for removing the element with lowest priority from the priority queue. However, a binary heap offers no ability to determine whether it contains a specific element. We expanded on this very point in the discussion of LINE SWEEP (Chapter 9), since this algorithm can only provide $O(n \log n)$ performance because it uses an augmented binary tree to implement the priority queue and still provides $O(\log n)$ performance for removing the minimum element. Another way of stating this principle is to beware of selecting an inappropriate data structure that will prevent an algorithm from achieving its best performance.

Table 11-3 shows the graph algorithms discussed in Chapter 6.

Table 11-3. Chapter 6: Graph algorithms

Algorithm	Best	Average	Worst	Concepts	Page
DEPTH-FIRST SEARCH	$V+E$	$V+E$	$V+E$	Graph, Array, Recursion, Backtracking	144
BREADTH-FIRST SEARCH	$V+E$	$V+E$	$V+E$	Graph, Array, Queue	150
DIJKSTRA'S ALGORITHM PQ	$(V+E)$ $\log V$	$(V+E)$ $\log V$	$(V+E)$ $\log V$	Weighted Directed Graph, Array, Priority Queue, Overflow	154
DIJKSTRA'S ALGORITHM DG	V^2+E	V^2+E	V^2+E	Weighted Directed Graph, Array, Overflow	158
BELLMAN-FORD ALGORITHM	$V*E$	$V*E$	$V*E$	Weighted Directed Graph, Array, Overflow	162
FLOYD-WARSHALL ALGORITHM	V^3	V^3	V^3	Dynamic Programming, 2D Array, Weighted Directed Graph, Overflow	166
PRIM'S ALGORITHM	$(V+E)$ $\log V$	$(V+E)$ $\log V$	$(V+E)$ $\log V$	Weighed Graph, Binary Heap, Priority Queue, Greedy, Array	171

Principle: Add Storage to Increase Performance

Many of the computations carried out by the algorithms are optimized by storing information that reflects the results of past computations. PRIM'S ALGORITHM for computing the minimum spanning tree for a graph uses a priority queue to store the unvisited vertices in order of their shortest distance to an initial vertex s. During a key step in the algorithm, one must determine whether a given vertex has already been visited. Because the binary heap implementation of the priority queue fails to provide this operation, a separate Boolean array inQueue is maintained to record the status of each vertex. In the same algorithm, a duplicate key array stores the computed distances to avoid having to search again through the priority queue. This extra storage on the order of $O(n)$ is required to ensure the efficient implementation of the algorithm. In most situations, as long as the overhead is $O(n)$, you are going to be safe.

Sometimes an entire computation can be cached to ensure that it never needs to be recomputed. In Chapter 6, we discussed how the hash function for the java.lang.String class stores the computed hash value to speed up its performance.

Sometimes the nature of the input set demands a large amount of storage, such as the dense graphs described in Chapter 6. By using a two-dimensional matrix to store the edge information—rather than using simple adjacency lists—certain algorithms exhibit reasonable performance. Also, you may note that for undirected graphs, the algorithms are made simpler if we assume that we use twice as much storage as necessary and store in the two-dimensional matrix information for edgeInfo[i][j] as well as edgeInfo[j][i]. Now it would be possible to eliminate this extra information if one always queried for edgeInfo[i][j] using $i \leq j$, but this would further complicate each and every algorithm that simply desired to know whether edge (i,j) exists.

Sometimes an algorithm is unable to operate without some higher-than-expected storage. BUCKET SORT shows its ability to sort in linear time simply by storing up to O(n) extra storage if the input set is uniformly distributed. Given that today's modern computers often have very large random access memory present, you should consider BUCKET SORT even though its memory requirements are so high.

Principle: If No Solution Is Evident, Construct a Search

Early pioneers in the field of artificial intelligence (AI) were often characterized as trying to solve problems for which no known solution existed. One of the most common approaches to solve problems was to convert the problem into a search over a (very large) graph. We dedicate an entire chapter to this approach because it is so important, and it is such a general technique for solving numerous problems. Be careful to apply it when no other computational alternative is available, however! You could use the path-finding approach to discover a sequence of element transpositions that starts from an unsorted array (the initial node) and produces a sorted array (the goal node), but you shouldn't use an algorithm with exponential behavior because numerous O($n \log n$) algorithms exist to sort the data. Table 11-4 shows the path finding algorithms discussed in Chapter 7.

Table 11-4. Chapter 7: Path finding in AI

Algorithm	Best	Average	Worst	Concepts	Page
DEPTH-FIRST SEARCH	$b*d$	b^d	b^d	Stack, Set, Backtracking	182
BREADTH-FIRST SEARCH	b^d	b^d	b^d	Queue, Set	190
A*SEARCH	$b*d$	b^d	b^d	Priority Queue, Set, Heuristics	195
MINIMAX	b^{ply}	b^{ply}	b^{ply}	Recursion, Backtracking, Brute Force	208
NEGMAX	b^{ply}	b^{ply}	b^{ply}	Recursion, Backtracking, Brute Force	214
ALPHABETA	$b^{ply/2}$	$b^{ply/2}$	b^{ply}	Recursion, Backtracking, Heuristics	218

Principle: If No Solution Is Evident, Reduce Your Problem to Another Problem That Has a Solution

Problem reduction is one of the fundamental approaches used by computer scientists and mathematicians in solving problems. As a simple example, suppose you wanted an algorithm to locate the fourth largest element in a list. Instead of writing this special-purpose code, you could use any sorting algorithm to sort the list and then return the fourth element in the sorted list. Using this approach, you have defined an algorithm whose performance time is O($n \log n$); although this is not the most efficient way to solve the problem—see the selectKth method described in Chapter 4 instead—it is correct.

Chapter 8 presented a set of problems that all seemed related, but there didn't seem to be any easy way to tie them all together. It is possible to reduce all of these problems into linear programming (LP) and use commercially available software packages, such as Maple, to compute solutions, but the reductions are complicated; in addition, the general-purpose algorithms used to solve LP problems can be outperformed, often significantly, by the FORD-FULKERSON family of algorithms.

We show in Chapter 8 how to solve a single problem type, namely computing the minimum-cost maximum flow in a flow network. With this algorithm in hand, the five other problems are immediately solved.

Table 11-5 shows the network flow algorithms described in Chapter 8.

Table 11-5. Chapter 8: Network flow algorithms

Algorithm	Best	Average	Worst	Concepts	Page
FORD-FULKERSON	$E*mf$	$E*mf$	$E*mf$	Weighted Directed Graph, Array, Greedy	230
EDMONDS-KARP	$V*E^2$	$V*E^2$	$V*E^2$	Weighted Directed Graph, Array, Greedy	

Principle: Writing Algorithms Is Hard—Testing Algorithms Is Harder

Because the algorithms we describe are predominantly deterministic (except for those from Chapter 11), it was rather straightforward to develop test cases to ensure that they behaved properly. In Chapter 7, we began to encounter difficulties because we were using path-finding algorithms to locate potential solutions that we did not know in advance. For example, although it was straightforward to write test cases to determine whether the GoodEvaluator heuristic was working properly for the 8-puzzle, the only way to test an A*SEARCH using that heuristic is to invoke the search and manually inspect the explored tree to validate that the proper move was selected. Thus, testing A*SEARCH is complicated by having to test the algorithm in the context of a specific problem and heuristic. We have extensive test cases for the path-finding algorithms, but in many cases they exist only to ensure that a "reasonable" move was selected (for either game or search trees), rather than to ensure that a specific move was selected.

Testing the algorithms in Chapter 9 was further complicated because of floating-point computations. Consider our approach to test CONVEX HULL SCAN. The original idea was to execute a BRUTE FORCE CONVEX HULL algorithm—whose performance was $O(n^4)$—and compare its output with the output from Andrew's CONVEX HULL SCAN. During our extensive testing, we randomly generated two-dimensional data sets uniformly drawn from the [0,1] unit square. However, when the data sets grew sufficiently large, we invariably encountered situations where the results of the two algorithms were different. Was there a subtle defect exposed by the data, or was something else at work? We eventually discovered that the floating-point arithmetic used by the BRUTE FORCE algorithm produced slightly (ever so slightly) different results when compared with CONVEX HULL SCAN. Was this just a fluke? Unfortunately, no. We also noticed that the LINE SWEEP algorithm produced slightly different results when compared against BRUTE FORCE INTERSECTION algorithm. Which algorithm produced the "right" result? It's not that simple, because using floating-point values led us to develop a consistent notion of comparing floating-point values. Specifically, we (somewhat) arbitrarily defined FloatingPoint.epsilon to be the threshold value below which it becomes impossible to discern differences between two numbers. When the resulting computations lead to values near this threshold (which we set to 10^{-9}), unexpected behavior would often occur. Eliminating the threshold entirely won't solve the problem, either. We ultimately resorted to statistically checking the results of these algorithms, rather than seeking absolute and definitive answers for all cases.

Table 11-6 summarizes computational geometry, covered in Chapter 9.

Table 11-6. Chapter 9: Computational geometry

Algorithm	Best	Average	Worst	Concepts	Page
CONVEX HULL SCAN	n	$n \log n$	$n \log n$	Array, Greedy	261
LINE SWEEP	$(n+k) \log n$	$(n+k) \log n$	n^2	Priority Queue, Binary Tree	270, 271
NEAREST NEIGHBOR QUERY	$\log n$	$\log n$	n	kd-tree, Recursion	283
RANGE QUERIES	$n^{1-1/d}+r$	$n^{1-1/d}+r$	n	kd-tree, Recursion	292

IV

Appendix, *Benchmarking*

APPENDIX

Benchmarking

Each algorithm in this book is presented in its own section where you will find individual performance data on the behavior of the algorithm. In this benchmarking chapter, we present our infrastructure to evaluate algorithm performance. It is important to explain the precise means by which empirical data is computed, to enable the reader to both verify that the results are accurate and understand where the assumptions are appropriate or inappropriate given the context in which the algorithm is intended to be used.

There are numerous ways by which algorithms can be analyzed. Chapter 2 presented the theoretic formal treatment, introducing the concepts of worst-case and average-case analysis. These theoretic results can be empirically evaluated in some cases, though not all. For example, consider evaluating the performance of an algorithm to sort 20 numbers. There are $2.43*10^{18}$ permutations of these 20 numbers, and one cannot simply exhaustively evaluate each of these permutations to compute the average case. Additionally, one cannot compute the average by measuring the time to sort all of these permutations. We find that we must rely on statistical measures to assure ourselves that we have properly computed the expected performance time of the algorithm.

Statistical Foundation

In this chapter we briefly present the essential points to evaluate the performance of the algorithms. Interested readers should consult any of the large number of available textbooks on statistics for more information on the relevant statistical information used to produce the empirical measurements in this book.

To compute the performance of an algorithm, we construct a *suite* of T independent *trials* for which the algorithm is executed. Each trial is intended to execute an algorithm on an input problem of size n. Some effort is made to ensure that these trials are all reasonably *equivalent* for the algorithm. When the trials are actually identical, then the intent of the trial is to quantify the variance of the underlying implementation of the algorithm. This may be suitable, for example, if it is too costly to compute a large number of independent equivalent trials. The *suite* is executed and millisecond-level timings are taken before and after the observable behavior. When the code is written in Java, the system garbage collector is invoked immediately prior to launching the trial; although this effort can't guarantee that the garbage collector does not execute during the trial, it is hoped to reduce the chance that extra time (unrelated to the algorithm) is spent. From the full set of *T* recorded times, the best and worst performing times are discarded as being "outliers." The remaining *T*–2 time records are averaged, and a standard deviation is computed using the following formula:

$$\sigma = \sqrt{\frac{\sum_i (x_i - x)^2}{n - 1}}$$

where x_i is the time for an individual trial and x is the average of the *T*–2 trials. Note here that n is equal to *T*–2, so the denominator within the square root is *T*–3. Calculating averages and standard deviations will help predict future performance, based on Table A-1, which shows the probability (between 0 and 1) that the actual value will be within the range $[x–k^*\sigma, x+k^*\sigma]$, where σ represents the standard deviation value computed in the equation just shown. The probability values become *confidence intervals* that declare the confidence we have in a prediction.

Table A-1. Standard deviation table

k	Probability
1	0.6827
2	0.9545
3	0.9973
4	0.9999
5	1

For example, in a randomized trial, it is expected that 68.27% of the time the result will fall within the range $[x–\sigma, x+\sigma]$.

When reporting results, we never present numbers with greater than four decimal digits of accuracy, so we don't give the mistaken impression that we believe the accuracy of our numbers extends that far. When the computed fifth and greater digits falls in the range [0, 49,999], then these digits are simply truncated; otherwise, the fourth digit is incremented to reflect the proper rounding. This process will convert a computation such as 16.897986 into the reported number 16.8980.

Hardware

In this book we include numerous tables showing the performance of individual algorithms on sample data sets. We used two different machines in this process:

Desktop PC
> We used a reasonable "home office" personal computer. This computer had a Pentium(R) 4 CPU 2.8Ghz with 512 MB of RAM.

High-end computer
> We had access to a set of computers configured as part of a Linux cluster. This computer had a 2x dual-core AMD Opteron™ Processor with 2.6 Ghz speed and 16 gigabytes of Random Access Memory (RAM).

The high-end computer was made available because of work supported by the National Science Foundation under Grant No. 0551584. Any opinions, findings, and conclusions or recommendations expressed in this book are those of the authors and do not necessarily reflect the views of the National Science Foundation.

We refer to these computers by name in the tables of this book.

An Example

Assume we wanted to benchmark the addition of the numbers from 1 to n. An experiment is designed to measure the times for $n=1,000,000$ to $n=5,000,000$ in increments of one million. Because the problem is identical for n and doesn't vary, we execute for 30 trials to eliminate as much variability as possible.

The hypothesis is that the time to complete the sum will vary directly in relation to n. We show three programs that solve this problem—in Java, C, and Scheme—and present the benchmark infrastructure by showing how it is used.

Java Benchmarking Solutions

On Java test cases, the current system time (in milliseconds) is determined immediately prior to, and after, the execution of interest. The code in Example A-1 measures the time it takes to complete the task. In a perfect computer, the 30 trials should all require exactly the same amount of time. Of course this is unlikely to happen, since modern operating systems have numerous background processing tasks that share the same CPU on which the performance code executes.

Example A-1. Java example to time execution of task

```
public class Main {
  public static void main (String[]args) {
    TrialSuite ts = new TrialSuite( );
    for (long len = 1000000; len <= 5000000; len += 1000000) {
      for (int i = 0; i < 30; i++) {
        System.gc( );
        long now = System.currentTimeMillis( );

        /** Task to be timed. */
        long sum = 0;
        for (int x = 1; x <= len; x++) { sum += x; }
```

Example A-1. Java example to time execution of task (continued)

```
        long end = System.currentTimeMillis( );
        ts.addTrial(len, now, end);
      }
    }
    System.out.println (ts.computeTable( ));
  }
}
```

The TrialSuite class stores trials by their size. Once all trials have been added to the suite, the resulting table is computed. To do this, the running times are added together to find the total sum, the minimum value, and the maximum value. As described earlier, the minimum and maximum values are removed from the set when computing the average and standard deviation.

Linux Benchmarking Solutions

For C test cases, we developed a benchmarking library to be linked with the code to test. In this section we briefly describe the essential aspects of the timing code and refer the interested reader to the code repository for the full source.

Primarily created for testing sort routines, the C-based infrastructure can be linked against existing source code. The timing API takes over responsibility for parsing the command-line arguments:

```
usage: timing [-n NumElements] [-s seed] [-v] [OriginalArguments]
      -n declares the problem size        [default: 100,000]
      -v verbose output                   [default: false]
      -s # set the seed for random values [default: no seed]
      -h print usage information
```

The timing library assumes a problem will be attempted whose input size is defined by the [-n] flag. To produce repeatable trials, the random seed can be set with [-s seed]. To link with the timing library, a test case provides the following functions:

void problemUsage( )
  Report to the console the set of [OriginalArguments] supported by the specific code. Note that the timing library parses the declared timing parameters, and remaining arguments are passed along to the prepareInput function.

void prepareInput (int size, int argc, char **argv)
  Depending upon the problem to be solved, this function is responsible for building up the input set to be processed within the execute method. Note that this information is not passed directly to execute via a formal argument, but instead should be stored as a static variable within the test case.

void postInputProcessing( )
  If any validation is needed after the input problem is solved, that code can execute here.

```
void execute( )
```
This method will contain the body of code to be timed. Thus there will always be a single method invocation that will be part of the evaluation time. When the execute method is empty, the overhead (on the high-end computer) is, on average, .002 milliseconds and is considered to have no impact on the overall reporting.

The test case in Example A-2 shows the code task for the addition example.

Example A-2. Task describing addition of n numbers

```
extern int numElements;      /* size of n */
void problemUsage( ) { /* none */ }
void prepareInput( ) { /* none */ }
void postInputProcessing( ) { /* None */ }

void execute( ) {
  int x;
  long sum = 0;
  for (x = 1; x <= numElements; x++) { sum += x; }
}
```

Each execution of the C function corresponds to a single trial, and so we have a set of shell scripts whose purpose is to execute the code under test repeatedly in order to generate statistics. For each suite, a configuration file is constructed to represent the trial suite run. Example A-3 shows the *config.rc* for the value-based sorting used in Chapter 4.

Example A-3. Sample configuration file to compare sort executions

```
# configure to use these BINS
BINS=./Insertion ./Qsort_2_6_11 ./Qsort_2_6_6 ./Qsort_straight

# configure suite
TRIALS=10
LOW=1
HIGH=16384
INCREMENT=*2
```

This specification file declares that the set of executables will be three variations of QUICKSORT with one INSERTION SORT. The suite consists of problem sizes ranging from *n*=1 to *n*=16,384, where *n* doubles after each run. For each problem size, 10 trials are executed. The best and worst performers are discarded, and the resulting generated table will have the averages (and standard deviations) of the remaining eight trials.

Example A-4 contains the *compare.sh* script that generates an aggregate set of information for a particular problem size *n*.

Example A-4. compare.sh benchmarking script

```bash
#!/bin/bash
#
#   This script expects TWO arguments:
#       $1  -- size of problem n
#       $2  -- number of trials to execute
#   This script reads its parameters from the $CONFIG configuration file
#     BINS    set of executables to execute
#     EXTRAS  extra command line arguments to use when executing them
#
#  CODE is set to directory where these scripts are to be found
CODE=`dirname $0`

SIZE=20
NUM_TRIALS=10
if [ $# -ge 1 ]
then
  SIZE=$1
  NUM_TRIALS=$2
fi

if [ "x$CONFIG" = "x" ]
then
  echo "No Configuration file (\$CONFIG) defined"
  exit 1
fi

if [ "x$BINS" = "x" ]
then
  if [ -f $CONFIG ]
  then
    BINS=`grep "BINS=" $CONFIG | cut -f2- -d'='`
   EXTRAS=`grep "EXTRAS=" $CONFIG | cut -f2- -d'='`
  fi

  if [ "x$BINS" = "x" ]
  then
    echo "no \$BINS variable and no $CONFIG configuration "
    echo "Set \$BINS to a space-separated set of executables"
  fi
fi

echo "Report: $BINS on size $SIZE"
echo "Date: `date`"
echo "Host: `hostname`"
RESULTS=/tmp/compare.$$
for b in $BINS
do
    TRIALS=$NUM_TRIALS

    # start with number of trials followed by totals (one per line)
    echo $NUM_TRIALS > $RESULTS
    while [ $TRIALS -ge 1 ]
```

Example A-4. compare.sh benchmarking script (continued)

```
    do
      $b -n $SIZE -s $TRIALS $EXTRAS | grep secs | sed 's/secs//' >> $RESULTS
      TRIALS=$((TRIALS-1))
    done

    # compute average/stdev
    RES=`cat $RESULTS | $CODE/eval`
    echo "$b $RES"

    rm -f $RESULTS
done
```

compare.sh makes use of a small C program, eval, which computes the average and standard deviation using the method described at the start of this chapter. This *compare.sh* script is repeatedly executed by a manager script, *suiteRun.sh*, that iterates over the desired input problem sizes specified within the *config.rc* file, as shown in Example A-5.

Example A-5. suiteRun.sh benchmarking script

```
#!/bin/bash
CODE=`dirname $0`

# if no args then use default config file, otherwise expect it
if [ $# -eq 0 ]
then
  CONFIG="config.rc"
else
  CONFIG=$1
  echo "Using configuration file $CONFIG..."
fi

# export so it will be picked up by compare.sh
export CONFIG

# pull out information
if [ -f $CONFIG ]
then
    BINS=`grep "BINS=" $CONFIG | cut -f2- -d'='`
    TRIALS=`grep "TRIALS=" $CONFIG | cut -f2- -d'='`
    LOW=`grep "LOW=" $CONFIG | cut -f2- -d'='`
    HIGH=`grep "HIGH=" $CONFIG | cut -f2- -d'='`
    INCREMENT=`grep "INCREMENT=" $CONFIG | cut -f2- -d'='`
else
  echo "Configuration file ($CONFIG) unable to be found."
  exit -1
fi

# headers
HB=`echo $BINS | tr ' ' ','`
echo "n,$HB"
```

Example A-5. suiteRun.sh benchmarking script (continued)

```
# compare trials on sizes from LOW through HIGH
SIZE=$LOW
REPORT=/tmp/Report.$$
while [ $SIZE -le $HIGH ]
do
  # one per $BINS entry
  $CODE/compare.sh $SIZE $TRIALS | awk 'BEGIN{p=0} \
      {if(p) { print $0; }} \
      /Host:/{p=1}' | cut -d' ' -f2 > $REPORT

  # concatenate with , all entries ONLY the average. The stdev is
  # going to be ignored
  # ---------------------------------------------------------------
  VALS=`awk 'BEGIN{s=""}\
      {s = s "," $0 }\
      END{print s;}' $REPORT`
  rm -f $REPORT

  echo $SIZE $VALS

  # $INCREMENT can be "+ NUM" or "* NUM", it works in both cases.
  SIZE=$(($SIZE$INCREMENT))
done
```

Scheme Benchmarking Solutions

The Scheme code in this section measures the performance of a series of code executions for a given problem size. In this example (used in Chapter 1) there are no arguments to the function under test other than the size of the problem to compute. First we list some helper functions used to compute the average and standard deviation for a list containing execution times, shown in Example A-6.

Example A-6. Helper functions for Scheme timing

```
;; foldl: (X Y -> Y) Y (listof X) -> Y
;; Folds an accumulating function f across the elements of lst.
(define (foldl f acc lst)
   (if (null? lst)
       acc
       (foldl f (f (car lst) acc) (cdr lst))))

;; remove-number: (listof number) number -> (listof number)
;; remove element from list, if it exists
(define (remove-number nums x)
   (if (null? nums) '()
       (if (= (car nums) x) (cdr nums)
           (cons (car nums) (remove-number (cdr nums) x)))))

;; find-max: (nonempty-listof number) -> number
;; Finds max of the nonempty list of numbers.
(define (find-max nums)
   (foldl max (car nums) (cdr nums)))
```

Example A-6. Helper functions for Scheme timing (continued)

```scheme
;; find-min: (nonempty-listof number) -> number
;; Finds min of the nonempty list of numbers.
(define (find-min nums)
   (foldl min (car nums) (cdr nums)))


;; sum: (listof number) -> number
;; Sums elements in nums.
(define (sum nums)
   (foldl + 0 nums))


;; average: (listof number) -> number
;; Finds average of the nonempty list of numbers.
(define (average nums)
   (exact->inexact (/ (sum nums) (length nums))))


;; square: number -> number
;; Computes the square of x.
(define (square x) (* x x))


;; sum-square-diff: number (listof number) -> number
;; helper method for standard-deviation
(define (sum-square-diff avg nums)
   (foldl (lambda (a-number total)
            (+ total (square (- a-number avg))))
          0
          nums))


;; standard-deviation: (nonempty-listof number) -> number
;; Calculates standard deviation.
(define (standard-deviation nums)
   (exact->inexact
    (sqrt (/ (sum-square-diff (average nums) nums)
             (length nums)))))
```

The helper functions in Example A-6 are used by the timing code in Example A-7, which runs a series of test cases for a desired function.

Example A-7. Timing Scheme code

```scheme
;; Finally execute the function under test on a problem size
;; result: (number -> any) -> number
;; Computes how long it takes to evaluate f on the given probSize.
(define (result f probSize)
   (let* ((start-time (current-inexact-milliseconds))
          (result (f probSize))
          (end-time (current-inexact-milliseconds)))
     (- end-time start-time)))


;; trials: (number -> any) number number -> (listof number)
;; Construct a list of trial results
(define (trials f numTrials probSize)
   (if (= numTrials 1)
       (list (result f probSize))
```

Benchmarking

```
      (cons (result f probSize)
            (trials f (- numTrials 1) probSize)))))

;; Generate an individual line of the report table for problem size
(define (smallReport f numTrials probSize)
  (let* ((results (trials f numTrials probSize))
         (reduced (remove-number
                    (remove-number results (find-min results))
                    (find-max results))))
    (display (list 'probSize: probSize
                   'numTrials: numTrials
                   (average reduced)))
    (newline)))

;; Generate a full report for specific function f by incrementing
;; one to the problem size
(define (briefReport f inc numTrials minProbSize maxProbSize)
  (if (>= minProbSize maxProbSize)
      (smallReport f numTrials minProbSize)
      (begin
        (smallReport f numTrials minProbSize)
        (briefReport f inc numTrials (inc minProbSize) maxProbSize))))

;; standard doubler and plus1 functions for advancing through report
(define (double n) (* 2 n))
(define (plus1 n) (+ 1 n))
```

The largeAdd function from Example A-8 adds together a set of n numbers. The output generated by (briefReport largeAdd millionplus 30 1000000 5000000) is shown in Table A-2.

Example A-8. largeAdd Scheme function

```
;; helper method
(define (millionplus n) ( + 1000000 n))

;; Sum numbers from 1..probSize
(define (largeAdd probSize)
  (let loop ([i probSize]
             [total 0])
    (if (= i 0)
        total
        (loop (sub1 i) (+ i total)))))
```

Table A-2. Execution time for 30 trials of largeAdd

n	Execution time (ms)
1,000,000	382.09
2,000,000	767.26
3,000,000	1155.78
4,000,000	1533.41
5,000,000	1914.78

Reporting

It is instructive to review the actual results when computed on the same platform, in this case a Linux 2.6.9-67.0.1.ELsmp i686 (this machine is different from the desktop PC and high-end computer mentioned earlier in this chapter). We present three tables (Tables A-3, A-5, and A-6), one each for Java, C, and Scheme. In each table, we present the millisecond results and a brief histogram table for the Java results.

Table A-3. Timing results of 30 computations in Java

n	average	min	max	stdev	#
1,000,000	8.5	8	18	0.5092	28
2,000,000	16.9643	16	17	0.1890	28
3,000,000	25.3929	25	26	0.4973	28
4,000,000	33.7857	33	35	0.4179	28
5,000,000	42.2857	42	44	0.4600	28

The aggregate behavior of Table A-3 is detailed in histogram form in Table A-4. We omit from the table rows that have only zero values; all nonzero values are shaded in the table.

Table A-4. Individual breakdowns of timing results

time (ms)	1,000,000	2,000,000	3,000,000	4,000,000	5,000,000
8	15	0	0	0	0
9	14	0	0	0	0
16	0	2	0	0	0
17	0	28	0	0	0
18	1	0	0	0	0
25	0	0	18	0	0
26	0	0	12	0	0
33	0	0	0	7	0
34	0	0	0	22	0
35	0	0	0	1	0
42	0	0	0	0	21
43	0	0	0	0	8
44	0	0	0	0	1

To interpret these results for Java, we turn to statistics. If we assume that the timing of each trial is independent, then we refer to the *confidence intervals* described earlier. If we are asked to predict the performance of a proposed run for $n=4,000,000$, then we can say that with 95.45% probability the expected timing result will be in the range [32.9499, 34.6215].

Table A-5. Timing results of 30 computations in C

n	average	min	max	stdev	#
1,000,000	2.6358	2.589	3.609	0.1244	28
2,000,000	5.1359	5.099	6.24	0.0672	28
3,000,000	7.6542	7.613	8.009	0.0433	28
4,000,000	10.1943	10.126	11.299	0.0696	28
5,000,000	12.7272	12.638	13.75	0.1560	28

In raw numbers, the C implementation appears to be about three times faster. The histogram results are not as informative, because the timing results include fractional milliseconds, whereas the Java timing strategy reports only integer values.

The final table contains the results for Scheme. The variability of the execution runs in the Scheme implementation is much higher than Java and C. One reason may be that the recursive solution requires more internal bookkeeping of the computation.

Table A-6. Timing results of 30 computations in Scheme

n	average	min	max	stdev	#
1,000,000	1173	865	1,274	7.9552	28
2,000,000	1921.821	1,824	2,337	13.1069	28
3,000,000	3059.214	2,906	3,272	116.2323	28
4,000,000	4040.607	3,914	4,188	81.8336	28
5,000,000	6352.393	6,283	6,452	31.5949	28

Precision

Instead of using millisecond-level timers, nanosecond timers could be used. On the Java platform, the only change in the earlier timing code would be to invoke System.nanoTime( ) instead of accessing the milliseconds. To understand whether there is any correlation between the millisecond and nanosecond timers, the code was changed as shown in Example A-9.

Example A-9. Using nanosecond timers in Java

```
TrialSuite tsM = new TrialSuite();
TrialSuite tsN = new TrialSuite();
for (long len = 1000000; len <= 5000000; len += 1000000) {
    for (int i = 0; i < 30; i++) {
        long nowM = System.currentTimeMillis();
        long nowN = System.nanoTime();
        long sum = 0;
        for (int x = 0; x < len; x++) { sum += x; }
        long endM = System.currentTimeMillis();
        long endN = System.nanoTime();
```

Example A-9. Using nanosecond timers in Java (continued)

```
        tsM.addTrial(len, nowM, endM);
        tsN.addTrial(len, nowN, endN);
    }
}
```

Table A-3, shown earlier, contains the millisecond results of the timings, and Table A-7 contains the results when using the nanosecond timer. The clearest difference is that the standard deviation has shrunk by an order of magnitude, thus giving us much tighter bounds on the expected execution time of the underlying code. One can also observe, however, that the resulting timings still have issues with precision—note the large standard deviation for the n=5,000,000 trial. This large deviation corresponds with the "spike" seen in this case in Table A-3.

Table A-7. Results using nanosecond timers

n	average	min	max	stdev	#
1,000,000	8.4833	8.436	18.477	0.0888	28
2,000,000	16.9096	16.865	17.269	0.0449	28
3,000,000	25.3578	25.301	25.688	0.0605	28
4,000,000	33.8127	33.729	34.559	0.0812	28
5,000,000	42.3508	42.19	43.207	0.2196	28

Because we believe using nanosecond-level timers does not add sufficient precision or accuracy, we continue to use millisecond-level timing results within the benchmark results reported in the algorithm chapters. We also continue to use milliseconds to avoid giving the impression that our timers are more accurate than they really are. Finally, nanosecond timers on Unix systems are not yet standardized, and there are times when we wished to compare execution times across platforms, which is another reason why we chose to use millisecond-level timers throughout this book.

Why such variation among what should otherwise be a rather consistent behavior? Reviewing the data from Table A-3, there appear to be "gaps" of 15 or 16 milliseconds in the recorded trial executions. These gaps reflect the accuracy of the Java timer on the Windows platform, rather than the behavior of the code. These variations will appear whenever System.currentTimeMillis( ) is executed, yet the values are significant only when the base execution times are very small (i.e., near 16 milliseconds).

The Sun engineers who developed Java are aware of the problem of timers for the Windows platform, and have no immediate plans to resolve the issue (and this has been the situation for nearly six years now). See *http://bugs.sun.com/bugdatabase/view_bug.do?bug_id=4423429* for clarification.

Index

Symbols

α (alpha), 217
≅ (approximately equal), 49
β (beta), 217
δ (delta), 49
~ (destructor), 44
ε (epsilon), 25
~ (package-private), 44
– (private), 44
(protected), 44
+ (public), 44

Numbers

15-puzzle, 201
19-Queens Problem, 307
4-Queens Problem, 306
8-puzzle, 176

A

Addition algorithm, 26
adjacency list representation, 141
AI (artificial intelligence)
    algorithms, 173
A[i] notation, 58
Akl-Toussaint heuristic, 262
Alexander, Christopher, 39
algorithm patterns, 40
    format, 41

algorithmic performance,
        measuring, 323
algorithms
    application example, 3–11
    domains, 46
    for memory allocation and
        deallocation, 9
    glyphs, 42
    performance, evaluating, 10
    potentially wrong, but with
        diminishing
        probability, 310–313
    principles defining usage, 314–320
        adding storage to improve
            performance, 317
        choice of data structures, 316
        construction of searches, 318
        decomposition of problems into
            smaller problems, 315
        knowledge of data, 314
        problem reduction, 318
        writing and testing, 319
algs.model.tree.BalancedTree, 132
    rotateLeft and rotateRight, 134
all pairs shortest path
        algorithms, 165–168
    Floyd-Warshall algorithm, 165–168
allPairsShortest( ), 167
AlphaBeta algorithm, 217–223
    game tree pruning, 219

We'd like to hear your suggestions for improving our indexes. Send email to *index@oreilly.com*.

AND/OR trees, 173
application domains, 46
approximation algorithms, 302
arrays, 14
A*Search algorithm, 194–203
   admissible functions, 200
   asterisk, 194
   compared to other path-finding
      algorithms, 204
   compared to other search tree
      algorithms, 204–207
   implementation, 198
   related algorithms, 204
Assignment problem, 248
augmenting paths, 242–245
   locating with Breadth-First
      Search, 235
   locating with Depth-First
      Search, 233, 234
AVL trees, 131

B

balanced binary trees, 8
Beck, Kent, 39
Bellman-Ford algorithm, 160–161
   compared to Dijkstra's
      Algorithms, 161
benchmark operations, 36–38
benchmarking, 323–335
   C test cases, 326
   example, 325
   hardware, 324
   Java solutions, 325
   Linux solutions, 326–330
   precision, 334–335
   reporting, 333–334
   Scheme solutions, 330–332
   statistical foundation, 323
BFPRT (Blum-Floyd-Pratt-Rivest-Tarjan)
      algorithm, 74–78
bfs_search( ), 152
binary decision trees, 61–63
   height, 61
   usage in BFPRT, 86
Binary Search algorithm, 112–116
   implementation in Java, 113
binary search trees, 129
Binary Tree Search algorithm, 129–135
   implementation, 132, 134

binary trees, 7
binary-search-tree property, 130
Bipartite Matching, 239–242
bitboards, 179
BoardEvaluation scoring function, 175
branching factors, 179
breadth-first blind searches, 179
Breadth-First Search
      algorithm, 149–153, 190–194
   augmenting paths, locating
      with, 234
   compared to other path-finding
      algorithms, 204
   compared to other search tree
      algorithms, 204–207
   implementation, 152
Brute Force Intersection algorithm, 279
B-Trees, 116, 129, 135
Bucket Sort algorithm, 93–99
   hash and numBuckets functions, 96
   implementation, 95
Buffon's needle problem, 279
buildHeap, 87, 90
bytecode interpretation compared to
      compiled code, 53

C

capacity constraint, 229, 249
case analysis, 18–22
   average-case, 21
   best-case, 22
   worst-case, 21
chaining, 121
   load factor, 125
checkers, 174
circle data, 266
class methods, 44
Coherence Test algorithm, 311
collation algorithm, 60
collision chaining, 116
collision handling, 127
collisions, 117
combinatorial games, 173
comparability of collection elements, 59
comparator function, 60
compiled code compared to bytecode
      interpretation, 53

computational geometry, 251
  assumptions, 255
  classic problems, 256–260
  comparison of algorithms, 319
  computation task types, 254
  Convex Hull Scan (see Convex Hull
    Scan algorithm)
  core concepts, 252
  LineSweep (see LineSweep
    algorithm)
  Nearest Neighbor queries (see
    Nearest Neighbor queries)
  problems and applications, 255
  range queries (see Range Query
    algorithm)
  static and dynamic tasks, 255
  three dimensions, 252
  types of input data, 251
confidence intervals, 324
constant performance family, 23
constants and instance size, 14
constructor methods, 44
Convex Hull Scan algorithm, 260–268
  data set distribution types, 266
  related algorithms, 268
  running times, 265
Counting Sort algorithm, 91–93
Cunningham, Ward, 39
cycles, 138

D

database inequality, testing, 311
demand satisfaction, 246
depth-first blind searches, 179
Depth-First Search algorithm, 142–149,
    181–190
  augmenting paths, locating
    with, 232–234
  board state symmetries, 186
  compared to other path-finding
    algorithms, 204
  compared to other search tree
    algorithms, 204–207
  edge types, 148
  open and closed board states, 181
  solution, 185
  vertices, data collection for, 145
DepthTransition, 184
design format, 43

design patterns, 39
  algorithm patterns, 40
destructor methods, 44
Dijkstra's Algorithm, 153–159
  compared to Bellman-Ford, 161
  dist[ ] and pred[ ] arrays, 153
  implementation for dense
    graphs, 157
    optimized version, 158
  priority queue implementation, 155
directed graphs, 136
domains, 46
DSLs (domain-specific languages), 46
dynamic programming, 165
dynamic typing compared to static
    typing, 53

E

edges, 136
Edmonds-Karp algorithm, 244
eHarmony matchmaking service, 252
empirical evaluation format, 44
Euclid's GCD algorithm, 32
eval program, 329
exit( ), 4

F

floating-point computations, 47–50
  comparing values, 48
  floating-point representation, 47
  performance, 49
  rounding errors, 47
  special quantities, 49
flow conservation, 229, 249
flow networks, 228
  vertex capacities and undirected
    edges, 238
  (see also network flow algorithms)
Floyd-Warshall algorithm, 165–168
Ford-Fulkerson algorithm, 227–242
  Bipartite Matching, solving
    with, 239–242
  lowest cost path search in Java, 243
  maximum flow problems, solving
    with, 227–238
    implementation, 231
    optimized implementation, 236

G

game tree algorithms, 172–176
    AlphaBeta, 217–223
    MiniMax, 207–213
    NegMax, 213–217
game trees, 175
    common interface for path
        finding, 176
garbage collection versus manual
        memory allocation, 53
GCD algorithm, 32
glyphs, 42
GoodEvaluator f*(n) function, 196
GPERF for C and C++, 129
GrahamScan algorithm, 263, 268
graph algorithms, 136
    all pairs shortest path (see all pairs
        shortest path algorithms)
    Breadth-First Search, 149–153
    comparison of, 316
    data structure design, 141
    Depth-First Search, 142–149
    minimum spanning tree
        algorithms, 169–170
    performance comparison of two
        algorithm variations, 141
    problems, 142
    single-source shortest path (see
        single-source shortest path
        algorithms)
graph analysis, 140
Graph Isomorphism problem, 312
graphs, 136–140
    adjacency list representation, 141
    connectedness, 138
    core graph operations, 142
    cycles, 138
    edges, 136
    storage issues, 139
    vertices, 136
growth rate of functions, 14–18
Guessing algorithm, 24

H

Hamiltonian Cycle problem, 312
Hash Sort algorithm, 97
Hash-based Search algorithm, 116–129
    comparable times to build hash
        tables, 127
    hash distribution using Java String.
        hashCode( ), 121

    implementation, 120
    loading a hash table, 123
    search time for various hash table
        sizes, 126
    searching for an element, 124
    statistics of hash tables created with
        examples, 126
    storage space, 122
hashing
    hash functions, 121
    hash tables, 116
    linear probing, 128
    quadratic probing, 128
Heap Sort algorithm, 86–91
    non-recursive versus recursive
        implementations, 90
heaps
    heap property, 86
    heapify function, 87, 90
    shape property, 86
hierarchical searches, 204
Hoare, C.A.R., 78
HPA* (Hierarchical Path-Finding A*)
        algorithm, 204
hypergraphs, 137

I

IDA* (IterativeDeepeningA*)
        algorithm, 203
IGameMove interface, 175
IGameScore interface, 175
IGameState interface, 175
IHypercube, 253
IInterval, 254
ILineSegment, 252
IMove interface, 178
IMultiLineSegment, 253
IMultiPoint, 253
INode interface, 176
INodeSet interface, 178
Insertion Sort algorithm, 63–67
    pointer-based values, 65
    usage in Bucket Sorts, 94
    value-based information, 65
instance of a problem, 12
instance size and constants, 14
IPoint, 252
IRectangle, 252
ISearch interface, 178
iterative deepening searches, 204
iterators, 106

J

Java benchmarking solutions, 325
Java interface and classes, 44
java.lang.ArithmeticException, 49
java.util.Hashtable class, 126
JPERF for Java, 129

K

kd-trees, 281–283
binary trees, compared to, 284
killer median-of-three, 100

L

linear performance family, 25–29
linear probing, 128
Linear Programming (LP), 249
LineState class, 277
LineSweep algorithm, 268–280
benchmarking, 279
implementation, 274
initialization phase, 278
LinkedList class, Java, 122
Linux benchmarking
solutions, 326–330
local transposition sorts, 67
logarithmic algorithms, 25
logarithmic performance family, 23–25

M

malloc( ), 4
behavior, investigation of, 9
mantissa, 48
manual memory allocation, 50–53
garbage collection, compared to, 53
Maple, 249
maximum flow algorithms, 229
Maximum Flow problem,
variations, 238
vertex capacities and undirected
edges, 238
(see also Ford-Fulkerson
algorithm), 229
mazes, solving, 142
Median Sort algorithm, 67–78
BFPRT algorithm, 74–78
implementation, 72
pivots, 69
memory leaks, 129
prevention, 3

memory-bounded searches, 204
method types, 44
MiniMax algorithm, 207–213
implementation, 209
Minimum Cost Flow problem, 246
minimum spanning tree
algorithms, 169–170
Prim's algorithm, 169–170
mixed operations, 35
ModGCD algorithm, 33
MoveEvaluation class, 209
MRU (Most-Recently-Used) paging
algorithms, 111
MST (see minimum spanning tree
algorithms)
Multiplication algorithm, 31

N

n log n performance family, 30
Nearest Neighbor queries, 280–291
implementation, 285–288
recursively constructing balanced
kd-trees, 284
NegMax algorithm, 213–217
analysis, 215
as basis for AlphaBeta, 219
consequences, 215
implementation, 214
input/output and context, 213
solution, 213
network flow, 228
network flow algorithms, 226
Assignment problem, 248
augmenting paths, 242–245
locating with Breadth-First
Search, 234
locating with Depth-First
Search, 232–234
Bipartite Matching problem, 239
(see also Bipartite Matching)
comparison of, 318
Ford-Fulkerson, 238
(see also Ford-Fulkerson algorithm)
Linear Programming, 249
maximum flow algorithms, 229
Minimum Cost Flow problem, 246
Transhipment problem, 246
Transportation problem, 247
Newton's method, 25
Nilsson, Nil, 175
NP-hard problems, 302

n-Queens Problem, 305–310
  19-Queens Problem, 307
  4-Queens Problem, 306
  implementation of Knuth's
      randomized estimation, 309
n-way trees, 135

O

offline algorithms, 302
open addressing, 127

P

parallel algorithms, 303
PartialHull class, 263
partition function, 69
  implementation, 70
  use in BFPRT, 78
  use in Median Sort, 69
  use in Quicksort, 82
  use in selectKth, 72
path-finding algorithms, 172
  A*Search (see A*Search algorithm)
  assumptions, 181
  Breadth-First Search (see Breadth-
    First Search algorithm)
  calculating available moves, 179
  comparison of, 318
  Depth-First Search (see Depth-First
    Search algorithm)
  game trees (see game tree algorithms)
  key concepts, 178–180
  maximum expansion depth, 180
  representing state, 178
  search trees (see search tree
    algorithms)
  static evaluation functions, 180
  using heuristic information, 179
path-finding problems, 174
patterns (see design patterns)
perfect hashing, 128
  hash functions, 120
performance costs, 14
performance families, 22–35
  constant behavior, 23
  less obvious performance
    computations, 32–35
  linear performance, 25–29
  log N behavior, 23–25
  n log n performance, 30
  quadratic performance, 30–31
  sublinear O(Nd) behavior for d, 25

pivots, 69, 79
platforms, 14
pointer-based information, 58
preprocessing, 254
Prim's Algorithm, 169–170
  implementation, 169
probing, 128
problem instance, 12
problem reduction, 318
problems, classifying, 251
programming and problem solving, 39
programming languages, choosing, 53
pseudocode pattern format, 42–43
Push/Relabel algorithm, 238

Q

quadratic performance family, 30
quadratic probing, 128
queries, 254
Quicksort algorithm, 78–85
  implementation, 82
  pivots, 79
  variations, 83–85
    partition, processing, 84
    pivots, selecting, 84
    subarrays, processing, 84
    using insertion techniques for
      small arrays, 84

R

randomized algorithms, 303–310
  estimating search tree size, 305–310
  estimating the size of a set, 303–305
  implementation of probabilistic
    counting algorithm, 303–305
Range Query algorithm, 292–298
  decisions at each node, 294
  implementation, 293
rate of growth of functions, 14–18
red-black binary trees, 8, 131, 135
rounding errors, 47

S

Samuel, Arthur, 180
Scheme benchmarking
    solutions, 330–332
Schmidt, Doug, 128
search algorithms, 105
  Binary Search, 112–116
  Binary Tree Search, 129–135

comparison, 315
Hash-based Search, 116–129
Sequential Search (see Sequential
    Search algorithm)
search tree algorithms, 172, 176–178
    common interface for path
        finding, 178
    comparison, 204–207
    Type A and Type B algorithms, 174
secondary storage, 58
Selection Sort algorithm, 85
sentinel, 110
Sequential Search algorithm, 14,
        106–111
    check for empty slots, 110
    implementation, 108, 109
    move to front, move up, and move to
        end on success, 111
    offline usage, 302
    parallel processing, 303
    performance, 110
shape property, 86
ShortestPathArray, Java
        implementation, 242
significand, 48
Simplex algorithm, 250
single-source shortest path
        algorithms, 153–164
    Bellman-Ford algorithm, 160–161
    comparison, 161–164
    Dijkstra's Algorithm (see Dijkstra's
        Algorithm)
skew symmetry, 229
slice data, 266
sort functions, comparing, 16–18
sorting algorithms, 57
    best-, worst-, and average-case
        performance costs, 61
    Bucket Sort, 93–99
    choosing a sorting algorithm, 99
    common input, 63
    comparable elements, 59
    comparison of algorithms, 100–103,
        315
        double benchmark
            results, 102–103
        string benchmark
            results, 100–102
    Counting Sort, 91–93
    double-precision floating-point value
        data sets, 99
    Heap Sort, 86–91

Insertion Sort, 63–67
local transposition sorts, 67
Median Sort, 67–78
preprocessing of input data, 99
Quicksort, 78–85
random string data sets, 99
representation of collections, 58
Selection Sort, 85
stable sorting, 60
terminology, 58
sparse graphs, 139
stable sorting, 60
state tree, 172
static evaluation functions, 180
static typing compared to dynamic
        typing, 53
String class, Java, 122
sublinear performance family, 25
supply satisfaction, 246

T

tertiary storage, 58
the, 44
Tiny-Puzzle (example), 181
tours, 302
Transhipment problem, 246
Transportation problem, 247
transposition tables, 204
Traveling Salesman Problem (TSP), 302
TrialSuite class, 326

U

UML class diagrams, 43
undirected graphs, 136
Unicode standard, 59
uniform data, 266

V

value-based information, 58
Voronoi diagrams, 281

W

war stories, 46
WeakEvaluator f*(n) function, 196
weighted graphs, 137
wrapper functions, 3

Z

zero-knowledge proofs, 311

About the Authors

George T. Heineman is an associate professor of computer science at Worcester Polytechnic Institute. His research interests are in software engineering. He co-edited the 2001 book *Component-Based Software Engineering: Putting the Pieces Together* (Addison-Wesley). George was the program chair for the 2005 International Symposium on Component-Based Software Engineering.

Gary Pollice is a self-labeled curmudgeon (that's a crusty, ill-tempered, usually old man) who spent more than 35 years in industry trying to figure out what he wanted to be when he grew up. Even though he hasn't grown up yet, he did make the move in 2003 to the hallowed halls of academia, where he has been corrupting the minds of the next generation of software developers with radical ideas like, "develop software for your customer," "learn how to work as part of a team," "design and code quality and elegance and correctness counts," and "it's OK to be a nerd as long as you are a great one."

Gary is a professor of practice (meaning he had a real job before becoming a professor) at Worcester Polytechnic Institute. He went to WPI because he was so impressed with the WPI graduates that he's worked with over the years. He lives in central Massachusetts with his wife, Vikki, and their two dogs, Aloysius and Ignatius. When not working on geeky things he...well he's always working on geeky things. You can see what he's up to by visiting his WPI home page, *http://web.cs.wpi.edu/~gpollice/*. Feel free to drop him a note and complain or cheer about the book.

Stanley Selkow, a professor of computer science at Worcester Polytechnic Institute, received a B.S. in electrical engineering from Carnegie Institute of Technology in 1965, and a Ph.D. in the same area from the University of Pennsylvania in 1970. From 1968 to 1970 he was in the public health service at the National Institutes of Health at Bethesda, Maryland. Since 1970 he has been on the faculty at universities in Knoxville, Tennessee and Worcester, Massachusetts, as well as Montreal, Chonqing, Lausanne, and Paris. His major research has been in graph theory and algorithm design.

Colophon

The animal on the cover of *Algorithms in a Nutshell* is a hermit crab (*Pagurus bernhardus*). More than 500 species of hermit crabs exist. Mostly aquatic, they live in saltwater in shallow coral reefs and tide pools. Some hermit crabs, however, especially in the tropics, are terrestrial. The robber crab, which can grow as large as a coconut, is one such example. Even terrestrial hermit crabs carry a small amount of water in their shells to help them breathe and keep their abdomens moist.

Unlike true crabs, hermit crabs do not have a hard shell of their own and must seek refuge from predators in the abandoned shells of gastropods (snails). They are particularly fond of the discarded shells of periwinkles and whelks. As they grow bigger, they have to find a new shell to inhabit. Leaving any part of themselves exposed would make them more susceptible to predators; in addition, not having a well-fitted shell stunts their growth. Because intact gastropod shells are limited, shell competition is an issue.

Hermit crabs are decapod (which literally means "ten footed") crustaceans. Of their five pairs of legs, the first two are pincers, or grasping claws, the larger one of which they use to defend themselves and shred food. The smaller claw is used for eating. The second and third pairs of legs help them walk, and the final two pairs help keep them in their shells.

Characteristic of crustaceans, hermit crabs do not have an internal skeleton but rather a hard exoskeleton of calcium. They also have two compound eyes, two pairs of antennae (which they use to sense smells and vibration), and three pairs of mouthparts. Near the base of the their antennae is a pair of green glands that excretes waste.

Sea anemones (water-dwelling, predatory animals) are often found attached to hermit crabs' shells. In exchange for transportation and a helping of the hermit crab's leftovers, sea anemones help to ward off the hermit crab's marine predators, such as fish and octopus. Other predators include birds, other crabs, and some mammals (man included).

Known as the "garbage collectors of the sea," hermit crabs will eat mostly anything, including dead and rotting material on the seashore, and thus they play an important role in seashore cleanup. As omnivores, their diet is varied and includes everything from worms to organic debris, such as grass and leaves.

The cover image is from Johnson's *Library of Natural History*, Volume 2. The cover font is Adobe ITC Garamond. The text font is Linotype Birka; the heading font is Adobe Myriad Condensed; and the code font is LucasFont's TheSansMonoCondensed.

Related Titles from O'Reilly

C and C++ Programming

C in a Nutshell

C Pocket Reference

C++ Cookbook

C++ in a Nutshell

C++ Pocket Reference

C++ The Core Language

Mastering Algorithms with C

Objective-C Pocket Reference

Practical C Programming, *3rd Edition*

Practical C++ Programming, *2nd Edition*

Practical Perforce

Programming Embedded Systems, *2nd Edition*

Secure Programming Cookbook for C and C++

STL Pocket Reference

O'REILLY®

Our books are available at most retail and online bookstores.

To order direct: 1-800-998-9938 • *order@oreilly.com* • *www.oreilly.com*

Online editions of most O'Reilly titles are available by subscription at *safari.oreilly.com*